Barça

Barça

A People's Passion

Jimmy Burns

BLOOMSBURY

First published in Great Britain in 1999
by Bloomsbury Publishing Plc, 38 Soho Square, London W1V 5DF
This paperback edition published 2000

Copyright © 1998 by Jimmy Burns

A CIP catalogue record of this book
is available from the British Library

ISBN 0 7475 4554 5

10 9 8 7 6

Typeset by Hewer Text Ltd, Edinburgh
Printed in Great Britain by Clays Limited, St Ives plc

To Julia and Miriam

Contents

'Only God knows how long we had to wait for that moment . . . it was an exceptional night . . . full of sentiment, emotion, feeling, and all without a second of rest.'

Johan Cruyff, 10th March 1999,
the night of the testimonial match at the
Camp Nou for him and his 'dream team'

'On Wednesday we celebrated one of the most important, I dare say historic, occasions in the life of FC Barcelona: we said goodbye to a manager and remembered a group of players who were famous. But this belongs to the past; it is history now.'

Josep Lluís Nuñez, president of FC Barcelona,
the day after the Cruyff testimonial

'There are a great many men dominated by the passion to rule others. But for this passion to flourish in all its fullness there need to be some fortuitous social circumstances, which may not always be coincidental but which, on the rare occasions that they do occur, ensure that this passion comes into its own.'

Gregorio Marañón

Acknowledgements

Although this book is not, and does not pretend to be, an official history of FC Barcelona, I am indebted to the co-operation offered by the club throughout my research and writing prior to and during its centenary year. Barça – past and present – responded generously to my requests for archive material, access to the stadium and interviews.

I am particularly grateful to Nicolau Casaus and Jaume Pares; to Jaume Sobreques and the staff of the library; and to Ricardo Maixens, Domingo Garcia, their secretaries, and other members of the press and information department.

I count myself fortunate that two key participants in the history of the club over the last three decades – Josep Lluís Nuñez and Johan Cruyff – separately agreed to be interviewed for this book.

Alfons Godal, Joan Laporta and Armando Caraben of the Blue Elephant were equally helpful in making themselves available for an alternative perspective on some of the more contemporary issues.

The project sprang from my own experience of Catalonia, from my interest in the career of Diego Maradona – subject of my last book – and from an idea conceived by my London editors, Penny Phillips and David Reynolds, who returned hugely enthusiastic from their first visit to the Camp Nou! The research took wings in Barcelona thanks to the encouragement of Gloria Gutierrez of the Carmen Balcells literary agency, and my editors at Anagrama and Empuries.

In Barcelona, Madrid, Buenos Aires, London, Amsterdam and Manchester, there were numerous people who agreed to be interviewed. Some of their names appear in this book, while others preferred to adopt a lower profile. I would like to make special mention – in no order of priority or seniority – of Carlos Tusquets, Cuqui Sarrias, Ricardo Huguet, Angel Mur, José-Maria Minguella, Dionisio Gimenez, Jaume Llaurado, José Oriol Comas, Jaume Rosell, Dolores and

Marti Anclada, Raimón Carrasco, Steve Archibald, Antonio Franco and Edwin Winkels (among others at *El Periódico*), the staff of *Marca* and *Expansión*, as also those of *El Mundo Deportivo, Sport, El País* and *La Vanguardia*. Eduard Boet and the team at TV3 were at all times a source of help and inspiration, despite their extremely heavy work schedule. My own memories were stimulated thanks to the good-humoured staff at Yorkshire TV who came up with the video.

Special thanks too to the Witty family and to Sue O'Connell for sharing their family history, to Simon Kuper, Tom Burns, Carlos Oppe, Tono Masoliver and Patrick Buckley – my unofficial 'advisory team' – for their criticisms and thoughts, and to Gary Lineker, Terry Venables, Bobby Robson, Jordi, Hugo, Henk, Leo and Consuelo for providing additional English, Dutch and Italian insights!

In London, David Snaddon, Peter Cheek, Bhavna Patel, Pedro Das Gupta and Neil McDonald of the *Financial Times* library and research department responded with patience and unflagging good cheer to my requests, as did my secretary Shah Chowdhury. Friends and colleagues who provided encouragement along the way were David and Samia Gardner, Maria Laura Avignolo, John Mason, Patrick Harverson, Nim Caswell, Charles Morris, David White, Richard Adams, Robert Graham and Alan Pike. Thanks again also to the editors and management of the *FT* – Richard Lambert, Andrew Gowers, Lionel Barber, Nick Timmins and Robin Pauley – for agreeing to give me the necessary time to write another book.

My London agent Caroline Dawnay was, as always, there to offer help and advice, as were Monica and the rest at Bloomsbury. To Kidge, and to Julia and Miriam, go my love and appreciation for their putting up with too many lost weekends, their companionship in between, and their helping me to recover at the end.

Foreword

This is the story and an anatomy of Football Club Barcelona, one of the world's most loved sporting institutions – an international passion.

No sporting motto is more appropriate than the club's own *Som més que un club*. Barça, as it is affectionately known by millions of fans around the world, has secured a number of successes both at home and abroad, but the loyalty and popularity it generates has for years had less to do with its success on the football pitch than with its transformation into a potent symbol of political and cultural identity.

Spain's *fin de siècle* – 1898 – may have meant the end of an imperial dream, but for the Catalans – for so long accustomed to defeat and humiliation – the year marked a turning point. The early twentieth century saw Barcelona's regeneration as one of Europe's most enterprising cities, with the appearance of a football club justifiably proud of its name. The growth of Barça as a sporting success projected the region's cultural and political revival to the outside world, as the club developed into the most revered symbol of Catalan nationalism as well as an expression of human rights. Repressed during the dictatorship of General Primo de Rivera in the 1920s and during the Franco years, it became a vehicle for a powerful collective identity, both defiant of dictatorship, and proud of a sporting language and expression that reached out, beyond the isolating frontiers of Spain, to Europe and beyond.

What this book is about is, like Barça itself, more than just a football club. It identifies and portrays some of the great moments of football history as played and managed by its collection of superstars. But its prime objective is to follow and dissect the human drama surrounding Barça's evolution as a political and sociological phenomenon, drawing on the testimony of key witnesses to bring alive the history of a collective experience.

This book began to form many years before it was written. I was born in Madrid, during Franco's regime. Mr grandparents' house, where I spent part of my early childhood, was on the same avenue as the Bernabéu stadium – but I was never a Real Madrid fan. As I grew older I became conscious of that club's identification with the Franco regime, and I felt I couldn't share in its politics. Later, once I began to go to school in England, I spent my family holidays in Catalonia, a region of Spain that was banned from speaking its own language in public and from waving its flags. I engaged with the small amounts of local culture that the regime allowed to manifest themselves: learning to dance the *sardana* at weekends, and later following Barça on TV. I eventually became a Barça fan for the same reason that I had *not* followed Real Madrid – its politics.

The point at which I realised what the club meant to the Catalan people, and to democracy generally, came while I was working on a documentary for Yorkshire TV on the new Spain that was emerging after Franco's death. Among the more moving scenes we filmed were those that portrayed the growing demands for self-government in street demonstrations, but no event impressed me more than a match between Barça and Athletic Bilbao in a Camp Nou stadium packed with Catalans and Basques, waving their national flags and expressing slogans and songs that had been banned since the end of the Spanish Civil War in 1939. Athletic was led out by its captain, the goalkeeper Iribar, who had campaigned publicly against human-rights violations and for the release of political prisoners. Barça had its own hero, in the person of one of the greatest footballers of all time, the Dutchman Johan Cruyff. This was not the opium of the masses, but pure adrenalin, passion deeply held and defiant – the kind that makes one happy to be alive. I've been drawn to Barcelona's Camp Nou ever since.

Before setting out to write about FC Barcelona, I registered a remark made some years ago by the Catalan author and Barça fan Manuel Vazquez Montalban: that much of what has been written about the club in his own country has tended to be introspective, almost obsessive in its unswerving loyalty to the subject, uncritical in its devotion, like a child playing over and over again with the same toy.

By birth, education and training, I believe I am in a position to look at Barça from a different perspective. My respect for and recognition of the club's standing in world football and its cultural and political tradition do not mean that I look at this phenomenon uncritically. I do not consider Barça any more sacred than any politician, king, or any other man-created institution, but rather a legitimate target of serious investigation and commentary. I hope that I have written a story that fans weary of the business of modern football can take some comfort in. I hope too that along the way it will break a few taboos, tell history as it really was, not as people would like it to have been. To that extent I hope that this book will be of interest not only to football fans, but also to readers who have never been to a football match in their lives.

1

Among the Believers

March 1998. English eyes blink in the brightness of a Mediterranean sun. Englishmen sit in the comfort of an air-conditioned bus, waiting to discover whether things are going to turn out as Doug said they would.

'If you love football and you love travel . . . you'll love this, mate,' Doug says on the plane over from London. A lifelong Spurs supporter turned adventurer, he's been doing it for sixteen years – following England, following English clubs in Europe (and beating up rival fans along the way), following Gazza when in Italy; he's a dedicated follower of the Glory Game, home and away. Some English fans see 'abroad' as an excuse to get drunk and have a battle. But Doug claims to be a little different. For all his passionate patriotism on England aways and his club loyalties on most Saturday afternoons of the year, it's a good game he is interested in, whoever plays it, and this one is going to be *the* cracker of the year: FC Barcelona v. Real Madrid.

On the plane there has been the odd couple who have looked at Doug with suspicion. The way his beer gut hangs over his bermudas, his shaved head, his face glowing with the first signs of alcohol, conjure up just one image: *hooligan*. And you can see, looking around at some of the others, why the odd couple might begin to wonder what might happen when this lot get to Barcelona. In normal circumstances one would have expected them to continue their journey to the tribal reservations of Tossa, Llloret, Mallorca, but they're staying in Barcelona.

On the bus, the odd couples shift uneasily in their seats when Dave, the tour operator, makes his first announcement since landing. 'Welcome to Barcelona, lads – or should I say lads and ladies. Unfortunately there has been a slight hitch with the tickets for the match. The club's chosen this weekend of all weekends to hold a vote on a motion of no confidence in its president, Mr Nuñez, and it would appear that some of Mr Nuñez's friends have taken some of our tickets to give to the voters . . .'

The word *wanker* can be distinctly heard whispered in a loud hiss from one of the rear seats.

For a moment Dave loses his flow, stops in mid-sentence, tries a smile, fiddles with the microphone, tapping it like a compère. 'Yes, you could say that . . . I mean . . . well, what I want to say is that there's nothing to worry about. Everyone will get a ticket, but it might be that some of you won't be sitting together as we'd originally planned . . . Priority, I'm afraid, must go to couples . . .'

'*Load of bollocks,*' the man in the rear seat says.

As the bus departs, Dave hands over the microphone to Carmen, a local guide. She talks like a taped language class. 'Welcome to Barcelona, the capital of Catalonia . . . of course we are proud of our football here, but there are many places to visit in the city – the Picasso Museum, the Sacred Family, the Rambla, the Olympic Village – and the weather is good, so you might want to visit the sea . . . there are nearby beaches at Sitges . . .'

As she rattles off her list, the odd couples begin to relax for the first time. Other occupants miss a collective heartbeat or two. It is the match, not the city, they have come to see and it looks as if it's going wrong before it's even started. 'This Nuñez, who the fuck does he think he is?' someone asks. The bus smells vaguely of stale beer and tobacco.

But when we reach the Hotel Princesa Sofia, things begin to look up. You can see the Camp Nou from here, and just seeing it puts your hair on edge. Milan's San Siro takes some beating, thinks Doug, but man this is one fuck of a stadium, rising up at the end of the tree-lined avenue like a sprawling giant. And now his enthusiasm is showing signs of spreading at last, and Dave sees that, and gives him a job to do. Doug is installed behind a desk in the foyer from where he hands out tickets neatly tucked into envelopes. And now the English can begin to take it in . . . the marble floors, and the chandeliers, and the staff in their trim uniforms picking up everyone's gear, and the large bar down near where Doug is, and the mini-bar stuffed with cans of lager and spirits upstairs in each room – which is larger than any room any of them have slept in in their lives – and yes, no it can't be, yes it can, it *is*

Terry Venables, fresh from a holiday in Alicante, walking through the hotel as if he owned it, like a man who enjoys good living.

It is more than ten years since Venables was *técnico* here, and his old friend, the vice-president of FC Barcelona, Joan Gaspart, is no longer the owner of the Princesa Sofia, but Venables still feels at home in the city, as he reminds me when we meet again. It was at the English Football Association's headquarters near Hyde Park in London that Venables had last talked to me at length not so long before. He was preparing the English squad for Euro '96 but seemed happy enough to discuss Gazza and Maradona and Barça, to talk about players who are above the ordinary, verging on the very special, and the need for a small bit of indulgence.

'Sure, I've got good memories of my time in Barcelona,' Venables tells me now. 'I keep coming back and they respond to me well. I get the feeling a lot of the time they like me better in Barcelona than they do in England.' I shall come back to Mr Venables later in the book, but for now the image that remains from that day in the hotel is of a bronzed and well-fed Englishman, very much at home both with the other *ingleses* – he greeted Doug and Dave like long-lost brothers – and with the Catalans who had begun to congregate. For despite the transfer of ownership to an American hotel chain, the Princesa Sofia in that year still conducts itself on special occasions like an informal headquarters of FC Barcelona. In the foyer and an upstairs conference room, cabals of club members and officials are forming, the gossip firmly focused on who is and who is not backing Nuñez. Only the arrival of Clemente, the Spanish national coach, with a senior editor of the Madrid-based mass-circulation sports paper *Marca*, serves as a reminder that there is also a match to be played later that afternoon.

Meanwhile, Dave has been giving me his thoughts on hooligan control. 'Give them a decent hotel, a good ticket to a good match, and throw in a fun weekend, and most of them won't get out of control.' I have told Dave that unlike Doug I need some convincing about the blurb in his travel brochure. 'If you love sport and you love travel . . . you'll love us,' it boasts. I am thinking about urine and beer, the two words a colleague of mine brought back from a forty-hour trip to Portugal and a game between Oporto and Manchester United, when Dave suggests that maybe I'd like to help out. 'Help out? What, like

Doug?' I ask. 'No, like what you are,' he says, 'a half-Spaniard who knows something about this city.'

And so, in the temporary role of Pied Piper, I lead a small group of *ingleses* downtown. Our destination is Tapa Tapa, a Mecca of regional and national culinary delights, where local beer is served like a flowing river if one agrees to dig into an altar of food. I order an extended round of beer and pick enough *tapas* to cover the table. No matter that several in our group are surprised that the filling in the *croqueta* is rather different from what's in a Cornish pasty, and that the *calamares a la romana* are not frogs' legs Roman-style, and that the *botifarra* is not a dog's turd but Catalonia's national sausage.

They devour the table with relish and ask for seconds, and thirds, while the local beer settles like a gentle tide. Among the few not dozing like so many Sancho Panzas is Ollie, a computer analyst from Liverpool. He tells me he used to go and see his local team every other week, but has given up because it has become too expensive. He is hoping this trip will be worth every penny, though. He's saved to have a weekend in the sun, to watch one of the great encounters of the football calendar. 'Football back home is in the hands of management and shareholders who don't care a shit about the fans,' says Ollie, downing another beer. 'I'm hoping what I'll see in the Camp Nou will pump up my enthusiasm. I've been told the atmosphere is great, genuinely popular.' By now it is the girls, not the boys, who are doing most of the talking – for I've forgotten to mention the discreet presence on the plane and the bus of Michelle, Sharon and Kate from Sheffield, taking a weekend away from their boyfriends and husbands and nicknamed by the group the Full Monty. As we slurp and guzzle away the afternoon, *las inglesas* declare in chorus, 'This is blooming marvellous.'

A carnival atmosphere is spreading through the town, the main protagonists seemingly drunk only on the incredible lightness of being Catalan on a day when Real Madrid are coming to town. They are gathering in groups along the Passeig de Gràcia, a wide and generous avenue where the people of this city flaunt their style and, thanks to the boldness and eccentricity of Gaudí, their architectural grandeur. As the writer Honor Tracy once observed, 'Barcelona . . . looks forward and out, she does not drowse and cackle like an old hen on an empty nest.

She busies herself with art and literature, she is willing to experiment and startle' – and, she might have added, she has Barça. Just across the avenue, half a dozen teenage girls painted with and wearing the colours of Barça giggle and dance an improvised rumba before disappearing into the metro. A family – grandparents, parents and children – similarly attired in Barça colours converse while eating ice-creams. A courting couple in Barça colours kiss, chase each other, play hide-and-seek behind the newspaper kiosk stacked with pre-match reports, until a newspaper headline seems to catch her eye. It reminds the reader that Real Madrid is out for revenge. The visiting side has not won at the Camp Nou in fifteen years. Which is another way of saying that Barça must not lose. 'Come on, it's time to go to the match,' she says in a voice that could have said, 'Come on, why don't we go to bed.' And off they go, down into the metro, she pulling him, meeting little resistance. It is Sharon, one of the Sheffield girls, who tells the *ingleses*, 'Come on, you pissed buggers, let's go, it's time for the game.'

Back in the Princesa Sofia, the principal courtiers and plotters of FC Barcelona have gathered to talk not about football but about power. Soon the votes will be counted in the latest electoral challenge against club president Nuñez – a no-confidence motion launched by an unfathomable coalition of opposing forces called the Blue Elephant. Nuñez is one of world sport's longest-serving rulers, as authoritarian and controversial as FIFA's Havelange and the International Olympic Committee's Samaranch (a Barça club member). Nuñez has been president of Barça since 1978. His staying power has proved longer-lasting than any of his predecessors', his regime more indestructible than that of any Spanish political leader since Franco. For more than twenty years he has presided over one of the fastest-expanding football clubs in the world, spending millions on an extraordinary array of world-class players, and an equally impressive catalogue of managers. Membership has grown to over 103,000. Nuñez, a developer who has made his fortune destroying old buildings and constructing new ones, stands on his record of growth. He is a little man who thinks big: the little big man who lays claim to personifying a regional aspiration, transforming the inferiority/persecution complex of Catalonia into the illusion of greatness. His enemies believe he has violated the essence of

Barça, manipulating the expression of Catalan nationalism to serve his passion to rule.

Image and what really lies behind it are what is at play in this vote. Nuñez wants us to believe that Barça's democratic structure has been consolidated under his rule, that his only interest is to serve club and country – that is to say, Catalonia – and that the club is answerable only to its membership. His opponents have taken to denouncing what they allege is Barça's subtle transformation into a personal fiefdom. In denouncing the despotic if miniature lion king, they have made their own emblem of a mammal that stands for virtue and responsible leadership: the elephant. With the colours of a new club in the making, deeply conscious of its roots, this elephant claims to show no abuse of power in the management of its enormous size, retaining an essential sense of nobility amidst nature's barbarous instinct of survival and the materialism of the modern world. These elephant tribesmen have declared no confidence in the way that Nuñez has built up his power base around official historians and sycophantic members of the board, no confidence in the way the club's accounts are rubber-stamped by a token annual assembly of members, and no confidence in what they perceive as the worst crime of all: the way in which Barça under Nuñez has lost its sense of its historic destiny to be *més que un club* – more than a club – in its expression of a collective political and cultural will.

Men in dark suits on the first floor of the Princesa Sofia discuss who voted for whom and why. The potential for mass mobilisation that is Barça has become the subject of political intrigue, the focus of calculation and manipulation by a few individuals with a vested interest in seeing that things remain as they are, and others who seek advantage from change. Occasionally, a local journalist – notebook, cassette recorder and mobile phone at the ready like instruments of war – can be seen making his way to the meeting, up the main staircase and down again, the messenger of a selectively perceived truth. Barça's mercenary. Whatever the message is, it is certainly not Johan Cruyff's. The Dutchman has flown in a few hours earlier from Amsterdam to cast his vote for the Blue Elephant. It is a stage-managed arrival, that of this liberator from abroad, for Cruyff works and lives much of the time in Barcelona, his son Jordi is named after Catalonia's patron saint, and his eldest daughter Chantal is married to a former Barça goalkeeper.

Johan has in fact as much right to be Catalan as many of the Spaniards who have emigrated here over the years. This Barça vote belongs to Cruyff as much as to any other club members, but in some ways it matters more.

The no-confidence motion is a convenient platform for Cruyff to exercise his ongoing grudge match against Nuñez, a battle between two proud and arrogant individuals who each claim to be in touch with the heart and soul of Barça. Cruyff brought some spectacular football to the Camp Nou as a player in the late 1970s. That period, along with the late 1980s and early 1990s when Cruyff returned as manager, is recalled as a Golden Age. Barça won the Spanish League championship four times in a row, and also secured the European Cup. Cruyff became Catalonia's adopted son, a privileged VIP. And yet he ended up being sacked by Nuñez when Barça lost the title to Real Madrid. He was cast in the role of insubordinate for having once suggested that the manager, not the president, ruled in the changing room.

1998 is clearly not 1978. Then, during the presidential elections, Cruyff had openly supported Nuñez's candidacy for president. It was a time of shared success and glory, big enough for two denizens of football politics each to claim a part. Now there are fans who look with fond nostalgia at the Cruyff years and wonder what has gone wrong. For Nuñez replaced Cruyff with Bobby Robson, an Englishman who was destined to fail because he failed to understand Barça. Under Robson, Barça bought Ronaldo, the most talented young player in the world, and lost him to Inter Milan, all in less than a year. Robson thought it was enough to win titles – he won three – forgetting that what the fans also wanted was a spectacle, something that Cruyff had understood instinctively.

And this is why, on this day in March 1998, Cruyff stirs emotions as he casts his vote in a way no goal ever did under Robson. Lean and bronzed, in an open-necked shirt and navy blue jacket, Cruyff looks every bit a star. Police strain to open a way for him as groups of fans surge towards table number 113. The fans clap, they struggle to touch him, young women gaze at him with ill-disguised sexual longing. Only a few dissidents, loyal to Nuñez, whistle and boo. One of them shouts, 'You're history.' But such is the bias of this particular crowd that even insults turn to compliments. 'It's our misfortune that you are history, Johan – we want you back. You're the best,' a fan shouts in reply.

Later that evening, a much younger Johan Cruyff slaloms his way towards the goal, a swallow in flight. The image of the Dutchman in Barça's Golden Age is flashed across a giant TV screen at one end of the stadium, high up in the upper terrace, where a few token Real Madrid supporters have been parked. In the final hour leading up to the start of the game, the thousands of Barça fans who have occupied the stadium are entertained with a filmed collage of the club's greatest moments, the feats of individual players presented like a litany of saints, the national and European cups held up like war trophies. Watching it, one realises the extent and scope of talent that have been Barça's, and the modest achievements it has secured through the years. There are memorable encounters between gargantuan rivals – Di Stefano and Kubala; the free kick at Wembley by Koeman; the magic of Maradona delivering a perfect goal, effortlessly. You would think, after watching such brilliance, that there would be little room for more. But Barça has built its collective passion on the expectation of something even better.

As it has been for nearly seventy years, it is one match above all others that galvanises the obsession with the victory of all victories. For days now, the local sports press and TV have been building up to this latest encounter between Barça and Real Madrid as if to the climax between two mythological giants. To suggest that this match matters rather more to one team than to the other is to lose sight of the endemic tension that drives the event, emotionally and commercially. As the writer Manuel Vazquez Montalban has put it, 'If Real Madrid didn't exist, someone would have had to invent it.' Real Madrid hasn't won a match at the Camp Nou in fourteen seasons. Barça's great rival from central Spain has hit bad form of late – eleven games without winning away – in the League championship, in the Champions' League, in the King's Cup. Were Real Madrid to lose again, it would consolidate Barça's position in the League, giving it an almost unbeatable five-point lead at the top, with one game fewer to play and an extra point in goal average. Real Madrid is out for revenge, it is out for survival; it has, in the words of the Chilean-born striker Zamorano, 'blood in its eyes'. Barça has a new manager and that says a lot, because managers in the club under Nuñez tend to come and go like the English King Henry VIII's six wives – 'divorced, beheaded, died; divorced, beheaded, survived'. The jury is out on van Gaal, a Dutchman lacking the humanity of Bobby Robson and the popularity of Johan Cruyff, both of whose heads have rolled in the space of less than two years. Barça may be at the top of the League, but the fans are unconvinced. They have watched the team pathetically founder in Europe, while continuing to play lacklustre football in the League, winning seemingly by default rather than by design. And no one has forgotten that this time two years ago, the team managed by Johan Cruyff was in with a chance of winning three competitions – the King's Cup, the UEFA Cup and the League – only to lose all three following a humiliating defeat at home against Atlético Madrid.

But to reduce this match to the immediate commentaries of rival form cards is to miss what a Barça–Real Madrid match is all about. 'It's something different,' writes José Vicente Hernaez in *Marca*, the Madrid-based sports daily, 'it's *the* match *par excellence*, it's the match of the year and of the century where you can bet on a win, a draw, or a defeat. Who is going to win? It's anyone's guess. It's a mystery. Don't believe anyone who says he knows. You've simply got to see it for yourself. It's more than just a match. There are three points to be played for, as well as the League championship. There is also the pride of twenty-two players out on the pitch, of the ten who are on the subs' bench, of the directors of the club, of the whole stadium, of the millions who are watching it on TV, and of another million who can't bear to watch it even on TV because they can't handle so much tension.'

So this is the motherfucker of them all, a War of the Roses, football against the enemy, the real Glory Game. As Robson remarked on the eve of a similar encounter in May 1997, it is the only fixture in the world that draws more than 100,000 fans twice a year. 'Throw into that equation all the history, the politicking and the media attention, and you're looking at a powder keg.'

One cannot begin to understand the phenomenon of Barça outside the context of Catalonia's relationship with the rest of Spain. Much of Catalonia's history is a story of humiliation and frustration, its aspirations as a regional power curbed and stamped upon by the centralising tendencies of Madrid, the potential of Barcelona as one of the great capitals of the Mediterranean never fully realised. Only at the beginning of the twentieth century did the formation of FC Barcelona by a group of enterprising Swiss and Englishmen bring into being the perfect vehicle for galvanising local pride, just at the very moment when Spain was suffering the trauma of the loss of its empire in Cuba and the Philippines. Barça offered the prospect of settling old scores, of defining a new frontier, more open towards Europe, from where the game had initially come.

The club drew its strength from troubled times, giving the region as a whole a necessary feeling of collective self-confidence. Whenever Madrid tried to impose itself, Barça drew its people deep into its bosom, offering protection like a medieval castle whose surrounding village is threatened by siege. Barça's identity was forged by persecution, its competitive edge by the obsession of proving itself better than Madrid on its playing fields, whether by winning or simply by stopping Madrid from winning. The history of Barça has its sharpest edges, its lowest and highest points on the grid of human conflict, whenever it and Real Madrid have played. It is a history reinvented again and again to the level of mythology, demigods fuelled by exaggeration and by propaganda, played out by symbols, heroes and villains, demigods and devils. Barça acquired its first martyr early in the Spanish Civil War, when the club president Josep Sunyol was executed by Franco's troops on a mountain road outside Madrid. It was a death foretold during the dictatorship of General Primo de Rivera in the 1920s when Barça was banned from playing for six months after the fans had greeted the Spanish national anthem with whistles. The repression became more acute during the Franco years. While Real Madrid became, in Catalan eyes, a symbol of dictatorship and the enforced unity of Spain, Barça was transformed into *more than a club*, a world in which people discovered a crude sense of what it is to feel Catalan, with loyalty and emotion.

Defining what Barça is has become more complex since Franco's death, although the myth has outlived the reality. Since the restoration of democracy, Catalonia has achieved a greater degree of autonomy than Northern Ireland, Scotland, Corsica, and the South of Italy, while Barça's ruling junta has achieved the kind of political and financial power only dreamed of by European parliaments. Since the 1996

Bosman ruling, which opened up the international transfer market, the playing fortunes of both Barça and Real Madrid have been determined not by Catalans and Spaniards but by Brazilians, Dutchmen, Germans, Frenchmen and, yes, some token Catalans and Spaniards. And yet the encounter between the two clubs is as passionate as it has ever been, the players merely actors on a stage that was erected many years ago and which no one wants to take down. In its crudest definition, the rivalry between the two teams sells newspapers, secures lucrative TV and sponsorship contracts, fills stadiums. As an enduring collective expression, it is in the Camp Nou that Catalans both forget and honour their history, and defy the loss of ideology in the modern world with their very own unity of faith.

English eyes blink in the brightness of a floodlit Camp Nou, at the sheer scale of the five-tiered terracing glowing under the black sky. The stadium has been dug deep into the earth, its turf elevated to give every game played on it the aura of a spectacle. In the changing room, players are preparing to take the final journey: along a small passageway lined with paintings by Catalan modern artists, and down the tunnel, with its chapel on the right and its iron grid down the middle separating the teams. Thirty-four steps down seem eternal, then eight steps up . . . Players emerge from the catacombs to conduct gladiatorial battle before the roar of the coliseum.

There are only minutes left before kick-off, and the eyes of the Barça fans are still on the video screen, with its flashes of skills and greatness, breeding a sense of invincibility before the enemy. The English, distributed around the stadium in small groups and couples, watch the heaving, whirling mass of foreign humanity around them, a vortex that allows for no dissent, that relegates the token hundred-odd Real fans to the most isolated heights of the Camp Nou – to be mocked there – and absorbs the visiting tourist into the adulation of a universal club. There is no space for neutrality, but the bias of the crowd is overwhelming, its fanaticism disquieting.

One team's supporters' intolerance of the other's takes different forms in the run-up to the game. Earlier in the day, the Real Madrid players have been forced temporarily to vacate their hotel after it receives a bomb threat from ETA. Later, their coach is attacked with stones as it makes its way towards the stadium. At 8.00 p.m., the Real Madrid players emerge first, to be greeted by an atmosphere that has been known to break weak spirits, an uninterrupted cacophony of boos, whistles and expletives. Only a hardened veteran of this encounter, Fernando Hierro, allows himself the cheek of lifting up his arm in a defiant greeting, fuelling even greater insults. The others seem awkwardly displaced, limbering up and passing the ball mechanically, nervously avoiding eye contact with the crowd, Christians to the slaughter. But this is but a mere tremor before the earthquake, a token wisp of smoke on the tip of the volcano, before the eruption that takes place as the blue and red colours of the Barça players spill out on to the pitch. Around the stadium, the crowd rises like a tidal wave, singing the club anthem, unfurling giant flags and paper mosaics, detonating thunderclaps. For some seconds, the stadium roars its loyalty as it is covered by a shower of paper ribbons and red and blue balloons, descending like friendly Martians, the members from space.

The sound of the Camp Nou rises from the centre of the earth, increasing in intensity as it spreads around the stadium. Just a few hours earlier, the club members have cast their votes on the motion of no confidence: in a forty-four per cent turn-out, just under 25,000 voted in support of Nuñez, with just over 14,000 backing the Blue Elephant. The result suggests that the president is losing his popularity, that the Blue Elephant strides are getting more self-assured. But for now, the internal battles are put to one side, and the war is once again declared against the common enemy. In its fanaticism, the crowd seems to abandon its democratic credentials, acting with the brutal uncompromising tones of a corporate rally. Every move played by Real Madrid is greeted with abuse, those of the team's Brazilian international Roberto Carlos with racist gorilla imitations.

Somewhere in the middle tier of the stadium sit two twenty-year-old Englishmen – Mark from Watford, and Gavin from Fulham. They are unshockable, but easily impressed. 'Great atmosphere, real passion,' says Mark. 'I've never had a piss like this in all my life, it's like a five-star hotel back there,' says Gavin, who has just relieved himself of the beer he drank at Tapa Tapa. There is a global audience of over 200 million watching the match, but these *ingleses* have managed to squeeze in to smell, hear and feel what it's like to be with a capacity crowd of over 100,000 Barça fans uncompromisingly backing one team. You feel that the world could begin and end here in these ninety minutes, played out by twenty-two players worth between them an estimated £220 million in buy-out clauses alone, that nothing outside really matters, really exists, beyond this gigantic orgasm of mass support.

The game itself is a bruising encounter of individual talent, sporadic runs at goal, brief instances of brilliance, and far too many mistakes, and yet not once does the game sink into mediocrity. Six minutes into the game, Barça's power horse Luis Enrique (a key protagonist politically, given that he was once a Real Madrid player) breaks through the midfield from just inside his own half, beats two opponents, then, anticipating a third challenge, serves Figo with an impeccable pass. The Portuguese's strike beats Real's German goalkeeper Illgner, but is just deflected by the right post. Two minutes later, it's Roberto Carlos's turn to rattle the Barça defence with a characteristic swerving free kick, which has the Dutch goalkeeper Hesp only just tipping it off to a corner. What transforms the game from an evenly balanced slug-out to a walkover is the red-card booking of Real Madrid's Hierro in the 51st minute.

In the history of Barça–Real Madrid games, the referee has always played a critical role, not so much in ensuring equanimity during the game as in responding to bias, or at least in seeming to do so. The corruption and partiality of Spanish referees during the Franco era is one of the many *bêtes noires* of Barça's official club history. Hierro's sending-off comes during a game when every foul by a Madrid player provokes a roar of protest from the Camp Nou, while similar gestures by Barça players are greeted with silence or applause. Several tackles by Barça players look as bad if not worse than those by Hierro, but none of them is sent off. After the match, Madrid's president Lorenzo Sanz cynically nominates the referee, Celino García Redondo from Asturias, as best player, a determining factor in ensuring the Catalan club's victory, having bent to the pressure of the crowd, a convenient scapegoat for the tactical weaknesses of the visiting side.

For without Hierro, Real Madrid loses its cohesion, is unable to rearrange its midfield and defensive formations and buckles before the inevitable onslaught led by the stars. The 69th minute sees a perfectly targeted centre from Rivaldo, transformed into a goal by a simple kick from Anderson. Twelve minutes later, Figo outmanoeuvres Roberto Carlos and scores a second with a devastating left-foot strike. Then, with minutes to go before full time, Figo combines with Rivaldo and Giovanni in a series of feints and passes that leaves Real's defence in tatters. On scoring the third, Giovanni gets a yellow card for taking his shirt off in celebration, but by then such disciplinary gestures by Mr Garcia Redondo seem irrelevant. The crowd thinks it is all over, and it effectively is.

Watching the stadium erupt, *los ingleses* can only marvel. The stadium seethes and trembles, cigar smoke rising like an offering to the gods; then the crowd pours back into the city, their city, their country, in their thousands, momentarily safe and secure – at least until the next encounter. There is no violence when a crowd is as one, and the token opposition has melted into the night.

Los ingleses are among the last to leave the stadium. By the time Mark and Gavin have stirred themselves, the tree-lined avenue named after Pope John XXIII that leads back to the hotel is almost empty. Where the Barça merchandise was earlier, there are prostitutes in short skirts, standing at intervals all the way down to the Camp Nou, like sentinels. 'Fuck me, if only I could speak the language . . .' says Gavin. Later still that night, Doug dreams of Gazza playing in a Barça shirt.

In the early days, when Barça was relatively a small club, and the stadium it played in was not the cathedral of football that is the Camp Nou but a much more modest piece of wasteland, those who couldn't afford a good ticket could still get an excellent view of the match by sitting on top of the wall that surrounded the pitch. Their legs hung on one side, and their asses on the other – good view, hard seat. Their asses were sore at the end of the game. Yet their enthusiasm never diminished. Players there were like the legendary Samitier, who would give them money on a good day. Their witnesses were those who happened to be walking or driving past the stadium during the game. They heard the cries of support, but nothing quite matched the sheer energy of those half-asses, bouncing like buoys on a turbulent sea. Those Barça fans who, despite their poverty, managed to maintain a loyalty to the club that was as rich as it was constant were nicknamed the *cules* ('asses' in Catalan).

In later years, thousands of Catalans got richer, a few remained very rich indeed, and the club got bigger, thanks to an expanding membership. The *cules* came from all social backgrounds, rich and poor. They found themselves no longer sitting on the wall. A majority were given seats, graded according to comfort, position and salary, passed down through generations. A minority were given pens to stand in, squashed together behind the goal or high up in the highest terraces, hundreds of dedicated madmen giving the sharp edge of genuine passion to the mass of self-complacency. These *cules* have always despised some of the *socios* who go to watch Barça as if to the theatre. The discreet charm of the middle and ruling classes is to this day to be found in the middle tiers: the women smelling of perfume and vaguely of mothballs, the men smoking cigars and, in the enclosure reserved for the members of the board and their guests, the politicians, the bankers, the lawyers and the businessmen – very few women among them – who relish the cocktails in the VIP lounge at half-time, make themselves available to the local TV, and know that the best time to be there is when Barça is winning well, and preferably against Real Madrid.

Now that the task has been accomplished, that Real Madrid has been sufficiently humiliated, that the past has been sufficiently avenged, it is time for expansion, for further conquest, for a club like Barça is much too big, much too proud, to settle for a victory at home. It wants titles that recognise a power that crosses frontiers, to hold up gleaming cups and say, 'We are the best in Spain . . . in Europe . . . in the world.'

In the 1997–8 season, Nuñez replaced Bobby Robson with former Ajax manager Louis van Gaal as Barça's chief coach. Van Gaal declared in his opening press conference, 'I have come here to do a job, and that is to deliver a system that will operate over the long term. We will be looking to win trophies from the very start, but to complete the project may take several years.' This season the club has had to trim its aspirations. Knocked out in the early stages of the Champions' League, it subsequently settles for victory in the finals of the much less prestigious European Super Cup. Within Spain, however, Barça is on a roll. The victory over Real Madrid has paved the way for its conquest of the Spanish League, and it now has the double in its sights, facing Mallorca in the finals of the King's Cup in Valencia. It's been a long time since it achieved the double – it last did so in the season of 1958–9, when the club had as its manager the mystical Argentinian Helenio Herrera, and other no less legendary players, such as Kubala, Suárez, Ramallets and Segarra.

A couple of months have gone by since that match in the Camp Nou against Real Madrid, and we are back outside the Hotel Princesa Sofia. This time it is not *los ingleses* but a group of *cules* who come together one morning near the taxi rank. They are boys and girls in their late teens and early twenties. With their sneakers, jeans and conversational effervescence, they are indistinguishable from the thousands of Spanish students who invade the British Isles in the summer. Only the blue and red of the Barça colours round their necks set their identity, remind the world why they've bothered to get out of bed. For those with a sense of passion, there is everything to cheer and whistle for, kilometres to travel, parties and sex to postpone, all for one, one for all, Barça, Barça, and nothing more. The *cules* prepare for their trip as if for battle, gathering provisions for the journey and for the match – videos, CDs, beer, banners, stickers, dope, printed T-shirts, thunderclaps, wine, Coke and vodka. The buses leave punctually at 10.00 a.m.

The *cules* have draped their flags over the windows: the colours of Barça, the colours of Catalonia, autonomous state, the colours of the movement for independence from Spain – a reminder that Barça is a broad church that accommodates a range of definitions as to what it is to be Catalan. The flags submerge the bus in half-light, isolate it from the outside world, making the emotions carried within it more intense.

A video begins to play against the background of a rock soundtrack by the Irish group Moving Hearts. It is a film on the IRA depicting the history of Northern Ireland as the organisation's 'courageous war of liberation' against the occupying forces of the British Army. It is blatant propaganda funded by French TV. 'Some friends of mine who were on holiday in Ireland last summer brought it back for me . . . it's got some real cool scenes, I mean look at that one,' says Pablo, one of the organisers of the trip. He has long curly black hair and dark eyes, and is trim, healthy and handsome, like a younger version of Barça's pin-up Miguel Angel Nadal. A group of hooded men are patrolling a Catholic estate in West Belfast, a sniper lies in wait as an army unit approaches, a mortar is fired across the hills of County Armagh, women shout obscenities at an English officer. 'The Irish have been engaged in a struggle for liberation just like the people of Catalonia,' says Pablo. As if to underline his point, he pulls out of a bag an Irish tricolour, and puts it alongside the Catalan flags. The video ends and is replaced by *The Full Monty*. Half the bus are soon pissing themselves with laughter. 'We like this film. It's one of our favourites. We like the humour, the music, and the way it shows men and women fighting back in adverse circumstances,' insists Pablo.

Only Oscar seems a little more subdued than when we last met near the estate agents' where he works during the day. It seems clear to him that although the team is winning games, the football it is playing is verging on the boring. I remember his telling me before that the most important day of his life was when Barça won the European Cup at Wembley in 1992. He is now gripped with a terrible sense of loss over one of the players who made that possible: Stoichkov. 'We are the Stoichkov generation. We liked his spirit, his game, his aggressiveness, his personality . . .'

We are less than an hour into the journey and already the bus is suffused by a fug of marijuana fumes mixed with tobacco smoke. The joint-smokers are in the rear rows, together with some of the heavier drinkers. While those in the front share occasional bottles of Coke and lager, those in the back are sipping wine with vodka. In my quest for the psyche of the *cule* I have started at the front and am working backwards. Across the gangway from Oscar and Pablo is Marc. Slouching in the seat he is sharing with his sleeping girlfriend, he explains why he has been a *cule* for as long as he can remember. 'I've been with Barça since I was a kid, from the moment I had a sense of being.' As he goes on talking, he sits up so that I can hear him better, letting his girlfriend's head fall like a rag doll's on to the flag-draped window. 'It was the year before Maradona came. I remember the first time I went into the stadium, thinking this place is going to eat me up, all the fans are going to eat me up. I was seven years old.'

All Marc can remember about the first game he saw is Simonsen. It was the 1981–2 season, a year recorded in the annals of Barça's official history as representing the paradigm of everything that is unforeseen and unforeseeable in football. Barça had fought hard throughout the season to get to the top of the League, despite the absence of the team's other foreign star, Bernd Schuster, who had been hacked by Athletic Bilbao's Andoni Goikoetxea. With six games left to play, Barça had a six-point advantage over its nearest rival, Real Sociedad. Then Barça not only gave two points away by drawing with Real Sociedad, but threw the League away altogether by losing four of the last five games. It was the kind of disaster that, because of its sheer impact and the shocked surprise among ordinary people, could only be compared to the end of the world.

But then something happened, as wonderful as a resurrection, something no *cule* could have imagined possible, however Catholic his upbringing. Barça, who had lost the League, after earlier losing the King's Cup, won the Cup Winners Cup against Standard Liège in the Camp Nou. Marc was there that day. At the beginning, the major part of the stadium taken up by the *cules* was restrained. Some of them were angry. But Barça played like a knight trying to win back his lover, desperately and courageously. 'Simonsen scored the first of two goals which took us to victory, that is what I remember,' says Marc. Maybe it wasn't his first game, maybe he was there too when the Basques got their comeuppance. But who wants to remember a mother's labour pains, when it's the birth that delivers life? Marc, like the rest of the stadium, forgave Barça that day, even if not everyone forgot.

The next year that figures in Marc's memory is 1992. It was a special year, that one – the 500th anniversary of Columbus's discovery of America. His statue near the waterfront in Barcelona is pointing towards the Mediterranean, towards Genoa, the place of his birth, as if the Catalans had wanted to puncture eternally the myth that he somehow belonged exclusively to Isabella of Castile. Instead Barcelona hosted the Olympics and put on a show that the whole world would marvel at, and the rest of Spain could only envy. But as far as Marc is concerned, that year is special not because of Columbus or the Olympics or Seville's Expo fair, but because that is the year he became a member of FC Barcelona. He had just turned eighteen – old enough to gain a little independence from his own family and to want to join a larger one. His membership card shows that he became the club's member number 90,000. Fingering it like a relic, Marc says, 'I think that watching Barça is better than watching a rock concert . . . it's the air I breathe in, intense and absorbing, ninety minutes of life and death.'

It was in 1992 also that Marc went to Wembley to watch Barça play in the final of the European Cup. There were 25,000 *cules* that day making the wish of their lives that Barça would beat Sampdoria. Full time and 0–0, and then *that* goal of Koeman's in the sixth minute of the second half of extra time. 'It was the best thing in the world . . . the goal, the people . . . Barça won that day because the *cules* were there in their thousands giving their souls . . . 25,000 candles lit to all the Virgins in the world so that Barça would win . . .'

In the bus, Marc is handing out the T-shirts of his fan club, the Peña Almogavers. On them are depicted medieval knights in full armour against a dark blue background. 'We're giving them away today because we want people to feel good, although we sometimes sell them – it's how we make money. You know who the Almogavers were? Catalan soldiers of the thirteenth century who conquered the Mediterranean. They'd go into battle on foot, holding their swords, and fight off whole armies on horseback. They were mercenaries for the King of Greece and on his behalf defeated the Turks. But then the Greeks started getting worried that the Almogavers were getting more powerful than they, and so they murdered their leader. The Almogavers swore revenge and razed the whole of Greece to the ground . . . they killed a third of the population. It was terrible.'

By now, we are half-way to Valencia and the bus pulls into a motorway service stop. The area is filled with hundreds of *cules* who are making their way to the match by road. It is like a caravan in the desert, a gathering at the water-hole, a sharing of tribal beliefs. The *cules* share some beers, break bread, piss together. They laugh and sing, small groups breaking out with a spontaneous rendering of the Barça anthem. It is a generally good-natured and joyful event, spoilt only by the presence of a small group of skinheads in dark glasses, leaning menacingly against the wall. Minutes earlier Marc has invoked images of conquest, plunder and revenge. However, with the exception of the *boixos*, nothing here points to anything but a peaceful day's outing. There is as much bluff as bluster as they sing together, '*Tot el camp es un clam, som la gente blaugrana* . . .'

Marc sings too, then says, 'We want Barça to conquer Europe just like the Almogavers did.' He is holding a small banner bearing the words '*Barça i Catalunya sempre al nostre cor*'. You see, it's one and the same thing – to be with Barça is to feel Catalan . . . that's what drives me. I've done so much for Barça, missed my exams, missed a whole year at college. You might say I'm fanatical. I like to consider myself someone who loves Barça with all my heart. If that's fanaticism, then I'm a fanatic.' And he joins a group of *cules* for another rendering of the anthem.

Among them are Bernard and José Miguel, who have been smoking marijuana and drinking since we left Barcelona. 'Don't think that some of us are all that different from the English fans – some of us will be out of our minds by the time the match begins,' Marc tells me before we board the bus again at the start of the last stage of the journey. I decide I want to talk to Bernard and José Miguel before they become incoherent, so I join them at the back of the bus. The air is smoky and pungent. Bernard is tall and drawn, shadows for eyes, ring on his ear. He has made a habit of repeating himself, when not giggling, or passing a half-lit joint between phrases, of speaking a language of defiance and subversion. Something tells me, though, that Bernard is not a fighter any more. 'My parents are right-wing; they are Catalans but they might as well be Spanish,' he says. 'I'm not like them – the most important thing in my life is Barça, it's Catalonia.'

The bus moves on, through orange groves and legends of *El Cid*. For no reason at all, or perhaps every reason, Bernard talks about Josep Lluís Nuñez, the president of FC Barcelona. 'Nuñez is a waste of time, like all his junta, he is just a money-spinner. They are extreme right. I ask myself, how is it possible that a guy belongs to Barça and then invests in a hotel named after the King of Spain? That shouldn't be. Those who vote for Nuñez are the rich. That's clear as daylight. And people are being conned. Wankers, the lot of them.'

Next to him, José Miguel, his eyes like discs, wants to talk football. He also remembers Wembley. 'Koeman had real charisma. He had grace, man, real class . . . what a fuck of a goal, man.' He was eight years old when his father took him for the first time to the Camp Nou. The first match he remembers was when Barça played Tottenham. A goal from Simonsen, who hit the ball with his chest, on his knees. 'I was very little and spent half the match not seeing a fuck because I couldn't see through everybody else . . . but I remember that goal because everybody got up. It was unforgettable.'

Bernard and José Miguel were *boixos nois* (our boys) once, members of the brotherhood of hooligans Barça-style who make more noise than anyone, and get into more fights. I ask them why they left. Bernard draws heavily on the joint, then, coughing, passes it on. We are entering Valencia, traffic cops gesticulating like unwound clockwork pieces, scattered pockets of *cules* making their way to the centre of town. Bernard tells me, 'When I joined the *boixos*, I thought they were left-wing and pro-independence. Then I realised they were the pits, man, that they were extreme right. It was the *boixos* who used to give it all for Barça and for Catalonia, but they are a disgrace now, man, they are Nazis who shit on Catalonia and forget that Barça is above all that – or should be.'

José Miguel confides that when he isn't watching football, he is handling dogs for a security company. It is tough work, dangerous at times. Control the dogs, and you can use them against the enemy. Lose control of them, and you're a dead man. He now tells me, 'There used to be a lot of dope with the *boixos*; now there are a lot of skinheads. In 1992 I think it was, there was a *boixo* called Jaro who was put in jail because he stabbed a French guy in the neck and in the heart. Seventeen stab wounds in all he and his mates were responsible for, and from that episode they developed this song which went something like this, 'El Jaro has got real balls, he fucked a Frenchman to death . . .'

As we arrive in Valencia, Marc is distributing *bengalas* (flares). They are officially banned in Spanish stadiums, but Marc has learned from experience that they are easy to slip through the security. He also believes that the people who make the rules know nothing about football. Marc knows only that a game without *bengalas* is like Christmas without presents.

Valencia is a city temporarily leased. It is occupied by thousands of *cules* and Mallorca fans who have travelled from the island in boats and planes. Catalans consider Mallorca an island off their coastline with a people who speak a similar language to their own. Mallorquinos consider themselves an island community, quite separate from Catalonia or any other part of Spain, with its own culture and traditions. In football the distinction is sufficiently blurred to prevent any serious outbreak of violence between rival fans. In Valencia, the most popular chant echoing through the city is 'Juve, Juve'. For more than anything else in the world the *cule* wants Juventus to beat Real Madrid in the European Champions' League.

Later, as the sun sets over the city of oranges, *cules* and Mallorquines gather outside El Bar Manolo, drinking, singing and occasionally having group photographs taken with the owner. The last time I had been with Manolo was at Wembley during the England–Spain match of Euro '96. That day, Manolo was the Spanish team's official cheerleader, his broad beret and drum essential reference points for the hopes and dreams of the 2,000 fans who had gathered to support Spain in section J behind one of the goals. Manolo inspired rather than incited, soothing the more aggressive fans with his benign smile, and urging all the Spaniards to dance and clap, giving the game its rhythm and its joy. But that was Wembley among the few Spaniards prepared to follow the 'national' team abroad. Many of the *cules* who have come to Valencia to cheer Barça would not be seen dead cheering the Spanish national team.

As things turn out, the Valencia game is played poorly. Van Gaal's team is seemingly made of expensive players who have yet to find their form or method. On balance, Mallorca play much better. They fight harder for the ball and work better as a team; they are robbed of victory in a penalty shoot-out. But the party that began early that morning has too much adrenalin in it for some of the *cules* to let it all go. Marc and the others wave their flags furiously, explode their flares, and taunt the riot police. They jump and push one another, their bodies only occasionally moving in some kind of shared rhythm, when they try to take everyone with them steaming down the terraces. They scream '*hijos de putas*' at the Mallorca players, at the police and at the referee, and unravel a Juventus flag, chanting, 'Juve, Juve, Juve.'

The biggest fix of all, however, is when King Juan Carlos appears in the VIP box. They give him a good whistle, which manages to make itself heard above the general applause.

2

Among the Believers (continued)

It is God v. Mammon – or so it seems. Mid-September, and in the city of Manchester the best and worst of this game we call football are gathered.

FC Barcelona has flown in for its European Champion's League encounter with Manchester United. Barça has got off to a bad start in the domestic League, some of its officials blaming its lack of strength and imagination on an extended hangover from the World Cup – an illness that seems particularly to affect Brazilians and Dutchmen. The more populist view, however, is that Louis van Gaal is to blame. He stands accused of more than just poor results and uninspiring football. He is disliked for the way he has carried out the hollandisation of the club, importing six Dutch players and three Dutch coaches. Worse still, as Simon Kuper points out in a profile for the *Financial Times*, 'Van Gaal has treated Barcelona's other players as if they were Dutchmen. He is like the expatriate business executive who cannot understand the local way of doing things. The man whose favourite word is *collectief* succeeded at Ajax thanks to a rigid tactical system in which each player carried out his task. To him that is the only way . . .' Yet Barcelona has several gifted players, among them the Brazilian Rivaldo who is capable of deciding a game alone, and Catalans from the youth team, such as 'Pep' Guardiola, who deserve to be taken more seriously and listened to more carefully.

But for once the club's performance does not seem to be the issue of primary concern, either for the club or for the team it is facing. Manchester – the town and its people – is in a state of shock. It is only a matter of days since local fans have been convulsed by the announcement that Rupert Murdoch, the Australian media magnate, has made a bid to buy Manchester United, one of the world's oldest teams, which prides itself on having built itself on the loyalty of its supporters and the efforts of its star managers and teams. There is a genuine fear that the club will lose its identity to a global business empire which treats human beings like cogs in a machine: a world muddled by complicated intercompany borrowings and financing and equally complex joint ventures, and simplified only in its ability to make of violence and sex marketable commodities. What the fans fear is only too clear in a handout from the independent Manchester United Supporters' Association. Decisions affecting the future of the club will be taken on the other side of the world. The club will no longer be independent. It will be owned and manipulated to further the interests of the Murdoch empire.

The fact sheet is distributed at a crisis meeting of the association on the eve of the big match. It quotes liberally from Geoffrey Green's book *There's Only One United*. The club that is about to be taken over by Murdoch is the same club that once upon a time turned you into a 'partisan holding your breath when the ball came sailing into your goal mouth, ecstatic when your forwards raced away towards the opposite goal, elated, downcast, bitter, triumphant by turns at the fortunes of your side'. It is also 'the club that turned you into a member of a new community, all brothers together for an hour and a half, for not only had you escaped from the clanking machinery of this lesser life, from work, wages, rent, dole, sick pay, insurance cards, nagging wives, ailing children, bad bosses, idle workmen . . .' United stands for something more than any other person, any player, any supporter. It is, as was written in the club programme of 1937, 'the soul of a sporting organisation which goes on from year to year, making history all the time'. All that seems about to be trampled on.

Into this state of romantically tinged nostalgia, of paranoia, of desperate vertigo, steps Barça, bringing with it its own dreams and illusions, manna from heaven, the good cop, the image of a club that Manchester fans would like to hang on to. It is an image that fits into a world neatly divided into black and white, with no space for shades of grey. This Barça now provides neat copy for those of us who want to add something to the thousands of words already written about the Murdoch bid with a study in contrasts. As the Manchester fans weep over the demise of their soul, they are consoled with the suggestion that it doesn't have to be this way. Barça holds the key to what was, what is, what still could be. The club remains, according to its statutes, faithful to the democratic principles of its founding fathers – a 'private association without profit motive, owned and controlled by its membership'.

In the lobby of the Hotel Jarvis Piccadilly, a large bald man with the look of a schoolteacher who has temporarily lost the pupils in his charge sits behind a large desk. His name is Moline and he works for a Barcelona travel agency called Viajes Marins. The agency has organised the travel arrangements of some of the *socios* who are in Manchester to watch the match. Some 150 of them have paid 149,000 pesetas for the privilege of flying in the same chartered plane as the team, and staying at the hotel, a monstrous concrete edifice off the city's main square. The cost includes bus transport to and from the match, and a place in the visitors' enclosure at Old Trafford. On the night before the big game, the visitors pay an extra £60 to see their team training at Old Trafford, while drinking Bucks' Fizz and eating a four-course meal in the ground's Stretford Suite. It is in fact the nearest glimpse they have had of the team on the whole trip, for on arriving at Manchester Airport the team and its management were taken to a location well away from the city.

Three hours before the game is due to begin, Moline is hoping his clients will turn up from their wandering around town. There is a sense of *déjà vu* about these last-minute hassles involving organised fans abroad. Earlier in the year, it was the English fans coming to Barcelona whom Moline had to deal with, Dave and Doug and the Full Monty. 'Yes, I remember it well, the last-minute problem with tickets – the ones we normally had reserved for the English agency were taken off us. It seemed as if they were being offered as an inducement to come to vote for Nuñez. Then this English girl, the daughter of the travel agent, got angry because I couldn't arrange for everyone to sit in the places she wanted. I tried to explain to her that this club of ours is owned by its members, who have a right to the seats they have always had. My grandfather is a member, so is my father, so am I, and we always sit in the same place. No one is going to tell us to move . . .'

Moline is telling his story about the English, when two young Catalans approach his desk. One of them identifies himself as the son of the club's vice-president, Joan Gaspart, and asks whether it is possible to make an extra space on the return journey to Barcelona for his friend. Moline would like to tell the kid to piss off, but he knows that to do that would probably mean losing his job. So he smiles instead, says there is no problem whatsoever, offers his service like the dutiful servant he is. Only when the two youths have gone does Moline regain some control over his own existence, gazing at the impossible list laid before him on the table. 'What do they think, that the plane is made of rubber, and we can just squeeze in anyone?' he grunts.

Upstairs in the hotel bar a group of somewhat less privileged *cules* are having some rounds of beer before the match. The oldest among them is José. He was born in 1938 in Almería, a desert land set against a generous oasis where the local civil governor refused to arm the workers the day Franco staged his uprising. 'Arm the people, but with what? Where do governors get arms to distribute to the people? The arms of the state are always placed in the power of the army, the governor had said. That was before the destroyer *Lepanto* with a loyal captain and crew on board secured the port for the Republic. Its guns had been trained on the civil guard and forced them to surrender.

That was at the start of the Spanish Civil War. José was only one year old when it ended, a year when life in Almería seemed to have changed irrevocably, with people captured, people killed, people victorious, people defeated. Much later Almería would become Texas-by-the-Sea, the place where American and Italian directors could film their spaghetti westerns cheaply. But for a while it was a dead part of Spain, deserted. José's family migrated northwards, escaping the poverty, to a land which had been conquered but not subdued, where there was less hunger and more jobs. As it proved for other southerners, this was not an easy rite of passage. They had to struggle for acceptance by those who had lived there much longer, who had suffered locally, who were reluctant to cede any part of their country to outsiders.

For José the past, like the present, is tied up with football. For only when his family began to follow Barça did they begin to feel a sense of belonging. To cheer the team, to pay homage to the individual skills of the players, to shout abuse at Real Madrid, was to confirm oneself as part of the local community and break through the alienation of being an emigrant. In the car plant where José worked, the politics the local union leaders spoke seemed to come not from Barcelona but from an internationalist textbook of workers' struggle. It was a difficult language to share beyond the factory gates. Only when José had himself grown old enough to be a *cule* – to go to the stadium whenever he could afford it – did he begin to lead a life that would allow him to say one day in Manchester, 'Catalonia means everything to me, that is why I am a *cule*.' And there is not much more that José can say on this day in September, even if he wanted to. He has cancer of the throat. His voicebox has been removed, and his words struggle to be coherent through a series of belches; one feels that he is saving it all up for the one word he desperately wants to say again and again as long as anyone can hear him: 'BARÇA!' The one time he says it to me, his stomach rises and pumps it out, as if he's drawn it out from deep within his soul.

In the group who are drinking with José, the girls are outnumbered by the boys, although it's the girls who do most of the talking – two of them, to be precise. Monica is Pre-Raphaelite – all blue eyes and tumbling hair. She is flirting with an English boy she met last summer in Lloret when I interrupt her and ask what makes a woman support Barça. 'My grandfather, my father are Barça fans' – male genes, in other words – 'and Barça *is* much more than a club. For historical reasons, the club is a way of saying that we do not want the rest of Spain to repress us – the stadium was the only place where we could express ourselves freely . . .'

Monica is twenty-two years old, which means that she wasn't even born when Franco died. So I ask, how can she possibly know all this? 'Because I was born into a community that lived it and because you go on feeling it. Whenever we sing the club's anthem, I get real goose bumps.' As for her favourite players, Monica names Bakero and Amor – because they play well and are not foreigners. 'We have too many foreigners in the teams these days,' she says, throwing a furtive smile at her *inglés*. Her friend, Maria, who is twenty-seven, recalls that she was three years old when she was first taken to the stadium. 'I have this clear memory of my father pointing out this player called Johan Cruyff and saying, "Look, look, look down there, isn't he amazing." I didn't know anything about football so I just sat there thinking how skinny he was.' Getting to know Barça better coincided with puberty and the first stirrings of domestic dislocation. She was twelve years old when the 'Hesperia mutiny' shattered Barça's sense of unity, and her own unswerving loyalty to her father. In April 1988, members of the team team met in Barcelona's Hotel Hesperia and demanded the resignation of the club president Nuñez, because of a row over payments that had been simmering for months. Nuñez responded by bringing in Cruyff as the new manager and replacing the majority of the team the following season. 'I was in favour of the players, of the way they were demanding change, and my father was backing Nuñez, so we had these blazing rows. I remember feeling so sad that the whole affair meant Schuster quitting,' says Maria.

So does she feel that Barça is fundamentally *machista* as a result? 'Sure,' she answers without hesitating. 'You know what the boys said to us the first time I and some girlfriends stepped into the bus to go and see a game with them? "You've come to clean the floor, darlings!" To this day, their favourite joke is to come up and ask us if we've cleared the rubbish yet. It's a kind of attitude that builds up outside the stadium, although once we're in there we're treated as equals. Somehow the boys think it's not cool to be seen to be friendly to you on the street, it's not hooligan enough. For them, women, Arabs and blacks are all in the same category – better not seen in Barça colours.'

Despite the drawbacks, Monica follows her team more than many *socios*; she rarely misses a League match and travels with the team abroad whenever she can. 'There is a typical *socio* who's quite happy just to be a couch potato and watch his team on his home TV, or who goes along to the stadium not because he wants to but because he feels he should be seen doing so. He smokes his cigar, he always sits in the same place – "Don't even think of moving my ass, this is my place and always will be," he says to anyone who tries to stir him. These people want a comfortable life, but they have no passion. Maybe that's why there are only a few of us here in Manchester.' Maria and Monica belong to a female supporters' club called the Amazonas – wild and defiant like the legendary women of the South American jungle who confronted the Spanish conquistadors and filled them with fear, then longing. 'We do our bit for Barça wherever we go. We lay our little grain of sand,' Maria says, before leading her *inglés* out of the bar, by the collar.

*   *   *

The other *ingleses* are exchanging local humour with the visitors in a pub just across the square. Alfons, clutching Blue Elephant pamphlets he has brought with him all the way from Barcelona, is looking for like-minded souls, beyond the sausage dripping with fat and beans and lukewarm local bitter he is having as a sign of solidarity. He dreams of a new popular alliance between Barça and Manchester United fans, joined in their passion for the game and in their determination to slay the dragons of men like Nuñez and Murdoch. The pub in late afternoon is filled with young couples snogging and middle-aged Irishmen taking a break from the bookies'. Two Manchester fans are propped up half drunk against the bar. 'May the best team win,' says Alfons, with a phrase he learned when he was a schoolboy. 'If we don't win, we'll fucking kill you,' says one of the *ingleses*. His friend points to the sports page of a tabloid paper in his hands, swerves, and belches. There is a story claiming that Jordi Cruyff has been spying on Manchester United and has passed on all its secrets to his old team. 'How's this for a laugh – as if Jordi had anything to give away. He's fucking crap, can't tell one boot from the other.' Alfons is told to watch out for Dwight Yorke.

Nearby, the betting shop has Manchester United as clear favourite to win. Some *cules* are placing bets that Barça will lose 3–0. Many more *ingleses* – actually, quite a few Irishmen too – are drinking nearer the stadium. 'We are here because we've won fuck all,' they chant. It's Murdoch who is looking every bit the winner, and Nuñez, for that matter; hard not to imagine them both in time laughing all the way to the bank, creaming off the profits from the revamped European Super League to which the two teams have their special invitations.

You can get a sense of the potential from the excitement generated by this match. As the *Guardian* columnist Jim White ponders, 'They don't come much bigger than these, the world's greatest football club owned by its 150,000 members spread across the planet from Vegas to the Vatican, visiting the world's greatest football Publicly Listed Company, soon to be owned by one man from Melbourne.' There is a Freddie Mercury anthem to the unbridled egotism of mankind which television has made its own. It spreads out from the stadium and across the city as unstoppable as nuclear fall-out: 'We are the champions . . . No time for losers!' it screams.

When they first catch sight of Old Trafford, the legendary 'Theatre of Dreams', some of the Barça *socios* are less than impressed. Compared with the Camp Nou, the stadium looks like an afterthought. Whereas the Camp Nou is one of Barcelona city's architectural giants, built on a wave of political and social ambition, Old Trafford is tucked away out in the suburbs, an oversized warehouse built amidst grey concrete and modest terraced houses. And yet there is no stopping Albert and his group of friends as they make their way into the stadium, long before it has been even half filled by the local supporters. Entering the visitors' enclosure, they are waving the Barça colours and singing the club anthem to a tune from *The Marriage of Figaro*, clapping as they go, making as much noise as they can. Albert is an Almogaver, a dedicated follower, unswerving in his loyalty, forceful in its expression, a very modern Barça crusader with his pot belly, hair tied in a bow, stringy beard, jean jacket and sneakers. He also feels enormous respect for Old Trafford – not its size, but its history. In coming he has realised the dream of one of his most longed-for pilgrimages. He and his friends have made their own way to Manchester, finding cheaper transport and accommodation than that offered to the 'VIP's by Viajes Marins. 'When you are my age you can't afford to pay 140,000 pesetas – and yet it's the youth that is the life-blood of the club.'

Albert's earliest conscious childhood memory is of being given his first Barça kit; he had wanted it so much, more than any other present in the world. It was to take some years before he could relive an occasion with such intensity: it was the farewell match for his idol Migueli. 'As far as I am concerned there's never been a player quite like him – great personality, great character. He was really strong; eleven players like him would have meant Barça winning many more trophies than it has done. He may not have had great technique, but he sure knew how to defend the club colours better than anybody. The day he played his last game, a friendly against Bulgaria, it was pissing with rain; I've got it stamped in my brain as if it was yesterday.'

There is a clear memory, too, of the European Cup final at Wembley on 20th May 1992, sitting behind the goalpost watching Koeman take the free kick against Sampdoria. 'You see the ball coming, straight at you, you see an Italian player trying to stop it and failing, and you're screaming "Goal" before it enters, and you go on screaming as the ball shakes the net and me and my mates are all hugging each other, rolling down the stand with crazy joy . . . you never forget that sort of goal, it's part of your life, a really important part.'

Albert is telling me this as we wait for the game to begin in the visitors' lounge by Bar 68. He sits on a bench facing a group of *socios* dressed impeccably in suits and lighting up cigars like generals considering whether to send in the heavy artillery to support the infantry. Looking at them, Albert lowers his voice and says, 'That famous phrase of ours – "we are more than a club" – I have my doubts. Sometimes in the Camp Nou there can be as many as 80,000, but only about 2,000 are actively supporting the team. The *socio* doesn't just want to see good football, he wants the team to win the whole time, something that is not possible. Anyway, for the team to do well you've got to get behind them, support them when they're down – what's the merit in backing the team only when it's winning?'

Albert is a romantic of the game – the team is above all other considerations in his life. He sleeps and wakes thinking only of the next time he can watch Barça play, of being there, of singing and cheering his heart out. But he has been touched by the Murdoch controversy, reinforcing his belief that Barça must hang on to basic principles if it is to survive the corruptive onslaught of the market. I ask him if he thinks the Blue Elephant attacks on president Nuñez are simply part of a power struggle. He sees such measures as a necessary refocusing on what really matters to the true *cule*. 'The elephant is defending ideas which a lot of us share. We realise that although the club should belong to the membership, most *socios* have very little control. We should have more democracy, a word that many members of the junta don't understand at all.'

Apart from the men with their cigars, there are two Manchester policewomen and several private security men keeping a discreet eye on Albert and his friends. And yet any possible fears that there will be trouble between rival fans prove groundless. For all the veiled threats that have been heard from the beered-up in the hours leading up to the match, the *cules* who have come to Manchester are too few in number and too respectful of their hosts to present any challenge to local fans. There is also a sense of underlining solidarity that cuts across club loyalties, an unwritten agreement to find a common cause against those who threaten the game's soul.

During most of the first half, the Barça fans grumble among themselves as they watch their club's star-studded team react with the inspiration of morphine addicts to the relentless attacking football of Giggs and Scholes, backed by Beckham. Watching Rivaldo fumble, and Giovanni miss his kicks, seeing how even Hesp's hands seem soaked with butter so easily does the ball slip from his fingers, the *cules* have a terrible sense of *déjà vu*, memories of a disastrous end to the previous season's Champions' League, when Barça conceded seven goals in two games against Dynamo Kiev and lost to Newcastle. The Manchester fans might have a buyer, but Barça has one too, a Dutch football coach called Louis van Gaal who thinks that to play good football you have to bring in foreign players and keep the local intake to a minimum. How apposite seems another pen portrait in that week's *Observer* by the half-Dutch writer Simon Kuper. He describes van Gaal as looking like 'a credible Devil with his flat nose, patently false teeth, and poor body language – a tall, stiff schoolmaster, with an unlikely penchant for extravagant gestures as when he famously asked a journalist, "Are you so stupid or am I so smart?" ' The Catalans just think van Gaal is rude.

A sense of collective mourning begins to stir as Ferguson's team steamroll their way through the midfield and defence. Thoughts turn on absent friends and heroes – players like Guardiola, Amor and Ferrer, who played on All Souls' Day four years previously at the Camp Nou when Barça beat Manchester 4–0. Bakero, who played in that match too, is in Manchester, but as a journalist. He has the sad look of a player who misses the adrenalin of the game. Ivan de la Peña, who so enchanted the *cules* with his imaginative touches and breaks from midfield, has left for Italy. Like all nostalgic longings, these dissipate as quickly as they resurfaced when van Gaal's team finds its form in the second half. Now it is Manchester who seem mesmerised by the skill and talent that wind their way towards goal. The *cules* wake as if from a bad dream watching Barça click into top gear, with a demonstrable brand of total football in which every individual player is in touch with a colleague's ability to exchange position, imaginatively and without strain. The interplay delivers players at ease with themselves and with each other, freeing up the defence and upping the tempo, with Rivaldo finding the space at last to show Old Trafford the star he really is.

The final score – 2–2 – is a fair reflection of a well-balanced contest. There is football at its best tonight, a wonderful night of European football with two of the world's great teams, the fans living the excitement of a game of fluctuating fortunes, a spectacle both absorbing and intense – worth it on its own terms and no one else's – where the dollar signs and the power brokers have no presence worth thinking about amidst the sweat of good players and the fans' sheer passion for the game.

The Manchester game is nevertheless a mere support act for the main event of the week – Barça's first game of the season against Real Madrid, in the Estadio Bernabéu on Saturday. This is a game that demands the presence of a different contingent of *cules*: hardened warriors, crusaders, fanatics like the Amazonas. Among the handful of supporters who have planned to be there is Maria. In Manchester, while waiting for the game at Old Trafford, she tried to explain why it was that so many men were too scared to make the trip to Madrid. 'You are asking me how and when we can meet. Well, I can tell you, it's not as easy as that with the Madrid game. Usually the police are waiting for us about fifty kilometres outside the city. They are there to escort you all the way to the stadium, although you feel like a prisoner being transferred to where you are hemmed in again. Even if you wanted to meet up with someone locally, they wouldn't let you.'

We were talking, Maria and I, in the relaxed atmosphere of a Manchester hotel bar. But the mere subject of the Madrid game made her tense, the sense of it too close for comfort. 'When you get to the stadium, all you hear are insults. They call us "Polish shits" because we speak Catalan and they want to make it sound as foreign as Polish. I've had Madrid fans taking their trousers down and facing me with their asses. If it occurs to you to fight back, you might as well forget it. The police are itching to lay into you . . . they take our flags away from us. They say that the independence flags are anti-constitution. That you can wave them in a foreign land but not in Spain . . . .'

Madrid is enemy country. The Bernabéu stadium is the castle

occupied by the forces of reaction, violent oppressors. No time for tourism here. Just the brutal reminder of a rivalry that has lasted for decades, fuelled by the authoritarianism and paranoia of one side or the other, maintained by a complicity of interests that range from the power of governments to the genuine faith of the ordinary fan in the team that has been inseparable from his or her life since birth. And lest anybody forget it, the media are on hand to stoke up the fires, to warm up the gladiators, to incense the crowds with suggestive headlines and tales of past defamations and present defiances – although you need historians and sociologists adequately to explain this, the most politicised football match in the world.

The coaches with the *cules* arrive three hours before the kick-off, 'protected', just as Maria predicted, by police vans in front and behind. There is a cordoned-off parking space for them, further protected by riot police on foot and on horseback, and by metal barriers. Only one coach appears to have lost its way, and parked itself away from the enclosure. Police move in on it, like hunters on their prey, shouting to its occupants to get out – and quickly. There is now a crowd of local fans gathering between the bus and the metal barriers. The police form a corridor through them and order the *cules* to walk along it, to the metal barriers and beyond. The *cules* run the gauntlet silently, each step accompanied by growing abuse. 'Polish shits', 'Catalan shit', 'Sons of bitches' are the most popular phrases. Some of the police appear to be smirking, the smiles wiped from their faces only when the visitors have got through to the other side of the barrier. For no sooner has the last *cule* done so than the Barça anthem is intoned, cheekily, defiantly, you could almost say with real balls were it not for the fact that women are singing too.

The new arrivals converge as bees on honey towards a tall, lean boy of military build with closely cropped hair. Hidden from the crowds behind the main group of buses, the boy is collecting wads of tickets from a man in a grey suit. He is a Barça official the club has appointed to 'liaise' with the fans. Several *cules* I have approached since getting into the enclosure have refused to answer any questions, referring me instead to the boy, identified as the leader of the *boixos*. The Barça official sees me coming and tells me not to take a step further. 'No one around here is making any statements. If you don't leave I'll call the police,' he says. Without prompting, two heavily padded policemen push me away. In an instant I glimpse a disturbing conspiracy of interests which is hard to equate with Barça's self-image of democracy.

There is time, though, to merge with other *cules*, out of range of central control. I have an advantage over a TV crew from Barcelona, the only other journalists who have managed to bluff their way into the enclosure: they have been told not to film, by the police, by the official, by the *boixos* commander who seems to wield so much ticket power. I wonder what it is that imposes this censorship, what fear of discovery lurks in the midst of this seemingly courageous crusade deep into the forbidden territory of public enemy number one.

There is genuine loyalty to be found here, good clean faith, un-adulterated by personal interest, but it struggles to keep free. One *cule* tells me he has joined up with some old friends after making his own way up from Granada. 'This match is pure adrenalin. You never get this feeling anywhere else. The biggest shot of my year,' he says. Another has come from Algeciras. 'Why am I here? Because my grandfather was a *cule*. He died before he could explain why he was. But I just grew up with the feeling. It never left me.'

As we talk, a skinhead with a *boixos* T-shirt approaches. I manage to engage him in a brief exchange before he tells the others to disperse. 'I've come from Barcelona,' he tells me. 'This is the big challenge of the year, that's why we are present here.' There are other skinheads, some with dark shirts and dark glasses. Were they not, some of them, speaking Catalan and sporting the Barça colours, they would be indistinguishable from the skinheads on the other side of the barrier, speaking Castilian and sporting the Madrid colours, trading insults, screaming, like a litany from hell, '*Indios y cules, indios y cules.*'

But now it is time to move. So come the orders from the Barça official, playing token collaborator to the local commander – an oversize police chief, trussed up in riot gear like a bit part from *Lethal Weapon*. The enclosure is filled with the staccato of horses' hooves in unco-ordinated step, and the crackle of short-wave radio. The police foot-soldiers gather the *cules* like so many heads of cattle, then begin to march them forward, instinctively prodding anyone who momentarily moves out of line. There is now a much bigger crowd assembled on the other side of the barrier, held back by another contingent of police.

'*Indios y cules, indios y cules*,' they chant, much louder than before. There is a short middle-aged man with a moustache and bearing an uncanny resemblance to Franco when young, who is screaming louder than all the others. Such is his excitement that he is sweating, shaking. When the first of the *cules* begins to file past with his police guard, the man aims a punch but misses. '*Hijos de putas*,' he spits out. The man is dressed neatly in a pale Corte Inglès summer suit. I imagine him as a bank clerk on weekdays. So I ask him, as I would ask for some pesetas for my pounds, quite matter-of-fact amidst the urban hysteria, why he feels so strongly at weekends, where he finds the passion to scream like this at some rival football fans who have come from the two extreme corners of Spain. 'Because they are not Spaniards, because they are *hijos de putas*,' he says at least twice over, before adding, 'This is the team of Judases.'

Now the *cules* – some one hundred of them – are walking up one of the stadium towers. The walkway spirals so that they come into view only now and then. Each time they do, the crowd who have been kept back by the police on the ground, looking up, scream more abuse. The higher the *cules* walk, the more confident they become, regaining their capacity to be themselves. The Barça anthem is intoned again, *cortes de manga* ('fuck off' signs) flourished, anti-Madrid phrases shouted. As they circle up and up they wave and taunt, they turn their backs, screw up their faces, clown-like. The crowd below gesticulate, shout back. It has become something of a game, to discover who has the biggest mouth, the most effective insult, the biggest balls.

In a side-street next to the stadium are gathered Barça's most militant sworn enemies, the *ultra surs*. They too have shaved heads and dark glasses among them, they too shout abuse, and threaten violence, as brutal and uncompromising as any the *boixos* can deliver. To that extent the two opposing groups complement each other, complete the circle in the necessary tribal conflict. Here in Madrid, it is the *ultras* who shout the loudest, their heads crowned with Viking hats, their arms outstretched in Nazi salutes. '*Sur, sur, ultra sur!*' and '*Barça, cabrón, saluda al campeón*' ('Barça, fucker, salute the champion'), they chant as part of their war dance, beers in one hand, *bengalas* in the other, jumping together. And as in Barcelona, it is a black player who is necessarily singled out for racial abuse, only this one plays for Barça and is best remembered locally for celebrating a goal with a *corte de manga* – the Spanish equivalent of a 'fuck off' sign. '*Giovanni, disfruta, tu madre es una puta!*' ('Giovanni, have a good fuck, your mother is a whore!') This is not enough for one of the younger ones among them, drunker than the others. He insists on invoking Hitler. '*Siempre facista, siempre Madridista, Sieg Heil!*' Then the others pick up the chant.

Later, in the Bernabéu, the *boixos* and the *ultra surs* continue to shout abuse across a stadium packed with Real fans. The song '*Que Viva España*' echoes across the stadium, Franco's most popular 'export' here reissued with a deliberate sense of provocation. As one of the *cules* tells me as he runs the gauntlet, 'These aren't two clubs. They're two nations, two people, two religions.'

3

Heart and Soul

RICARDO HUGUET: the philosopher

In order to talk about Barça, Ricardo Huguet has chosen to meet me not in his office, but in Via Veneto, one of Barcelona's better restaurants.

It seems only natural to discuss Barça over food, because next to football there is nothing in which Catalans take so much pride as the local cuisine. That we should eat at the upper end of the market also does not seem out of the ordinary. For Huguet may not be a millionaire, but he is not exactly poor. He is a businessman, and in this part of Spain men have worked hard to make sure that business not just makes money but means money too, in a different way from the 'slothful aristocrats' of the South and the '*arrivistes*' of Madrid. Huguet himself has made money making paper – a sharp entrepreneurial thing to do, given that Catalans also read a lot: newspapers, books, tax bills, and pages and pages devoted to Barça.

There are several things that make Huguet typical of his class. Regularly he meets with fellow businessmen – he is close to employers' organisations and is an adviser to several companies – and, over a meal, discusses the economy, Catalonia's relations with Madrid and the rest of Europe, the latest speech by Jordi Pujol (the Catalan President to whom he is close), the value of the euro, the value of their shares, the value of his shares . . . But amidst the politics, the economics, the sociology, Barça is one subject that is never far away. For Huguet is not just an entrepreneur, he is also a *cule*, his membership of the club a key point of reference for his sense of democratic Catalan nationalism.

These days there are a lot of businessmen around who may eat and look like Huguet, but not so many who claim that the football club they are devoted to is one of the most important parts of their lives, who can speak with heart and soul about sharing in a people's passion, without seemingly aspiring to owning shares in it.

Even if he wanted to, Huguet would not be able to buy shares in Barça, because the club is defined by its own statutes as a non-profit-making association belonging to its members. But Huguet does not believe he is tilting at windmills. For over a decade he has publicly opposed Josep Lluís Nuñez, Barça's president, and the way he has increasingly turned the club into a personal fiefdom. 'The difference between Nuñez and the rest of the club membership is that he does not belong to Barça. Nuñez *is* Barça – or at least thinks he is – Barça conceived as a small big state and made in his image, so that we are all merely his subjects. The world is divided between those who are for him and who vote for him, and those who are against him – those he condemns as anti-Barça. This is both the cause and the origin of his megalomania. He acts like a head of state,' Huguet wrote in the Catalan newspaper *El Periódico* in July 1997.

Huguet resists subordination to the Nuñez regime not just on a point of political principle, but because he regards himself not just as a *socio* but as a *cule*, indivisible from other true believers. I am glad we have settled for a lengthy lunch because I need to be convinced of the genuineness of his position. As we sit down at table he begins a lengthy case for the defence.

'If I'd been born in Burgos, because of my class and professional interests I think I would have been fairly uninterested in football. I like music, I read more than fifty books a year, I write, I'm a qualified engineeer . . . you could say not the typical qualifications for a fan. But the one thing that has been central to my life is my Catalanism.'

'I see . . .' I venture cautiously, but Huguet has finished eyeing the menu, and is on a roll of verbal and physical self-expression, which tolerates no extended interruption barring that of the head waiter taking the order.

'Let me try and explain. My friends who know me pretty well ask me, why am I such a fanatical Barça fan? How is it that I get so stressed out, do some real mad things for the club?'

He orders some good local wine, and we both choose some tender steaks. The waiters circle like butterflies around the heavy tableware of silver cutlery and porcelain. At other tables, there are other businessmen – with each other or with their mistresses. The restaurant lives or dies on its discretion. The longer I take in my surroundings, the more incongruous seems the setting, a planet removed from the wild crusaders I have encountered in Manchester, Valencia and Madrid.

Yet Huguet claims to have an instinctive feeling for his club. 'Well, the answer is that I feel profoundly Catalan, that is to say I believe there is such a thing as a Catalan nation with its own history and cultural roots, and that Barça is the product of historic circumstances which Catalonia has experienced for a century. So that Barça for me is a point of reference for the frustrations that we as a people have had to suffer. And Barça too has helped provide a sense of identity to a lot of people who have settled here . . .'

Catalanism can thus be acquired and does not have to be innate; it is something that any settler can aspire to – it has to do with language, feelings, a state of belonging to Catalonia as a nation. Huguet is trying to articulate a collective sentiment, a question of faith, which as the Catalan author Manuel Vazquez Montalban has put it, is 'as irrational as a pilgrimage to Lourdes'. It is a faith that none the less draws into its soul a mass of new converts anxious to make something of their lives: immigrants from the poorer parts of Spain who came to Catalonia following the Civil War, 100,000 in the 1940s, and another 400,000 in the 1950s. The immigrants were brought into a society that was unable to express its language and music, that was banned from electing its politicians, and yet struggled to maintain a sense of being with its collaborators and opponents of the Franco regime. FC Barcelona became the mother church, capable of absorbing Catalonia, and its capital in particular with all its schizophrenia.

The immigrants got the toughest jobs, some of the worst houses, they formed urban ghettos where they struggled to hang on to some of their traditions, where Spanish rather than Catalan was spoken not because it was mandatory but because it brought memories of abandoned villages and hamlets elsewhere in Spain. And yet supporting Barça was the way of feeling part of something that went above the mediocrity of life, of submerging in the wider universe, of being able to cry and laugh and not be punished for it. It was also a way of being seen to give thanks, for the immigrant cannot survive long if he is deemed to be ungrateful. Thanks to Barça, the immigrant could hold his head high on Sundays and say, I am a Catalan although I come from Andalusia. It is here that I have developed the ability to sell my labour and choose how I spend my scarce leisure hours – following one of the greatest teams in the world. This is where I have learned the little culture that I can share with others; this, ultimately, is my land.

These thoughts drifts over the table as the waiter – Andalusian by origin – is with us again, topping up our glasses, enquiring whether the food is to our taste. And yes, one feels there is more empathy than servility in his actions, drawn as he is to our table by Huguet's speech, so it seems to him at least, a ray of sunshine amidst dull clouds.

Huguet is half-way through his steak. The bottle of wine is half drunk. 'To be a *cule* is to express a sentiment that goes beyond sport. It has to do with a feeling of community, of shared culture, of patriotism. Of course, one could separate Barça from this and maybe still have a great club, but what you'd sacrifice along the way would be its popular support. I'm talking not just about the more than 103,000 members, but also about three or four million people who don't go to the stadium because there is no room, who, whenever there is a match, follow it closely, are spiritually connected to the stadium. I think this is what makes Barça such a special club and what makes me an addict of the club, because the addiction I suffer is the profound sense of being Catalan.'

The waiter withdraws our empty plates, and comes back with a trolley of cakes and mousses. We opt for coffee. In the short interval in which our table rests empty, Huguet tells the story of a Barça fan that has stuck in his memory. He cannot remember the exact year, although the period he recalls has a starting-point of particular significance in the history of the club. It was in November 1953 that Francisco Miro-Sans took over as president of Barça, with the pledge to build a new stadium. What was to become known worldwide as the Camp Nou was inaugurated four years later, with an initial capacity for 93,000 spectators. Its construction was testimony to Barça's transformation into one of the great European clubs with a mass following. In the first half of the decade, Barça became the undisputed leader of the Spanish League, fuelling local pride with a series of competition successes at home and abroad. It won two successive League championships, thanks to the inspiration of a memorable front five made up of Basora,

Manchon, Moreno, César and Ladislao Kubala – the subject of nostalgic serenades to this day and of whom there will be more further on.

In the 1950s, walking in the Pyrenees, Huguet came across a shepherd, with his sheep spread out on a patch of deserted mountainside. The shepherd was sitting on a rock, holding a small radio to his ear, listening to a Barça match. 'The shepherd had never in his life gone beyond his mountain village in the Pyrenees but he felt connected through his radio, and felt as much a *cule* as the rest of us.'

The wine bottle is empty. The lunch is complete and, so it seems, Barça has helped us cross the social divide.

ANTONIO FRANCO: cule and journalist
You do not have to have a meal to discuss Barça with Antonio Franco. He is a giant of a man, bearded, full-bodied, broad-shouldered; he talks and acts with the generous enthusiasm of a satiated soul, who has taken his fill of life. Franco – no relation to Francisco – is a *cule* who happens to be a journalist, as opposed to a journalist who writes about Barça. The distinction is important. It has to do with the differentiation between genuine faith and opportunism. In Barcelona, hundreds of journalists make a living thanks to Barça, their wages and terms of employment intimately linked to the fate of the club, their public expression conditioned not necessarily by what they genuinely feel but by what they know they have to write if they are to survive professionally. In addition to the main Catalan newspapers, *Avui*, *La Vanguardia* and *El Periódico*, and a plethora of local magazines, newsletters and special editions, *Sport* and *El Mundo Deportivo* – the two Barcelona-based tabloid daily sports newspapers – devote more than thirty pages between them to Barça, while the local TV station, TV3, which is broadcast in Catalan, lives and breathes Barça in its sports coverage and regional news items. Contractual negotiations between the station and the football club were a source of tension in the 1980s, but relations later stabilised, with the two institutions discovering a shared interest in a mass audience of loyal Catalans. The football club's importance was underlined by TV3's decision to mark Barça's centenary by devoting a forty-three-part prime-time series to the club from November 1998 to November 1999. As Eduard Boet,

one of the programme's producers, told me, 'Football is a way of making politics entertaining.' And Barça sells. Barça is politics. Barça is advertising. Barça is merchandising. No marketing strategy of any Catalan newspaper or magazine can ignore this.

This Franco carried Barça within him before he could even write his name. His uncle was captain of Barça immediately after the Spanish Civil War and before Antonio was born. It was with his uncle that Antonio went to live at the age of nine, when his mother fell ill with hepatitis. One of the rooms in his uncle's house was full of trophies, and newspaper cuttings, and old photographs of Barça days. 'I call one of my earliest childhood memories the five-to-one. That was the five stickers of Spanish club players I'd offer in exchange for one sticker of a Barça player,' recalls Antonio.

His maternal grandfather had been a mayor of the Catalan town of Lleida before the Spanish Civil War. When the other Franco came to power, Lleida was brutally repressed. Antonio, although he was born after the war, nevertheless feels to this day that he 'lost a war before I was born'. That feeling underlines his passion as a *cule*, and his commitment to democracy as a journalist. Football became a way of hanging on to a semblance of existence during years when the Catalan language was banned, of rediscovering a sense of pride in what one could claim, in part, as one's own. Antonio moved from childhood towards manhood during the 1950s, a time of some glory at Barça thanks to players like Kubala, Evaristo, Eulogio Martinez and Sandor Koscis, 'the Golden Head'. These were years when Barça won both the League and the European championships under the tutelage of Helenio Herrera. Antonio learned to love not only watching the game, but also playing it, long before he trained as a journalist. His generation is one of the last who can remember kicking balls in the streets of his neighbourhood, in that kind of carefree way the inhabitants of Third World shanty towns still do. He was never exactly nimble with his feet, but he had a good touch, and his commanding physical presence from an early age made him a formidable defence against most of his contemporaries. Football also provided a good weapon for dealing with the enemy, a regime to whom the concept of free expression was anathema.

Look around Antonio's office and it's not hard to guess what generation he belongs to: plaster-cast caricatures of the Beatles copied from *Yellow Submarine*, a reproduction of the front page of the *New York Times* with the report on the Kennedy assassination and, most telling of all, a photomontage of the main *dramatis personae* of a key moment in Catalan history, the transition to a post-Francoiste democratic government in 1976. Politics is defined in football terms. Under the heading 'Catalonia's National Football Team 1976', photographed portraits of well-known local figures are stuck on to figures of players with the red and yellow Catalan colours and in team formation. The poster is an image as much of an obsession with football as of the inherent contradictions of local politics, the game of which is inherently Catalan. For these players range from left to right, from radical opponents of the Madrid government to collaborationists, maverick strikers and cautious defenders, not to mention those who in the words of the poster have definitely been transferred to Madrid – Catalans so close to Franco the ruler as not to deserve any other colours than the starched white of Real Madrid.

Consider the Catalan national team *circa* 1976 as identified in the poster: Cassia Just (goalkeeper); Josep Badia (*suplente titular*); Joan Colomines (*suplente titular*); Jordi Pujol (*defensa central*); Josep Pallach (*mig volant dret*); Joan Raventos (*mig volant esquerre*); Heribert Barrera (*defensa dret*); Armet-Comudella (*defensa esquerre*); Sole Barbera (*delanter centre*); R. Trias Fargas (*extrem dret*); anonimo y con los ojos bendados (*extrem esquerre*); Lluís Xirinacs (*interior esquerre*); Assemblea Catalunya (*entrenador*); Josep Terradellas (*president*); anonimo pero vestido de militar (*director técnico*); Viola, Samaranch, Udina Martorell, Santacreu etc. (*definitivament traspassats a la seleccio central madridista*).

During the Franco years, Antonio wrote about football under his real name, and about politics under a pseudonym. What in others may have evolved into schizophrenia was thus resolved into a productive duality, in which the shortcomings of one identity were compensated by the conviction of the other. It seemed a happier existence than that lived by many of his colleagues: the sportswriters who suppressed their political feelings and wrote about nothing other than Barça (the more uncritical the article, the greater the reward neatly stashed in a brown envelope and delivered once a month), and those so submerged in politics as to anaesthetise their love of football, radical in their commitment yet sacrificing a necessary passion for life somewhere along the line.

Antonio does not forget, as some of his countrymen do, the betrayals and the brutalities of the past. But part of his memory is tied up with gentler things. Thus he recalls, with a deep belly-laugh, two key moments of his marriage: the first was on the day of his wedding and involved his borrowing at the last minute a Barça tie from Marti Filosia, a friend who played as centre-half for the club when Vic Buckingham was manager. The second had Antonio insisting that his honeymoon should include watching two matches played by Barça – against Elche and, of course, against Real Madrid.

Antonio is and has always been a political animal, but one with a wide generous field in which to exist and engage other humans. He has a simple political instinct for the power of football, and the particular place that Barça has in the game. He sits in the Camp Nou, experiencing much the same feelings as any other dedicated *cule* – ecstatic elation if the team plays well, morbid depression if it plays badly. He can follow it up by eating well or not being able to eat anything at all. He has travelled with his team to foreign lands, painting his face with blue and red stripes, and submerged himself in the collective being of Barça. It is ninety minutes with all the ups and downs of life, and even death, sheer enjoyment, appalling agony.

When I meet Antonio in April 1998, he has just finished reading Nick Hornby's *Fever Pitch*, the English bestseller of the 1990s about an Arsenal fan's obsessive loyalty. While he loves the book, he thinks the obsession of Arsenal fans a pale reflection of the political intensity that drives the loyalty of *cules*, a cultural expression that far outlives even the most memorable of games. 'I don't know if you can call us tribal. I don't like the word. I prefer to see myself as part of a collective *fiesta* in which I can celebrate the great opportunity of being surrounded by others who feel the way I do. The club belongs to us; we are linked to it as if it were a vital element of our existence.'

Every success is worth a few defeats, and Barça has had its fair share of memorable victories, which is why Antonio can still smile a lot and keep his weight, despite having the responsibility of editing one of Catalonia's most widely read newspapers, *El Periódico*, which is published in two separate editions – Catalan and Spanish. These days he writes editorials about politics, not about football, and he goes to watch Barça play not as a journalist but as a fan, sometimes painting his face with the club's colours, all the more to be part of the masses. It's his way of making sure he can still feel the world that matters to him, without lies.

KUBALA: the old man and the sea

Midday in late May 1998. A piece of wasteland with four goalposts near the Camp Nou. Beneath a scorching sun, old men are playing football on a dust pitch, disorganised and rebellious like children of the shanty town. Among the players there is one old man, his bare chest reddening in the sun, holding a T-shirt in one hand, who seems to be working harder than all the others, hobbling up and down the right wing, shouting for the ball. He is clearly struggling with his bow-legs and with a skin as scarred and ribbed as a ploughed field in drought. Yet this eccentric tramp at one point dribbles superbly with the ball stuck to his feet, before delivering a perfectly angled shot into goal. It is at this sublime moment that I am reminded that the player is Ladislao Kubala, one of the great figures of international football, and that the motley crew he is kicking a ball around with is made up of other Barça veterans.

As I watch this collection of middle-aged men and grandfathers huffing and puffing in the first heat wave of the local summer, I struggle to understand their motivation. It is more usual for men of their age to sleep a lot, to watch TV, to sit on benches watching life go far too quickly by. Men of their age struggle in anonymous hospital beds with breaking bones and failing prostates, and grumble to their wives about jobs they no longer have. Some of them take Viagra. When not taking pills, they allow others to take control of their leisure time – bossy daughters, upstart sons, grandchildren far too unruly to play with. That is, if they are still around, and not dead.

'Laszi' has an explanation of sorts when I meet him in the 'social office' of the FC Barcelona Veterans' Association, of which he is president. No sooner have we introduced ourselves than he lifts his suit trousers to the knees to reveal the close-up of battered skin I have glimpsed from a distance. 'Look at this . . . that's seven operations for you – and still it seems things aren't quite the way they should be. I speak with the doctor and he says that whenever I walk I put strain on my bones and he has to do something about it because otherwise my bones get worn out. The older one gets, the more problems, but I go on playing because I don't want the other "grandads" knowing about it, because if they found out they'd give me nothing but trouble. So they don't know anything and that way we are all happier when we play together.' He speaks Spanish rapidly, with the clipped accent of an Eastern European, the words of his anatomy lesson running over each other like those of a lecturer on overdrive.

The 'office', with its long meeting table and chairs, its TV, bar, and one wall lined with trophies, seems too small to contain his energy. Laszi finds it difficult to keep still. But if he is there at all it is out of a sense of camaraderie towards the others, most still far less charismatic than he is and with less dramatic tales to tell. For it is here, when not playing like children on the parched earth, that the Barça vets come to share old memories, forging a unique solidarity in a shared sense of times past and passing.

Listening to Laszi I am reminded of what Angel Mur, another veteran I have met separately, recalled about him. Mur was the club's masseur when Kubala played for Barça. 'I remember a game when I had to take care of Laszi. They'd fucked up his knee God knows how many times. I told him he just couldn't go on playing with the injuries he had, but he begged me to put him right so he could go on playing. "I want to play, I need to play," he kept saying. So I put together two pieces of cardboard and a bandage and fixed him the best way I could. He went out on to the pitch and played till the end of the game.'

It's in this way, perhaps, that Laszi would like to be remembered – as the seventy-one-year-old vet still capable of sweating it out for his club mates just as he did at the peak of his career, the incorrigible crusader always ready to do battle with the toughest of opponents. Yet to probe a little deeper into Laszi and the world of the veterans reveals a little more of what Barça was and what it has become.

Ladislao Kubala was born in Hungary in 1927 to Slavic parents. To this day he insists that he was born into poverty – his mother worked in a factory, his father was a bricklayer – and that football success came to him from an early age. 'At the age of fifteen I was playing in the First

Division and at the age of seventeen I was picked to play in the Hungarian national team,' he tells me, more matter-of-fact than boastful. The official history of Barça, which describes Kubala unreservedly as 'the most charismatic Barça player of all times, notes simply that he played respectively for two Hungarian clubs – Ferencvaros Bratislava and Vasas of Budapest, with whom he signed in April 1948.

On 25th January 1949 he left club and country and fled from Communism to the West, initially to a US military zone in Austria, then to Italy, where he began playing again with a local team called Pro-Patria, in the town of Busto Arsizio. Back in Hungary, the club reacted to his defection by denouncing him as a delinquent and a fraudster, which from their perspective seemed justified enough – he had, after all, done a bunk with the ink still wet on a contract with Vasas. The denunciation had a political edge to it. It was backed by the Communist-dominated Hungarian Football Federation, which managed to secure a formal extradition request on account of Kubala's alleged financial crimes, his fleeing from the country without permission and his failure to do military service. World football's governing body, FIFA, backed the Hungarians and imposed a one-year international ban on Kubala.

With the evidence of hindsight, the ban was a blessing in disguise. Faced with the new restrictions on his playing as a professional, the Italian club temporarily ceased paying him. Kubala once again packed his bags, this time moving with his young wife to Cinecittà, a refugee camp under US military administration, in January 1950. Soon after arriving there, Kubala met with some of his fellow countrymen who had similarly fled Hungary, and with them formed a football team called Hungaria. That summer he travelled to Spain for the first time on what was to prove the most defining journey of his football career. Three figures conspired to make it so: Armando Muñoz Calero, the head of the Spanish Football Federation; the Barça manager Pepe Samitier; and General Francisco Franco.

'My team was called Hungaria because we were four or five Hungarians playing in it,' recalls Kubala, as the other 'grandfathers' recover from their sun-filled game, 'but there were also Czechs, two or three Croatians, a few Russians . . . they'd all escaped from Communism.' He is speaking in rapid-fire phrases, his misty blue eyes fixed on distant memories as if he's afraid that they might escape him when he least expects it. Of late he has found it increasingly difficult to remember things from one day to the next. 'We travelled to Madrid to play in a friendly against a Spanish squad that was getting ready for the World Cup. Samitier was in the stadium and he watched me play. Afterwards he came up and said, "Why don't you come with us to Barcelona?" And I told him, "I'd would love to but FIFA does not allow me to play as a professional and I've left my country without authorisation." Then he said, "Don't worry, we'll fix it." '

The simple humanity was typical of Samitier – better known as El Sami – one of Barça's most legendary players turned cigar-toting, good-living manager; the warm glow of the Mediterranean embracing the exile from Eastern Europe. According to other witnesses, the thaw was helped along by Kubala's extraordinary capacity for hard drinking, which in time was to become as much part of the legend as his football skills. El Sami's efforts to draw Kubala away from the clutches of Real Madrid, which also showed an early interest in signing him, were conducted largely in an alcoholic haze through which Laszi often barely knew whether he was coming or going, let alone where from or to. According to an account written for *La Vanguardia* by Lluís Permanyer, El Sami was helped in his endeavours by a Hungarian friend of Kubala's, a swimmer called Zalyoni. 'On this strategically important occasion, Zalyoni encouraged Laszi to have a tipple or two,' wrote Permanyer.

Following the game in Madrid, Hungary travelled to Barcelona to play against the city's 'other team', Espanyol. It was June 1950. It was then that El Sami made his final move to ensure that Kubala did not take up the offer made by Real Madrid. According to Enrique Llaudet, the former Barça president, the circumstances surrounding Kubala's seduction by El Sami verged on the farcical. 'Kubala came to Spain thinking he was going to be signed by Real Madrid, but because he was half pissed he didn't really know whether he was coming or going. If Kubala had one weakness it was that he drank too much – whisky, wine, whatever he could get his hands on. Well, as things turned out, there was a real confusion on the train and Kubala – with that way of speaking that was so typical – suddenly turns to Samitier and says,

"Hey, we go to Madrid, don't we?" "Sure we are," says Samitier. "But the sign says 'Barcelona'," insists Kubala. And then Samitier says, "Don't you worry. We are going to the club now." And that is how he brought us Kubala.'

By all accounts, Kubala was able to strike a hard bargain when it came to the actual moment of signing for Barça following the match with Espanyol. When he sat down at the table with the president of Barça, Augustin Montal Galobart, to negotiate the final terms of the contract, Kubala took a piece of paper out of his pocket and said the first thing that came into his head. 'I want this,' he said. The piece of paper was a copy of the draft contract Real Madrid had prepared for him. The contract Kubala signed with Galopart made him the highest-paid player yet in the history of the club. Although Kubala spent the next nine months without playing a League game with Barça because of the FIFA ban, by the end of the 1950–1 season he had earned 647,850 pesetas for playing in just thirteen games. Next to him the best-paid member of the Barça squad was the team's new Czech coach Daucik, Kubala's brother-in-law, whose hiring formed part of the deal El Sami had helped negotiate.

The ban on Kubala's playing professional football was lifted at a meeting between FIFA and Spanish football officials in Madrid on 2nd April 1952. Subsequently Kubala was given Spanish nationality. Kubala's confirmation as player and resident in the Catalan capital – in the midst of a continuing rivalry between Barça and Real Madrid – was resolved thanks to the *bête noire* of Catalan nationalism, the Franco regime. The paradox was the product both of Samitier's friendships with members of the Madrid political establishment and of the Cold War context in which the Spanish government was developing its policies. 'Pepe Samitier and Muñoz Calero of the Spanish Football Federation, who had a post in FIFA, got involved in the affair and resolved it,' Kubala tells me as we sit in May 1998 in the veterans' club-within-a-club, down in the basement of that great symbol of Catalanism which the Camp Nou has become. When the Hungarian talks of his friend 'Pepe' Samitier, his blue eyes glaze over even more than usual. 'I loved him a lot. My father died before I escaped from Hungary so that Pepe became like a father to me. He loved me like his own son.'

Samitier was a subject of much admiration, too, for certain members of the Franco regime, not least the old general himself, who had watched El Sami's brilliant days as a footballer. Franco was easily convinced that Kubala's presence in Spain could do no harm to his cause. Like Samitier, the Hungarian had no nationalist axe to grind. In political terms what mattered was that he was a defector from Communism whose tales of Communist persecution fitted nicely with Spain's new Cold War alliance with the United States, a strategic link which helped Franco break free from the international isolationism he had been plunged into immediately after the end of the Civil War in 1939.

Kubala's starry-eyed role in the Cold War – a mere pawn in a game of global politics way beyond his understanding – is nowhere more evident than in a filmed dramatisation of his life called *The Stars Search for Peace*, which was keenly distributed by the Franco regime after he had been given Spanish nationality. In it Kubala and Samitier play themselves, their voices and those of others dubbed over in heavy Castilian accents. The film reproduces a somewhat romanticised old Hollywood-style version of Kubala's escape from Hungary, sanitising his drinking bouts, and transforming the world of football into a glossy fantasy made up of sickly condescending saints.

This is all part of a history that Catalans to this day find it hard to come to terms with. In the words of Vazquez Montalban, they move between 'amnesia and memory'. In Barça's authorised histories, much is made of Kubala the player helping to forge the club's sense of self-worth and pride, separate from and defiant of the political horrors identified with Real Madrid.

Certainly there is some evidence that not all non-Catalans shared Franco's sympathies with Kubala. In an article published on 18th May 1952 in the newspaper *El Correo Español*, a sportswriter called José-Maria Mateos commented, 'In Spain we do not need players who learned the game under Communism,' and followed this with a stream of critical references to the Hungarian-born nationalised Spaniard who had begun to make his mark, playing for Barça. Mateos claimed that Kubala used his elbows and tried to monopolise the game too much. According to Barça's official historian Jaume Sobreques, the article 'had an immediate impact on most of the

country and created a black legend. It was not only a new way of
attacking Barça, which at the time seemed invincible on the pitch, but
also defined Kubala's future. For the rest of his career, the Hungarian
was the object of relentless persecution in Spanish stadiums: an
organised butchery of fouls that would have broken a player without
his physical strength. In every game, Kubala was the player who had
to be cut down, and his persecution was Barça's persecution, and
Catalonia's as well.'

Others prefer to look back at Kubala's glory years with a deeper
sense of his inherent humanity, a personality that defied political
typecasting and which left to its own devices would have resisted a
transformation into a political icon or target. Kubala was first and
foremost a great player who brought to Barça a combination of skills
that the club had until then rarely seen in one player. He was quick on
and off the ball, demonstrated extraordinary control when dribbling,
showed an unrivalled vision of the game, knowing when to pass, and
was always accurate in his shooting. He was as devastating with his left
foot as he was with his right, and proved a master with the dead ball,
curling his free kicks over the densest of walls. If he played hard off the
field as well as on it, it was because he worked hard, sweating it out
with each game, inspiring his team-mates with his toughness and
determination to win.

Most of Kubala's admirers draw a veil over his later years, which he
spent on a series of short and not hugely inspired spells training clubs
around the world from Malaga to Saudi Arabia. Some Catalans have
not totally absolved him for the year or so he played for Espanyol
alongside his old rival Di Stefano. He was not a success during his year
as manager of Barcelona in the early 1970s. Only in the 1992
Olympics in Barcelona, when the Spanish football team he helped
train won the gold, did his star shine bright again. Since then Laszi has
been living with his memories and off others who warmed to his
generosity of spirit by organising more than one benefit match in his
honour to help him out financially in his old age. Both as a player and
in retirement, his own sense of charity towards his family and to those
he considers less fortunate than himself has meant his living his final
years with no glamour and some hardship. His financial difficulties
have sometimes given rise to problems in his relationship with a club

that has come to be ruled by men obsessed with value for money. But Laszi keeps his worries from the public eye.

At the end of a frenetically delivered monologue, he excuses himself and says that he has to attend a meeting outside Barcelona. He leaves me with a personal appreciation of his contemporary the great English international Stanley Matthews: 'There are English players I really respected as adversaries. I had a special admiration for Stanley Matthews – he worked so hard and had such great vision and potential.' And he is full of praise for some of the Barça players he formed a team with, players such as Segarra, César, Biosca and Manchon. He remembers 'the way I've shared my life with them, not just on the field but off it too. They've been like brothers to me; they were all great.'

He then moves around the room, bidding farewell to the other veterans, pumping their hands and embracing them like brothers-in-arms. 'I will never forget my team-mates, nor what Barça did for me. They got me out of a concentration camp, and gave me all the support I could have possibly wanted. When I go to the stadium, they still treat me as someone who was born here in Catalonia, with real warmth. All this has given me a lot of satisfaction.' He gives a final collective farewell to all in the room, turns and walks out, dragging his battered legs with him.

No doubt when Laszi dies Catalans will come out in droves to say goodbye to the first of the 'foreigners' who gave them so much joy on the pitch, and such innocent amusement off it, and who in the end made up for his small betrayals by coming home, choosing to live among them.

Watching him disappear into the day after our conversation, I cling on to the man, not the myth. I remember the late Helenio Herrera, one of Barça's most memorable coaches, recalling how once, when the team arrived at Barcelona Airport from a trip abroad, a customs official asked Kubala if he had anything to declare. Kubala said, 'Yes, two bottles of whisky.' The official asked him where they were. Kubala pointed at his stomach and said with a broad grin, 'Do you want to take an X-ray?'

And then there is Angel Mur, whose memory was of finding Kubala drunk out of his head only hours before a critical match. 'I put him in a cold shower, gave him a massage with pure alcohol, and made him drink a cup of black coffee before putting him to bed for a few hours. Later he got up and went and played as if nothing had happened.'

FUSTE: home-bred

The history of Barça is punctuated with famous foreigners, some of them more controversial than others, none of them lacking exceptional talent. They are the big earners, the headline makers; they command fiercely dedicated followings among the fans, which then break out into civil wars between supporters and detractors. Sometimes it is easy to forget that others have made important contributions to the club, local players who have carried the colours of Barça from an early age, fought their hearts out, led their lives with minimum publicity, with moments of inspiration you can count on two fingers, yet in spirit and loyalty perhaps as deserving of being part of that great pantheon of heroes reserved for the likes of the Kubalas, the Cruyffs, the Maradonas, the Ronaldos . . .

I am reminded of this on this day in May when among the veterans about to play across the dust I meet a quiet, unassuming ex-Barça player, the one-time forward José-Maria Fuste. Some time previously I have been warned by another former Barça player, 'El Lobo' Carrasco, that 'the secrets of the club changing room are sacred'. But I now find myself unwittingly penetrating that inner sanctum. Fuste has told me to meet him there.

I find him half naked, a middle-aged body still reasonably in shape among the sagging forms of other more elderly former team-mates. Here among the smells of oils, disinfectant and cologne, the strip lights and the white polished walls, there is no room for boasting or prudery among those who have known each other for too many years, who retain, now as then, a calm communion with the matrix that is Barça, who draw strength from familiarity and comfort from shared memories.

On other days, Fuste works as a public relations executive for Codorniu, the Catalan *cava* (sparkling wine) company, but coming here to kick a ball about is his way less of escape than of keeping in touch with a part of himself. For Fuste is one of those players whose career as a footballer is inseparable from his time at Barça. In retirement he has become a point of reference for fans and former players who do not want to lose their roots in a world that seems at times to be on fast forward.

Born in Lerida, Fuste joined the club as a schoolboy aged twelve. Because he came from outside the capital, he was housed with a local family, one of several at the service of the club. Nowadays, the Masia – the youth home – is one central building, but at that time the schoolboys were housed in separate family flats. The club paid for his housing and local school lessons in return for regular training lessons. 'I think for a footballer who joins as a schoolboy a club as big as Barcelona it is very difficult to reach the first team even though that is his maximum ambition. I was lucky that at the age of seventeen I began playing in the first team.'

Hungarians led by Kubala and Argentinians led by Di Stefano were the undisputed stars of his youth years, but from an early age Fuste was conscious that the club's greatness had also been reinforced with home-grown talent. The *cule*, above all the immigrant *cule*, appreciated the duality, recognised it as something he could identify with. Fuste never aspired to Kubala's talent and skill, still less Di Stefano's, but he was an essential part of the machinery; the rest of the team could rely on his hard work; his passes and goals often decided victory or defeat. 'With Fuste, Barça works well' was the popular phrase. Fuste half-jokingly used to say that that also meant that if Barça didn't work, he was to blame.

Fuste joined the club in 1953 and left it in 1972. *Cules* do not have it in their nature to celebrate the achievements of Spain's national squad – many Catalans feel they should have a squad of their own. And yet the fact that Fuste played for Spain shows that it was not just in Barcelona that he was valued. Fuste played in the World Cup in England in 1966. Thanks to his equaliser, Spain nearly beat West Germany in a very tight Group match played in Birmingham. (West Germany eventually won 2–1.) But it was in July 1968 that Fuste earned his place in the gallery of Barça's heroes, as part of the team that beat Real Madrid 1–0 in the final of the Generalissimo's Cup (named after Franco) in the Bernabéu stadium. The match was recorded in the history of the club as the 'final of the bottles' because of the objects that disgruntled Real fans threw at the Barça players.

During his time as a player there, Barça had five presidents and seventeen coaches. 'Enrique Llaudet [1961–8] was the best president I had, in every respect. He was a great guy. My favourite coaches were Herrera and Michels.' He puts it down to a question of personal taste and experience. On the individual performances of these personalities the reader will find more later in this book, but for now, Fuste has this to say about the Barça of times past and times passing, as he rests for a while on the changing-room bench.

'When I started playing for Barça, things were different. The footballer was a person who enjoyed sport and didn't think about other things. Today the footballer is a person who can still enjoy the sport but who has a value on him in monetary terms, and it is that which affects his life. Money is in the midst of things. In the early days there was less pressure, less TV. Sometimes there is so much pressure these days that a footballer can't play his best because of it.'

In 1989, Fuste – then president of the Barça veterans' association – joined in a failed electoral challenge to Nuñez spearheaded by Sixto Cambra, a Catalan nationalist who claimed, as did others, that the club had been turned into a personal fiefdom of the president. By so doing Fuste had unwittingly moved from sport to power politics over which he personally had very little control.

Cambra was a thirty-six-year-old economist who came from the textile sector that had delivered the presidents of an older tradition. He was closely associated with the world of tennis, a bastion of the Catalan upper classes. His involvement in the politics of Barça was given behind-the-scenes encouragement by Jordi Pujol, the president of the Generalitat, following a series of meetings held in the Palau de la Generalitat. Those attending the meetings included Catalonia's PR and marketing guru José-Maria Gené, and two individuals who had played important roles in FC Barcelona during the 1970s, Josep Lluís Vilaseca, the local sports minister, and Joan Granados, the head of TV3.

It was decided that the best strategy to adopt would be not for Pujol to back Cambra openly but for key sectors of his government to offer some covert support. As one insider told me, 'At those meetings, the view that emerged was that it was good that Cambra should engage in a test of strength with Nuñez, although there would not be any declaration of war emanating from the Generalitat.' While Pujol viewed Nuñez as a political rival, he did not want to invest publicly too much in the Cambra campaign for fear that its failure would backfire on him politically. As things turned out, Cambra lost the election, despite having the backing of a large campaign fund and important sectors of the local media, not least TV3.

When I met Fuste ten years on, he had seemingly left the world of political intrigue behind him. Fuste was back doing what he knew best: playing football in a veterans' game. As he put on his boots and got ready to join Kubala and the others, I got a clear sense that his heart still lay with the club and not necessarily with those who run it. 'Barça is easily the best club in the world because it represents a country, Catalonia, and this is something that gives it its extraordinary potential. You only have to open its accounts to realise that we've really got it covered. What we've lost a bit is our sense of identity. I don't share the same feelings as the people who are running the club. They want to run this club like a company, when I don't believe that they should. For me, Barça is an exemplary football club. We don't get paid dividends, not because the money is not there but because we don't want it. I'm happy to be a member and that's it, and that's what makes us different from other clubs. I played for a club that represented its people during Franco's dictatorship, and it was here in this stadium that we could shit on the regime if we really wanted to. There are some people who don't understand that, or maybe don't want to understand it.'

In football, one of the hardest things for a player is to hang up his boots, and then to decide what to do next. Not everyone is a natural for TV; few have the intellect and imagination to share their own skills with others as managers. And yet for all his loyalty, Fuste claims to have had no problem in making the break. 'I am involved in commerce. I don't train any more, although I do play now and then. There was a time when Barça was playing so badly that I stopped coming to the stadium. It was towards the end of Venables's time here. He was a nice guy, a great guy, but I thought the kind of football he taught was a disaster. I don't like English football – you know, the long ball stuff. I like quick passing and quick touches. I started going again when Cruyff returned. Now he really *did* know how to play good football, and he knew how to make people play good football.'

Another foreigner, I think loudly to myself, letting the word 'foreigner' echo across the changing room, empty now except for Fuste and me. For the first time since we began talking, I seem to have touched a subject that troubles Fuste. A frown is drawn across his lean, dark features.

'If there is one problem with this club it is that it has tended to exaggerate the importance of its foreign stars. I think there have been better Spanish players around who deserved as much if not more appreciation – players like Juanito Segarra and Luisito Suárez. Why is it that the history of Barcelona seems to belong to foreigners? There are non-foreigners who have stayed with the club for twenty years or more, probably played better, and yet hardly even figure in the stickers. It's a huge bloody injustice.'

Fuste gets up from the bench, draws his socks up, and heads for the exit. His anger will make him play well today.

TINA SAMITIER: the widow

When the veterans don't meet to play football together, they sometimes meet for a celebratory dinner. Among them sits a widow, Tina, with fading good looks, who carries the memory of a footballer within her like a precious gem. It is in his memory that she will be, as long as they live, the veterans' guest of honour, for the history of the Barça they identify with is intimately linked with the legend of her late husband, Pepe Samitier.

In her flat, Tina tells me about her life with Samitier. It is a small apartment, simply furnished, with none of the trappings of wealth of more contemporary football wives. *!HOLA!* magazine would be hard put to find space for its cameras. Apart from in her memory, his presence is stored beneath her bed, in an old suitcase filled with photographs she is happy to share only with those she trusts. She is an attractive, well-preserved middle-aged woman. It's difficult to identify her as the widow of a man who died more than twenty-six years ago, until she reminds you that she was only a teenager and he thirty years older when they first fell in love. 'Before I met him, I wasn't all that interested in football. My parents weren't Barça fans. They supported Espanyol. My family was more into wrestling and boxing. Every week we'd go to the Plaça d'Espanya to watch the wrestling . . .

Thursdays, Saturdays, Sundays. I remember the crowds walking along Sants Street . . .'

She and Samitier met while she was working in a bakery. He used to visit relatives nearby and take them cakes. It was pure circumstance that initially marked their lives. 'He was no longer playing at that time. He was technical secretary at Barça – a member of staff, a worker like anybody else. He had to travel, look at players, look at teams. He was still an idol. People would stop us all the time – because we used to walk a lot – and they'd say, "Look, look, it's El Sami!" We never had a car. Either we were driven by friends or we'd go by taxi. When he died they had him lying in the chapel in the stadium for two days so people could see him. I've never seen so many taxi men. I think all the city of Barcelona's taxi men filed past his coffin. They turned up dressed in the uniform they had in those days. I'll never forget it. It was like a special tribute from a group of people who really loved him.'

Pepe Samitier died on 5th May 1972. He had made his début playing in the Spanish First Division at the age of sixteen. The Uruguayan author Eduardo Galeano has drawn this portrait of a Barça legend: 'In 1918 he signed with Barcelona in exchange for a watch with a dial that glowed in the dark, something he'd never seen, and a suit with a waistcoat . . . a short time later, he was the team's ace and his biography was on news-stands all over the city. His name was on the lips of cabaret *chanteuses*, bandied about on the stage and revered in sports columns where they praised the "Mediterranean style" invented by him.

'Samitier, a striker with a devastating shot, stood out for his cleverness, his domination of the ball, his utter lack of respect for the rules of logic, and his Olympian scorn for the borders of space and time.'

I would add that Samitier's ability to rise above the ground, and hit the ball with extraordinarily contorted shots, earned him the nickname 'the Lobster Man'.

The Samitier Tina married in Nice in 1966 was a pale reflection of those glory days. El Sami, as we have noted earlier, was still a strong personality capable of using friends and influence to secure the most controversial contracts. But the apparent zest for life that drew him to a woman much younger than himself responded to a sense of disillusion with the same club that had once turned him into an icon. 'They threw him out of Barcelona because of envy. The same thing happened when he was a player thirty years earlier. It had nothing to do with his ability. It hurt him a lot. He felt very down, betrayed, the worst that any person can feel. He never forgave the people who did it. Pepe had a good memory. When they threw him out, Bernabéu [Santiago Bernabéu, president of Real Madrid] said to him, "Why don't you come home." Bernabéu treated him like a brother.'

Samitier's close links with Real Madrid, to which I shall return in a later chapter, belong to a past some Catalans would prefer to forget or ignore. But Tina's testimony is a valid insight as much into the humanity of her husband as into the contradictions that formed part of Barça's history during the Franco regime. To ignore it is to accept that history can only be written in halves.

'We never spoke about politics because Pepe was completely apolitical. He left Spain during the Civil War because everyone was leaving and because he was half famous and because he was afraid of being caught up in the repression. I remember once when we'd been married for a while Pepe came back from a trip abroad and said, "You'll never guess who I bumped into in the airport. I think it was Santiago Carrillo [head of the Spanish Communist Party who lived in hiding during the Franco years]." He wasn't shocked, just interested in a purely human way. He didn't really worry about who he met. He was by nature open and down to earth. To Franco he used to say things like "My General, you've put on a bit of weight," and he'd tap him on the tummy.'

Thinking of what so many *cules* have been telling me along the way of my research, I ask her whether El Sami shared their vision of Real Madrid as the living symbol of centralised repression. 'No, he was above all that. He was a free man, a sportsman,' she answers.

When people ask Tina if she feels any links at all to Barça, she reminds them that two or three times a month she shares a supper with the veterans, footballers she learned long ago to admire and trust. 'I've stayed attached to Barcelona because I haven't got married again in twenty-six years. Maybe if I'd fallen in love with someone else, I would have gone on being attached to Barcelona, but in a different way. Call it destiny, but if I'd married again I would have led a very different life . . .'

So after all these years she has forgiven the club, if not some of those who treated her husband in the way they did. Before leaving, I ask Tina to leave me with her favourite image of El Sami. She says, 'Pepe is like the history of Spain. Talk to people in Barcelona today about Samitier and everyone remembers him. And he earned that playing as a footballer many years ago.'

JOSÉ-MARIA MINGUELLA: the agent

Forty-odd years of Barça history is a long time, and to no one more so than José-Maria Minguella. The man has come a long way since – when he had just turned five years old – his dad made him a member of the club: membership number 6061. As one of the world's leading agents, he has made a fortune out of the business of football, his growth and success personifying Barça's own transformation into a money-spinning machine struggling to keep hold of its soul before the relentless onslaught of the market-place.

We meet at his house, a modern, multi-level whitewashed building surrounded by a large garden in the exclusive neighbourhood of Pedralbes. Like so many other houses in Pedralbes, that of the Minguella family hides from the passing world behind an unassuming façade. From the street, the Minguella residence is simply a long wall and a small door. Its true nature is apparent only from within. The rich and successful of Catalonia are more discreet than their peers in the rest of Europe. Nevertheless the area, with its protected, anonymous entrances, is perched on a hill, so that its inhabitants live their lives looking down on the city, a constant reminder that on the scale of social status, they are very definitely high up.

The most modest thing one can say about the Minguella residence is that it is more discreet than the palace nearby where one of his clients, Diego Maradona, lived when he played at the club in the early 1980s. Agents the world over cannot afford to be seen to be living in greater luxury than the players they deal or have dealt with, and it's in the nature of the money they make that it travels far and fast, rarely keeping still. Alan Sugar, the chairman of Tottenham Hotspur, once told me, 'A lot of agents are spivs – they divert funds to special bank accounts, take money from both sides involved in the deal. Some of them are absolute crooks – no doubt about it.'

Minguella is not universally liked in Barcelona. Some distrust the amount of money he appears to make; others his apparent obsession with making it. A few are prepared to question in whispers the way he makes his money, although if there is any suggestion of illegality it has not been made public. Certainly there are also people owing Minguella a favour or two, which most of the time gives the impression that he is beyond good or evil, as much a part of the Barça landscape as any good player or prominent local journalist. By his own admission, Minguella began to see money moving from an early age. The home where he spent his childhood was next to Barça's old stadium of Les Corts. The boy looked up towards the sky one day and noticed that Les Corts had been made redundant, the decision taken to build a bigger, better stadium, the Camp Nou. The extension of bricks and mortar conveyed a simple message: the more money you make, the bigger you become, and the bigger you are the more money there is to spend.

As we begin to reflect on Barça's history, Minguella moves unprompted into a world of stars. 'Barça has had three great stars: one was Kubala, and because of him they built the Camp Nou; another was Cruyff, who ensured that the stadium got filled; and the third was Maradona, thanks to whom the stadium had to be extended from 90,000 capacity to 120,000. These three players forced the club to think big. I've got a very clear theory about all this. People become members, they're fans, and it's said that Barça is "more than a club", and people are very devoted, but when a team hasn't got big stars, people stop going to the stadium. That's why I always say that a big club like Barça is built on big stars, and these big stars have to have some important players playing alongside them.'

Minguella is self-effacing about his own start with Barça, claiming that it was the result more of good luck than of design. He had studied law at university and had become the trainer-manager of the university team when in 1970 Barça signed Vic Buckingham as the club's new manager. 'One day the club call me and tell me that they need an interpreter who also happens to know something about football. The club secretary Hector Carrera rings me. God knows why they thought of me. I didn't know much English. I'd been a couple of summers in England and that was it. But I said I'd do it because I wanted to get near the first team. If they'd asked me to interpret Chinese, I would have also volunteered.'

The day after the phone call, at 9.00 a.m. Minguella walked into the changing rooms at the Camp Nou and introduced himself in English to Buckingham. The boy who had been born under the shadow of Les Corts never looked back. The early press conferences proved chaotic affairs, with Minguella's limited English barely serving Buckingham as he faced a barrage of questions from local journalists. But the two men struck a good personal relationship. While Buckingham died some years back, Minguella retains fond memories, crediting the Englishman with many of the insights on the game he has carried with him into the newspaper columns he occasionally writes.

'Vic managed to convey to the players the sense that they were in a big club, and that when they had the possession of the ball they had to completely forget about the opposition. It was an attacking mentality. He didn't want his players using up their energies in thinking who they should mark. His view was that the first defence the team should count on was the last player to lose the ball. But only if a player lost the ball should he think about defending. Vic also had a great sense of humour. One day one of the members of the club's ruling junta came down and started telling him what he thought was a better way for the team to play. Vic just stood there watching him until he'd finished talking and then said, "I couldn't agree more. In fact I am so in agreement that I suggest that you, sir, turn up at nine o'clock tomorrow morning and train the team." ' On hearing this, the official begged Buckingham's pardon and beat a hasty retreat.

In the one year Buckingham was at Barça (he cut short his contract after suffering repeated back problems), the club won the Generalissimo's Cup and narrowly missed winning the League after being held to a draw in a crucial end-of-season game against Real Madrid. Buckingham was replaced as manager by the former Dutch international and Ajax player Rinus Michels. Under him, Minguella moved to full-time duties as one of the trainers of the first team. 'With Michels it was four really intense years at all levels, training, seeing players, seeing teams, drawing up contracts. Then I went for a year as club secretary to Hercules, the Alicante club. With all that experience I pretty well learned what had to be learned about the world of football.'

Instead of going back to his old job, Minguella decided to start working as an agent, although the practice was still subject to an official FIFA ban as not serving the interests of football. What had begun as a three-year leave of absence became a lifelong obsession – to control the destiny of important players and assure himself of their thanks at all times. While never losing his love for the game, the world in which Minguella began to operate was determined by the crude equation of offer and demand. He started to travel a lot, and with each trip he would bring back a player – either pledged or in person. Latin America became his favourite hunting ground. 'It was a job that I liked because it gave me freedom to operate. It allowed me to stay within football while not being seen to have too much of an official tie with the club management.'

It was a freedom and a distance that Minguella learned to manipulate according to what best served his interests. When Josep Lluís Nuñez ran for president of Barça in 1978, Minguella calculated correctly that Barça was entering a more aggressive entrepreneurial stage where the money would be made available if he could deliver star potential. He helped organise Nuñez's election campaign.

Two years earlier, in Argentina, Minguella had caught his first glimpse of Diego Maradona as a sixteen-year-old playing in a First Division match – the youngest player ever to do so. 'The kid was on the small side, although big-headed. Apart from that you didn't have to be a genius to realise that Maradona was something special. When I came back to Barcelona I talked to the club secretary, Jaume Rosell, and told him, "I've just seen this youth, a sixteen-year-old who I think is going to turn into something pretty special." Days later I got a letter back from Rosell, and you know what it said? It said, "We can't pay a million dollars to a youth." '

Rosell was replaced as secretary of the club when Nuñez won the election in 1978. Minguella continues his story: 'In 1978, Maradona was left out of the Argentinian World Cup squad and Nuñez was elected president of Barcelona. At that time I was very close to Nuñez because I had helped him with his election campaign. He'd asked me for advice, and I'd given it to him. I felt that what Barça needed was a foreigner, above all a forward. It was then that I suggested we have another try to get Maradona.'

Only in 1982 did Maradona finally come to Barça. The intervening four years saw Minguella involved in negotiations essentially aimed at making sure that anyone remotely involved with the player should make money. Thus one interest was balanced against the other, complex financial transactions worked out to take advantage of unstable local exchange rates, and the grim human-rights violations and corruption of Argentina's military regime conveniently ignored.

Looking back on those years in the comfort of his home, Minguella admits that torture and the 'disappeared' were the last things on his mind when he went to the Naval Mechanical School, one of Buenos Aires's most notorious concentration camps, to try to persuade Navy Admiral Carlos Lacoste to allow Maradona out of the country. 'At that time the only thing that people talked about was football. I'd fly into Argentina, book into a hotel, talk around the place, eat some barbecued meat . . . To tell you the truth we had a hell of a good time.'

The day he went to the Naval Mechanical School, no one suggested there was another Argentina, that of the screams of pregnant women having their babies snatched from them, and of the helicopters filled with prisoners, hovering above before throwing their human cargo drugged and blindfolded to their deaths in the waters of the nearby River Plate.

'The place where I was told to go and meet Lacoste was weird. There was a big gate and a small spy window. Some soldiers came out and after five minutes of checking my papers they let me in. Before me there was a long dark passage and at the end of it a naked light and a small office. I was told to sit there and wait . . .'

Invoking national sovereignty, Lacoste temporarily blocked Maradona's transfer to a 'foreign country', but this did not deter Minguella from making sure that the player stayed within his sphere of influence. On 13th February 1981, Minguella helped broker a deal whereby Argentinos Juniors loaned out Maradona to another Argentinian club, Boca Juniors, until 30th June 1982 – the eve of the World Cup in Spain. Boca paid US$4 million, in addition to assuming $1.1 million of Argentinos Juniors' debt. 'I had a good relationship with Boca and so it occurred to me it would be a good idea to say at one point, "Why don't we sign up Maradona but on the assumption that he won't be in Barcelona until two years' time?" That was the contract I helped sculpture.'

By January 1982 Minguella was so confident of clinching the player that he rang up Nuñez and suggested Barça make another direct approach. By then, the local Argentinian currency had suffered a thirty per cent devaluation against the dollar, putting Minguella in a much stronger position to put together a deal that Nuñez would consider worthwhile in dollar terms. Barça, meanwhile, engaged the services of Carlos Tusquets, a banker by training who was the club's financial administrator, and together he and Minguella worked out an $8-million contract, purchasing bonds traded through the New York Stock Exchange to minimise the real cost to Barça of the transaction. It was the kind of dubious speculative trading that under the Argentinian military came to be condemned as the 'bicycle', because of the way it was used to launder illicit funds. But when it came to Maradona's transfer, all involved were more than happy to 'pedal' furiously.

Among the Argentinians who witnessed the Maradona negotiations was Settimio Aloisio, at the time a member of the board of Argentinos Juniors. Aloisio was horrified at the way the Maradona contract ended up a carve-up of commissions and special payments. He told me, 'In the end, Maradona's transfer to Barcelona turned into a Persian market in which everyone was trying to make money – hundreds of thousands of dollars were played with. It was a very degrading spectacle.'

Minguella insists that he personally did not make much money out of the deal – a claim impossible to verify with any accuracy. He has, however, no regrets about helping to put it together. On the contrary, he looks back on it as one of the highest points of his career as an agent. 'It's difficult for me to admit this, but yes, I guess you could say that the Maradona contract was a big point of departure for me. It got huge publicity. I never looked back.'

Just looking at Minguella, I find it difficult to match the person to the job. He is quietly spoken, intelligent, thoughtful. He doesn't drink. During two lengthy interview sessions he has no difficulty in sharing the intimacy of his office and his home – both housed under the same roof – with me. I am allowed to overhear his telephone conversations – striking this deal and that across the Atlantic and beyond, arguing terms with faceless Brazilians and Eastern Europeans. He does not hide his arguments with his Argentinian partner, less good-humoured than he and seemingly forever at odds with him over ways of making money. One day while we are talking, he confides, 'What some people don't understand is that you can't ask for $20,000 when you know that something is really only worth $2,000. You have to maintain some semblance of credibility in this business.'

Later, using a special security key to unlock the entrance to his living quarters, Minguella shows me around his large sitting room – filled mainly with videos and a large digital screen – and the small kitchen and dining room where he and his family share their quieter moments together. There may be a lot of secrets known only to himself and some of his players; it's hard to dig them up in Pedralbes.

What makes Minguella disconcerting is the way he seems completely at ease with a business that each day it develops threatens to turn football into just one more commodity to be picked up, traded and, if necessary, discarded when it gets beyond its sell-by date.

If one of our meetings extends through half an afternoon and well into the evening, it is partly because the phone rarely stops ringing, part of a hectic schedule that continues without a break for most of Minguella's year. Here is an average week in the life of José-Maria Minguella as described by him in one of his extended monologues: 'On Wednesday I'm going to the final in Valencia, on Thursday I've got a ticket for Brazil – I'm talking to someone in Chile to see if they can meet up with me in Brazil . . . I've just come back from Munich. I went on the two o'clock flight, I stayed there for an hour and a half and then caught the next plane back. At nine o'clock I was back here. We've got various offices abroad. They are there to keep me in touch with what's going on, although I try to see a player personally.'

Minguella, like many other agents, has managed to take advantage of the freeing-up of the transfer market as a result of the historic Bosman ruling. To that extent he is inseparable from the big money machine that is European football generally. But he is also very much a symbol of what Barça may become more like in the future. Some of

Barça's best players have passed through his hands, including the Spanish internationals Nadal and Amor, and Stoichkov and Romario. That his column in *Sport*, one of the capital's leading sports papers, is written with a sharp and seemingly acerbic pen, extending criticism of the club whenever he feels like it, reflects a certain power. His agency has some one hundred players on its books, the largest number Spanish, but also a growing number of foreigners originating in all parts of the world from the Ukraine to Brazil.

Being a powerful football agent by day, and a shooting-from-the-hip columnist at least once a week, gives Minguella plenty of opportunity to further his interests. Bobby Robson was among those who distrusted him, but in the end Robson didn't go the distance, and Minguella is still there. 'The business of football has become globalised, and an agency like ours has to be everywhere,' he says. From his perch up in Pedralbes, he is watching the world with a telescope, while constantly venturing out in search of the big prize.

Minguella likes to sound like Jerry McGuire, the American agent played on film by Tom Cruise, who considers himself a protector, not an exploiter, of his clients. 'When a player comes to see me, I've got to explain a few things to him so that we can be in agreement. When he tells me that he wants me to look after his wife, I'm the one who has to sort things out; it's the same if he doesn't like the house he's got and wants to change it. I've got one thing for sale: my service.'

But talk to him a little longer and you realise that this is only one level of his existence, that the life of the agent is racing to keep up with the money machine that is turning and turning, thanks to TV. 'When TV didn't exist, a club's income was, say, ten and it would spend eleven. With the arrival of TV, the revenue is, say, 1,000 and the club spends 120. Where's all the money gone? It's gone on players and their managers.'

He doesn't add the word 'agent', so I ask him, how much money does José-Maria Minguella make in a good year?

'When I was with Buckingham, I helped out with the schoolboys and earned half a million pesetas. Nowadays I can be making four or five million pesetas a year in commissions . . . I'd like to give you more precise figures, but you've got to understand, this work is not like any other work.'

It sure isn't.

Before leaving Pedralbes, I wonder aloud how long Minguella thinks he can keep this up, and where it's all going.

'Maybe,' he says, deadly serious, 'one day I might present myself as a candidate for the club presidency.'

4

Roots

On Christmas Eve 1899, eleven men stepped out on to a race track in the neighbourhood of Bonanova to play a game of football wearing the blue and red colours of what in time would grow into the biggest sporting institution in the world – FC Barcelona.

In contrast to its opponents on that day, FC Catala, the team could boast little genuinely Catalan about it beyond its being named after the regional capital. While FC Catala was made up mainly of Catalans, the majority of Barcelona's players were foreigners, notably Englishmen. The Anglo-Saxon contingent included a goalkeeper called Brown; the club's first president, William Wild; and two brothers, Arthur and Ernest Witty.

Two weeks earlier, a game between FC Barcelona and an improvised collection of enthusiasts, drawn from various locally based English companies – Barcelona's official début – had been able to muster only ten players on each side. The second event was altogether a more organised affair, with Barcelona strengthening its side with the only truly free transfer of a foreigner in its history: Arthur, the elder of the two Witty brothers, scorer of the winning goal by *los ingleses* in the inaugural match.

The encounter on Christmas Eve was followed closely by a hundred or so local football fans. Barcelona dominated the game, its players controlling and passing the ball with greater skill, and opening up greater attacking opportunities inside the Catalan half. The 'Spaniards' were nevertheless described as 'heroes' in one local newspaper account for the bravery of their individual defence in the face of a more co-ordinated superiority. Barcelona won 3–1, with one of its goals the subject of some dispute, given that the referee overruled a linesman's opinion that it had been handball. On balance, the game proved a Christmas treat, enjoyed by the crowds as much as by the players on both sides, as reported in this eyewitness account:

'The fans were full of admiration and enthusiasm. They watched the players pass the ball firmly and decisively, passing it with skill from one half of the pitch to the other, the ball moving backward and forward in a series of combined moves . . . but perhaps the most pleasing aspect of the *fiesta* was that everyone ran a lot and consumed a great deal of oxygen, and that all the body-blows and falls were without serious consequence. Such was the quality of the game that a few jockeys, who happened to be exercising their horses, detained their charges to watch the players, so impressed were they by the sight of their varied colours set against the green of the turf. Thus did these riders contribute to the splendour of the scene, unconsciously paying just homage to this great and novel sport which with such spirit has taken hold among us.'

In the context of football's wider audience at the time, what was remarkable about Catalonia's discovery of football and the English 'connection' was not that it existed but that it had been so late in coming. By the time Barcelona was formed in 1899, dozens of English, Scottish, Welsh and Irish towns had been represented on the football pitch for over two decades. The game had also already been exported to South America – an export as typically 'British' as Lancashire cloth, Birmingham engineering and City of London loans. As Eduardo Galeano recalls, 'It arrived on the feet of sailors who played by the dikes of Buenos Aires and Montevideo, while Her Majesty's ships unloaded blankets, boots and flour, and took on wool, hides and wheat to make more blankets, boots and flour on the other side of the world . . .' He adds, 'The English of Montevideo and Buenos Aires staged Uruguay's first international competition in 1889, under a gigantic portrait of Queen Victoria, her eyes lowered in a mask of disdain. Another portrait of the queen of the seas watched over the first Brazilian football game in 1895, played between the British subjects of the gas company and the São Paulo Railway.'

As in Latin America, football in Spain had initially followed the imperial flag, taking hold in that part of the country where British mercantile interest was most concentrated. Spain's first football club, Huelva Recreation Club, founded in 1878 – twenty-one years before FC Barcelona – was geographically at the opposite end of the country to the Catalan capital. Football was brought to the Andalusian port by English sailors and the managers and workers of the nearby tin and zinc mines owned by the British conglomerate Rio Tinto, and was quickly learned by the local population.

Football took hold only belatedly in Catalonia, partly because of the nature of local politics. The working classes were embroiled throughout the nineteenth century and well into the twentieth in a seemingly endless cycle of repression and violence that left little time to watch, let alone learn, an innovative sport. As for the middle classes, while they enjoyed something of an economic boom in the last dozen years of the nineteenth century, their bourgeois paradise was overshadowed in the 1890s by escalating strikes and anarchist-inspired bombing campaigns. It was the middle classes, none the less, who toyed with Catalan nationalism, speaking their own language alongside Spanish, and selective in what they would and would not surrender to 'foreign' influence.

The inherently inward-looking conservatism of Barcelona's local rich in their attitude to leisure has been well defined by the Australian writer Robert Hughes, in his portrait of the emblematic Puig family. 'No television, radio, cinema; instead, the decorous sound of the piano, as Señora Puig and her daughter tinkled out a four-handed piece for Papa. Parchesi was played, and whist. Increasingly, middle-class women read: mainly sentimental novels, but the menu widened a little as the Church began (slightly) to relax its all-encompassing injunctions against anything foreign . . . As for open-air sports, wives did not play them, though some rode a little and even accompanied their husbands to shoots on properties like Eusebi Güell's at Garraf, south of Barcelona. Athletics consorted badly with the dignity of women, and even worse with the imposing waistlines of their husbands. Life was essentially sedentary, ruminant and processional. The only opportunity to work up sweat was in bed or at one of the enormous formal balls that were the seasonal delight of the bourgeoisie. Nor were spectator sports popular in turn-of-the-century Barcelona. Football clubs had only just begun to come into existence . . . The lower classes had their bars and cabarets and dance halls, a seamy and raucous night life concentrated in the Barri Xino [Chinatown] and the demonic spine of the Parallel. Their betters had the café, the club, the promenade and better brothels . . . Señor Puig spent most of his daylight hours away from home, in the office or in the handsome establishments that had sprouted everywhere in the Eixample, along Passeig de Gràcia and down the Rambla that catered to the boulevardier with time on his hands.'

Among the local bourgeoisie, there were those for whom the sight of men in short trousers was morally reprehensible. If and when they practised sport – and this was on rare occasions – it was to ride horses, shoot, or play tennis – in long trousers and in groups restricted to family and close friends. On the few occasions they caught a glimpse of some of the rough-and-tumble of a hard-fought football game egged on by an increasingly excitable crowd, they viewed it as a painful reminder of the militancy that simmered in the cramped urban dwellings of their employees.

No such misgivings seem to have been shared by Barcelona's first foreign players, who regarded football as a pleasurable form of exercise, a welcome break from the rigours of office life and trade. The Witty family, two of whom played for one of the club's first teams, had emigrated to the Catalan capital from England in the middle of the nineteenth century and set up a shipping business, acting as agents for all the British merchant vessels that sailed in and out of Barcelona. The family firm survives to this day.

The family members most closely linked with football, Arthur and Ernest Witty, were born in Barcelona but educated at Merchant Taylors', one of the more ancient English public schools, where sport was regarded as an important part of a young man's development. In a very particular way, Merchant Taylors' had the game of football built into its tradition. Founded in 1561 during Queen Elizabeth I's reign, the school had had as its first headmaster Richard Mulcaster, a fine classical scholar who was also an early figure in the history of football. In an age when there was still a very exaggerated store set by learning to the exclusion of all else, Mulcaster proved himself a true man of the Renaissance, insisting that the body should be trained as much as the mind if a human being was to reach his or her full potential. His programme for securing a rounded human personality included every kind of exercise: dancing, wrestling, fencing, walking, riding, jumping and, last but by no means least, football.

In *Positions*, a personal manifesto written soon after he became headmaster, Mulcaster resurrected the practice of football from its existence as one of the most popular pastimes of ordinary Londoners – despite its periodic repression by the authorities on the grounds of keeping public order. He wrote, 'The football game could not possibly have grown to the greatness it is now if it had not been beneficial to health . . . football strengthens the body and helps weak humans by much moving and thickening of the flesh.' A very different view was taken at the time by the Royal Exchange, which banned the sport after disqualifying it as a 'disorderly exercise'. At this establishment as in other parts of seventeenth-century England, any men or women caught practising football were threatened with imprisonment. It is not clear to what extent pupils of Merchant Taylors' were at the time prepared to buck the trend by following their headmaster's example. The school's official historian Frederick Draper comments, 'How much boys played football or whether they played it at all, we do not know.'

What *is* known is that by the end of the nineteenth century, when the Witty brothers were pupils there, Merchant Taylors' had a long-established tradition of good sportsmanship, with the then headmaster William Baker as dedicated as Mulcaster to 'training the body as well as the mind'. Baker, an old boy himself, served as headmaster from 1870 to 1900. Two years after taking office, he wrote to parents and pupils, 'I would like to foster a corporate and public spirit among the boys by drawing them together in common amusements and giving them common interests. I regard such an arrangement as desirable for the healthy development of the boys' character and as furnishing a wholesome corrective to the narrowing effects of excessive competition.' By then, football in England had become more of a working-class sport, with 'football' in public boarding schools like Merchant Taylors' played under the separate rules and regulations of the Rugby Union. And yet it was their enthusiasm for sport generally, and their respect for it as an integral part of their lives, rather than their focus on any one sport in particular, that Englishmen like the Wittys transferred to Barcelona.

In the spring of 1998, I went in search of the club's beginnings to Castelldefels. As one makes one's way south beyond the urban sprawl of the capital, some twenty kilometres along the highway, this is the first place of reasonable peace one can find. In an old people's home discreetly located in a quiet residential neighbourhood, I met Arthur

Witty's surviving son, Frederick. He was an old man clearly in the final phase of his life, hard of hearing, and struggling to rekindle the memory of times long past.

With his tweed jacket and silk cravat, and heavily accented Spanish only occasionally being brought into his conversation, Witty seemed the epitome of a post-imperial Englishman abroad, as proud as he was conscious of his father's very particular position in local society – so much part of it, and yet not part of it. Sitting on the veranda, we were surrounded by men and women holding on to to their existence with pills and tubes, but as I took him back over the years his eyes seemed to brighten with the image of energy and enthusiasm that his father had been. Although the sea breeze was building up and it was getting chilly, he resisted going back up to the room he shared with his bedridden wife. The old man wanted to play for a while with life. When I asked him to tell me a little about his father, he scarcely paused for breath.

Old team photographs of FC Barcelona show that the physical bridge between the Victorian English public schoolboy and the Catalan bourgeois was Arthur Witty's dark hair and full moustache. *Donde hay pelo hay alegría* – where there is hair there is happiness – went the old local proverb. Socially stiff and restrained the Catalan bourgeoisie may have been at times, but in their display of hairiness they hoped to signify their virility.

Witty showed his masculine energy and vitality in abundance. 'My father was about five foot ten and very strongly built,' the son-turned-old-man began to recall. 'When he was at school he played rugby as a forward. Then he came out to Barcelona and played football as a fullback. Rugby was impossible in those days because none of the sports grounds was fully turfed, whereas with football you could learn quickly enough to kick a ball around on any surface.' Thus did the public schoolboy learn to control and run with the ball on the kind of uneven wild surface that in time would produce stars from shanty towns and beaches.

The first Englishmen to play football in Barcelona did so on a fairly *ad hoc* basis, improvising games between employees of the companies they owned. It was a world within a world, self-assured and exclusive. Things might have stayed that way a great deal longer than they did had it not been for the role played by another 'foreigner', who shared

no such post-colonial idiosyncrasy. He was a Swiss by the name of
Hans Kamper, and on 22nd October 1899 he placed a short advertisement in the local sports newspaper, *Los Deportes*: 'The said Kans
[Hans] Kamper is keen on organising some football games in Barcelona and encourages anyone who feels enthusiastic enough about the
sport to make themselves present in the offices of this newspaper, any
Tuesday or Friday in the evening between the hours of nine and
eleven.'

Kans (Hans) Kamper was to adopt the Catalan name Joan Gamper,
the title under which he has been acknowledged as the true founder of
FC Barcelona. Kamper was in fact a Swiss businessman who had ended
up living in Barcelona more by accident than by design, according to
his son, Joan Gamper Jr. His aim had been to set up some trading
companies in Fernando Póo, but he had been persuaded by an uncle to
stay on in Barcelona during a stopover while the ship he was sailing on
replenished supplies. The job he took locally was that of chief ac-
countant of a local tram company. He was subsequently to make his
fortune trading in sugar, coffee and cinnamon. But his place in history
was assured by the love of football he brought with him from his native
Switzerland, where he had helped set up a team. Football was fast
becoming a popular sport among the Swiss, as it had already become in
France and Britain. Kamper had played as captain for FC Excelsior and
had then become one of the founding members of FC Zurich. His
advertisement in the Barcelona press was an attempt to pull together a
team from the various foreign and local enthusiasts distributed around
the capital.

Gamper's instinctive enthusiasm for the game is reflected in this
anecdote of his early days in Barcelona left by his son: 'One day, he was
making his way as usual by train to his office in Sarria when he saw a
group of youths kicking what appeared to be a ball on a piece of
wasteland. My father got off the train at the next stop, and joined in
the game. At one point he kicked the ball with such force that he broke
it. My father was very apologetic, and promised he would replace it
with a proper ball. He in fact ordered two from Switzerland, and gave
one to the youths. I think they must have been the first real footballs to
reach Barcelona.'

Among those who came forward at an early stage to join up with

Gamper were a fellow Swiss, Otto Kunzle; the Englishmen Walter Wild and brothers John and William Parsons; and two Catalans, Lluís d'Osso and Bertoméu Terradas. The founding meeting, held on 29th November 1899 in the Solé gymnasium, Number 5, Montjuïc del Carmen Street, mirrored football at its best. Of the eleven footballers present, the majority were foreigners. The days when such gatherings would be stimulated only by money and legislation were still far off. All that mattered was a common unadulterated enthusiasm for the game.

In the early years of the twentieth century, not all sport played in Barcelona could lay claim to such universality. Tennis, for example, was the preserve of the moneyed classes, and notably subject to British exclusiveness. The Witty I conversed with at the old people's home in Castelldefels, whose uncle, Ernest, as well as playing for FC Barcelona had been a champion tennis player, had chosen to spend the last years of his life among Catalans. But earlier generations had not always been so democratic. 'I think the game that really caught on among the English out here was tennis,' he told me. 'They played on their own courts. English men and English women. Some of the Spaniards tried getting in, but the English weren't very keen . . . Why? Because it wasn't done in those days – even though some of us were members of the Barcelona tennis club, which was really a Spanish club from the start.'

That the Wittys got involved with football in Barcelona was thanks to Gamper's personality, as Ernest's brother Arthur recognised in a rare interview given on the occasion of Barça's golden anniversary, in which he said, 'It was all Joan Gamper's work. The rest of us didn't do very much. He had the idea, and then inspired us with his enthusiasm. His powers of persuasion were very great. That's why we all followed him.'

Only in one respect, symbolically significant, have the Wittys challenged the Gamper legacy. While the Barça crest is eminently Catalan – the cross of Sant Jordi, the patron saint of Catalonia, and the red and yellow stripes of the Catalan nation – the Wittys have questioned the assertion made by several official histories of Barça that the club colours were inspired by Gamper. Arthur claimed he drew on his old school colours for the maroon and blue that were to become Barça's. In correspondence with Arthur's son Frederick in 1975, the school's then headmaster Reverend H.M. Luft reinforced the claim. In a letter, which I have seen, Reverend Luft states, 'I think it is very likely that the present colours of Football Club Barcelona (maroon and blue) are ultimately derived from our original colours here. The Waterloo Rugby Football Club was founded by two of our old boys, the Hall brothers, and in 1882 the club was given colours of dark blue with red stripes. The School Rugby Football Club chose to have the slightly different colours of chocolate and blue in 1885, though they had originally played in red and blue jerseys. I think they changed their colours so as not to be confused with the rapidly developing Waterloo Rugby Football Club, which was made up entirely of old boys of Merchant Taylors'. I would therefore say that you are probably completely right that your father and your uncle together transferred the original colours of our club to Barcelona when they founded the football club there. It is likely that in the late 1880s there was no such colour as maroon and that it was probably called dark red.'

Certainly in their response to Gamper's calling, the Wittys seemed subconsciously to absorb the ideals of distant headmasters, playing the game not so much to beat their opponents but to share in the sheer fun of it. 'The person who really got my father and uncle interested was that chap Gamper,' Frederick confirms in his conversation with me. 'One day he got in touch with them and said, "Look, there are other people who want to play like you, why don't we play together?" He was that sort of man, outward-going and very nice. The English who lived in Barcelona – well, they were English – they played any sport, for the sake of it. They played football just like they went rowing or sailing, or played tennis. Gamper had won medals as an athlete and as a cyclist in Switzerland, but when he came here he was only really interested in football, he was devoted to it. At first the English had their team, then Gamper formed his . . . After that, more and more Spaniards got the idea and wanted to play too. That's how things developed . . .'

We had drunk a cup of tea, night had fallen. The other old people had retreated inside. The bird-song had given way to invisible crickets, their sound as repetitious and inevitable as a clock's. Witty shivered with the frailty of a child but seemed still reluctant to move inside. There was memory left in him still. I asked him just how seriously his father had taken football, what role it had really played in his life, beyond the legendary image of the moustached team player, upright and defiant like a cavalry officer on the brink of victory.

Witty stared beyond me into the night, paused a little, then returned his face into the light, smiling, his pale cheeks grown ruddy in the chill air. 'He never did any specialised training – none of that stuff you see these days, with players having orders shouted at them by coaches acting like camp commandants. But he knew how to keep fit, and did so.' While they played for Barcelona, the Wittys lived alongside Catalans and foreigners of similar social standing in the Passeig de Gràcia, the parade ground of the upper middle classes, developed during the late nineteenth century as a place of fashion and elegance. On weekends – and when he was not playing football – Arthur broke free from the urban conformism and did a very typically English thing: he'd lead his family, walking, all the way to the top of Tibidabo, Barcelona's highest vantage point on the Collserola massif, and back again. Most locals made the trip by private vehicle or public transport. But Witty did it because he enjoyed the exercise.

The Wittys may have displayed a certain cultural schizophrenia, but their contribution to the early development of Barcelona as a football club is beyond dispute. The football they played together with Gamper showed skill and toughness in equal measure. Gamper was probably the best player. Arthur Witty recalled years later, 'Without a doubt Gamper was the best centre-forward. He had an extraordinary control of the ball and dribbled better than anybody. He was also a great striker. He scored more goals than anybody else. He'd run a lot, lifting his knees up; he gave an image of huge potential that I've seen in very few players.'

Among the more controversial early encounters involving these players was that between Barcelona and its local rival Catala on 11th February 1900. By fielding a team made up of locals and Scotsmen, Catala had effectively cast aside its pretence of being the only truly native team, but the game proved a turning-point by breaking with the somewhat restrained form the game had taken until then.

Barcelona beat Catala 4–0, with three goals scored by Arthur Witty and one by Gamper. But the final score was reached only after a bruising contest between the two sides, with Englishmen and Scots engaged in a dual reminiscent of ancient battles off the pitch. Tensions flared when Harris for Barcelona brought down Gold, one of Catala's Scottish players, with one of the most brutal tackles ever witnessed on Catalan soil. Gold got up limping but with enough strength and anger in him to deliver a series of body-blows to Harris. A general punch-up followed, the violence of which would have made the local anarchist demonstrations look like a picnic. Both Harris and Gold were expelled by the referee, and the two teams barely managed to regain their composure before the final whistle.

Once the heat of the moment had passed, Witty grew reflective. As captain of Barcelona, he felt responsible for having allowed the game to degenerate the way it had, and he promptly tendered his resignation. This was rejected by Barcelona's management board. Instead, Barcelona announced that it would not play another game against Catala for a whole year.

In October of that year, a short news item published in the local newspaper *La Veu de Catalunya* announced that Barcelona had rented a piece of land near the Hotel Canovas between the streets of Dos de Maig and Independencia, to serve as its first permanent playing field. It measured 200 metres by 130, and the rental included the use of two of the hotel rooms by players and club members. The use of the property was reported as an important symbolic act, confirming that Barcelona was a sporting institution that was more than the simple fantasy of a handful of enthusiasts. It showed the determination of Gamper and his friends to turn it into a permanent feature of the city. Ernest Witty played his part in reinforcing the seriousness of the project. He travelled to England and returned with a suitcase of standardised leather balls and a referee's whistle, just in time for the inaugural match played at Canovas against Hispania, another local team. With the exception of those that Gamper had managed to have sent from Switzerland, the balls used by Barcelona until then had been crafted in a somewhat haphazard manner by a local saddler more used to measuring horses than watching football. The match was also the first time that the Barcelona players sported their blue and red shirts.

After a year's rental of the Hotel Canovas site, Arthur Witty proposed a further expansion of the club's premises, in step with Barcelona's evolving reputation as the city's best-organised and most successful team with a dedicated following of fans. Drawing on his experience of English fields and gardens, Witty initially planned a manicured turf prepared with well-sown and fertile grass. This was abandoned after it was judged too expensive. But the piece of wasteland acquired by the club on the Horta road, between La Sagrera and Guinardo, was flattened with rollers, and loose stones and clumps of weeds carefully removed to make the surface as smooth as possible. An adjoining farmhouse was converted into a clubhouse with changing rooms for the players, while special parking spaces and entrances were added to accommodate the spectators. The ground was still a far cry from the Camp Nou, but it was no longer reminiscent of a shanty-town wasteland.

On 26th December 1904 Witty took another leaf out of the book of English football. He marked the occasion by organising a game of sufficient interest to draw fans away from the domestic indulgence of the festive season. He arranged the first international match ever played in Barcelona, between the club and Stade Olympique of Toulouse. Barcelona beat the French 4–0, with Gamper the undisputed star of the match, scoring two goals.

In terms of footballing skills – a combination of acceleration, toughness and ball control with goal-scoring potential – there was little to choose between Gamper and the Wittys. But the Swiss's direct involvement in the club's affairs outlasted by over a decade the Englishmen's, once Barcelona replaced its founding players with new ones. Only much later and with some regularity would other Englishmen come to have a similar impact on Barcelona's football life. 'My father remained a member of the club to his dying day,' recalled Frederick Witty. 'In retirement he used to go along and watch the team playing, until TV came and he chose to watch most of the games at home. He did keep in some personal contact with club officials, but he never really talked about football at home and was certainly never interested in the financial side of it all. He was interested in playing while he was young and fit enough to play. In a way, football became an incidental part of his life.'

Long after he retired from playing, Arthur Witty was often approached by Catalan business friends and invited to join the club's board of directors, but he appears to have become increasingly reluctant to do so because of what he thought of as the club's increasing politicisation. He belonged to a generation moulded by the British Empire, dedicated to commerce and administration, and always mindful of maintaining self-control, which was perceived as a dedication to the notion of 'fair play'. The truth was that football as conceived by Witty was never intended to become the mass sport of obsessive fanatics it is today. Nor did this colonial Englishman display an understanding of why football in Catalonia was destined to be political. This was clearly reflected in an interview he gave shortly before his death:

'What I dislike is all this excess of passion, and the partisan attitude of the crowd. This habit of protesting every decision that goes against the team, and of applauding whenever the same foul is committed by one of our people, is neither just nor sportsmanlike. Nor is the habit of taking on the referees. The referee is the only authority there is on the football pitch and should be respected.'

While the Wittys kept their distance, Gamper devoted most of his adult life to ensuring Barcelona's growth as a club worthy of respect and support in a region of Spain he felt had adopted him both professionally and emotionally. He served as the club president for five terms between 1910 and 1925, although he remained close in spirit to it for much longer than that, effectively from its foundation in 1899 until his death in 1930. While he lived, Barcelona grew from its *ad hoc* beginnings into one of Spain's major football clubs. On the occasion of the club's silver anniversary, in 1924, it was Gamper who was marked out for special tribute. Under his guidance, Barcelona had won twelve Catalan championships and five Spanish championships. Club membership had grown to close to 12,000. It was a remarkable achievement for a man who had initially had to struggle against local indifference, and had on at least one occasion personally intervened to save the club from terminal crisis.

Barcelona's nadir and Gamper's finest moment was in the summer of 1908. The club had lost through retirement some of its better players and had temporarily failed to find replacements capable of keeping up its performance. Throughout the season it had moved from one defeat to another. Its popularity had dwindled, and with it its finances. At an extraordinary meeting attended by a handful of members, the president Vicenc Reig resigned, while the treasurer Francesc Sanz proposed that the club dissolve itself. Just before the final vote was taken, one of the few Englishmen left in the team, Wallace, asked whether there was anyone present prepared to save the club from extinction, adding that if such a saviour existed he would be guaranteed the unanimous support of the players. Gamper rose to his feet and delivered what was to go into the annals of the club's history as a seminal declaration of principles: 'Barcelona mustn't and cannot be allowed to die. If no one is willing to do the job of saving it, then I will personally take it on from now onwards.'

No sooner had the meeting endorsed him once again as president than Gamper set out on an exhaustive personal crusade to rescue the club and put it on a sounder financial footing. Virtually cap in hand he went visiting personal business contacts, friends, and those he knew simply as loyal enthusiasts of the game like himself, asking them for funds. In return he promised to build the club into something worth watching by continuing to improve its ground facilities, investing in good players, and drawing up fixture lists that involved international as well as local matches.

Gamper was a man in touch with the times, particularly the social and political changes taking place in Catalonia. These made the development of a popular and genuinely local football team an event waiting to happen. Gamper's devotion to his adoptive Catalonia was recalled years later by his son, Joan Gamper Jr, in words that marked out an essentially different territory to that trod by the Wittys. Recalling his childhood with his father, in an interview published in 1974, Gamper Jr said, 'The language we usually spoke at home was Catalan. From the moment he fixed his residence in Barcelona his main objective was to become a Catalan citizen like everybody else. He learned Catalan perfectly, although he was never as good speaking Spanish. That's why he came to be known as the "Swiss Catalan" or the "Catalan Swiss".'

For centuries, the adoption and promotion of Catalan as a language – not a dialect – distinct from Castilian had been viewed as a key cultural symbol of local identity separate from the rest of Spain. Gamper's enthusiastic use of it reflected his identification with a Catalan nationalism that was entering a period of growth in the early part of the twentieth century and which in time would turn to FC Barcelona as one of its most passionate expressions.

The first years of Barcelona's existence as a club coincided with the 'great leap forward' of political Catalanism. Anti-Madrid sentiment was fuelled in the very year of the club's foundation. In the previous year, 1898, the imperial power of Castile had irrevocably ended with a failed military defence of its colonies in the Caribbean. At a time when other European countries led by England were successfully carving up Africa and Asia to suit their colonial designs, Spain had lost Europe's longest-surviving empire stretching back four hundred years to Christopher Columbus.

The disintegration of the imperial dream meant that more and more Catalans came to question the nature of their dependence on the rest of Spain, in particular Madrid. In 1901, a new Catalanist grouping, Lliga Regionalista, won four of the seven parliamentary seats for Barcelona, with a fifth going to the non-Lliga Catalanist Republican, Pi Maragall. A familiar pattern developed, with the Spanish army – the self-proclaimed guardians of national integrity ever since the Napoleonic wars – attempting to curb Catalan dissidence, only to stir its popularity.

On 23rd November 1905, a satirical magazine in Barcelona called *Cu-cut!* published a cartoon seemingly celebrating the growing political success of the Catalan parties in contrast to the apparent failure of the Spanish military as demonstrated in Cuba. The cartoon showed a large crowd making its way into a sports stadium for a celebratory party, being watched in the foreground by a fat man and a ornately uniformed officer. 'What are they celebrating here with such a big crowd?' asks the fat man. 'The Victory banquet,' replies the officer. 'Victory? In that case I suppose they must be civilians.' The magazine was closed down for insulting the honour of the military, but the clash only succeeded in stirring Catalan sentiment. That the incident had been provoked by an image depicting Catalan enthusiasm for sport would not have been lost on Gamper in those days of trial and error on the football pitch. However much the army may have disapproved of the notion, the idea was forming in the collective subconscious that politics and sport could be part of the same cultural identity.

FC Barcelona's projection as a Catalan team developed in opposition to the team that established itself as its undisputed local rival within ten years of its foundation in 1899: Espanyol. From its inception, Espanyol challenged the middle-class backers of Barcelona and the way they appeared to claim a monopoly on civil and patriotic virtue. Espanyol assumed the full title of Real Club de Fútbol and made King Alfonso XIII its patron. The juxtaposition of royalty and Spain in the Castilian language reflected a social reality: that in the city of Barcelona, there were monarchists and Spanish-speakers who wanted to go on living in a part of Spain and not become separate from it. In its early days, Espanyol made much of the fact that none of its players was a foreigner – born outside Spain, that is – although by 1911 it had three Englishmen playing for it. Espanyol had the royal crown on its club crest. Barcelona had the Catalan colours. And while Barcelona's team colours were argued over by Swiss and Englishmen, the Espanyol players came out in their first games dressed in long trousers and a shirt and tie.

Initially, Espanyol's symbols and dress codes were aimed at appealing to those who felt vulnerable and distrusted change, who needed reassuring that football was not about to split society apart. But the club's very existence came increasingly to be seen as a crude insult by Catalan nationalists who supported Barcelona, making encounters between the two teams a recipe for division and violence. One of the earliest violent incidents occurred during the derby played by the two teams in the 1909–10 season. Espanyol, the host, scored first, then Barcelona drew level. No sooner had the second goal been scored than hundreds of Espanyol fans invaded the pitch, surrounding the referee and threatening him with a lynching. Fearing for his life, the referee could think of nothing better to do than blow his whistle and declare the Barcelona goal a handball. The match was subsequently abandoned before half-time when all eleven Barcelona players walked off the pitch in protest.

It became a rarity for the local derby not to be engulfed in some controversy or other. Increasingly the scraps between players, the confrontations between rival fans and the verbal warfare between the respective managements came to reflect deeper social and political tensions. These surfaced with a vengeance during a match between the two clubs on 23rd November 1924. The detonator was the sending-off during the first half of Barcelona's star player Samitier after he had punched a member of the Espanyol team. The referee's decision was greeted with a roar of disapproval, followed by thousands of coins which rained down on the ground. The game, for ever remembered as the 'match of the coins', was cancelled, provoking a fierce debate between the two clubs' managements, conducted through the local media, as to who had been most to blame. Then in an unprecedented move the military authorities ordered that the game be played again, with no supporters allowed into the stadium. The ban only incensed the rival fans even more. As the match got under way behind closed gates, they massed outside the stadium and spent the evening engaged in a pitched battle.

The stadium had only recently been built, its commissioning a powerful symbol that FC Barcelona had outdistanced Espanyol in terms of its support. Les Corts had been inaugurated on 20th May 1922. This brought to fruition one of the first pledges made by Gamper when he personally undertook the rescue of the club at Barcelona's make-or-break extraordinary meeting. With a seating capacity of 20,000 and a covered stand for a further 1,500, Les Corts dwarfed any other stadium in Catalonia, and compared favourably with other venues in Europe. Its opening was a sell-out. Joining the crowds of supporters was the entire local political establishment, including the mayor, Ferran Fabra Puig and the president of the local government (the Mancomunitat), Josep Puig. Barcelona had come a long way since that first kick-about between Swiss and Englishmen. It had become an institution clearly identified with local Catalan politics.

Within a year, however, the Madrid government and King Alfonso XIII had voluntarily abdicated before a military *coup* led by General Miguel Primo de Rivera, an emotional patriot of the old school. The core of his political personality lay in a hatred of politics and politicians and a fondness for wine and women. 'I know how little I am worth and I recognise Divine Guidance which allows one who could not govern himself to govern twenty million Spaniards,' the Andalusian-born Primo declared soon after taking power. The dictator considered his greatest enemies anyone who toyed with the idea of becoming more separate from Madrid, by pursuing their own devolved government and speaking their own language. Political Catalanism in all its manifestations came into his firing line, making a clash with FC Barcelona inevitable.

The occasion was a benefit match on 14th June 1925, which Barcelona had organised to raise funds for the Orfeó Català, a choral society set up to carry on the work of the father figure of Catalan music in the 1860s, Josep Anselm Clave. Although Primo de Rivera had spent his first days in power forging tactical alliances with some of the richer families of Barcelona, he had stirred the passions of thousands more Catalans by closing down their local government and banning the use of their language. Days before the match was due to take place, he banned any tribute to the Orfeó Català, although he allowed the match itself – between Barcelona and Jupiter – to go ahead.

Those angered by the measures included the majority of people who packed Les Corts that day in June. The mood of defiance was signalled by the presence in the executive box alongside the Barça directors of two prominent Catalanist politicians, Francesc Cambo and Joaquin Ventosa Calvell, together with the founder of the Orfeó, Lluís Millet Pages. But it surfaced dramatically at half-time when a band of English Royal Marines, arranged for the occasion by the Wittys and the officers of a visiting Royal Navy vessel, played the first notes of the Spanish national anthem. From the stands rose a collective whistle while those in the executive box remained sitting in silence. The bemused Marines stopped playing, and could think of no alternative but to strike up the first bars of the English national anthem. The crowd broke into spontaneous applause. The event would in normal circumstances have been almost farcical. But there was no denying the seriousness with which the authorities interpreted it. A military edict issued within days of the match by General Joaquin Milans del Bosch, Catalonia's newly appointed captain-general, fined the Barça directors and imposed a six-month ban on Barcelona's activities as a club and as a team.

Not all those who filled Les Corts the day the English band played on were there to make a political statement. Many were there too to pay tribute to the promise that had begun to be shown by a generation of new players. The 1920s with its recurring pattern of repression and reaction – closures, censorship, strikes, demonstrations – inevitably politicised life inside and outside the stadium. But it was a period also when Barcelona experienced unprecedented days of football glory and transformed itself into the popular Barça of mass following.

The football imported and played by eccentric foreigners as a hobby had verged on the elitist. Gradually it had come down to earth, attracting an increasing number of locals to the game. The sport linked long-resident Catalans with more recently arrived migrants from other parts of Spain, and crossed class barriers, connecting the middle classes with the factory workers. Catalan society had historically taken pride in its architects, painters and writers. It was also respectful of its artisans. Thus the footballer – he who could make magic with his feet and even his hands – grew to be accepted and respected as another creative talent.

During this early period, Barcelona relied on a succession of foreign managers to learn the tactics and strategy long practised by more experienced European teams. The club's first full-time coach was an Englishman, John Barrow. He was replaced in 1917 by another Englishman, Jack Greenwell. From then until World War II, Barcelona was coached by two Hungarians, Jesza Poszony (1924–5) and Franz Platko (1934–5); an Irishman, Patrick O'Connell (1935–6); and four Englishmen, Ralph Kirby (1925–6), Jack Dormby (1926–7), James Ballamy (1929–31) and Greenwell for a second term (1931–3). But while the 1930s were to be overshadowed by politics, the 1920s was a decade marked by the success of the team made possible by the brilliance of individual, mainly home-grown talent. According to a report in *El Mundo Deportivo* in 1919, Barcelona's full complement of players was made up of a majority of forwards – a total of thirty-five. This compared with twenty-eight midfielders, fourteen defenders and nine goalkeepers, a composition that was reported as evidence of the team's overall emphasis on attacking football. The majority of the first-team players were Catalan, with the rest originating from elsewhere in Spain.

Barça players learned their toughness, fitness and goal-scoring skills – as well as team discipline – from their foreign coaches. But to these imported lessons they added some of their own language of invention, learning to possess the ball as much as kick it, quickening the pace, and throwing their energies into a sort of native dance of legs and hands in flight, which had one dual purpose – to entertain and score goals. Barça's popularity expanded in parallel with the club's growing sense of self-worth, in both political and sporting terms, the passion of its following fired by the pride the fans took in seeing men like themselves join the pantheon of team heroes.

One of Barça's first local heroes, Paulino Alcantara, was born in the Philippines but lived in Barcelona from the age of three. He joined the club in 1912 while studying medicine. Alcantara proved himself a sharp and powerful shooter, a versatile forward capable of scoring as many goals with his left as with his right foot. As one of the team's youngest players, Alcantara formed a highly effective tandem with a brilliant winger, Emilio Sagi. Both men helped Barcelona transform itself into one of Spain's leading teams, a strong contender for both Catalan and Spanish championship titles.

In 1915–16, the team won the Catalan Cup and narrowly missed winning the Spanish, blaming biased refereeing for its defeat in the final against the team destined to be its most bitter rival – Real Madrid. Such was Alcantara's popularity that the team's English coach, Greenwell, narrowly escaped being sacked the following season. Barça's lacklustre performance was blamed by the fans on the fact that he had dropped Alcantara from the first team in a series of crucial games.

Alcantara got his comeuppance the following season, helping Barça to a psychologically crucial 3–0 victory over Espanyol, the Cup holders and as ever a source of considerable political friction. According to an eyewitness account by Barça fan and historian Daniel Carbo, the game played on 12th May 1918 was 'an afternoon of explosive triumph, not so much because of the result achieved but because of the majestic way in which Barcelona played, reducing to impotence the opposition'.

Alcantara hung up his boots to become a full-time doctor on 3rd July 1927. In his fifteen years of playing for Barça, he scored a total of 356 goals, making him the highest goal-scorer in the history of the club. His many legendary moments include one during an international between

Spain and France on 22nd April 1922: one of the shots he kicked into goal was delivered with such force that it perforated the French net.

Another early hero of Barça, already referred to in an earlier chapter, was Pepe Samitier, more popularly known as El Sami. He made his début playing with Barça at the age of seventeen, on 31st May 1919, in an age when the players had yet to wise up to the business of football. Much later, Samitier would become the highest-paid member of the team, as Barça players moved from amateur to professional status, but his humanity endured. He was never short of time for the fans, particularly the younger, poorer ones with whom he always identified more than did some of the stiffer-collared members of the club's administration, who he suspected had no interest in the game at all other than as a source of social prestige and money.

Samitier had just turned twenty when the nine-year-old son of emigrants from Argentina, Nicolau Casaus, tried to see him play for the first time. When I interviewed Casaus towards the end of the twentieth century he was titular vice-president of the club and, now in his nineties, Barça's 'grand old man'. 'In 1922, I was nine years old and was living in a town in the province of Barcelona called Igualada,' he remembered. 'They'd organised a friendly between Barça and Igualada, and Samitier came to play. In those days you had to pay twenty-five centimos to get into the stadium, but I couldn't afford it. So what the boys and I did was organise ourselves into porters. When the team bus arrived we ran along and offered our services. I had the good luck of picking up Samitier's suitcase. He thought I was a funny kid – fat and small as I was then – but he made me a member of the club there and then.'

Among the quainter exhibits in the Barça museum at the Camp Nou is the simple first contract Samitier signed with the club: his agreement to play in exchange for a watch with a dial that glowed in the dark and a three-piece suit, neither of which he had ever possessed. Innocent and naïve Samitier may still have been, but the world he was entering was far from being so. His first match with Barça was a friendly between the club and an 'Allies team', made up of players from the three footballing nations that had emerged victorious from World War I – England, France and Belgium.

It is known that one Christmas during that war, English and German soldiers briefly came out of the trenches, laid their arms to one side and played a game of football. But for most of Europe that had been but an instant in a long nightmare when those for whom football had only recently arrived died in their thousands on the battlefields of the Western Front. Very different had been the experience in Catalonia, where the local economy prospered enormously as a result of Spain's neutrality. The Catalans who supported Barça as it developed its dream team had the time and money to make profits and enjoy football, a privilege denied to most of those fighting the war. They included the owners and managers of local textile companies, who were to have a powerful influence on the development of the club. They – among others – supplied the coats worn by French soldiers, and saw the profits from cotton exports double as a result. During this period, too, workers saw their salaries boosted by increased productivity, while shopkeepers increased their profit margins with higher prices. Much of the activity represented quick profits rather than sound expansion, but it is safe to say that World War I did Barça no harm.

Only afterwards, when the speculative nature of the war 'boom' fuelled dramatic price rises and unsettled labour relations, did Barça reconnect itself with the reality as experienced by the wider international community. In the early 1920s, the club found it difficult to persuade foreign clubs to come and play against them because of the periodic outbreaks of strikes and more serious political violence on the streets of the Catalan capital.

And yet despite the politics, or maybe because of it, the 1920s came to be recorded in the club's history books as its first Golden Age, a source of escape as much as an expression of pride for Catalans. They were by no means united in terms of either the nature or the intensity of their political allegiance, but they joined in the excitement of watching some wonderful Barça players – football at its best; the kind that Italian Marxist Antonio Gramsci praised with the phrase 'this open-air kingdom of human loyalty'.

El Sami was an early exponent of 'total football'. He was taken on as the linchpin of the team's defence. As things turned out, there was no position off-limits to him, as he feinted and dribbled his way from one end of the field to the other, baffling his opponents, and often leaving his team-mates to a purely supporting role, shifting their own positions to accommodate his talent. Such was the force of his personality on as well as off the pitch that only the foreign coaches exercised limited control over him. The one Catalan coach who coincided with him as a player during the 1920s, Roma Forns, felt duty-bound to let his star player dictate who should play and how. Josep Obiols, one of Samitier's team colleagues, later recalled, 'Samitier was the one who formed the team, who was the boss in every respect on the pitch and in the changing rooms, because Forns was a nobody. Samitier decided who played and who didn't play. He once even withdrew Alcantara because they had a disagreement, even though some would say he was a better player.'

Much has been written about the birth of the most beautiful football in the world – not in Europe, but in Latin America. But El Sami's touches with the ball were as effortless as any seen on the fields of Buenos Aires and Montevideo, his movement as elastic as that of any Brazilian. After Alcantara, he scored more goals in his fifteen years with the team than any other player in Barça's history. His *langostas* – kicks bicycle – made him an acrobat with a ball at his feet. He was the subject of one of the earliest football biographies, a bestseller on the news-stands of Barcelona, while he was still midway through his career. Subtitled *The Stars of Football*, the book was called *Samitier: The Magician of the Ball*. The dust cover drew attention to the 'inimitable style and marvellously original technique' of the midfield international.

El Sami's natural good looks, charisma and sheer love of life meant that the stadium was often too small to contain his energies. A favourite anecdote friends continued to repeat long after his death recalls one of many cheeky encounters Samitier had with the Barça management. While hitting the town late one night with a group of team-mates, confronted half-way down the Rambla by two directors of the club, Samitier joked back, 'You're asking me what's going to happen to tomorrow's training? Well, I've got a question for you, gentlemen: what are you two doing here and how come you're up so late to ask me the question?'

His stardom coincided with that of Carlos Gardel, the most famous of Argentinian tango singers, with whom he developed a close friendship. Both men maintained a hugely popular mass following, despite developing a taste for the glitter and glamour of high society and a dalliance with intellectuals and artists. When Gardel came to Barcelona as part of a Spanish tour in the mid-1920s, his interest and friendship were drawn to two figures who in their different ways had become icons of Catalan culture: the first was Santiago Ruisinyol, the Catalan writer and painter, and focus of Barcelona's radical circle of impressionist artists; the second was Samitier.

By age and temperament Gardel was more at ease with Samitier, who helped introduce him to the delights of Barcelona's 1920s night life, so imitative of Paris with its café culture and dance halls. Samitier was always a great walker – although Gardel learned the secrets of the Rambla initially not from the football player but from a Catalan barman he met in Buenos Aires. Throughout the '20s the two men kept up their friendship, with the footballer inspiring tangos written in his name, and the musician in turn going to see his friend El Sami play whenever his tour plans coincided with a Barça game. Samitier and Gardel were similar characters – popular extroverts, each a genius of his profession – who may have carried complexes within them, but who in their attitude to the outside world showed a refreshing irreverence towards all that was forced or typecast. They were society's darlings, and yet never allowed themselves to become prisoners of one set or another. They were rebels without a cause other than life itself. One expressed this with his football, the other with his songs. Their friendship turned into a powerful synergy, linking the sport of the masses to the music of the individual heart.

Gardel was killed in 1935 in an air crash in Colombia. In Spain, the Civil War was close to breaking out, and Samitier together with the rest of his team colleagues was preparing to go into voluntary exile. The only survivor of the crash was Gardel's personal assistant, who was a Catalan. Although badly burned and disfigured, he recovered sufficiently to give an interview one day in which he revealed himself as the man who had first introduced the tango singer to football. It was as if he felt destined to survive that crash in order to pay lasting tribute to the Samitier–Gardel connection.

One of the mysteries that Gardel carried to his grave was his ancestry. No one ever knew who his parents were or where he was born, and that added to his popularity in Argentina, for in a sense it made him belong to everyone. But while in Barcelona, Gardel occasionally used to boast that one of his parents was Catalan although he was born somewhere in France. Catalans loved him for that. So did Samitier.

Among other Barça heroes of this period was the legendary goalkeeper Ricardo Zamora, one of Samitier's best friends among the players. Zamora joined Barça in 1919, at the same time as Samitier. He had made his début two years earlier at the age of sixteen, playing for Espanyol. He was still a schoolkid wearing short trousers, but he soon adopted a dress code that marked him out as one of the great eccentrics on the field as much as off it. Strikingly handsome, he would put on a white polo-neck jumper and broad cloth cap before taking the field. He said it was to protect himself from the sun and the blows of his opponents, but it made him look like an Argentinian on his way to play polo in an English winter.

Zamora was fearless, throwing himself at the feet of attackers, or venturing out with the ball, often leading a counter-attack well into the opposite half of the pitch. Rare was the game that he ended without his hands and body covered in cuts and bruises; rare, too, a match lost because of a mistake made on his part. 'Over the years,' writes Galeano, 'the image of Zamora in those clothes became famous. He sowed panic among strikers. If they looked his way they were lost: with Zamora in the goal, the net would shrink and the posts would lose themselves in the distance. For twenty years he was the best goalkeeper in the world. He liked cognac and smoked three packs a day, plus the occasional cigar.'

In a sense, both Samitier and Zamora exteriorised Catalonia's and Barça's *alter ego*. By tradition, Catalans have reflected on the differences that set them off, individually and as a 'nation'. There is a part of themselves that believes in *seny* – roughly translated, 'common sense', but probably still best reflected in Samuel Johnson's definition of what he called 'bottom': 'an instinctive and reliable sense of order, a refusal to go whoring after novelties'. But the other side of the coin to *seny* is what Catalans recognise as *rauxa* – an uncontrollable emotion, an outburst, any kind of irrational activity. Both Samitier and Zamora seemed to have more *rauxa* than *seny*.

In his early days with Barça, they called Zamora the 'Divine One', but his place in the club's pantheon has its dissenters. Many fervent Catalanists have never forgiven Zamora for returning to his old side at Espanyol within three years of playing for Barça. It was at Espanyol that the goalkeeper in many ways always felt more at home, because of his self-proclaimed status as a Spaniard first and foremost.

Zamora was replaced as goalkeeper by a foreigner, who joined the long line of non-Catalans who have made a major contribution to the club. He was the Hungarian Platko. His strength of character and bravery on the pitch have been assured a lasting testimony thanks to the presence of the Spanish poet Rafael Alberti at one of Barça's more memorable encounters. It was in Santander on 20th May 1928, a game between Barça and Real Sociedad of San Sebastián, the first of three games needed before Barça won the Spanish Cup. In his memoirs, *La Arboleda Perdida*, Alberti recalls what inspired him to write a poem he called 'Ode to Platko':

'It was a brutal game between Catalans and Basques with the Cantabrian sea as a backdrop. Football was being played but so was each side's sense of nation. The violence of the Basques was the worst. Platko, the giant Hungarian goalkeeper, defended the Catalan goal like a bull. There were demonstrations, the police beat people up, there were injuries. At one point Platko was set upon by the Real players and he lay there bleeding, clutching the ball, almost senseless. He was carried off the field by his team colleagues amidst cheers and protests, leaving his fellow players shattered by his absence. Platko came back on again before the end, his head all bandaged up, determined to get killed. The effect he had on his team was instantaneous. Within seconds Barça had scored the winning goal.'

As the 'Ode' would later put it, 'No one will forget Platko, no, no one will ever forget that golden bear from Hungary.'

The night of that legendary day when Platko played in Santander, Alberti, accompanied by his friend the writer and essayist José-Maria de Cossio, joined up with the players and a group of Barça supporters for a celebration in a local hotel. They sang 'Els Segadores', the Catalan anthem, and waved Catalan flags. They also listened to tangos sung by a *cule* who had travelled all the way from Buenos Aires: Carlos Gardel. Later that summer, Gardel's love of partying, and the temptations to which the players succumbed during the night life of Buenos Aires,

5

Death in the Afternoon

The impressive granite, pine-coated mountain range of Guadarrama outside Madrid is popular with middle-class Castilian holiday-makers and with Americans tracking the footsteps of Ernest Hemingway, whose novel and the film *For Whom the Bell Tolls* for ever linked the Spanish Civil War with the heroics of Gary Cooper. Yet for Catalans with a memory this is the setting, too, for a real-life heroic sacrifice during that traumatic conflict that so divided Spain: the execution of Josep Sunyol, president of FC Barcelona, executed without trial by Franco's soldiers.

Sunyol was born in 1898, the year Spain lost her empire, into a family well known in Catalonia for its riches and its politics. His father, Jorge, was a major shareholder in Spain's main sugar refinery, his uncle Idlefons one of the leading luminaries of Catalan nationalism in the early years of the twentieth century. Josep got himself a good education, qualifying as a lawyer, thanks to his father, but from early adulthood appears to have been more inspired by his uncle in choosing politics rather than sugar as his main interest in life.

In a very real sense one of Sunyol's first 'political acts' was becoming a member of FC Barcelona in 1925. It was two years on from General Primo de Rivera's *coup d'état*, and in the midst of a sustained campaign against Catalanism. The restrictions placed on FC Barcelona by the dictatorship included a ban on the use of the Catalan flag in the stadium, the registration with the police of all membership files, and the obligatory use of the Spanish language in the club's announcements. In a separate decree, permission was granted to the club to stage a post-match pilgrimage of thanksgiving to the Virgin of Montserrat, but with the proviso that this applied only to the Spanish championship final and not to the Catalan one. The authorities specified that club members could make their way to the shrine in the mountains outside Barcelona by train or car. Those who chose to go in their own vehicles were allowed to do so only on condition that they kept a minimum distance of two kilometres from the next car, to avoid a mass gathering.

To be twenty-seven and choose to join the club in these circumstances, as Sunyol did, was a youthful way of buying a ticket well into Catalan roots, as a mark of identification with the struggle against Madrid-inspired authoritarianism. In fact Sunyol had already become involved in Accio Catala, a movement of left-wing Catalanism determined to break with the more conservative politics favoured by some of Catalonia's big business. Inevitably politics and sport became increasingly linked in his life, as Catalan politicians put increasing emphasis on civic society based on a local culture.

In 1928, as the Primo de Rivera regime was entering its death throes, Sunyol became a member of Barça's governing board, while doubling up as the president of the Federation of Associated Catalan Football Clubs, in which the club already had a strong role. He also took to writing newspaper columns on football – less focused on match reports than on the politics of the sport. He developed the practice in his newspaper *La Rambla* once the Primo de Rivera regime fell in 1930, paving the way for the return of constitutional politics and a Republican state.

By then, some conservatives and leftist intellectuals in Catalonia, as elsewhere in Europe, were suspicious about the place football was claiming in people's lives. When they looked at the fights between Barça and Espanyol supporters, the occasional clashes between fans and the Civil Guard, the brawls involving players, conservatives saw only a mob culture of riff-raff revolutionaries. For their part, some on the left echoed Karl Marx in their witness of what they feared was the 'opium of the masses', distracted from the class struggle by an increasingly powerful drug called football.

Sunyol used *La Rambla* – which took the unprecedented step of splitting its front page on a daily basis between sport and non-sport news items – to appeal to a new social order where football and politics, far from being in fatal contradiction to each other, formed an essential part of a truly democratic society. The alleged role model, hardly surprisingly, was Catalonia and specifically Barça. Prior to its closure as a result of the Civil War, *La Rambla*'s identification with the club was symbolised by its tradition of marking up on a giant board Barça's score whenever the team played away. In the days before prime-time TV rights, loyal fans would turn up and celebrate victories at Number 13, Rambla de Canaletes. The address is today that of the Nuria restaurant, near the Plaça de Catalunya. Along the Rambla *cules* still meet regularly to discuss football and politics, while the area generally has survived as a place for celebrations and demonstrations, not least when Barça wins a title.

In an early manifesto, Sunyol explained what was meant by the newspaper's joint slogan 'Sport and citizenship': 'To speak of sport is to speak of race, enthusiasm, and the optimistic struggle of youth. To speak of citizenship is to speak of the Catalan civilisation, liberalism, democracy, and spiritual endeavour.'

So much for the rhetoric. In reality, politics and football during this period mirrored each other in terms of division and instability so that neither Catalonia nor Barça really gained much. Matters were not helped by the world economic crash of 1929. A deep depression brought on by the fall in the stocks and shares he had so successfully speculated in over decades led Barça's founding father, Joan Gamper, to suicide. The management of the club opted for personal survival by transferring the cost of the crisis on to jobs and wages. Barça's administrative staff were laid off, while some of the club's star players, such as Samitier, were dropped from the first team with the excuse that they were too old. Such a view was not shared by Real Madrid, who were quick to entice El Sami to play for them in the midst of a bitter unresolved row between him and the Barça management.

Beyond the stadium, Catalans became caught up in a political situation that daily grew more complex and frenzied, as the left wing won one election and then another, deepening divisions with conservative nationalists and moderate Republicans who feared the country was lurching inexorably towards revolution of one kind or another. What became rarefied into an almost obsessive political climate coincided with a drop in membership numbers at Barça. The downward trend partly reflected the loss of earnings in a time of recession, but it also suggested that too many Catalans were simply too caught up with arguing in the streets and in parliament to take time off to watch football.

Sunyol himself was elected as a deputy in the new parliament in Madrid in the summer of 1931 as a representative of a new party of the Catalan left, Esquerra Republicana de Catalunya. The following year Catalonia was granted a new political framework by Madrid, with a large measure of devolved power and all its cultural liberties guaranteed. Esquerra became the largest party in the Catalan parliament with forty-seven per cent of the vote. Yet Sunyol's position of power as a leading figure within Barça did not go unchallenged within the club, nor by implication his vision of a society in which Catalan voters and football fans could march hand in hand towards Utopia.

Part of the problem was that while Esquerra claimed to be the true voice of Catalonia, there were those linked to Barça who considered themselves politically opposed to Sunyol and yet Catalans as well. They regarded Sunyol's call to citizenship as presumptuous and arrogant, and the attempts of his allies to monopolise the future of the club as tantamount to a very unsporting attempt at a palace *coup*. Tempers flared following the publication in November 1932 of a leading article in the pro-Esquerra newspaper *La Humanitat* that accused a majority of the Barça management board of being conservative reactionaries linked to the Lliga Regionalista. According to the article, the club directors whom it named had betrayed the essence of Catalanism and Barça, defined as Republican and democratic in spirit and revolutionary in action. And in a football equivalent to a call to arms, it urged the club membership to vote with its feet and force their resignation. In reply the management board spoke as one, claiming that while some of the directors might indeed be sympathisers of the Lliga, this did not stop them from belonging to a club defined essentially as 'apolitical but always prepared to stand up for the human rights of Catalans'.

The battle between the left and right for the soul of Barça continued throughout the early 1930s, against the background of deepening political agitation throughout Spain. In December 1933 the anarchists in Catalonia attempted with limited success a 'revolutionary strike' which was intended to collectivise land and a few local factories. The following October, Catalan reaction to the emergence of a conservative government in Madrid took the form of a regional uprising, and the proclamation by the Catalan regional government under its president Lluís Companys of 'a Catalan state within the federal republic of Spain'. The uprising was suppressed by the army division stationed in Barcelona, and Companys imprisoned. The military intervention passed off reasonably peacefully compared to that in the region of Asturias. There, anarchists looted priceless treasures in Oviedo Cathedral and murdered as many priests as they could lay their hands on. Then an uprising by miners was brutally suppressed by Moorish troops and soldiers of the Spanish legion under the overall command of a rising star in the military hierarchy, the newly appointed chief of staff General Francisco Franco.

Ever since he had begun writing for *La Rambla*, Sunyol had gone out of his way to present himself first and foremost as a Catalan patriot rather than a party dogmatist, with a belief that democracy could best be served by Catalonia ruling itself by democratic means and with its cultural roots unfettered. He had watched with a growing sense of historical inevitability Barça develop from its somewhat closeted, over-dignified beginnings to a Catalan club commanding a mass following. As football had become a popular passion it had to some extent ceased to be the preserve of conservatives. By instinct Sunyol would have preferred Barça to develop as part of a root-and-branch democratisation of society, making of it a club both for and of the people. But his vision struggled to survive as political emotions and ideologies hardened on both the left and the right.

Sunyol became president in July 1935, the latest in a line of six presidents since Gamper had formally left the post in 1925. In his acceptance speech, Sunyol declared that he would endeavour not to let politics get in the way of his work for the club. The fact was, however, that for all his love of sport, Sunyol was primarily a politician, and regarded Barça as a means to an end, rather than an end in itself. He had been re-elected to the Spanish parliament as deputy of Esquerra Republicana Catalana in November 1933 on a platform directly opposed to Catalan conservatives, some of whom had run the club's affairs during a period of maximum glory. Although he had benefited from his own links with Barça in boosting his campaign in the Catalan capital, Sunyol had subsequently distanced himself from the club's affairs, partly on health grounds, yet at the same time claiming that he was too busy with his career as a deputy. When he finally did accept the presidency of Barça, it was in the hands of a majority of people who shared his political opinions. His acceptance speech seemed to indicate that those within Esquerra considered that only they knew what was best for the club. Such certainties were to prove less a virtue than a liability as Catalonia was drawn into the Civil War.

In strictly football terms the Sunyol presidency did bring off one significant *coup*. It helped temporarily reconcile Samitier with his old club, offering him more money, although the player had little time for the radical politics sweeping through the Catalan capital. El Sami returned in early 1936 to an enthusiastic reception at Les Corts stadium, where thousands of devoted fans turned up for a benefit match in his honour between Barça and Sidenice of Czechoslovakia. The match ended in a 1–1 draw, with Samitier scoring for Barça, much to the joy of the stadium. But it was to be years before the club was able to recover the form of its '20s glory days. Although its superiority over Espanyol at the time ensured the validity of its claim to be the best club in Catalonia, it was unable to win the prize it had always yearned for – the League championship. Barça's encounter with Real Madrid in the Mestalla stadium of Valencia in June 1936 proved especially humiliating. Despite playing with ten men for most of the game, Real hung on to a 2–1 lead. Barça's attempts to equalise came closest in the final minutes of the game but were thwarted by a spectacular save made by the ex-Barça goalkeeper Ricardo Zamora.

One can only speculate as to whether Barça's performance as a football team during this period would have been any different had a political storm not been building up around it, drawing those who claimed to have the club's interests at heart deeper and deeper into its bloody eye. In February 1936, a Popular Front electoral coalition between Communists and Socialists was swept to power, and Sunyol was elected for the third time to parliament. The suspended local governments were restored to office, and the prisoners taken during the uprising of October 1934 released, and Lluís Companys returned in triumph to Barcelona. But Spain was on the brink of war with itself, with sectors of the military secretly planning to overthrow the government from the moment of the Popular Front's election victory.

*   *   *

On 18th July 1936, the day the Spanish Civil War began, with a military *coup* co-ordinated by General Mola (Franco was proclaimed leader on 1st October), FC Barcelona was on summer vacation, a traditional break between the end of the Spanish and League championships and the beginning of the seasonal 'friendlies'. The club's coach was Patrick O'Connell, a former captain of Ireland, who before coming to Spain had had a distinguished footballing career playing for Irish and English teams as a strong and talented centre-half. O'Connell's early days were with Dublin's Stranville Rovers and Belfast Celtic. In Scotland he played for Dumbarton, while in England he played for Sheffield Wednesday and for Manchester United. It was with Belfast Celtic, a predominantly Catholic side that was eventually disbanded because of the Troubles, that O'Connell learned a thing or two about sport and nationalism and its extremes. He was not unprepared for the turbulent times he encountered in Catalonia. He is thought to have been out of the country when the Civil War broke out, probably back in his native Ireland, although he soon returned to Barcelona.

At Barça, O'Connell replaced as manager the legendary Hungarian goalkeeper Platko, after a successful term of office at Betis where he had taken the Seville club to the top of the Spanish League. One of Platko's 'star' acquisitions, inherited by O'Connell, was the Uruguayan Enrique Fernandez. He was also abroad, savouring native delights he similarly missed: large chunks of free-range meat charcoaled over a wood fire. Most of the club's senior management, staff and players were in Barcelona and neighbouring towns such as Gerona, and on the Costa Brava.

Among the most disappointed by the brutal interruption of a sporting life was Angel Mur, the groundsman at Barça's Les Corts stadium. The son of emigrants from Aragon, Mur had been given the job after being rescued from his military service by a scout for Barça's amateur athletics team. The scout had watched Mur easily outpace two of the team's faster runners during a benefit sports day organised by his regimental commander. I interviewed Mur in 1998 in one of the changing rooms of the Camp Nou. Now well into his eighties, he had continued training long past his retirement. Remarkably, his memory of a traumatic point in Spanish history was as clear and full of anecdote as his body appeared still fit and full of life:

'The day the Civil War broke out I was getting ready to go to Montjuïc where I was down for the 3,000-metre steeplechase in the so-called People's Olympics. The idea was that the games would be staged as an alternative to Hitler's Olympics in Berlin. The Barcelona Olympics were declared an act of solidarity with international youth and in favour of peace, progress and well-being, although because of the troubles it ended up getting cancelled. Instead of going to the races, I stayed at home, and didn't poke my head out for two days. They were shooting all over the place. All day long people were going backwards and forwards across the city carrying pistols and rifles. I didn't feel anything politically. I was a sportsman, not a politician, and my race had been cancelled.'

Such a sentiment was not quite shared by the directors of Barça when they met in extraordinary session after urgently cancelling their vacations. Some of them, led by Sunyol, had after all made no secret of their allegiances to the Republic and Catalan nationalism, causes that were now under direct threat from the *coup*-mongers. There was also the added concern that a worsening political and economic climate would make it impossible to run the club effectively as one of the region's major sporting institutions. While the club's administrative offices were near the city centre, its prime asset, the stadium, was at that time in a less densely populated neighbourhood nearer to the outskirts of Barcelona and vulnerable to occupation.

At the meeting the board, with extraordinary restraint given the gravity of the circumstances, opted for pre-emptive surgery rather than euthanasia. For practical and cost reasons, they told the Uruguayan international Fernandez not to return from Montevideo, and cancelled negotiations on a pending contract with one of his fellow countrymen, Raul Villalba. Barça's other foreign player at the time, the Hungarian Berkessy, was also taken off the team's books.

The club's governing board voted to continue in office and it was decided that the club would continue playing at least at regional level, pending developments in the war. It was a gesture of faith in Barça as a political and cultural entity. But the fate of the club was complicated not simply by virtue of being identified with a political and social movement, but because of the nature of the Civil War. Far from proving a definitive victory for one side or the other, from the outset it fragmented Spain into various zones, officially controlled by one camp or the other. The victims of the war on both sides were not all of them necessarily guilty on account of their politics. Some of them were caught up in the conflict by mistake or simply bad luck. The only certainty was that any part of Spain could become a killing field.

The shots Mur heard in those days were mere echoes of the battles raging on the streets of Barcelona. At 5.00 a.m. on 19th July, General Fernandez Burriel seized the principal squares and public buildings of Barcelona and invited General Goded to fly in from Palma de Mallorca to take command in Catalonia. But anarcho-syndicalist workers and Catalan federalists, armed and led by loyal Assault and Civil Guards, retook the city in an orgy of bloodshed. Among the early victims was retired General Joaquin Milans del Bosch, who had spent part of his military career as an equerry to King Alfonso XIII. In the summer of 1936, Milans del Bosch was ninety years old, long past involvement in the military affairs of his country, and he had no direct involvement in the uprising plotted by Franco and others. But a group of Catalan anarchists remembered him as the general who eleven years earlier had ordered the closure of Barça's football stadium. Milans del Bosch was shot without trial. Three days later in Madrid, thousands of anarchists, spurred on by news of Goded's surrender, stormed the city's main military barracks and lynched those officers within who had supported the *coup*.

Among those arrested by anti-Francoists in those early days of revolutionary fervour was Samitier, the 'star' player of the 1920s, who had chosen to take his holiday break in Madrid. Like so much of what happened in the Civil War, quite why Samitier was arrested is not clear. He had, after all, only months earlier been given a euphoric reception in Barcelona, in tribute to his contribution to Barça's glory years. On the other hand, as has been noted earlier, El Sami was never in fact the Republican Catalan nationalist some of Barça's revisionists would have liked him to be. It is possible that those arresting him equated him with the forces of reaction and had already learned that one of El Sami's biggest fans was General Franco.

What is beyond doubt is that the fullest, somewhat propagandist, account of Samitier's 'escape' from possible execution appeared in *Marca*, a sports newspaper that backed Franco. *Marca*'s first weekly edition appeared just before Christmas 1938 on the streets of San Sebastián after the Basque country had been overrun and occupied by Francoiste forces. Its main purpose was to act as the official organ on sports matters, and to turn the mass following of football, in particular, away from the politics of the left and towards the right. *Marca* gave generous coverage to El Sami's dramatic escape from the hands of the 'reds', after he had lived in hiding for days after the outbreak of the war. He was detained by members of the anarchist militia, but eventually released. Samitier left for France on a warship, and, according to the account that appeared in *Marca*, arrived into exile with 'two suits, a lot of hunger, and exhausted'.

It was in the French coastal town of Nice that Samitier met up with another Barça veteran, Ricardo Zamora. The star goalkeeper's experience of the Civil War had proved even more theatrical, with the Francoiste side openly exploiting Zamora politically as a martyr for the cause, the man who had effectively turned his back on Catalan nationalism by choosing to play his best years with Espanyol. (In fact Zamora's politics were as ambiguous as Samitier's. Two years before the outbreak of the Civil War he was given a medal of the Order of the Republic. Much later, during the Franco regime, the right honoured him with the Great Cross of the Order of Cisneros.)

In late July 1936, days after the Francoiste forces had taken control of the town of Seville, the local edition of the conservative newspaper *ABC* reported that the bullet-ridden body of Zamora had been found in a ditch near the Rubio Institute in Madrid's Moncloa district. Seville's new military governor and the man who had helped launch the *coup*, General Queipo de Llano, wasted little time in using his regular propaganda broadcast on the radio to include Zamora, 'the nation's goalkeeper', in a list of prominent cultural figures allegedly murdered by the 'reds'. There were even Masses organised in his memory in traditionally clerical towns like Valladolid that had also swung behind Franco.

In fact Zamora was alive and well, so alive that as soon as the rumours of his alleged 'execution' began to spread, a group of militiamen went to where they knew they could find him, arrested him, and took him to Madrid's infamous Modelo prison. The building was one from which prisoners were lucky to emerge alive, but according to

Zamora's own memoirs, the player was saved thanks to his football. Guards and militiamen, whose time was normally spent selecting lists for execution, were delighted to have such a sports hero in their midst. They brought a ball along and organised matches in the prison's main yard.

Zamora was eventually released thanks to the Argentinian Embassy, which interceded on his behalf. He spent a few days in the Embassy before travelling to Valencia, where he too took a ship bound for France, together with his wife and son Ricardo – who years later would follow in his father's footsteps as a goalkeeper, playing for Mallorca. His flight from Spain had a touch of farce about it. According to his personal account, Zamora left the Embassy in disguise – he had grown a beard and wore dark glasses – hoping to evade the attention of the militiamen who regularly stood guard outside the building. He was just getting into the car that was to take him to freedom, when one of the militiamen came up behind him and tapped him on the shoulder, saying in a jocular way, 'Hey, Zamora, *hombre*, what you doing with that beard?' The goalkeeper was allowed to move on anyway.

In Nice, Zamora and Samitier played for the local team. On 8th December 1938, Zamora was back in Spain, in San Sebastián. The day was one of the most important in the traditional Catholic calendar: the Immaculate Conception of the Virgin Mary, whom Franco's Spain had already claimed as her protector. The occasion was a benefit match between 'Spain' and Real Sociedad to raise funds for Francoiste soldiers. Zamora was given star rating by the authorities, although the 'Spain' team was devoid of Barça players, past or present. An official advertisement stated that this was the first time that Zamora had played in Spain since the 'glorious uprising'. The favoured son had come back into the fold, with honours.

A very different fate befell Josep Sunyol, the man who had been elected president of FC Barcelona in 1935. Within days of the outbreak of the Civil War, at the beginning of August 1936, Sunyol set off by car for Madrid via Valencia. Sunyol's last act as Barça president appears to have been his attendance at the 30th July meeting of the management board, where it had been decided to suspend further player contracts while maintaining the activities of the club as normally as possible. The purpose of Sunyol's journey south appears to have been strictly political: to meet and talk to like-minded Republicans who still retained a measure of influence in areas of the country that had thus far successfully resisted the military uprising. He also planned to visit some volunteers who had been enlisted in a Catalan column to defend Madrid from the Franco military offensive. At least one official Barça historian has suggested that he was also on club business, arranging transfers, but this seems unlikely given the nature of the conflict then gathering steam.

The most accurate chronology of Sunyol's movements at this time has him arriving in Valencia on the afternoon of 4th August, and within twenty-four hours driving on to Madrid. From there, he set off for the Guadarrama hills in a chauffeur-driven car lent to him by the local military authorities loyal to the Republic. The car was flying the Catalan flag in recognition of Sunyol's status as an elected deputy and of the fact that Barcelona, which he represented, had so far defended itself against the uprising.

By this stage in the war, the peaks of Guadarrama and its lower-lying hills had become one of the key battlegrounds for the control of Madrid. The military insurgents had taken several major towns, including Burgos, Valladolid, Salamanca, Segovia and Zaragoza. Under a plan drawn up by one of the main commanders, General Mola, who had marked the uprising by taking Pamplona on 18th July, the insurgents had launched a two-pronged offensive with the aim of capturing the two main northern approaches to Madrid – the pass of Somosierra and a second pass known as the Alto de Los Leones. Part of this offensive was diverted east of the capital to Guadalajara, where another front had opened up. But a substantial number of troops had continued south to the mountains north of Madrid to engage on and around the Alto de Los Leones. Here they had dug in with bunkers, trenches and machine-gun posts to continue fighting a war of attrition with militia units sent out from Madrid. It was a complex and not easily identifiable patchwork of military units that spread out across the hills on either side of the pass. The situation was made all the more confusing by a relentless campaign of propaganda waged by the contenders which often distorted news from the front.

In setting off from Madrid that day in August, Sunyol appears to have been following other politicians and journalists who, out of a mixture of curiosity as to what was really going on and solidarity with the troops, had engaged in a somewhat dangerous form of 'war tourism'; dangerous because the nature of the military situation made it uncertain exactly which part of the mountains belonged to which side at any given time. Sunyol's car had driven through the town of Guadarrama, and was beginning the ascent of the mountain when he came across a military post. At this stage it would not have been unreasonable for Sunyol to believe – in accordance with the information supplied to him by the chauffeur from Madrid – that he was still in safe territory, and that any opposing forces were dug in further up towards the Alto de Los Leones, and on the other side of the pass. Whatever he may have been thinking, Sunyol somehow managed to find himself on a stretch of road controlled not by militiamen from Madrid but by Falangist troops loyal to the Franco uprising. He was detained and subsequently shot dead, late in the day of 6th August 1936.

The first report suggesting that Sunyol might be dead was made by Catalan officials working for the Madrid parliament. Without naming any sources of information, the report simply stated, 'According to information provided to us, he was executed by firing squad on 10th August by the [Francoiste] rebels ... after kilometre 50 on the Corunna road.'

Sensitive to the propaganda war that continued to dominate official lists of victims, Catalan newspapers were at first cautious. On 11th and 12th August, *La Vanguardia* and *La Humanitat* respectively simply expressed concern about Sunyol's 'disappearance' and appealed to those with more information to provide it. The Catalan Football Federation meanwhile issued a statement expressing its 'firm desire and hope that our friend Sunyol will soon find himself returned to his normal sporting and political activities in our country'.

Sunyol's fate continued to be the subject of contradictory speculation for months. Some reports claimed that he was a prisoner of the Fascists in Burgos; others that he had fled to Switzerland, suffering from morphine addiction. The precise circumstances of his death remained a mystery throughout the Franco years. Following Franco's death in 1975, advertisements placed in the letters column of three

Spanish newspapers – *El País, Ya* and *ABC* – by a Catalan investigating reports that Sunyol had been killed in Guadarrama led to hundreds of letters being written by veterans of the conflict who had been in that area, or by their descendants. Several of the letters gave a very vivid description of the fighting in the area on both sides, but not one claimed to have seen Sunyol or heard of his whereabouts at the time.

It is the testimonies given by two Catalan militiamen and a Francoiste sergeant, which were published in a newspaper in Barcelona and another in Valladolid respectively, that have been taken most seriously by investigators. It is far from conclusive, but the work done by Antoni Strubell on archive material that was ignored for many years during the Franco regime has been sufficient to put some flesh on the myth of Barça's most notable 'disappeared'.

The testimonies given by opposing sides in the conflict concur that Sunyol probably met his fate at the hands of soldiers stationed in a small roadside workers' hut, temporarily transformed into a military post, on the outskirts of Guadarrama town. Ironically, the hut had been locally nicknamed La Casilla de la Muerte (The Little House of Death) before the war began, because of its situation by a sharp bend in the mountain road notorious for fatal accidents involving lorries bringing fish from the North.

As far as those responsible for his death were concerned, the nearest they came to assuming responsibility for it was in a curt statement of registration read out in a military court on 28th September 1939 during Sunyol's posthumous prosecution by the Francoiste state for 'political crimes': 'Sunyol, a well-known figure of the left, and a deputy of parliament representing this political tendency, at the beginning of the month of August of 1936 travelled to Madrid knowing that by doing so he would be taken prisoner by our national troops in Guadarrama, and that the authorities would subject him to summary trial before giving him the maximum sentence.'

Two months later, a report published by the Catalan headquarters of the Falange movement, which had taken control of the city following Franco's 'liberation', referred to Sunyol's links with local football. The report was indicative of the political reaction that Barça would be forced to endure during the Franco regime: 'For a time he was president of Barcelona football club, and was responsible for the clear anti-Spanish line which the club adopted.'

Remarkably, it was not until 1996, on the sixtieth anniversary of Sunyol's disappearance, that the first detailed investigation into its circumstances was published, in the form of a book written jointly by the Catalan journalist Carles Llorens and two academics, Josep-Maria Solé and Antoni Strubell, a graduate of Oxford University. They made use of many formerly unavailable documents and newspaper archive material, and of a political willingness within the club to have the truth published that had not previously prevailed.

In Franco's Spain, Sunyol was virtually taboo in political terms. In his native Catalonia, the post-war years saw successive presidents of Barça agreeing to collaborate in a generalised amnesia, downplaying Sunyol's role as politician and president to the point almost of eradication, for fear that his memory might rekindle the politicisation of the club leftwards. Even after Franco's death in 1975, not all Catalans considered Sunyol a subject worth discussing too openly or frequently. He still smacked of revolutionary separatism when a pragmatic accommodation with Madrid was required. The fiftieth anniversary of his execution, in 1986, was completely ignored by the club, eight years after Josep Lluís Nuñez's ascendancy to the presidency.

It was in 1994 that an article in the Catalan-language newspaper *Avui*, by the journalist Josep Llado, and other reports by Strubell raised the subject of Sunyol, paving the way for a series of articles and letters – many written by members of the club – urging that he be properly remembered and recognised. The Nuñez presidency initially refused to bend, no doubt seeing in the campaign a conspiracy by its opponents. Its formal response came in a letter to a member of the club who on behalf of many others had asked for a special tribute to Sunyol to be organised by Barça. The letter, signed on 13th February 1996 by Nicolau Casaus, the vice-president, omitted any reference or commitment to the tribute, and appealed instead to the unity of the club.

Far from defusing the campaign, the attitude of the club presidency stirred matters up even more, with the pro-Sunyol lobby stepping up its campaign with a vengeance. Among the more militant campaigners grouped around Els Amics de Josep Sunyol was Francesc Gordo, a member of Barça since 1940 and the son of one of Sunyol's contemporaries. The memory of the assassinated president had been engraved on his memory from childhood. Gordo told me, 'I was eight years old in 1936. Sunyol used to come to my house often and he used to say to me jokingly, "Be good or you'll get into trouble." Then the war broke out and one day my father came to my room and said, "I'm sorry, but that nice man who always asked you to keep out of trouble can't come any more. They've shot him." That really shocked me. When the war ended, his death was covered up, forgotten, because too many people were implicated in one way or another and people were afraid.'

There was no fear in the issue of the Catalan weekly *El Temps* that appeared on 29th April 1996. The magazine devoted several pages to Sunyol, openly accusing the presidency of Barça of seeking to remove his legacy from the history of the club, and detailing the obstructions they had put in the way of those campaigning on his behalf. A massive poster campaign around Catalonia, coinciding with the local saint's day Sant Jordi, drew its inspiration from the magazine's hard-hitting cover: 'How to Kill a President', the posters proclaimed. Fan clubs throughout Catalonia began to raise their voices in protest.

By the summer of 1996, the sixtieth anniversary of Sunyol's death, president Nuñez had concluded that the controversy was doing his image no good, and decided to give in to pressure. In June he agreed that a member of the ruling junta and the club official historian, Jaume Sobreques, should be present alongside several leading Catalan politicians, including the president of the Catalan parliament, at the unveiling of a commemorative monolith in Guadarrama, near to where Sunyol was believed to have been killed. And yet the attitude of the Nuñez presidency remained cautious rather than generous. During that summer's Gamper tournament in Barcelona's Olympic stadium, a memorial pamphlet, partly written by Nuñez and paid for by the club, was distributed belatedly – on the second day – after being temporarily mislaid in a cupboard at the stadium. The silence in Sunyol's honour that preceded one of Barça's matches lasted under half a minute, considerably less time than was devoted to honouring Soto, a *boixos nois* leader with a criminal record who was killed in a car crash.

*   *   *

While researching this book I retraced Sunyol's final hours, driving out of Madrid and towards the mountains, with the aid of a map put together by Antoni Strubell, the Oxford graduate who had investigated his death. The area has been swept and modernised since my childhood days in the late 1950s when I and a long-term friend – an Anglo-Spaniard like myself – used to play in the old Civil War bunkers and trenches, picking up occasional pieces of rusting armoury and smuggling them back to London. It was hard for my friend and me – for we were together again and sharing in this journey – to turn back time even further, but the knowledge we now had of Sunyol's fate fuelled our imagination, drew us emotionally to the spot in a way that responded to something deeper than simple childhood nostalgia: a need to rediscover history.

A straight road across an arid plain leads from Madrid to the town of Guadarrama. It is on the outskirts of the town, in a small clearing among some pines, that a monolith rests with the simple inscription 'José Suñol Garriga: Barcelona 21–VII–1898; Guadarrama 6–VIII–1936'. Those who created it chose to use the Castilian version of the names Josep and Sunyol, and to avoid any mention of his role either as a Catalan politician or as president of Barça, for fear that it might draw the attention of local Fascists and be destroyed.

In fact, the location does not mark the spot where Sunyol was killed; it was picked as part of a political compromise. The owner of the land where the death is believed to have occurred refused a request to have the monolith placed there, insisting that any monument to the Civil War dead should include one to his son, who was killed by Republican militias in the same area. (The request seemed to overlook the fact that a few kilometres down the road was the huge cross and basilica built by Franco for the Civil War dead, El Valle de los Caídos – the 'Valley of the Fallen'.)

Following the landowner's refusal, the local mayor of Guadarrama – a member of the ruling centre-right party Partido Popular – offered a piece of land owned by the municipality. The monolith was unveiled there on 4th June 1996, with the local Civil Guard making the unprecedented gesture of presenting arms when the Catalans sang their national anthem.

Spain may have changed, but not completely. I follow Strubell's map, as the route begins its climb. What in Sunyol's day was known as the Madrid–Corunna road is today the N-VI. A kilometre or so beyond the town comes the first sharp bend in the road, the tree-covered countryside rising on one side, and sloping down into the valley on the other. Then the road straightens out again. The two main landmarks mentioned in the soldiers' testimonies are just over a kilometre apart: after the bend in the road, La Casilla de la Muerte, and further up the hill, a stone fountain called La Fuente de la Teja. The fountain is still there, but La Casilla has long since been removed. In its place is a large military sanatorium built by Franco for his victorious army after the war.

When we visited the place, there were a couple of young conscripts at the main entrance, supposedly on guard duty, playing cards and listening to rock music on a radio. 'Do you know what went on here during the Civil War?' I asked them. 'That's a long time ago. If I didn't have to do my military service, I wouldn't be here. I'd be with my friends back in Madrid,' said one. 'Well, of course, everyone knows that quite a lot of fighting went on up here in the mountains,' the other said. These boys supported Atlético Madrid. Neither of them had ever heard of Josep Sunyol, let alone the fact that he had been executed within metres of where they were playing cards. No one had ever told them.

On 15th August 1936, Angel Mur, the amateur sportsman who had seen his hopes of participating in the People's Olympics dashed, took some pre-emptive action against the Civil War's frustrating his life even further. That morning he was on his usual duty as a groundsman at Barça's Les Corts stadium, when he noticed a group of people putting up posters at the entrance, declaring the club's imminent expropriation by the anarchist workers' movement CNT-FAI. He immediately rang the club secretary, Rosendo Calvet, who in turn contacted all the other club officials.

Mur and Calvet were in no doubt as to the meaning of the posters. In the days following the successful defeat in Barcelona of the military uprising, the Catalan capital had been plunged into a social revolution. Initially with the passive acquiescence of the regional government, large sectors of local industrial, commercial and cultural life were put in the hands of workers' committees. Among the first institutions to be targeted in this way, because of its anti-Catalan reputation, was Espanyol football club. The planned move against Barça appears to have been motivated simply by a desire to put the club's not inconsiderable financial assets and mass appeal firmly in the control of the revolutionaries – most of whom had little time for football.

In response to the threat, Barça's management board announced that very morning that it had dissolved itself and been replaced by a 'workers' committee' which had spontaneously sprung up within the club. And five days later, on 20th August, a spokesman for the committee told the Barcelona sports newspaper *El Mundo Deportivo*, 'The take-over of the club responds to the imperatives of the profoundly revolutionary situation we are living in, which naturally the club must abide by. We are studying a plan whereby Barcelona will act for the greater good of sport in line with its history. We shall function within the new legal framework that has been set up in response to the seditious military and Fascist uprising.'

Far from signifying that Barça had decided to become Europe's first genuinely collectivised football club, the statement was encouraged by the club's old guard to discourage the anarchists from taking too great an interest in the club. For the committee, which included Mur and Calvet, formed part of a clever plan by certain directors of the club to keep a measure of control while giving the appearance that Barça had become part and parcel of the egalitarian society to which the anarchists and their allies in the Socialist UGT trade union aspired.

As Calvet himself later recorded in his history of the club, two months after the committee's formation he and Mur were joined by three former directors as representatives of the *socios* or members. Their idea was that Barça should remain as broad a church as possible and not succumb to what was regarded as the financially and socially counterproductive obsessions of class conflict.

In its first months of activity, the club's new organisational structure seemed to work miracles. Football continued to be played despite the continuing battles, executions and imprisonments. But for all the efforts at achieving a semblance of normality, Barça increasingly came to be affected by the divisions and tensions in the country generally. The first casualty of the conflict was any concept of a national league.

With towns up and down Spain falling into the control of opposing armies, the playing of games became strictly localised, and the transfer of players extremely limited. Politics took precedence over the organisation of matches, with teams expressing their loyalties to local rulers and playing benefit matches for the soldiers of the protecting forces.

By October 1937, Franco's Spain had official control over some of the country's best-known teams. They included Sevilla, Betis, Zaragoza, Celta, Deportivo La Coruña and Athletic Bilbao. The fact that the country was still immersed in the Civil War, and that many people living in Spain opposed Franco, was seemingly judged irrelevant by FIFA, world football's governing body. In late 1937, FIFA recognised the status of the new National Football Federation of Spain, which had been set up with the blessing of Franco's generals.

Anti-Franco forces meanwhile took control of Real and Atlético Madrid, purging the clubs of politically suspect officials. Real's president, Santiago Bernabéu, sought asylum in the French Embassy and subsequently went into exile to avoid being executed by the militia. Both clubs played some football, but not very much. There were not too many teams to play with. The Madrid stadiums were periodically requisitioned for Soviet-style sports demonstrations, but by the end of the war had fallen into disuse.

The redrawing of the political map led to extraordinary reversals in club policy in the early stages of the war, such as the two Madrid teams applying to play along with Barcelona in the Catalan League on the basis that both towns had initially managed to fight off Franco. The application was turned down by Barça. Its officials argued that such an encounter would undermine the traditional Catalan 'national' spirit of the competition. One wonders what Sunyol, had he survived, would have thought of such a display of Republican solidarity!

The Catalan championship went ahead in the first year of the Civil War with five teams instead of the usual twenty, after a controversial meeting in which Barça and Espanyol opposed a recommendation by the Catalan Football Federation that it should be played with the participation of numerous amateur teams. According to one account of the meeting, 'on the table around which sat the various delegates were pistols and machine guns, some of which appeared to be pointing at Barça and Espanyol'.

These were turbulent times. For a while Barça managed as best it could, given the circumstances. A reduced number of loyal *socios* kept coming to the stadium; football went on being played, with the club keeping the younger players as occupied as possible so that they wouldn't be drafted to the front. What else could Barça do but try to keep going? For many of those most closely associated with the club, football was not just a much-loved sport, it was a way of survival, which is why they played on, trying not to think too hard about the politics of one side or the other.

However, the club could not avoid a financial crisis, with gate receipts falling off and an increasing number of the club membership, the *socios*, not paying their dues. While many Barça supporters remained loyal to the club, they were too caught up in the war politically, and had to prioritise their spending on essential goods. There were other Catalans who were politically sympathetic to the Franco cause, and would have rather been seen dead than participated in an organisation ruled by a workers' committee, however much its founders saw it as a smoke screen to maintain its independence. Their time would come.

What is beyond doubt is that Barça's survival as an organisation became increasingly at risk because of political developments beyond the stadium. By the middle of 1937, the spontaneous revolution so loved by the anarchists was being crushed by Stalinist Communists who feared that the war effort would disintegrate without discipline and central control. The way divisions arose within the left in Barcelona, leading to a second terror within the city, with factions fighting one another and executions being extended on the basis of Marxist disagreements, has been well documented in George Orwell's *Homage to Catalonia*.

Orwell's sympathies for the international struggle of the working class had been strengthened by his experiences down British mines. Full of enthusiasm and ideology, he had signed up with Trotskyite anti-Franco forces at the end of 1936, joining a POUM (Workers' Party of Marxist Unity) column on the Aragon front. But within months he returned to Barcelona, to find the Communist Party and left-wing libertarians embroiled in a bloody battle for control of the city. Orwell described the scene in Barcelona vividly:

'In Barcelona, during all those weeks that I spent there, there was a peculiar evil feeling in the air – an atmosphere of suspicion, fear, uncertainty, and veiled hatred . . . Over the POUM buildings the red flags had been torn down, Republican flags were floating in their place, and knots of armed Assault Guards were lounging in the doorways. At the Red Aid centre on the corner of the Plaça de Catalunya the police had amused themselves by smashing most of the windows . . . Down at the bottom of the Ramblas near the quay, I came across a queer sight: a row of militiamen, still ragged and muddy from the front, sprawling exhaustedly on the chairs placed there for the bootblacks.'

In such circumstances, FC Barcelona struggled to find a new recipe for survival. Its 'workers' committee', either as a genuine concession to anarchist thinking or simply as a bourgeois disguise, could not long continue. The Communists were calling for nationalisations rather than collectivisations, with no guarantee that institutions like Barça would not be taken over by central government. Among the institutions that were appropriated was Sunyol's newspaper *La Rambla*.

In early April 1937, officials and players at Barça were looking towards the future with a deepening sense of vertigo. Those at the club felt an increasing sense of being besieged by the political situation, of gradually losing control. Then, suddenly, came a lifeline, in the form of an invitation from a Mexican basketball-player-turned-businessman, Manuel Mas Soriano. Barça was invited to travel to Mexico and play a series of matches with leading local teams. The deal was that the club would be paid US$15,000 in cash and have the return flight and all other expenses paid for.

To the majority of the committee and the players the offer seemed heaven-sent – it not only offered a temporary solution to the club's cash-flow problems, but also allowed them to escape from a political situation that could no longer guarantee their safety. That Angel Mur, the groundsman, managed to be included in the trip was thanks to a mixture of good luck and Irish humour, as he recalled in an interview with me many years later:

'I was on the pitch doing some gardening duties when Mr O'Connell came up and said, "Good day to you, Mur, I've got something I want to discuss with you." My first thought was that he was going to complain about the state of the grass, that maybe I hadn't hosed enough or something like that. Instead, he said, "We've got a problem. We're going to Mexico and our masseur has left us. I thought you'd make a good replacement." I stood there looking at him, hardly believing him. Then I said, "Me? But what do I know about massage? I'm a groundsman." He looked at me, smiled and said, "Don't worry, you can learn. I'll teach you what to do in emergencies." And that's how I ended up going to Mexico with the team, with a suit I was given by one player, and a suitcase I was given by another player. I was also lent some clothes. I bought myself a couple of books on the anatomy of the human body and got to learn something about the vulnerable parts . . .'

In Mexico, Barça was given a warm official reception by the authorities and the local press. The country had given asylum to several Spanish exiles from both sides in the Civil War, and saw some parallels between its own revolutionary experience and the upheaval that Spaniards were experiencing. Coming as the team did from a region in Spain that was still resisting the Franco uprising, the tour had a political edge to it: Barça represented Catalonia, but also *Republican* Catalonia, although the essential meaning of that word was becoming daily more confused back home.

On the first night in Mexico City, the visitors got a bit of a shock. Arriving at El Casino Español, a Spanish dining club, they saw the Franco flag flying over the entrance. Inside, their hosts – a group of Spanish businessmen who had been living there since before the outbreak of the Civil War – accosted some of the players, asking them how many Francoistes had been executed by the 'guillotine' that they erroneously claimed had been set up in a central square in Barcelona. Some of the businessmen called for a boycott of the tour. The encounter turned out to be less serious than it at first seemed, with the local Spanish community generally rallying round the Barça team and hundreds of Mexicans turning up for the games.

It was the rainy season in Mexico, and it usually rained in the second half of the day, so the games were played in the mornings. In the afternoons, the players went to movies or played cards or some other game in the Hotel Continental where they were staying. After the traumas of the Civil War, the Mexican trip was like an extended holiday. No one seemed in any great hurry to return to Barcelona – the news coming from there seemed to go from bad to worse. So a tour that in normal circumstances could have been over in three weeks went on for two months. During this period Barça played six matches, of which they won four.

At the end of the tour, a local newspaper, *El Universal*, commented, 'We can't say that Barcelona is the best team in Spain, but what we can say with absolute certainty is that of all the Spanish teams that have come to Mexico, it's Barcelona that has made most friends here. One of the reasons it is held in such high esteem is that it played pretty well; but it is also because the players behaved like true gentlemen.'

Mur not only learned to massage the players, but assumed an additional role in order to help everyone out financially. He undertook to raise funds at dinner gatherings with the local community by singing traditional songs from his native Aragon. That his repertoire included music from Madrid's popular operettas the *zarzuelas* mattered not an iota to the Catalans, still less to their Mexican hosts. Mur's passionate intonations moved some of them to tears. The trip proved romantic in another respect too. One of the players, Ventolra, fell in love with the niece of the Mexican President, Lazaro Cardenas, married her, and opted to stay in the country.

After Mexico, Barça moved on to the United States. It was a lower-profile trip and even less taxing, for football of the kind that was already played widely in South America and Europe was not a popular sport north of the Rio Grande. The team played four games that September in 1937: one against the local Latino community repre-sented by Hispano of Brooklyn; two against a ragtag selection of Italians, Irishmen and other European immigrants representing New York and the US; and the fourth against a team put together by the local Jewish community. All expenses were paid for again, although this time the club settled for a symbolic additional cash payment of only US$500, as well as a token political gesture whereby the local (Republican) Spanish Ambassador, Fernando de Los Rios, officially opened the US tour at the start of the match against Hispano. Hardly surprisingly, Barça won all four games.

By the end of September, though, Barça had run out of places to escape to. For four months, the team had lived in a kind of fantasy time capsule which kept them insulated from the detailed realities of the Civil War. Some consciences had long since started to prick. There was money in the kitty, but simply to spend it in these circumstances would have been a betrayal of the principles of civic duty that Barça had absorbed from men like Witty, Gamper and Sunyol.

Calvet, the club secretary, had masterminded the tour. He now drew the tourists together to a meeting and offered them a stark choice: they could choose to go back to Barcelona or to remain away from it, effectively as exiles. Out of sixteen players, four chose to follow Calvet, O'Connell, Mur and the team doctor, Amoros, back home. Of the twelve who chose not to, a majority returned to Mexico, and three opted to exile themselves temporarily to France. The decisions did not in themselves reflect a greater or smaller loyalty to the club, for there was an underlying acceptance that the future of the club would only really be resolved once the Civil War was over. Players responded much more to different calculations about what might happen next in Spain and how that might impact on their lives individually. To the extent that there was a common denominator at all, it was based on self-interest and a basic instinct of survival. This was behind Calvet's intelligent decision not to take the $12,500 clear profit made from the tour back with him to Barcelona, where it would have run the risk of being expropriated on behalf of the revolution. Instead he had it transferred to an account in Paris, to be held as security against the club's future needs.

It was a decimated club that struggled to reorganise itself after the tour. It was difficult to generate enthusiasm when a growing number of Catalans were beginning to ask themselves not *if* Franco would march into the city, but when. Franco's air force was stepping up its bombing attacks by the week, destroying buildings and killing hundreds of civilians and military personnel. On 16th March 1938, just before midnight, a Fascist bomb fell on a building near the centre of Barcelona used as a social club by Barça officials, staff and *socios*. Because of the lateness of the hour, the building was empty of people except for the porter, who had taken cover just before the military strike. Miraculously he survived the bomb with only minor cuts. He emerged half naked and dazed from the rubble. When, later, club officials came to see what else had survived, they found that most of the club's archive of

6

Survivors

In the history of football there can be few conversations as melodramatic as the one that took place in Barça's Les Corts stadium the day a small company of Francoiste soldiers arrived there with the intention of turning it temporarily into a military camp.

The officer leading the soldiers was greeted by Rosendo Calvet, the Barça secretary, who had so dextrously managed the club's affairs through *coups*, revolutions and counter-revolutions. Calvet told him, 'Sir, before you is a temple dedicated to the cult of sport and physical culture. We have respected it throughout the war. Now, it is up to you to decide what to do with it.'

Calvet had prepared himself for the worst. Even as they spoke, summary executions were beginning to take place elsewhere in Barcelona as the victorious army consolidated its hold on the city. Public spaces and buildings were being unilaterally requisitioned as part of the 'military regime'. Les Corts seemed an open invitation to the dozens of armoured vehicles and their occupants looking for some free parking space; anyone connected with the club a potential victim of the firing squad.

However, according to Calvet, the officer had this to say: 'Rest assured, young man, that we will not be the ones who will undermine what you yourselves have conserved.'

That conversation, as immortalised in the official history of the club, is not the kind Shakespeare would have subscribed to, even on an off-day. It may be partly or wholly apocryphal. Nevertheless, the version has survived more than sixty years in the club archives as a reminder that Barça was not by nature confrontational; only circumstances and the attitudes of certain individuals had made it so.

Two months after that alleged conversation, on 29th June 1939, Les

Corts staged its first match under the Franco regime. The match was a 'friendly' played between a Spanish team dressed in the blue and red colours of Barça and Athletic Bilbao's youth team. The inaugural kick of the game was entrusted to the daughter of General José Solchaga, who had helped 'liberate' Barcelona for Franco. Not surprisingly, the Spaniards beat the Basques 9–1. The encounter mocked a team's colours and was clearly aimed at anaesthetising any sense of pride or identity among aspiring Catalan and Basque nationalists.

The match was preceded by a ceremony of tribute to the new state, a typical Fascist celebration full of smiling blond dancers and bombastic speeches. The organisers bluntly proclaimed its purpose as that of exorcising the stadium of malevolent separatist spirits, submerging the institution of FC Barcelona under the all-encompassing political, social and cultural umbrella of Franco's Spain. The main speaker was Ernest Gimenez Caballero, one of Franco's chief ideologues, who had helped draft the regime's 'decree of unity' at the end of the Civil War. In the words of Franco's biographer, Paul Preston, Gimenez Caballero was 'along with Salvador Dali and Luis Buñuel one of the fathers of Spanish surrealism. He was also one of the first Spanish Fascists in the late 1920s and put his manic talents at the service of Franco during the Civil War, reaching delirious heights of sycophancy.' The occasion in Les Corts was tailor-made for his talents. In taking on the role of exorcist, Gimenez Caballero took up where General Milans del Bosch had last been – purging the spirit of Catalanism with an act of terrifying political eccentricity.

In his speech, Gimenez Caballero spoke like a man who was himself possessed, paying tribute to a Catalonia that had been 'redeemed' by a glorious army, and to a football club that had in the past been diverted from the path of light by malignant spirits opposed to Madrid. He ended declaring that the air in the stadium 'smells of flowers and empire'. The exorcism was complete. Cries of '*Viva el Barcelona!*' and '*Viva España!*' rang out through the stadium.

Among the first measures taken by the regime was to scrap the Catalan championship, and rename the Spanish championship the Generalissimo's Cup in honour of Franco. Barça, meanwhile, found itself having to conform to the new political reality in other ways. The club's book of accounts shows that in the week leading up to the ceremony in Les Corts, Barça officials bought six records of Francoiste national anthems, a new crest representing the Francoiste state, Falangist banners, and several portraits and posters of Franco and the Falangist leader, José Primo de Rivera, who had been executed by left-wing militias during the Civil War.

Beyond the stadium, those who had opposed Franco or continued to do so were brutally repressed, and the places of local officials who had been loyal to the Republic occupied by hand-picked Francoistes. An estimated 10,000 were executed within the first week of 'liberation', with another 25,000 meeting a similar fate later on. The scale of the killings was such as to disturb the conscience of one of Mussolini's officers whose troops had helped take Barcelona for the Fascists. General Gambara told his headquarters that Franco had 'unleashed in Barcelona a very drastic purge'. Along with the killings came the change of street names that made any allusion to a local identity; they were replaced with the names of conquering generals. And in a particularly cruel blow to many local people, Catalan was banned as an official language.

Among those with every reason to remember those days with particular distaste is Nicolau Casaus, who signed up as a member of Barça in 1922, aged nine. Casaus became vice-president of Barça following Franco's death. In an interview with the author while still in office, the ninety-year-old Casaus spoke with the authority of a generation that can with justification still claim to feel the Spanish Civil War in its blood:

'The Civil War generally for Catalonia signified a tremendous confrontation, but the post-war period was probably worse. During the war we managed to resist the gathering storm, but when the Francoiste troops came in, that's when we started having a really bad time. The atmosphere was such that people in the regime saw FC Barcelona as a focus of Republican resistance, so that those who had fought on the wrong side in the war suffered as a result. I am a case in point . . . I never considered myself political as such. I acted with a social conscience. I was president of the Catalan journalists' union. I used to edit a magazine called *Horizonts*, and write some very anti-Franco articles under the pseudonym of Oswald. I felt all I was doing was standing up for the rights of my union, but because of that I came to be considered an enemy of the state. When the Civil War ended I was arrested and condemned to death by a military tribunal. For seventy-two days I was in prison, waiting for the knock on the door, listening every day to dozens of my comrades being taken out and shot . . .'

Casaus made enemies then, and has had them for most of his life. Not all Catalans accepted him as one of them – he was born in Argentina. Like so many personal histories of the Spanish Civil War, his has never been entirely believed by those who fought on the opposite side. And yet he is also widely respected for upholding Barça's traditional values. He is in charge of more than 500 supporters' clubs Barça has around the world. But his enemies say he cries too easily. The author Vazquez Montalban calls him 'a formidable character actor – he is like Marlon Brando, capable of acting the role of ostrich one day or a florist the next, he can be an ashtray or any personality he feels like, even Christopher Columbus'.

Casaus sticks to his own version of history, and his history, whether real or mythical, has become part of Barça's, as symbolic as Sunyol's execution. It is not true, he insists, that it was thanks to an uncle of his, Archbishop Modrego Casaus, that he was saved from the firing squad. Instead, according to Casaus, this is what happened:

'. . . then the knock did come, only it was from a prison official who said that all the journalists who were detained had to write a report on how conditions had changed since some nuns had turned up to help out . . . I wrote that things had really improved, that the food had got better, that we were being treated more humanely. I didn't write that soon after I had arrived, the director of the prison, Isidro Castellon Lopez, had given a speech to all of us who had been condemned to death in which he'd said, "You lot are a quarter-piece of a lump of shit and I'm going to see to it that you are all shot!" The fact was that they loved my report so much that they put me in charge of the prison stores and commuted my sentence. I was released in May 1944, after serving five years.'

Among the many Catalans who were not so lucky was their president, Lluís Companys, who was betrayed to the Gestapo, extradited to Barcelona from his exile in France, and executed on 14th October 1940 after a summary trial for 'military rebellion'.

*   *   *

The inevitable political suspicion that Barça came under in the aftermath of Franco's victory was underlined in assessments made of the club by the security police, which were used to brief government ministers and officials in their formulation and implementation of Catalan policy. One lengthy file accused the club of being political and by definition subversive and separatist. Among the pieces of supporting evidence was the club's historic rivalry with Espanyol, which the police described as the only football club in Catalonia that was genuinely patriotic. 'In the matches played by these two clubs,' the police stated, 'the Barcelona supporters would label the Espanyol fans as foreigners simply because they spoke Spanish.'

Other parts of the police file focused on the club's support for the autonomous Catalan government and the involvement of some of its senior officials in local politics during the Republic. Among the 'subversive' crimes committed was the laying of floral wreaths by Barça directors and players at the statue of Rafael Casanova on 11th September, the Catalan 'national' day. After the end of the Civil War, no attempt was made to apologise for or to clarify the death of Sunyol. On the contrary, Sunyol was a leading character in the black legend served out by the police. It had not been forgotten, for instance, that in 1935 Sunyol and his fellow directors had supported a campaign to free dozens of left-wing political prisoners arrested during a popular uprising against Madrid's conservative rule. The day the prisoners were freed, according to another police file, they were received by representatives of the club, waving Catalan flags and singing the Catalan anthem *Els Segadors*. As for the Civil War, the police reported that 'on the Aragon front, the national troops [i.e., those loyal to Franco] had captured from the "reds" a Catalan flag with the inscription "To our heroic comrades in the Ebro from the members of FC Barcelona".'

Once the Civil War ended, the new regime wasted little time in stripping the club of its political and cultural identity. Among the early measures taken against the club was a decree, issued by the government's regional office for propaganda, changing its name from Football Club Barcelona to Barcelona Club de Fútbol. FC Barcelona had been the name picked by the club's founding members, led by Joan Gamper, in honour of the contribution made to the early development of the game by Swiss, like himself, and Englishmen. But the Franco regime insisted that the use of English was an affront to Spain's sense of nationhood, and wanted to mark the break with the past with a new name for which it could claim responsibility. The move had nothing to do with football. Instead it responded to the political paranoia that accompanied Franco's triumph in the Civil War.

Franco wrapped his victory in the illusion that Spain under him would recover the imperial grandeur she had lost in 1898, particularly in North Africa from where he had helped launch the uprising. The Caudillo's loathing of Communism, liberal democracy, freemasonry and separatism was matched by a resentment of Britain and, to a lesser extent, France, which he held responsible for Spain's international subservience. In the words of Paul Preston, 'Accordingly in the flush of victory and inflated by the incessant chorus of adulation, he saw himself as the natural partner of Hitler and Mussolini, one of the new leaders who would reorganise the world on a more equitable basis.' In a real sense, dispensing with the English in Barça's nomenclature gave Franco double satisfaction: it humiliated the Catalans and cocked a snook at the British.

Next to the club's name, there was nothing as symbolic of Barça's roots as its colours and crest. There is no doubt that if Franco had known then what some of us know now – that perhaps the red and blue may have had their beginnings in an English public school – these too would have been changed. Instead, the newly appointed sports authorities and propagandists of the regime focused on the crest's four red bars on yellow, decreeing that these should be reduced to two. In this way the Catalan colours were absorbed into those of the new Spanish state.

Such measures were part of the 'exorcism' considered by the regime to be a necessary process of purification of a club that had become over the years inseparable from the politics of Catalonia. However, the break with the past had to be accompanied by steps to ensure that the future would always belong to the Francoiste state and that any potential dissidence be buried once and for all. There was therefore no question of allowing anyone remotely sympathetic to the cause of Catalanism anywhere near the administration of the club. Armed with their secret files, the police did their bit in vetting potential Barça officials.

Nicolau Casaus was among those who had his application to take a more active role in the club's affairs blocked for many years, on the grounds of his dissidence prior to and during the Civil War. By 1954 Casaus was none the less actively involved in the Penya Solera, one of the most important of the supporters' associations. In that year he was almost expelled from Spain for 'insulting Franco' in a social club, popular with players and supporters, owned by the Penya. In his defence before General Felipe Acedo Colunga, the then governor of Barcelona, Casaus claimed that all that had happened was that he had asked someone to move a portrait of Franco from its position above the main door and to take it instead to a nearby meeting room, because it tended to fall down on the floor every time someone slammed the door. With help from several friends close to the regime, he was eventually exonerated.

Three years later Casaus was considered by the regime a sufficiently safe pair of hands to be allowed to head the organising committee for the celebrations marking the opening of the Camp Nou. The ceremony was attended by several Franco officials, including José Solis Ruiz, the secretary general of the Movement (Franco's party); Felipe Acedo, the unelected governor of Barcelona; and Josep-Maria de Porcioles, the unelected mayor of Barcelona. Casaus got one of his dearest friends from Madrid, José-Maria de Cossio, to give the keynote speech in honour of Barça, eulogising it as a unique cultural phenomenon with a special meaning to Catalans. Cossio was a member of Spain's prestigious Royal Academy, a well-known expert on bullfighting and football fan, and supportive of the regime. Casaus had calculated correctly that Cossio would be allowed by the authorities to speak more freely than a Catalan.

At that time, registration details of individual Barça members dating back several decades were filed at police headquarters, with membership itself sometimes being used as an excuse for discrimination. Among the many who experienced this was Francesc Gordo (whose father had been a close friend of Sunyol, the club's executed president). Gordo's first application for a Spanish passport – in order to leave the country – following World War II was rejected by the authorities. Only eight when Sunyol died in 1936, Gordo had subsequently become a member of Barça. This, as a passport official later explained to him, made him suspect as a citizen with potentially dissident leanings.

It was for the same paranoid reasons that Barça, following the Civil War, had imposed on it a management board hand-picked by the regime. The board was made up of pro-Franco Catalans, outright Falangists and military officers – among them a captain of the Civil Guard's anti-Marxist division – acting initially as a 'caretaker management team', then as a permanent ruling junta under the presidency of Enrique Pineyro, the Marquis of the Mesa de Asta, a man who knew next to nothing about sport, and had never seen a football match in his life. He had, however, fought on Franco's side as a serving officer during the Civil War; he was chosen on the basis of his loyalty to the regime.

Pineyro was an affable aristocrat, with some political sense, who wanted to show that behind the strident ideology of the regime lay elements of pragmatism. He reflected this in his inaugural speech as president to his fellow board members on 13th March 1940. He deliberately steered clear of any triumphalism. Instead his words were carefully framed (if patronising in the extreme), appealing to a sense of complicity and pride, by holding out the prospect of sporting greatness without the politics. This was not so much an olive branch as an iron fist not very subtly hidden in a velvet glove.

The regime wanted the abandonment once and for all of any notion that Barça was more than just a club. The hand-picked board was there to ensure that there could be no return to the days when the club could be used as a political Trojan horse against the government of Madrid on behalf of Catalan nationalism. Equally, the regime was conscious that football as a mass sport was something that could be turned in its favour, and that if crowds were to be drawn to Les Corts again, Barça would have to have a team worth watching.

Among the first measures of the Pineyro administration was to make gestures of reconciliation to some of the players who had chosen to remain abroad rather than return to the Civil War at the end of Barça's tour of Mexico and the US. Under a military decree issued following Franco's victory, exiled sportsmen – particularly those with declared left-wing or separatist sympathies – faced a six-year ban from any team activity if and when they returned to Spain. Pineyro saw the ban reduced to a token number of months in the case of Barça players who had indicated a willingness to rejoin the team and were not considered potentially subversive in political terms. Among the first to return to the fold, in 1940, were Escola, Pedrol and Raich. Of the three, Raich was the only playing member of the Mexican tour who had had to leave Spain because his conservative Catholic sympathies made him a potential target of the anarchists. Balmanya was another member of the Mexican tour who returned after having his six-year ban reduced to two years. He eventually became coach of the Spanish national team while Franco was still alive.

In addition to its policy of bringing back some of those abroad, the club was able to use some of the money it had successfully saved from the tour to enlist some new players, including two powerful new forwards, Mariano Martin and César Rodriguez, and Mariano Gonzalvo III, who came to be regarded as one of the most talented centre-halves of the 1940s. The club's Irish coach Patrick O'Connell was replaced by Josep Planas, a Catalan, the first in a line of Spanish and South American coaches which lasted for most of the 1940s and 1950s. Despite his varied and promising young career as a player in Britain and Ireland, his championship win with Betis, and his extraordinary survival of the Spanish Civil War, O'Connell died destitute and forgotten in London in 1959, aged seventy-two.

Rather different was the fate of the Witty family. Arthur Witty, one of Barça's founder players, did all he could to keep his Barcelona shipping business going. Far fewer ships now came into Barcelona from England, but he had built up stocks of a whole range of British products which sold well locally, given the difficulties the besieged Catalan economy faced in maintaining normal trade. 'When the Civil War broke out,' recalled Arthur's son, Frederick, 'we had quite a lot of capital in reserve and a very good business going in a variety of British household products, from soaps to chocolate. We traded in tea, whisky, that sort of thing, and during the Civil War developed other markets. For example, we sold strips of rubber for shoes, which were in short supply. Of course we owed some money to our suppliers overseas, but they realised that it was all chaos over here and took our word for it that we would pay them back once the war was over.'

While Barça was forced to form its own workers' committee, the

Wittys were covered by an agreement reached by the regional government and the British Consulate for the protection of eighty-seven
British-owned firms in Barcelona. Once the Civil War had ended, life
became more complicated for the Witty family firm. It was a difficult
period, marked by a settling of accounts by the victors against those
who had agreed to go on working with the regional government. There
was also a thriving black market in which the more unscrupulous took
advantage of the shortages of food and basic materials suffered by the
bulk of the local population.

Arthur Witty left Barcelona half-way through World War II, leaving
his business ticking over in the hands of a lawyer friend. He returned
after the war was over, when Franco's regime needed compliant
traders to help break out of the isolation that some democratic
countries imposed on him. Arthur Witty recovered his status as one
of the city's best-known shipping agents, and together with his brother
opened one of Barcelona's most popular sports shops.

The Witty saga has an interesting postscript, which I discovered
belatedly during the research for this book. Arthur's son, Frederick,
with the encouragement of his father and a military attaché friend of
his in the Madrid Embassy, left Barcelona at the start of the Spanish
Civil War, and went to work for the British mining company Rio
Tinto, near Huelva, home of Spain's first football team. From an early
stage in the Civil War, Rio Tinto was in an area occupied by the Franco
forces. With the compliance of its British management, it sent over half
its entire output from the mines to help bolster Franco's military
machinery. The company's backing of Franco ignored protests by
Aukland Geddes, one of its most prominent shareholders and a
sympathiser with the Republican side. Geddes accused Rio Tinto's
board of directors of being composed of 'violent Fascists'.

When World War II broke out, Witty was one of several Rio Tinto
employees who enlisted to fight for the Allied cause. He spent the rest
of the war in London, working in Section V – the Iberian section of
British intelligence, run at one point by the double-agent Kim Philby.
Part of the Iberian section was run out of the Madrid Embassy, with
agents all over Spain, including in Barcelona, as documented by a
member of the staff at the time:

'An annexe of the Embassy harboured the secret services, a mixed bag, smooth SIS professionals mixed with rather jolly and cynical fruit shippers ... later joined by another section, SOE, mainly young merchant bankers from the City ... they were apparently making contingency plans in the event of a German invasion ... a highly effective department, working in its own, was responsible for the reception and safe shipment through Spain to Gibraltar of escaped prisoners of war and other military personnel who managed to evade the occupying army. A network of escape routes from northern France down to the frontier serviced by gallant men and women – mostly French – was responsible for the transit of some hundreds of Allied troops and airmen.'

This 'member of staff' was my father, the late Tom Burns, who, as he said of his own appointment in Madrid, chose 'not to take the diplomatic train as a way out but to go underground in Spain'. I could never have imagined that in researching Barça's roots, the tortuous route of discovery would lead, in a sense, back to him.

Football in Spain as popular pastime was nowhere more vividly identified by the Franco regime that in its first extensive authorised encyclopaedia on the subject. Called simply *Fútbol* and laid out in numerous volumes each the size of a thick Bible, the enterprise had the endorsement of the officially controlled Federation of Spanish Football, and the blessing if not the ghosted authorship of General José Moscardo, defender of Toledo's Alcázar during the Civil War, who became the Count of the Alcázar de Toledo once it was over, as well as holding the government post of Secretary of State for Sport.

For a while Moscardo was also Captain-General of Barcelona, so it is perhaps not altogether surprising that the volume dedicated to the history of individual Spanish clubs should describe that of Barcelona Club de Fútbol (as it had been renamed by the regime) in terms that ignore its involvement with the politics of Catalonia, while paying some tribute to its record as one of Spain's better clubs in strictly footballing terms. There is no mention of the closure of Les Corts stadium during the dictatorship of General Primo de Rivera, or of the club's president Sunyol – executed by the army Moscardo helped organise and lead – or of the purges that took place at the end of the Civil War. The most generous and accurate comment to be found about the club refers to 1919 when Barcelona had 'undoubtedly the best team in Spain', with players like Samitier, Zamora and Alcantara, and its winning of both the Spanish and the Catalan championships.

More revealing of this account penned in the mid-1940s – although not published until 1950 – was the assessment made of the growing popularity of the game by a loyal servant of a regime that arguably stood or fell on the relative compliance or subjugation of the mass of Spaniards: 'That Football, written with a capital "F", has become the great spectacle of the masses is something that today no one doubts. All over the world – and especially in Europe and in Central and South America – football creates more passion than any other sport. Every Sunday, millions and millions of fans of all ages go to the stadium to support their favourite team, to let themselves go in the sheer excitement of the competition . . .

'Spain could never be an exception. Among us, if there is one spectacle that can seriously compete with bullfighting in terms of its passion, it is, without any doubt whatsoever, football. Who would have thought this fifty years ago when the sport, which was then referred to by the English word "football", was a simple distraction for a few gentlemen of leisure. And yet here it is today, the favourite sport of all Spaniards. Football has taken its emotion to even the most remote parts of Spain, with even the smallest hamlet boasting a team of its own, even if the local population have never seen a bullfight. But it has also extended its popularity across society, generating the interest of even the most distinguished sectors who until now felt distanced from the game . . . Today, every town has its team and the town's reputation is intimately linked to the glory of those players, for it is around eleven men that fans multiply and passion is born . . . which is why stadiums have to get bigger to accommodate the growing crowds who want to see the game. There is no such thing as a crisis when it comes to football, or its fans.'

Football was expressed not just as simple diversion but as Empire, the Francoiste regime consolidating its control over the regions, making of sport its instrument of unification and neutral politics for the masses. The statistics tell their own story. In the aftermath of the Spanish Civil War, the membership of FC Barcelona increased dramatically. Previously the number of members had peaked in 1924, during the dictatorship of Primo de Rivera, but it had fallen to 9,587 by the time of his death. It fell consistently during the years of the Republic leading up to the Civil War and during it: 7,719 (1936); 5,248 (1937); 4,150 (1938). At the end of the war it had fallen to 3,486. Yet by 1942, membership had reached a new peak of 15,400.

Who were these post-war members who signed up in their thousands for a club 'purified' of its dissident elements by the Fascist state?

They were certainly not, in the main, those who had fled across the Pyrenees rather than face repression for their political beliefs, among them the more militant Catalans who during the Republic had spent more time on politics than on football. Catalans formed the bulk of the estimated 450,000 exiles from Spain between February and late April 1939. The exodus from the Basque Country and Andalusia paled into insignificance compared with the flight from Catalonia, the nature of which was shocking enough to move a German military officer to describe it as a 'road of suffering'.

What then of those who had stayed behind? As has been noted in an earlier chapter, Barcelona resisted the military uprising of 1936, and Republican Catalonia formed one of the main focuses of opposition to the Fascists throughout the Civil War. And yet there were many Catalans who, on grounds of ideology, religion or pure self-interest, supported Franco. Some of these left Catalonia at the start of the Civil War, and joined up with the uprising, while others kept a low profile, privately gambling on Franco's ultimate triumph. According to the Catalan deputy of parliament Ignasi Riera, these 'Catalans of Franco' were drawn from a wide spectrum of local society, from big business-men to small traders. They included churchmen, journalists, bankers and lawyers, whose collaboration helped the Franco regime rule in Catalonia with relative ease until the dictator's death in 1975.

The day Franco's troops entered Barcelona is vividly described in Joan Thomas's book *Falange, guerra civil, fraquisme*: 'The troops were received enthusiastically by a good part of the local population who had opted to stay and not flee towards the French border. It was because of this that one of the first military communiqués issued that day referred to the "unbelievable enthusiasm" that troops had en-countered. The expressions of joy came most evidently from the sector who had always been sympathetic to the Franco cause, but also from a larger part of the local population who simply felt relieved on realising that this was the end of the war – a war that had caused huge suffering, with the situation reaching a crisis point by January 1939: by then, in addition to the rationing of food, essential products and electricity, there was the burden of an increasing number of refugees newly arrived from the south and west of Catalonia.'

How many of these 'Catalans of Franco' became members of Barcelona Club de Fútbol following the Spanish Civil War is impossible to quantify with total accuracy, although it is certainly not true that they all signed up for the traditionally more 'Spanish' local club, Espanyol. In their applications, new members identified their profession, not their political affiliation. Although war veterans who had fought for Franco did identify themselves as such, one can reasonably assume that they would not have been the only *socios* who supported him during the conflict. Equally, among the new members who made no mention of their war record, there would have been Catalans who were anti-Franco but had no wish to broadcast the fact too openly – at least in the early years of the regime – for fear of imprisonment or even execution. If all these factors are taken into account, a reading of the membership records gives part of the picture, but not the whole of it.

These records show that the membership books remained officially closed for the first five months after Catalonia fell to the Francoiste offensive, a period during which the conquering generals and their civilian cohorts consolidated their grip on the population. The club's affairs were put in the political deep-freeze, and only brought in from the cold once a very different atmosphere was reigning in and around Las Corts. Barcelona was opened to new members on 13th July 1939, following the Fascist 'act of purification'. Nearly four hundred new members registered within the first three months of the new regime. The biggest group – more than a quarter – were industrialists and traders, followed by students, while the rest were drawn from a wide range of professions, crafts and manual labour. The list included lawyers, doctors, accountants, hairdressers, waiters, chauffeurs, pharmacists and metal and agricultural workers. Of the nineteen who had openly declared themselves to be Francoiste war veterans in order to qualify for a reduced rate of membership as well as freedom from harassment, ten were 'traders', three were students, and the remaining four a butler, a teacher, a photographer and a scrivener.

7

The Enemy Within

To judge by the post-war newsreels – a favourite propaganda weapon whose use Franco learned from the Germans – Las Corts had been converted overnight into a passive theatre of orderly entertainment and harmless encounters between competing teams: not a flag or banner in sight, thousands of spectators in suits applauding respectfully, a few men in uniform here and there, and then the players, doing the one thing they had been called upon to do and nothing more – play football and obey the referee.

According to one eyewitness, 'There was nothing glorious or ostentatious about the club then, although there was an element of nobility among those who worked for it. Some of the players turned up to train by tram or by bicycle; the team travelled to away games on a coal-gas-fired bus. We used to keep the coal in the stadium and then load the bus before the players got on . . . There were players I remember for their humanity – Samitier giving a poor boy at the gates of the stadium some money to buy himself some shoes; Kubala forever followed by seven or eight Hungarian refugees whom he basically fed and clothed . . .'

There were no Catalan flags or slogans of political protest. The crowd bayed like sheep, collectively but with no visible sense of common identity beyond those eleven players slogging it out on the pitch, like so many anonymous gladiators, one or two of them getting more applause than the rest – for really making his shirt sweat, for chasing the ball. In the crowd, hearts and souls had been distributed between those who did not care and those who feared to care too much too openly, not just about the football, but about what lay behind it.

'Politically no one said a thing openly,' recalled the same eyewitness. 'There were about ten Civil Guards who would turn up and sit by the pitch and stay for the whole match, as if everything was quite normal.

But you knew there were people in the crowd who said nothing overtly political for fear that the man next door might be a plainclothes policeman or some collaborator.'

And yet the silence was deceptive. Somewhere in that crowd on some Sundays there was at least one militant spirit who had slipped through the Fascist 'purification' of Les Corts – a man with a memory, who had escaped the regime's general anaesthetic. Many years later, in 1998, one of the unassuming *cules*, Gregorio Lopez Raimundo, now an old man, told me this with the conviction of personal experience. He had insisted on coming to meet me in preference to my looking for him – a practice from his years of living clandestinely.

As we moved towards a new millennium, Lopez Raimundo had recently given an interview to *El País*, which struck me as full of insight about the direction of world politics, as if history was reaching a crisis point: 'Russia is being ruled by a drunkard. But even more alarming is how the United States and the Western world have wasted the opportunity presented by the end of the Cold War to help civilisation, to bring about real progress in the world . . . I wrote once that one day there will be a new Viking invasion, but this time the hordes will be coming from the south and will finish us all off . . .'

In the hotel where we met, I probed a less well-known part of Gregorio Lopez Raimundo's life: as the dedicated fan of FC Barcelona. The fact that he was born in Aragón, and not in Catalonia, is in itself a reminder of the contribution emigration has made to the development of the club. The emigrant arriving in Barcelona was given a job and a home. But to get a sense of solidarity, of genuinely belonging to the community, he had to go church, join a trade union, or go to Les Corts. Gregorio became a Communist and a Barça fan – a club that, rather like religion, could accommodate rich and poor, but which had a genuine mass following. To back the football team was to belong to a community, no longer to feel an outsider in the region that had offered you a job and a home but little real warmth beyond the stadium and the trade union – although Gregorio claims to have carried the blood of a *cule* from an early age:

'In my childhood I wasn't very good at playing football, but I loved it. When we lived in Zaragoza, the local teams never got very far in the Spanish championship so we always had a second team that we supported. My brother was a big fan of Athletic Bilbao, but I supported Barcelona. Initially I think it was because they seemed to have the best stickers, but I think what really got me was watching a championship semi-final in Zaragoza between Barcelona and Arenas. I think it was in 1927. It was the last time that the "great three" – Alcantara, Samitier and Sagi – played together. It was a sensational match that went into extra time. Barça lost 4–3. They were my idols, and from that day I really felt fanatical about Barça . . . I also remember that the first time I ever listened to the radio was to listen to a match the club was playing . . .

'Then I came to Barcelona, to follow my father's profession, as a tailor's apprentice. It was 1931. I was seventeen. Three years later, there was the miners' uprising in Asturias, and here in Catalonia we proclaimed our Republic . . . I didn't become a member, but I went to see matches. I couldn't afford the membership. Wages were really low in those days; what I earned at the beginning was barely enough to cover the cost of my rent. I started earning a little more and with that little more I'd buy myself a ticket to Las Corts. It cost three pesetas in those days. My wage was five pesetas a day . . . Then the war came and for me Barça and football virtually disappeared, although I do remember that the government was keen on the club touring abroad to help the cause . . .'

Lopez Raimundo's trade-unionist brother was killed during the fighting that developed between anarchists and Communists. It was in those days that the Catalan Communist Party, the PSUC, was created. Lopez Raimundo says he has a clear conscience first as a soldier fighting against Franco and then as a militant member of the Communist Youth. In *Homage to Catalonia*, George Orwell blamed totalitarian Stalinists for the betrayal of Catalonia's libertarian revolution. But Lopez Raimundo's version of history is necessarily different: 'The PSUC played a very important role in the war. It fought with a lot of courage and with a lot of deaths in the internal struggle of the left . . .'

With the end of the war, Lopez Raimundo went into exile, from where he continued to oppose Franco. He returned in 1947, secretly crossing the border from France with a false passport, and joining the 'clandestine struggle' against the Francoiste state in Barcelona. His main task was to help reorganise the leadership of the party after more than one hundred militants had been arrested, four of them summarily executed.

'They were dangerous times. We had to be very careful who we met and how. They were constantly watching us, following us. And yet even then I felt like watching football, and went to Las Corts on a number of occasions. Strange at it may seem, in Las Corts I felt protected in a way that I didn't in the street where I was always looking two hundred metres ahead in case I recognised a policeman . . . There was another big difference for me between the street and the stadium in those days. Out in the city, Fascism was very visible – the names of the streets, the Falangist crests, the portraits of Franco, the flags – but in the stadium you were among the masses and I felt – maybe I was imagining it, but I felt it all the same – that everyone around me was really anti-Fascist deep down, at least where we were standing. Maybe things were a little different where people were sitting; the club management was pro-regime, hand-picked no doubt, but not the fans – they identified themselves with a democratic Catalonia.'

Just how different were the experiences of those who sat and ruled FC Barcelona and those who stood and dreamed of solidarity can be gauged by that of Enrique Llaudet, probably the most unapologetic of presidents who presided over the club fortunes during the Franco years. Llaudet came from one of Catalonia's most powerful industrial families, whose textile company was one of the region's biggest. Enrique served as Barça's president for two successive terms between 1961 and 1968, although his links with the club predated his presidency by decades. The official club history describes him as 'a passionately Barcelonist textile industrialist'.

Since the early part of the twentieth century when the club had grown into one of Catalonia's major institutions, the name Llaudet had never been far from the machinations of those who ran the club, the Llaudet money exerting a powerful counterweight whenever Barça showed signs of veering towards the left. The Llaudet view on life was essentially patriarchal and conservative – the opposite of those for whom Catalanism was a vibrant political dynamic. There was never any doubt which side they would back once General Franco staged his uprising.

The surviving grand patriarch, Llaudet was recovering from a stroke and in a wheelchair when I interviewed him in 1998 in his palatial family apartment – a veritable museum of tapestries, paintings and hunting trophies and skins. But as he sat in his office, a portrait of Franco giving some Barça players a cup just behind his head, there was enough memory left in at least part of his brain to convey his side of history, with as much passion as that displayed by his political opponents.

'When the Civil War broke out I was arrested by the "reds" and condemned to death, because I was right-wing, a property-owner, and because I was trying to slip out of the country. I was in fact a nineteen-year-old student at the time, although at university I was considered a Falangist by left-wing students. I think my father must have a good contact among the police because I had my sentence commuted and was sent instead to a convent near Manresa which had been converted into a prisoners' camp. I worked there for a while as a bricklayer, although everything I built turned out crooked. I managed to escape dressed as a soldier, thanks to the prison warden's daughter whom I befriended. It was she I think who left me a door open . . .

'That first night I sought shelter in a nearby farm shed. I was hiding in the hay, with the town being bombed from the air, when I suddenly saw some soldiers. At first when I heard the sound of the soldiers I though they were "red" militias. But then I saw they were wearing red berets which meant that they were *requetes*, our side, and that the captain was a friend of mine . . .'

In Catalonia, the Civil War was drawing to an end, the taking of Manresa by groups of *requetes* (right-wing royalists) confirmation that the whole region was close to being subdued by forces loyal to Franco. Llaudet made his way to Vic, where he was reunited with his father and a group of fellow loyal Francoiste Catalan businessmen. They had heard that Communist troops were burning factories and bridges as they retreated towards the French border, and were worried about their own interests going up in flames.

'One of the group, who was unmarried, had a factory about two kilometres from the ones we owned in what was called the Llaudet colony. He turned to my father and said, "Pepito, what are we going to do now? At our age, how can we begin all over again?" My father replied, "You can do what you like because you have no family. But I've got no choice," then, turning towards me, said, "I've got no choice but to keep going because of him." After the war we got the factory going again, and when I got married my father ordered me to spend my honeymoon working . . .'

If there was a divine right of Barça presidents, it would undoubtedly belong to the Llaudets. Among the portraits and documents in Enrique's house is a menu card for a six-course dinner at Chez Martin, one of Barcelona's oldest French restaurants, to which his father – who was vice-president of Barça – took him decades ago along with some of the club's first directors. He remembers Joan Gamper, Barça's Swiss-born founder, as a boy at court remembers the ageing emperor of a long-ruling dynasty: 'What do I remember about Gamper? That he used to give me chocolates – those that have made Switzerland so famous. He used to give me a chocolate every time I went to the stadium with my father.'

To this day Enrique Llaudet boasts of his term in office as an example of shrewd financial management: he paid off some of the debts incurred from building the Camp Nou, and sensible politics helped keep Catalonia on the right side of Franco. 'I am the only president who said goodbye to everybody from the centre of the stadium. My forerunners and successors usually came in through the front door only to have to escape from the back.' He did not add that if in the early years he had discovered that Gregorio Lopez Raimundo was in the terraces, he would no doubt have handed him over to the police, but he did say this:

'I never felt remotely pressurised by Madrid. If anything I had nothing against the regime getting involved. Whenever we had our board meetings, I always insisted that the government representative sat on my right, and was more than happy that he and all of us should conduct our business in Spanish, not Catalan. I didn't want to be political. You see, I was conscious that among my 80,000 members I had people who were right-wing and people who were left-wing, people who spoke Spanish and people who spoke Catalan – so my conscience was clear. Nowadays, everyone who goes to the presidential box is a politician – it makes me sick.'

All of this tells us the following about FC Barcelona in the post-war years: that it was controlled by a management who were politically submissive to Madrid and by a sector of Catalonia's entrepreneurial class – mainly from the textile sector – who considered that the club's best interests were served by keeping it out of radical politics. But the club was by no means simply a political eunuch exploited by Franco and driven, on his behalf, by the local business community. Its support base, made up not just of members but of others who identified with the club but could not risk adding to their police file, was politically and socially diverse. Which is why, during the Franco regime, the passion of the people continued to be fuelled as much by events off the pitch as by those on it, and Barça always did remain more than just a club, not just a piece of opium for the masses.

Franco may have believed he was ridding Las Corts stadium of the evil spirits of Barça's Catalan past, but he was mistaken in concluding that football could only be of benefit to his regime. For it was in the intensifying rivalry between the club and Real Madrid that many Catalans managed to exteriorise their resentment of Franco's repression, finding a new political expression capable of restoring their sense of pride. The bogyman was dressed in white but there was no doubt that he had horns and a long tail, however much Real supporters tried to confuse the issue by nicknaming the players the *meringues*.

As far as Barça fans were concerned, Real Madrid was not just backed by Franco, it *was* Franco, while for many Real Madrid fans, FC Barcelona was, as it always would be, separatist scum – a bias that extended itself through much of Franco's Spain, outside Catalonia. Barça veterans like Fuste remember it well: 'There were always those who wanted to mix up with politics those of us who just wanted to get on with playing football. As a Catalan I felt that they screamed phrases at us which I didn't like and which affected me, even though I still enjoyed the game. In a sense I felt proud that they felt a need to insult us. It made me feel that we did really represent another country, another nation, even though the words they used were pretty horrendous. From 1941, the year I was born, until the day I retired from football, they always screamed the same insults.'

One of the most dramatic incidents in the history of the two clubs occurred in 1943, during the semi-finals of the Spanish championship, renamed the Generalissimo's Cup in Franco's honour. The first round was played in Las Corts. In the previous season, Barça had blamed its poor performance in the League championship – it was nearly relegated – to biased refereeing, with the popular notion that referees were under specific instructions from the regime's sporting officials to act against the Catalan club. Barça had nevertheless recovered some self-esteem by winning the Generalissimo's Cup, and came out with every intention of not letting the title go. Real Madrid for its part took to the field with equal determination to concede as few goals as possible, by whichever means proved most effective.

Barça scored three goals. The game was marred by some reckless tackling by four Madrid players, Moleiro, Querejeta, Souto and Corona, including a kick at the stomach of the Barça star of the time, Escola. Despite his having to be withdrawn in agony on a stretcher, only a free kick was given as a reprimand. Indeed, much of the refereeing appeared once again to be biased against the Catalans, fuelling their local complex of persecution and the determination to protest against it. When not applauding the goals, the Catalans gathered in Las Corts spent most of the game whistling and booing at the Madrid players and the referee.

Among those who reported on the game was a former Real Madrid goalkeeper, Eduardo Teus, who before the end of the Franco regime would become coach of the national team. Teus was known as an emotive character; he was eventually to drop dead of a heart attack in the press box of Bilbao's San Mames stadium while watching a match between his team and Athletic Bilbao. But even by his standards, what he had to say about the Las Corts match would survive as one of the most irresponsible pieces ever written in the history of sports journalism.

With the undisguised intention to provoke, he wrote a lengthy article in *Ya*, a Madrid-based newspaper, exaggerating the behaviour of the Las Corts crowd as a co-ordinated political conspiracy against the state. 'The crowd in Las Corts,' he wrote, 'whistled at the Madrid players with the clear intention of attacking the representatives of Spain.' He also claimed – inaccurately – that the referee had overlooked a much greater number of fouls committed by the Barça players. (Conveniently overlooked was the fact that anti-Barça bias among Spanish referees had become so blatant and systematic as to have forced even the Francoiste Barça management to issue a note of protest to the Spanish National College of Referees – a protest note that was unsurprisingly not even responded to, and effectively ignored.)

The Teus allegation was the beginning of a campaign in *Ya* and other Madrid newspapers aimed at stoking up anti-Catalan feelings prior to the return match, which had the blessing of the regime. Far from defusing the sense of impending crisis, the management of Real Madrid issued an eve-of-match statement reminding its fans of the alleged lack of sportsmanship shown in Les Corts by their Barça rivals, and accompanying this with an unconvincing appeal for calm. Even as the statement was being issued, free whistles were being handed out to local fans together with tickets, while the Barça team were treated to an unannounced and terrifying visit by the Director of State Security, José Finat y Escriva de Romani, the Count of Mayalde.

The security chief told the Barça players, 'Do not forget that some of you are only playing because of the generosity of the regime that has forgiven you for your lack of patriotism.' The message was deliberately ambiguous, leaving half the changing room in a state of accentuated pre-match paranoia. Some of those present did not hesitate in putting the worst interpretation on the visit. This was that the players' behaviour was expected to extend to losing the match. Any attempt to put up a fight would lead to Raich, Escola and Balmanya – the three players who had left Spain during the Civil War – having their police files 'reconsidered', together with their future in Spanish football.

The Barça players also received a visit from the referee, who warned that any act of indiscipline would be dealt with harshly. By now the Chamartin stadium was packed with local fans, a simmering cauldron of *madrileños* out for revenge beneath the fierce, unforgiving rays of the Castilian sun. At 4.30 p.m. the home team ran out on to the pitch to be greeted by a roar of approval. But even louder were the whistles and protests that met the Barça players the instant they appeared, and accompanied their every move during the match.

Among those watching the game was Barça's masseur Angel Mur. Years later he recalled his horror: 'The night before the game we had to change our hotel, and even then we didn't leave it all evening because we were convinced we would be lynched. Then the game came, and our goalkeeper was so petrified of being hit by missiles that he spent most of the game as far forward from his goal as possible, allowing the Madrid players to strike at the net from all directions. Not so far from where we were sitting, there was a man dressed in military uniform who kept on screaming through the game, "Kill these red Catalans, kill these Catalan dogs." At one point I interrupted him and said, "Look, I may not have been born in Catalonia, but I feel I belong to it, and I'll go on working there because it is separate from the rest of Spain." The officer shouted, "You separatist son of a bitch!" and told me I was under arrest for sedition. It was at that point that the Marquis of the Mesa de Asta, the president of Barça, intervened, telling the officer to leave me alone. The Marquis had been picked by the regime and was a personal friend of Moscardo's, but the officer didn't recognise him. "Who do you think you are?" the officer said to the Marquis. "You're under arrest as well – come with me." Then the Marquis took out his credentials, and told the officer, "I'm terribly sorry, officer, but it's you who have to come with me." '

Barça lost the match 11–1. Post-match reports in the local press were euphoric, led by the unflagging correspondent for *Ya*, Eduardo Teus, who described the result as the 'most resounding victory in the history of Real Madrid.' According to his detailed report of the game, the match was evenly balanced for much of the first half, despite a brilliant early goal by Real. Within minutes of the start, one of Real's most imaginative players, Sato, collected the ball well inside his own half and, in a surprise exchange of position with one of the forwards, switched to the wing and swept down the length of the pitch, the ball close to his feet, before crossing to the winger Pruden, who struck goal.

Teus went on to describe how, despite this early goal, Barça put up a strong resistance in defence for most of the first half, repelling wave after wave of intrusions by Real. Only belatedly did the visiting side, outmanoeuvred and exhausted, succumb to Real's relentless attacking football and goal power. The match, according to this version of events, effectively turned with Real's second goal, scored in the 31st minute with a powerful strike by the club's Basque centre-forward, Barinaga. By half-time, Real had scored six more.

In the second half, Real consolidated its lead with a vengeance. 'Real beat Barcelona,' Teus commented effervescently, 'in a tenacious struggle for superiority, paving the way for its victory with its eight goals in a fantastic first half. And it was made possible because this Madrid is a team with nerve and muscle. It had already proved itself such in the first game in Las Corts in the midst of the storm, and here in Chamartin it finally overcame all adversity, without fear of confronting the enemy, with a real attacking fever as well as courage in defence, the kind of style we have come to identify with Athletic Bilbao.'

While full of praise for the winning team as a whole, Teus singled out Real midfield players Moleiro, Sauto and Ipina for their speed on and off the ball and their ability to cover the ground with 'serenity, nerve and precision', and the club's Basque centre-forward Barinaga for his impeccable touch and his devastating goal-scoring. Teus conceded there was noise in the stadium, but insisted that he had played in the face of more aggressive crowds in his time as a player and his team had won. 'There are countless examples of teams who have had to play in adverse circumstances like these and who have not succumbed,' he wrote, while pointing out that in the first half-hour of the match the Barça players had played with the same level of noise for thirty minutes and conceded only two goals.

A somewhat different perspective of the game was recorded in a post-match report by Catalan-born Juan Antonio Samaranch. The man who would one day become president of the International Olympic Committee was assigned to cover the match by the newspaper *La Prensa*, part of a Spanish-wide media chain owned by the Falangist movement and totally loyal to Franco, whom the Samaranch family had fully supported during the Civil War. Samaranch was already better known then as a sportsman than as a sportswriter, but the piece he wrote that day came to be regarded by his fellow Catalans as one of his most memorable and indeed rare contributions to the cause of truth and democracy.

Instead of toeing the biased pro-Madrid line adopted by Teus and others, the young Samaranch attempted to judge the game from a purely sporting perspective, concluding that the intimidation of Barça had been quite unprecedented and of such a powerful nature as to have made it impossible for there to be a proper game of football. Crucially,

Samaranch took issue with a key decision taken in the first half by the referee: the sending-off of one of Barça's key players, Benito, which he claimed was completely unjustified and responded solely to the wishes of a partisan crowd. It was at that moment that the avalanche of goals began, with Barça as a team effectively deciding that it was not worth their while putting up any resistance.

'Perhaps if the final result had been 4–0, it would have been possible to blame this or that player,' wrote Samaranch. 'But a ten-goal difference is too incredible for there not to be an alternative explanation. If Barça had played really badly, the result would have been different. But it was not a question of playing badly or well. Barça simply ended up by not playing at all. Individual players were fearful of making even the most innocent of tackles because of the crowd reaction and therefore hardly touched their opponents . . . It was frankly sad having to watch the spectacle of a Barcelona forcefully reduced to impotence by the coercion of the crowd . . .

'. . . I won't deny there was some merit in Real Madrid's playing. Its midfield was marvellous, and the team as a whole dominated the match, but on reflection, one has to admit that it's not difficult to look great if you haven't got anyone playing against you (a children's team would probably have had more of an impact than Barcelona did in this match) . . .'

Samaranch at the time remained, as he would always, a Francoiste Catalan who continued to declare his belief that Catalonia was not a nation in its own right but an inseparable part of Spain. He wrote as a hobby, and was not an accredited journalist. His reaction has survived as a curious piece of objective reportage by a man whose own democratic credentials were somewhat limited. It was no great loss for him to be told by *La Prensa*, after the match, that his services would not be needed for the foreseeable future. He carried on with his politics, his sports, and his contributions elsewhere, eventually reappearing in *La Prensa* in 1952 with his daily coverage of the Helsinki Olympics.

Real Madrid and Barça were fined 25,000 pesetas each for their alleged part in the disturbances at Chamartin, while Barça was given an additional fine of 2,500 pesetas for the lack of respect shown to the Real Madrid players in the first leg at Las Corts.

As far as Barça was concerned, the most positive result of the whole saga was the conversion, of sorts, of the Marquis of the Mesa de Asta. So outraged was he by the crowd behaviour in Madrid that he wrote a lengthy letter of appeal against the sanctions imposed on his club by the very authorities who had given him his job in the first place. The appeal was rejected, and the Marquis resigned within a year, having won some respect among his former enemies. He remained an aristocrat and a Spaniard to his death, but within Barça he is remembered as someone who treated the club with some sympathy.

The rivalry between Barcelona and Real Madrid so manifest in those two encounters in 1943 has continued unabated to the present day, although its political component was at its sharpest during the years of the Franco regime, when Real Madrid was identified by the Catalans as the club of the dictator, and in the aftermath of Franco's death in 1975, when Catalan political leaders used Barça to consolidate their push for regional autonomy from the Castilian-led state. The bad blood that ran through every encounter between the two teams was a constant over more than half a century, the changing rhythm and scope of its spilling a matter of degree rather than substance. For while not all games were characterised by the same level of violence on or off the field, there was rarely an encounter in which both sides could claim a level playing field. It did not matter whether the game was played in Barcelona or Madrid, or how well; support would always be intensely partisan. Real or imagined, accusations of bias against the referee would always be present. The loser would feel cheated, the winner rather less than magnanimous in victory.

It was a rivalry that, while having its roots in politics, became driven by a momentum of mutual creation. It fed on itself, reflecting the growing popularity of football as a sport. The teams came to dominate Spanish football, with the biggest stadiums in the country, and the most extensive media coverage, their commercial weight assured by the ambition that drove them to seek conquest both within and beyond their national borders.

During the 1950s the rivalry achieved new levels of intensity, as both Barça and Real Madrid led Spanish football's drive into Europe. As has been noted earlier, Ladislao Kubala, one of the great Barça heroes, belongs to this period. His transfer to Barcelona, organised by the 'apolitical' Pepe Samitier, was given a helping hand by Franco because it served his propaganda: Kubala arrived as a refugee from Soviet Communism, at a time when Franco's foreign-policy interest lay in an anti-Soviet Cold War reconciliation with the West. Kubala's stardom also increased the mass appeal of Barça's football, channelling the energies and the passions of the population away from the streets and into a bigger stadium. While savage repression had been the regime's main instrument against its opponents at the end of the Civil War, it subsequently encouraged more subtle forms of maintaining itself in power, gradually realising the potential of football as a means of social pacification.

Franco's favourite pastimes were movies and football. While he was always only too happy to hand out the Generalissimo's Cup in person – whether it was won by Barça or Real Madrid – he often relaxed in his El Pardo palace, watching Spain's *Match of the Day* on TV. The first live broadcast of a Real Madrid–Barça match was in February 1959. Legend has it that it led to such a rush for television sets the week before the game that there was a virtual sell-out in both the capital city and Barcelona. Franco himself, when not watching TV, also like millions of his fellow countrymen spent time filling in the pools, which he signed for a while under a pseudonym, Francisco Cofran. Franco won the pools twice. 'It is somehow difficult to imagine Hitler or Mussolini doing the pools,' comments his biographer Paul Preston.

While Franco skillfully derived maximum advantage from the international triumphs of Spanish clubs, and used football as a political sedative domestically in many Spanish towns, Barça never fully succumbed to a state of political inertia even at points of greatest crisis. This was evident during the first organised protest in Spain after the Civil War, in March 1951. The protest, over increases in the price of tram tickets in the city of Barcelona, led to a mass boycott of this form of transport, student demonstrations, and some worker unrest – for which the by then Communist leader and Barça fan Gregorio Lopez Raimundo was arrested and tortured. Barça itself went ahead and played a League match against Racing of Santander in Las Corts. But the crowd did not disconnect itself from the protest outside. Hundreds of leaflets backing the boycott were distributed round the terraces, and when the match was over as many fans ignored the empty trams that the regime had placed near the stadium, choosing to walk home instead as a mark of solidarity.

This sense of solidarity was not dented by Kubala's arrival. It was around Kubala's charisma and footballing skills that Barça overcame its post-war loss of confidence and shattered organisation, developing its strongest and most successful team since the days when Samitier and Alcantara played. Kubala made his début international appearance in Las Corts, three months before the tram strike, with two consecutive friendly games against the West German champions, Frankfurter Spot Vernam. Kubala was the undisputed star of the two games, which Barça won 4–1 and 10–4. He scored six goals, and was a principal architect of another five, showing a combination of strength and control with the ball the likes of which had not been seen before in Las Corts. 'It would appear,' the local newspaper *Destino* commented, 'that with Kubala has arrived a new style of playing football . . . The public came out of these matches in a state of amazement. Such was the intelligence shown by the player on and off the ball that it appeared he'd been playing with the team all his life.'

Kubala's inspiration helped Barça win the Generalissimo's Cup on 27th May 1951, beating the Basque team Real Sociedad 3–0 in the final held in the Real Madrid stadium. The game was ignored by the local fans, but enthusiastically followed by Catalans and Basques. Trains that later transported the *cules* back to Barcelona had painted on them '*Visca el Barça*' – '*Viva Barça*' in Catalan, in open defiance of a government ban on the use of the language in public.

In the 1951–2 season which followed, Barça went on to win the Spanish double, and the Copa Latina (played by the Spanish, Italian, French and Portuguese champions), together with two summer tournaments, the Martini Rosso and Eva Duarte tournaments. Kubala missed some of the games through injury, but once again emerged the 'star' of the team, responsible as he was for some of the most memorable moments of football. One of them was a League match against Athletic Bilbao, renamed Atlético de Bilbao by the regime but still exclusively Basque in its team composition. The club at the time was, together with Barça, considered to be playing the best football in Spain. Kubala scored the one and only goal of the game, in the 24th minute of the second half, picking up a pass just inside his own half, dribbling the ball with a mixture of skill and sheer strength through various Bilbao defenders – the toughest in the business – before striking home a powerful cannon-ball shot which brought the stadium to its feet.

In another memorable League match, this time against Gijon, Kubala played after an extended absence because of injury. His extraordinary powers of recovery gave Barça a 9–0 win over Gijon, with Kubala himself responsible for no fewer than seven goals – a new record in Spanish football.

Kubala's performance was no less impressive against foreign competition, so that he played a key role in raising Barça's international profile. In the Copa Latina, Kubala's Barça overwhelmed Juventus 4–2, even though the Italian club had until then been considered the best team in Europe. Barça won the finals against the French champions, Nice, in Paris, 1–0, a much harder-fought victory assured by a goal from Kubala's main rival in the team, César. Thousands of *cules* crowded into the Parisian stadium – those from Barcelona and other parts of Catalonia joining up with local exiles in a show of Catalan solidarity. Back in the Catalan capital, the success of the team was greeted euphorically by even bigger multitudes, as great in number as, if not greater than, those who had greeted Franco's troops at the end of the Civil War.

The 'season of the five cups' is remembered as something of a rite of passage by the Barça faithful, as a time when the club not only played great football, but also showed that it had survived the regime's repression with its roots intact. Many years later, in 1989, Juan Manuel Serrat, one of Catalonia's most talented musicians, wrote a song of tribute to Kubala. A passionate *cule*, Serrat felt as close to Kubala in spirit as the Argentinian tango singer Gardel had been to Samitier. As Serrat sang, 'For me there was no one like Kubala . . . I was happy to play with him, carry his portrait in my wallet . . .'

Serrat, however, belonged to a different generation from Gardel's, and his political commitment was much stronger. Born in 1943, in Poble Sec, a poor suburb of Barcelona, the son of an immigrant, Serrat grew up among the shortages of the post-war years, looking towards a future that would one day be inescapably without Franco. Kubala's days of glory coincided with Serrat's adolescence. Serrat's 'football' song – written fourteen years after Franco's death – remembered a time of loyalty and defiance by fans amidst the nobility of its players, when Catalans hung on to their sense of identity thanks to Barça.

For most of its history, Barcelona had aspired to be considered Spain's most outward-looking and European city. The dream had been shattered somewhat by the Civil War, when revolutionaries on one side, and Fascists on the other, had sought to impose Utopias of their own: hammers and sickles, and then the arrows of the Falange movement, had appeared painted on walls and were raised on flags. The *cules* who followed the team's success in 1952 to Paris during the Copa Latina waved Catalan flags, and danced together with their French neighbours. Thanks to football, they had rediscovered a language and expression that reached out beyond the isolating frontiers of Spain to Europe and beyond.

8

Against the Enemy

At the time when Barça was basking in its first experience of European glory, an equally unprecedented footballing success was taking place across the Atlantic in a country better known for the quality of its cocaine.

Colombia had turned into football's equivalent of El Dorado since its new League had turned professional in 1948. Local business barons spent fortunes building up local teams into some of the best on the continent, importing star players from countries such as Uruguay, Brazil and Argentina, who had become experienced practitioners of the game, as well as a smaller number of Europeans. By the early 1950s, the first team of Millonarios of Bogotá – eight Argentinians, one Brazilian, one Peruvian and one Colombian – had established itself as the best in the country, making a spectacular if short-lived contribution to the growing reputation of South American football. Between 1949 and 1953, Millonarios won the local championship four out of five times, in 1951 without losing a single game, thanks to one player, above all the rest: an Argentinian called Alfredo Di Stefano.

This extraordinarily talented forward had already made his reputation in his native Argentina playing for River Plate, in an attacking formation of such devastating efficiency that it was nicknamed *la maquina* (the machine). In Colombia, he was the master ingredient in a blend of football's magic realism – the sport of fantasy, imagination and native instinct. With Di Stefano in their midst, Millonarios fans claimed they had elevated football to an art, calling their team's performance out on the field a 'ballet in blue', the ball passing from one player to another with such precision and speed as to leave the opponent often just standing and watching in admiration.

Di Stefano himself personified 'total football' long before the term had entered the official lexicon of the modern game, as Eduardo

Galeano's portrait of the player makes clear: 'The entire playing field fitted inside his shoes. From his feet the pitch sprouted and grew . . . he ran and reran the field from net to net. He would change flanks and change rhythm with the ball from a lazy trot to an unstoppable cyclone; without the ball he'd evade his marker to gain open space, seeking air whenever a play got choked off . . . He never stood still. Holding his head high, he could see the entire pitch and cross it at a gallop to prise open the defence and launch the attack. He was there at the beginning, during, and at the end of every scoring play, and he scored goals of all colours . . .'

It was another magician of the game, Barça's Pepe Samitier – 'El Hombre Langosta' of the 1920s – who watched Di Stefano play against Real Madrid during a triumphant tour Millonarios made of South America and Spain. Samitier had long since retired as a player, but at the time was effectively Barça's chief scout, as a member of the club's technical staff. The year was 1952. Watching Di Stefano play, El Sami had no doubt that with the Argentinian playing alongside Kubala, Barça would become unstoppable in its quest for unrivalled greatness, both at local and at international level. Not surprisingly, however, Samitier was not the only person in Spain to be impressed by Di Stefano. The evening before the match against Millonarios, Real Madrid's president, Santiago Bernabéu, emerged from sharing a radio programme with Di Stefano and, with characteristic bluntness, said to a local journalist, 'This guy smells of good football.' It was the beginning of the extraordinary struggle between FC Barcelona and Real Madrid to get their hands on Di Stefano, the greatest forward of a generation, and one of the true 'greats' of international football, the outcome of which was to be a turning-point in the history of the two teams.

Bernabéu was a hard-nosed Civil War veteran, a man of considerable ambition and with a visceral dislike of Catalan politics. When the Spanish Civil War broke out, he was denounced as a Fascist by a fellow member of the Real Madrid board and narrowly escaped execution by the militia by taking refuge in the French Embassy. He later joined up as a cadet with Franco's troops and fought in the division commanded by General Agustin Muñoz Grandes on the Catalan front. 'I was in the reconquest of Catalonia, the reconquest of an independent Catalonia

for the greater glory of Spain,' he later recalled, adding that in his view
the problems of the Catalans had no other solution than domination
by Madrid.

His dream, once the war was over, was to build the biggest football
stadium his country and most of Europe had ever seen, as a symbol not
just of the growing popularity of the sport but of Madrid's status as the
'centre of Spain' – a Spain which, under Franco, had emerged victorious from the Civil War with illusions of imperial grandeur. Bernabéu
invited bids for the project of building the stadium within two years of
his appointment as president of Real Madrid in 1943. The panel drawn
up to consider the bids from various Spanish companies was headed by
Pedro Muguraza Ontanon, the architect of El Valle de los Caídos, and
Javier Barroso Sanchez-Guerra, an ex-goalkeeper of Atlético Madrid,
who as the first president of the Spanish Football Federation under
Franco had facilitated Bernabéu's appointment as president of Real
Madrid. The company chosen to build the stadium was Huarte, who
had, surprisingly enough, built El Valle de los Caídos. So much for
competitive tendering!

The Santiago Bernabéu stadium was inaugurated just before Christmas 1947. For the remaining twenty-seven years of Franco's rule, the
final of the Generalissimo's Cup would be played there, with the
exception of three years – 1957, 1963 and 1970 – when the game
coincided with a visit by Franco to Catalonia and it was played in
Barcelona. Ironically, however, in the first season of its use, Real
Madrid, the club for whom it had been built, played so badly that it
narrowly escaped relegation. It would take another six years before
Bernabéu had secured Di Stefano, the one player who guaranteed
filling the stadium.

Di Stefano's transfer to Real Madrid in October 1953 followed nine
months of tortuous negotiations, the bulk of which involved Barça's
trying to reach an acceptable deal with Millonarios and with the
player's Argentinian club, River Plate, which technically owned
him. The negotiations were initially entrusted by the management
of FC Barcelona to a Catalan nationalist lawyer, Ramón Trias Fargas,
who knew Colombia well. Trias Fargas's father, Antoni, a Catalan
doctor, had gone into exile at the end of the Spanish Civil War, and
was a shareholder in Millonarios. Ramón Trias Fargas's other cre-

dentials were that he was an expert in commercial law and, most importantly, was a strongly committed Catalan who was acutely sensitive to the political implications of Spanish football.

Such was the political intrigue surrounding the negotiations, once FC Barcelona had reached an initial memorandum of understanding with River Plate, that Trias Fargas used a secret code when communicating with his father by telegram. As he explained to him, in a letter, 'As you know, FC Barcelona has come to an understanding with Di Stefano and the Argentinian club River Plate. It would seem that Real Madrid was trying to get in on the act, but Barça has managed to get in first. Football in our country has become a very important issue, as it is the only way we can collectively convey our regional aspirations. Therefore the Di Stefano question is a national problem. That is why the telegrams are being sent in code form. We know for a fact that our telephones are being bugged by the government of Madrid, which claims to be defending the integrity of the Spanish state.'

In a subsequent report he wrote on the whole affair, Trias Fargas blamed the difficulties he faced in reaching a deal on Barça's own management. His own good contacts with Millonarios, which he planned to build on through patient and honest negotiation, were undermined early on by Barça's decision to involve the former player Samitier, who in turn brought in a Colombian friend of his, Joan Busquets, to speed up the talks. Busquets was an unfortunate choice given that he was a director of CF Santa Fe, the other main Bogotá club and rival of Millonarios, and seems to have acted in a way designed more to sabotage the deal than to secure it. Busquets issued an extraordinary ultimatum to Millonarios: either the club accepted a modest offer for the player, or FC Barcelona had the consent of the player to take him to Catalonia anyway. When Millonarios refused, Busquets went to work organising Di Stefano's escape. During a tour by Millonarios of neighbouring Venezuela, the player announced that he was not going back to Colombia, despite the fact that he owed the club $5,000. Within weeks, on 17th May 1953, he arrived in Barcelona, together with his family, and the local press were soon claiming a done deal that would pave the way for the most glorious partnership in the history of FC Barcelona: Kubala–Di Stefano.

In fact, while River Plate had given its consent to Di Stefano's transfer to Barcelona, it had made it conditional on Millonarios's agreement. The Colombian club was furious as a result of Busquets's bullying tactics, and because of what it perceived as the player's breach of trust in not paying his debts. The negotiations were complicated even further by Barça's increasingly confused strategy in the affair. Trias Fargas, who had been appointed with the assurance that he would be able to pay all that he felt was necessary to secure Di Stefano, now began to find his negotiation undermined by Barça's president, Marti Carreto, who doggedly rejected a figure whenever it was agreed between the lawyer and the Colombians. Trias Fargas at one point thought he had the deal in the bag, when Millonarios president Alfonso Senior backed down from his demand for a transfer fee of $40,000 and seemed poised to accept a revised offer from Trias Fargas, under which FC Barcelona would pay closer to its original offer of $10,000, in addition to assuming Di Stefano's debts and agreeing to play a match against Millonarios, the proceeds of which would go to the Colombians. Again Marti Carreto intervened, insisting that $10,000 was the total amount he was prepared to pay, with no additions or concessions.

Trias Fargas subsequently claimed that Marti Carreto's obstruction-ism could not be attributed solely to unreasonableness or incompe-tence, and implied that the whole negotiation had fallen victim to a conspiracy orchestrated by Real Madrid with the blessing of the government. There was much talk at the time about the Barça manage-ment's being infiltrated 'at the highest level', and Marti Carreto's having felt pressurised by telephone threats and the intimidation of a private detective firm.

No firm evidence was ever produced to support any of this. How-ever, what is not in doubt is the speed with which Real Madrid moved to exploit the divisions and inconsistencies in its rival's negotiating strategy, making its own approach to Millonarios. It is also known that the government from the outset took a dim view of the prospect of Kubala and Di Stefano playing together for Barça rather than for Real Madrid – a view that translated itself into an increasingly public role in the affair: when the two clubs were still negotiating in parallel with Millonarios, the Spanish Football Federation introduced a new law banning the acquisition of foreign players, a move deliberately aimed at effectively giving the government a role as broker. Barça and Real Madrid were told that Di Stefano would be excluded from the ban, but only so long as the two clubs agreed to the Federation's proposal that Barcelona abandon its efforts to clinch the player for itself and instead agree to share him with Real Madrid. Under the deal, Real Madrid would have Di Stefano in the seasons 1953–4 and 1956–7, while FC Barcelona would have him in the seasons 1954–5 and 1957–8, at the end of which all the parties would try and reach a fresh agreement as to what to do with the player in the medium to long term.

Marti Carreto and his counterpart at Real Madrid, Santiago Bernabéu, signed the deal on 15th September 1953. A week later, Marti Carreto resigned, such was the storm created by the deal with his own management and among Barça supporters. In his resignation letter, the outgoing Barça president claimed that he had always had the club's best 'sporting and financial' interests in mind, and that he had effectively been left with no other option by the Federation. The interim management board that succeeded him, pending the election of his successor, opted to scrap the deal altogether, surrendering Di Stefano to Real Madrid in return for a compensation payment of 4.4 million pesetas. The prevalent view within Barcelona was that Marti Carreto had at best fallen victim to a cynical ploy by Madrid to control and manipulate Barça's ambition, at worst secretly collaborated with it.

Certainly, the whole episode was an appalling humiliation, showing Barcelona completely outmanoeuvred in its effort to secure a major international star without help from the government. With the evidence of hindsight, however, one can also see how in the end Barcelona may have fallen victim to its own pride in deciding to pull out of the deal altogether, rather than opt for the Solomonian agreement put forward by the Spanish Federation. While the motive for the latter may have been to ensure that Real Madrid could get what it had failed to secure through direct negotiation with Millonarios, it nevertheless also guaranteed that Barcelona would have something of Di Stefano too. As things turned out, they lost him completely, and Barça supporters to this day have been left with the pain of comparing the dream of what might have been with what actually happened.

In practice the illusion had an extension of ninety minutes, when, on

26th January 1955, Di Stefano played alongside Kubala wearing the Barça colours. The occasion was a charity match on behalf of Barcelona's School of Journalism, against the Italian team Bologna and played in Barça's Les Corts stadium. The *cules* hovered in dreamland for ninety minutes that day watching the two players – their youthful speed and strength still intact and as complementary on the pitch as they were friendly off it – deliver an unprecedented exhibition of football skill and imagination. The Barça team beat Bologna 6–1.

Many years later, a sense of what might have been, thanks to these two players, and what was lost through no fault of their own but because of officials – some of whom had never kicked a ball in their lives – was conveyed to me by Kubala. It was the day I watched him stumbling through the dust in a veterans' game, alongside colleagues who even in their dreams could never have played like Di Stefano, that the old Hungarian war-horse told me, 'The Di Stefano transfer was a bit of a disaster compared with mine as far as Barça was concerned. Alfredo came to Spain with some of the same problems that I had – Real Madrid wanted him, he didn't have Spanish nationality, he'd left Colombia without authorisation – but things turned out differently. I think the problem was that there were certain people in Barça who didn't show enough patience to resolve the situation. All I know is that I personally really wanted Alfredo to join our team; he was a friend, but much more than that: the rare occasions when Alfredo and I played together there was a real chemistry, a fantastic understanding between us.

'The trick with Alfredo was that you had to give him complete freedom of movement and a colleague who knew how to back him up. We'd take turns going forward, but always supporting each other. We were constantly changing positions. This meant that we were always with the ball, and always creating problems for our adversaries, particularly when they tried to mark us. Alfredo and I were always two against one, and that made the game seem easy . . . Of course I usually had Alfredo playing against me, and he was always a dangerous adversary, and an extraordinary player, quite unlike any other. He had speed, technique, and a great vision. He also knew how to sacrifice himself for the good of the team. He was always a great example to the younger players.'

Di Stefano was destined to play a great many more games as Kubala's adversary than as his team-mate. And so, because of circumstances beyond their control, these two players came to personify one more stage in the history of enmity between Real Madrid and Barça, teams that for political and social reasons came to represent more than just football clubs to each other, in a tragic extension of their sporting rivalry.

Kubala's star was at its zenith when Di Stefano's began to create Real Madrid's own very special firmament. Thanks to Kubala, Barça had won the League championship in the 1950–1 season and the 'triple' – League, Spanish and the Copa Latina – in 1951–2, making a real mark in Europe. But it was Barça's League championship win in the 1952–3 season that earned Kubala virtual mystical status. He helped the team win it after a miraculous recovery from tuberculosis which some doctors had predicted would end his career as a footballer for ever. The day of his 'reappearance' in Las Corts, supporters were treated to a festival of goals thanks to Laszi's inspiration: 8–0 against Zaragoza. As a newspaper report noted at the time, 'When Kubala was diagnosed with his illness, there was general anxiety, comparable only to what Catalans feel when they put the price of bread up. When he recovered, people were so happy that it seemed as if everyone had got a sudden wage rise.'

The *cules* loved him for it, shouting '*Hala, hala, Kubala!*' in his honour, and making the Las Corts stadium seem too small for the mass passion he generated. It was because of Kubala that the club hatched its plans to build a bigger stadium than Real Madrid's – the Camp Nou. Pepe Samitier, the Barça player who achieved heroic status in the 1920s and the man who was instrumental in securing FIFA's critical authorisation of Barça's contract with Kubala, said of him during those days of glory, 'Kubala has been the great pillar which has sustained the growth of support for football in Catalonia. People sometimes ask me if there is a comparison to be made between Kubala and Di Stefano. I will simply say that no one like these two players has until now produced football of such beauty and entertainment. Thanks to Kubala, we have a team that is technically much improved. To my generation, Kubala was the best of all Barça players. Before his arrival a lot of good football was played in Barcelona, but he was the first to give it real class. Thanks to him, football moved from being an operetta to become an opera.'

It was not just Kubala's footballing skills that won the respect of his fellow players and endeared him to the *cules*, but also his personality. He had an extraordinary capacity to take punishment and go on playing – to deal with pain, in other words, as has been noted in an earlier chapter. His strength and sheer will-power ensured a usually prompt recovery from his drinking bouts, which he himself never considered a sign of personal weakness but part of the bonding process with the rest of the team. In the early years, management chose to turn a convenient blind eye – although not always. In December 1955, two days before a European Fairs Cup tie between Barcelona and Copenhagen, Kubala led a group of team-mates away from the club's training camp and on a drinking spree that ended in a brothel in the city's notorious red-light district, the Barri Xino. Several of the players were suspended, while Kubala temporarily lost the captaincy of the team. It later emerged that the club management had become so worried about his occasional acts of wildness that they had hired a private detective agency to monitor his private life.

Apart from his periodical hard drinking, however, there was not much else they could blame Laszi for, other than a kind of incurable romanticism that seemed so refreshingly to contrast with the repressive atmosphere and imposed austerity of the early period of the Franco regime. He was not fickle with money, but always maintained a healthy irreverence towards it, never allowing himself to be spoilt by it. He earned more than any other member of the team, but he shared with others as much as he spent on himself. Once someone stole 200,000 pesetas from his car. 'Don't worry about it,' he told the police. 'All I hope is that the money does the person who's taken it a favour.'

Years later the Catalan musician Serrat would pen his poem, recalling 'those times'. He sang about the moments of magic offered by Kubala and the other components of Barça's front five – Basora, César, Moreno and Manchon – who flourished thanks to his inspiration and team spirit, in contrast to the feelings of despair, isolation and underlying resistance that many Catalans experienced under Franco.

Nostalgia often helps to soften the set-backs of the past, and through

Serrat's image of liberation through football – as indeed his portrayal of Kubala as Catalan gladiator, suffering the blows and insults of his detractors, which the club's official historians have emphasised – Barça has tried to compensate for the reality of defeat and failure that befell it following the Di Stefano transfer controversy. In its first season with the Argentinian player, Real Madrid won the League for the first time in twenty-one years, a title it defended with honour the following year. It was the start of an extraordinary record of success lasting two decades, which included five successive European Cup victories, establishing the men in white as the undisputed stars of international football. Beyond Catalonia, the period is considered unequivocally to have been the Golden Age of Spanish football. Many Catalans, however, to this day look back on it as an age of trickery, when the cards were unfairly stacked against Barça, a team that in different historical circumstances would have achieved better results than the chequered record of the '50s and '60s: the League in 1952–3, 1958–9 and 1959–60; the Spanish Cup in 1953 and 1957; and two European Fairs Cups, in 1958 and 1960.

A typical if partisan view of the period that followed Di Stefano's arrival in Madrid is expressed in the massive official history of Barça written by a member of the current management board, Jaume Sobreques. 'Barça supporters are conscious of various realities,' he comments, 'among them the fact that Real Madrid was the favoured club of the regime and therefore had political backing and with it the support of the referees. There was no doubt at all that to win a championship Barça always had to catch up with the generous number of points which were fixed beforehand in Real Madrid's favour. The facts confirmed this theory.'

Around the anniversary of his military uprising, 18th July, Franco made a habit of drawing up an honours list of those deserving medals for being good and patriotic Spaniards. On that date in 1955, the Caudillo did not hesitate in giving all the Real Madrid players the Imperial Order of the Yoke and Arrows – the symbols of his movement. The medals were given officially in recognition of Real Madrid's victory in the Copa Latina. No such honour, of course, had been given to Barça when it won the European tournament in the glorious season of the 'three cups'. The following season, in recognition of Real

Madrid's entry into the more ambitious European Cup, the club was given the Gold Medal of the City by the regime, and its president, Santiago Bernabéu, the Grand Cross of Civil Merit. Thus was Bernabéu able to add to his collection of military decorations won for helping to 'reconquer' Catalonia during the Civil War.

Real Madrid's international projection coincided with an easing of Spain's diplomatic and commercial isolation, the United States in particular leading the West's reconciliation with Franco, who in turn agreed to the placing of US military bases on Spanish soil. As a result, Real Madrid came to be viewed by the Francoiste regime as an important instrument for building diplomatic bridges. In this it had the backing of FIFA and UEFA, world football's governing bodies, whose commercial interest lay in bringing about the global expansion of the game, depoliticising it whenever politics got in the way. An early example of this strategy was the decision to allow Partizan of Belgrade to play Real Madrid in 1955 even though at the time there were no formal diplomatic links between Spain and the then Communist-dominated Yugoslavia. In the words of Fernando Maria de Castiella, who served as Foreign Minister under Franco, 'Real Madrid is a style of sportsmanship. It is the best embassy we have ever had.'

It was a role that Real Madrid had thrust upon it rather than one it openly sought. If anything, there were occasions when the players wished that no such identification with the regime existed, as when on certain European Cup ties away from home they found themselves shouted at by demonstrations – not of opposing fans, but of local left-wing militants, some of whom were not remotely interested in Real Madrid's value as a football team. Di Stefano – a nationalised Spaniard but an Argentinian born and bred, who has never lost touch with his roots in the shanty neighbourhood of Buenos Aires – to this day resents the extent to which he and other players of his generation were exploited as political pawns. 'I am a footballer; I am not interested in talking about politics, particularly when people ask me about the games we played against Barcelona,' he told me.

And yet what is undoubtedly true is that Di Stefano and his Real Madrid colleagues moved around Spain with rather fewer problems than the Barça players. While Di Stefano was projected as a national hero, Kubala was jeered at on some of his club's away games by local fans who regarded Barça as a traitor to the national cause. 'Foreigner, go back to your country! We don't want players made by Communism!' and 'Ladislao, you're a crank!' were among the comments made by fans who conveniently overlooked the fact that Real Madrid's glory years were brought about in large part by foreigners, not by Castilians – Di Stefano from Argentina, Puskas of Hungary (the same country as Kubala), Kopa of France, Canario of Brazil and Santamaria of Uruguay. Barça was not helped by the bias of the press. Outside Catalonia this was overwhelmingly antagonistic. But even among local Barcelona journalists, there was a strong contingent who wrote anti-Barça pieces, proudly displaying on their lapels the Franco military insignias from when they had fought for him in the Civil War or done their military service.

Another advantage that Real Madrid had during those years was television. Gradually introduced during the 1950s, it was completely controlled by the regime, with its coverage throughout the country selected and planned from the Spanish capital. Real Madrid was given a great deal more air time nationally than any other Spanish team, with the TV commentators specially picked for their rabid nationalism. As Charly Rexach, one of the most popular players in Barça history, told me, 'Today you can go to any town or city of Spain and meet people who support Barça. But in those days you belonged to the team of the town or city you lived in or else you supported Real Madrid. That was because people identify with the football team they can see, and Real Madrid was the team that was most visible in Franco's Spain. Barça was very visible in its own stadium, but only Real Madrid was promoted as Spain's club.'

But TV contributed to a less than even playing field in an even more critical sense. The primitive way in which the games of the 1950s and 1960s were filmed – without the combination of multi-camera, zoom, and video play-back that has become such an essential part of the modern game – meant that fouls were never re-examined. It was therefore possible for a referee to make a mistake and not face an extended public reprimand. This was a huge potential advantage to Real Madrid, when the referees were deliberately biased in the club's favour or against Barça.

The fact that, despite the absence of modern TV at the time, a number of dubious if not deliberately unjustified referee decisions were noted by live witnesses, and have been recorded and passed down through generations as a key part of Barça official history, is in itself testimony of the club's enduring sense of collective identity. For the bent Spanish referees are, together with Kubala and the hidden traitors of the Di Stefano negotiations, the key *dramatis personae* in the tragedy of Barça's fall from greatness.

Of a long list of questionable decisions through the years, the majority occurred in matches involving Barça and Real Madrid, although Barça saw itself as a potential victim of discrimination in any game played away from its own stadium. In a League match played between the two main rivals on 13th November 1955, Barça dominated the game, although each side conceded a goal. In the first minute of injury time at the end of the second half, Real Madrid's right full back, Marquitos, had a winning goal allowed despite – according to the Catalan witnesses present – being clearly offside and going on to push the Barça goalkeeper to one side as he confronted him.

Less than a month later it was Athletic Bilbao, the third main contender for the League title, that was given a helping hand in a match against Barça, in more ways than one. The match was a crucial one: Bilbao was at the top of the table, leading Barça by just one point. The half-time score was 1–0 in Barça's favour. Ten seconds into the second half, the club's newly acquired Uruguayan from Millonarios, Villaverde, broke through the Bilbao midfield and, with metres to go, dribbled past a final defender – Garay – and the goalkeeper, Carmelo. Then Garay turned and threw himself at Villaverde's running feet, effectively tackling him to the ground, and deflecting the ball. The referee whistled a goal kick! Utterly demoralised by the decision, Barça went on to lose the match 2–1. Bilbao clinched the title a few days later, frustrating Barça's dream of competing in Europe once again.

On the few occasions when a referee was forced to take a decision more sympathetic towards Barça – usually on the club's home territory and amidst huge protests from the local crowd – a punitive measure would normally follow the match, again with a bias against the Catalans. Such was the case during a memorable early encounter between Barça and Real Madrid led by, respectively, Kubala and

Di Stefano. On 21st February 1954, the two teams played the second of their seasonal matches. In an earlier round, Di Stefano had marked his first match against Barça in the Bernabéu with a brilliantly versatile performance, leading his team to a 5–0 victory. But at Les Corts, Barça hit back with a vengeance, scoring five goals after Di Stefano had scored one in the opening minutes of the first half. The game deteriorated after a scuffle involving Kubala and several Madrid players had developed into an assault by the latter on the referee. Despite the stadium calling repeatedly for the Madrid players to be sent off, they were allowed to play on, together with Kubala.

Once the game was over, Kubala escaped with only the usual critical report from the Madrid press – seemingly lacking firm evidence of any wrongdoing. But the Spanish football authorities had their way anyway. Barça was fined 10,000 pesetas; one of the Barça players was suspended for four games; and another five of his colleagues received further individual fines. Real Madrid as a club was left untouched, with just two of its players receiving minimal fines.

And yet it is one referee's decision, more than any others, that marks a watershed in Barça's history: that taken on 6th June 1970 in the Camp Nou by the young Basque-born Emilio Guruceta. The occasion was the second leg of a quarter-final Spanish Cup tie between the two big rivals, which had taken on even more importance than usual because both teams had failed to win the League. The first leg had resulted in a 2–0 victory for Real Madrid – with one of the goals disputed by the Barça fans and even by some of Real's own players.

In the Camp Nou, 100,000 Barça fans receive the visitors for the second leg with a loud and sustained whistle. After a shaky start, Barça takes the lead just before the end of the first half with a goal scored by Rexach. In the sixth minute of the second half, Barça seems well on its way to its second when the fateful decision is made. Guruceta awards a penalty to Real Madrid after one of its players, Velazquez, is brought down by the Barça defender Rife. Guruceta is trailing well behind the Madrid attack and positioned thirty-five metres from the spot where Velazquez falls when he blows the whistle. The stadium, which claims to have seen what has happened only too clearly, erupts in protest. The entire Barça team, led by the goalkeeper, Reina, insists through a persistent cacophony of sound that Velazquez was tackled and fell more than three metres outside the penalty box. Some of the fans begin to throw cushions towards the pitch.

When Guruceta, backed by his linesmen, ignores the protests, some of the Barça players, led by Rexach, Rife, Terres and Reina, walk off the pitch – on to which cushions are now raining down. They are ordered to return by their coach, the Englishman Vic Buckingham. Near him the police presence is being reinforced, with officers looking towards the terraces with increasing apprehension. After the penalty has been successfully scored by Amancio, Guruceta sends off the Barça player Eladio for applauding the goal ironically and telling Guruceta to his face, 'You're a Madrid stooge, haven't you got any shame?' It is nothing compared with the insults being shouted by the fans behind and on either side of the goal. 'You can stuff the Cup up your ass,' one shouts. 'Sons of bitches,' larger groups chorus.

Play resumes, but only as long as the ball stays in play. When the ball is kicked into the terraces, the fans hang on to it. Among those watching the game is Manuel Vazquez Montalban, the Catalan author, *cule* and member of the PSUC, the local Communist Party. Montalban will turn what happens next into literature. He will write it up in a courageous essay for the magazine *Triunfo*, itself a victim of censorship during the Franco years.

'. . . Guruceta continually stops play and orders the latest wave of cushions to be removed. It becomes increasingly difficult to do so. Twenty, thirty thousand cushions fill the night with strange colours, and behind them the first of the fans begin to advance towards the pitch. Mr Guruceta is beginning to look worried. No one has touched him, but now that some 5,000 fans are surrounding him, someone must have said something to him because suddenly he is running against the stop-watch and he is running as fast as Juan Carlos used to in a good match, not caring how much of the pitch he has to cover or about the steps into the changing room. Now the pitch belongs to the people, five, six, ten thousand people parading with their Barça flags, shouting the name of the club, marching towards the presidential box. The spectacle is bigger than any match you've ever seen – the colours of summer, the enthusiasm of countless bodies, the green turf, the cushions like so many poppies, the dark blue night, fireworks, Barça flags, and an intimate, total, collective satisfaction, so much so that

even the middle classes with their cigars are shouting at last, at last . . .
Today is a *fiesta*. You can breathe freedom, and the night has the most
favourable of colours. The public shout, clap, sing, "Barça, Barça,
Barça" . . . and then suddenly some secret bugle must have warned
that things are going to change. The rectangle is plunged into darkness
and there follow other noises, other shouts . . . The colours have
changed. The first of the fires appear . . . the straw of the slashed
cushions is flaming, setting fire to the advertising boards . . . The cries
have turned bitter . . . The public disperses . . . But strange angers have
been born . . . A group of fans pass by me, shouting, "Barça, Barça,
Barça . . ." '

The unprecedented pitch invasion had taken place five minutes
before full time, with the two teams level and Barça on its way out
of the Cup, the simmering frustration of the *cules* boiling over. The
more militant among them later engaged in a running battle within the
Camp Nou and in the nearby avenues, with the riot police using the
extremely brutal tactics developed through the years of dictatorship.
Dozens of fans were beaten indiscriminately, some seriously injured,
amidst cries of '*Policía asesina!*'

The 'Guruceta case' was charged with symbolism, a liberation after
a long period of self-restraint, a time when Barça seemed to assume
once again its political mandate on behalf of a repressed Catalonia.
What is remarkable is not that the explosion took place but that it was
so long in coming. One explanation is that by 1970, Barça was being
run by a management team, part of which strongly identified with the
growing calls for democratic rule and political autonomy for Catalonia.

Indeed, it was a sense that the protest expressed a majority feeling
among the fans that forced the Barça president, Agustin Montal, to
adopt a tough stance over the whole affair, insisting on his club's right
to be treated with equanimity and launching an unprecedented attack
on the alleged corruption of the Spanish football authorities. In a
statement to the media, in the aftermath of the match, Montal
declared, 'For too long the College of Referees, the Spanish Federation
and all the other official bodies have allowed things to happen that
should never have been allowed in our football stadiums . . . The
members and supporters of FC Barcelona felt profoundly hurt and

insulted by the shameful and unjust role played by Mr Guruceta. One should on no account decree the punishment of 100,000 spectators for what occurred . . .'

Such language had never been used by any of Montal's predecessors during the Franco regime. On the contrary, Franco had counted on the collaboration of a succession of Barça boards and officials close to them, together with the fear of repression that still paralysed many Catalans in the early years, to maintain his grip on Spanish football. Enrique Llaudet, president of FC Barcelona from 1961 to 1968, as has been seen in a previous chapter is blunt about his Francoism. Others were as close to the regime, but certainly less honest. Any objective examination of the Di Stefano affair leaves a serious question mark as to whether the president at the time, Enric Marti, really had the interests of his club at heart, or whether, as Trias Fargas suggests, he was playing to another master's tune. Between Marti and Llaudet came Francesc Miró-Sans, president from 1953 to 1961. One of his first acts on taking office was to send a personal telegram to Franco's chief of staff with the words, 'On taking the office of president of Football Club Barcelona I would like to convey to His Excellency the Generalissimo my profound support and respect.'

I have touched already on the fact that one of Franco's favourite players was Barça's Pepe Samitier. The friendship between the two continued throughout the 1950s when Samitier was Barça's chief scout and technical secretary, a position that helped him maintain an influence within the club that, in parallel with the manager/trainer's, extended from the board of management through to the players. El Sami's playing days achieved legendary status. He helped make Catalan football popular. To this day he has never been held accountable for his Francoism by the Barça faithful, perhaps because to denounce him would be like denying a part of themselves.

There is no doubt, however, that Franco considered Samitier not just a friend but a political ally within Barça, and that he exploited the friendship to counter the suggestion that he was by nature and principle biased against the football of Catalonia. On the few occasions Franco held a personal audience with the Barça board, he insisted that Pepe Samitier be present. Samitier himself stayed on at Barça as long as his own influence was not challenged within the club. When it was, in

1959, he had no moral qualms about transferring his services as scout and technical secretary to Real Madrid, as he had earlier done as a player.

In Franco's Madrid, Samitier felt as much at home as he had been in Barcelona. He maintained a broad range of friendships within the permitted establishment, from liberals such as my maternal grand-father, Gregorio Marañón, to General Muñoz Grandes, a man of far less human qualities. Having played football as a young man (before abandoning it because of a broken leg), Marañón never shared the disdain for the sport evinced by other Spanish intellectuals like Ortega and Unamuno. And politically he was a great deal more sympathetic towards Catalans than Muñoz Grandes. The General had helped Franco's assault on Catalonia before leading the Francoiste Division Azul (Blue Division) on the Russian front in support of Hitler, for which he was decorated by the Führer with the Iron Cross, and rewarded by his own Caudillo with the Ministry of War. Muñoz Grandes's only real interest in FC Barcelona was the fact that some of those who had fought with him in the Division Azul had declared themselves supporters of the club. It was through Santiago Bernabéu, himself a veteran of the assault on Catalonia, that Samitier appears to have been introduced to Muñoz Grandes. Many years later, Samitier's widow, Tina, told me this about the first meeting she had with the General at his offices in the Ministry of War:

'It was during a trip that I made to Madrid before getting married. I was twenty-two years old and Pepe was technical secretary of Real Madrid. Of course he was in love and wildly enthusiastic about us getting married, but the difference in our ages – more than thirty years – meant that a lot of people were scandalised. Most people were against me until they got to know me. Muñoz Grandes was a bit like that. Pepe had told him that he was in love and wanted to marry a very young girl. Muñoz Grandes said he wanted to meet me on such-and-such a day at such-and-such an hour. So the day came and the two of us went to see him at his offices of the Ministry of War. When we entered his room, Muñoz Grandes stood there looking at me and said, "You are very beautiful," and he made me turn round in front of him. It made me feel as if I was an exhibit. The truth was that no one trusted me. Nowadays people just wouldn't treat you like that, I suppose.'

Protests against the regime there were, but they never got as out of the authorities' control as in 1970, perhaps because Franco's strategy when it came to the politics of football was more subtle than the paranoia of many of his opponents made it seem. By allowing Barça to function, he divided and ruled, exploiting the political confusion of the Catalans at a time when football was growing in popularity. His intention was never to prevent Barça from winning titles, for his interest lay in building the national sport on the rivalries of the big teams, not despite them. Bernabéu was his natural home but his political instinct took him on occasions to Las Corts, and later to the Camp Nou, a lion's den that only belatedly recovered its political roar.

Whatever the conspiracies – imagined or real – that pervaded Spanish football during the Franco years, they were not the only explanation for Barça's misfortunes. The fact that Real Madrid during the 1950s produced brilliant football and won titles at home and abroad cannot be put down to a government plot. Although it was clearly given a helping hand on occasions by referees and officials – and to that extent was a product of the times – the team did well because it was made up of players of exceptional talent and skill, capable of taking on and beating the best in Europe. The main components of that golden Real, Di Stefano and Puskas, were, in the words of Keir Radnedge, editor of *World Soccer* magazine, 'creators and finishers, of a standard rarely seen before or since'. But one thinks back too on the strength and ability of defenders like Santamaria and Marquitos, and on the speed, and touch, of the left-winger Gento. If Catalans have found it hard to honour Real Madrid's performance during those years, the reason has less to do with sport than with politics.

It is no less true that Real Madrid's record in title-grabbing during the 1950s and Di Stefano's global reputation have tended to over-shadow the fact that Barça also built up a not unimpressive team, which during the same decade kept itself near the top of the Spanish League, won the Generalissimo's Cup five times, and secured the European Fairs Cup in 1958, crushing the London XI 8–0 over a two-legged final tie played in the Catalan and English capitals. Kubala was undoubtedly the star, a natural goal-scorer who developed to an art form the effortless way in which he kicked a dead ball without a run-up.

Barça also came to have other players of international calibre, such as the goalkeeper Ramallets – the natural heir of the legendary Zamora in terms of his ability to block goals, if lacking Zamora's style; Luis Suárez, a creative inside forward and superb organiser of the game, one of the great 'names' of Spanish football; and Basora, a winger as fine as Gento whenever he hit form. Among the foreigners Barça had were the other great warriors of Hungarian football, Czibor and Kocsis, and the Uruguayan striker Villaverde. 'In football there are engineers and workers; I am the engineer,' Czibor said once, boasting of his own speed and extraordinary control of the ball. Kocsis was called 'the Golden Head' by the *cules* because of the way he used the strength in his neck to head home goals at acrobatic angles. As for Villaverde, he came to Barcelona from Millonarios with the handicap of being proclaimed at the outset Barça's answer to Di Stefano. He never quite lived up to the expectation, but he proved a good team player, contributing with skill and passion to some of his team's better matches.

9

El Salvador

The arrival in the spring of 1958 of Helenio Herrera as Barça's new manager marked the beginning of one of the most dynamic if fleetingly successful periods in the club's history. Herrera temporarily pulled Barça out of the humiliating doldrums it had fallen into when faced with the white avalanche from Madrid. Barça's outgoing manager, a popular former player from the war years, Domingo Balmanya, had been sacked – despite the club's victory in the Fairs Cup – for failing to win the League. Barça had finished seven points behind Real Madrid.

One year earlier, Bobby Charlton had been so struck by the quality of Di Stefano and his Real Madrid team that he had confessed a measure of relief at being left out of the Manchester United team that played against them in the semi-finals of the European Cup. 'I thought, these people just aren't human,' Bobby reflected. 'It's not the sort of game I've been taught.' From the start of his contract, however, the Argentinian-born Herrera showed no such self-doubt. On the contrary, he was possessed of an extraordinary belief not just in his own unique qualities, but in his capacity to use these to bring out the best in a team he considered had the potential to play as well as – if not better than – Real.

Herrera, like the French writer and philosopher Albert Camus, had grown up in French North Africa. Both men developed a philosophy on life through their football. 'I learned that the ball never comes when you expect it to,' wrote Camus. 'That helped me a lot in life, especially in large cities where people don't tend to be what they claim.' Herrera played alongside Arabs, Jews, Frenchmen and Spaniards – an experience he described as a 'school of life'. To Barcelona, he brought a widening horizon.

Of the Barça of the late 1950s, Herrera said, soon after his departure, 'This was the most extraordinary group of players I have ever had to deal with in my career. With such human material I could not possibly argue. All one could do with it was to win every competition in which the team participated. Until now, the triumphs achieved by Real Madrid at home and abroad have intimidated the team. Real Madrid has shown itself the king of entertainment, perfect in almost every way, and intelligently managed. However, Barça has a team that can keep up with the best of clubs.'

During his two-year stint at Barça, Herrera took the team and shook it to its roots. He used his powers of psychology to motivate a team that all too often had stumbled under the burden of its own history, too easily believing that games were won and lost at the bequest of a conspiratorial government, rather than because of the relative strengths of the competing teams. The transformation in the way the team saw itself and confronted the outside world was so quick as to raise suspicions all around the Herrera camp. There was talk of trickery, secret rituals, drugs. Local journalists who couldn't stand Herrera's arrogance and obsession with money dubbed him – among other things – 'the pharmacy cup coach'. They alleged that the team's medical staff had their bags stuffed with every conceivable performance-enhancing substance, during a time when dope-testing in football was still a long way off. Officials and players I have talked to deny this, although this may reflect the absolute loyalty that Herrera secured rather than the complete truth as taken by the manager to his grave.

One of the Barça players successfully groomed through his youth by Herrera was the Spanish international Fuste, who recalls, 'Herrera was a really nice guy and also a manager who knew how to train. He was serious at his job but had a good sense of humour, and knew how to get the best out of his players. All that stuff about him giving us all drugs is all lies. What he was was a good psychologist, which is what a coach needs to be if he is to handle a team properly. He knew how to make the best use of the resources he had at his command.'

Herrera believed that those who suspected drugs did so because they did not have the imagination or scope of experience that would have allowed them to explain his approach to the game. Certainly Herrera's football of motivation was nothing if not eccentric. They called him 'the Magician' because his words and actions were those known to mothers and priests and officers, but never witnessed until that time anywhere near the football pitch. His press conferences had the intensity and following of religious events, his unwavering opinions about players and opponents designed to lead his men over the parapet.

Herrera tended to be disdainful of other managers for their failure to engage with their players and to bring about a real change in their attitude to the game. 'Too many managers limit their role to little taps on the players' shoulders as they are about to go on to the pitch, or making the occasional patriotic speech, which, while maybe warming up the hearts of some players, only serves to cool the muscles of the whole team.' His pre-match warm-ups, like his training sessions, became so legendary that people – in their thousands – paid to see them, or as much of them as they were allowed.

As the players change in the dressing room, cups of tea are passed round. The tea does not taste like English tea, but of strange spices and herbs. The players have been encouraged to believe that this witches' brew, produced from some South American or Arabian potion only Herrera knows about, will give them peace of mind and strength of spirit. Fifteen minutes before the big game, Herrera gathers his players around him in a circle. Throwing the ball at each in turn he screams a question, looking at every player directly in the eyes: 'What do you think of this match? How are we going to play? Why are we going to win?' The questions follow one after the other, round the circle, with increasing passion, until manager and players have worked up a collective sweat, as if they are doing a tribal war dance. At a signal from Herrera, the players break away, sprint, then rejoin the circle, as though drawn by some hidden force, each with his arm round the next player, declaring to Herrera, to themselves, to the huge stadium that awaits them, 'We are going to win! We are going to do it together!' It is a public commitment that each makes, as it is when they finally gather around their manager one last time, each touching with one hand the football he holds, swearing nothing less than victory . . .

From early on Herrera claimed to be able to look into the heads and hearts of each of his players, and to be able to turn this to the team's best advantage. He encouraged superstition as long as he could control it, nowhere more so than in the case of Luisito Suárez – the player he considered the 'legitimate heir' of Di Stefano. One of several 'tricks', as

Herrera put it, that he liked to encourage while at Barça, in order to keep morale high and to influence events favourably, was this: 'I knew that Luisito was ferociously convinced that a glass of wine, when spilt during a meal, meant an announcement that he would score a goal. Naturally I was not going to wait passively for this to occur, so whenever he wasn't looking I would give the glass a good tap and exclaim in a loud voice so that he could hear me, "What a pity we've ruined the tablecloth!" Luisito would immediately run up, dip his finger in the spilt wine, and then with it touch first his forehead, then the tip of his shoe . . .'

Despite his eccentric mind games, Herrera also had a genuine knowledge of the game; he was certainly more experienced and visionary than any of his predecessors at Barça, and on a level with some of his 'star' successors. It was while at Barça that he experimented with some innovative attacking football, using inside forwards at wing-half to turn some of the easier matches into goal sprees. Herrera never saw any contradiction between the football he played at Barcelona and the *catenaccio*, a system whereby the sweeper stays behind the defence, with the rest of the team marking man to man and letting the opposition attack. In his view, the *catenaccio* got a bad reputation as being synonymous with a defensive style of football only because it was misused by others. In his system, he always insisted, while the centre-backs in front of the sweeper were markers, the fullbacks had to attack.

At Barça, Herrera professed an intimate knowledge of his players' qualities, and weaknesses, and forged his bold tactics around this perception. He was generous with the *cantera* (the youth system), those players whose adolescence had been spent learning at Barça, players such as Olivella, Gensana, Gràcia, Verges and Tejada. 'We owe them many of our victories; they played not just with class but with absolute dedication to the club colours,' recalled Herrera in his memoirs, *Mia Vita*. His regular line-up included players like Martinez, 'a man of iron, a real tank – the ideal man to disturb the defence with the added virtue of knowing how to do the things his adversary least expected . . . His main defect was his tendency to get fat. That was partly psychological, partly the fault of his trainer.' Of another leading Barça player, Evaristo, the analysis was that he was 'unsuitable for the captaincy, but nevertheless possessing a varied and irresistible dribbling technique'. Herrera added, 'He was also incomparably quick in getting a vision of the game and how it would pan out, as well as clever and calm and possessing a kick of aggressive precision.'

Herrera was similarly full of praise for the two recent foreign arrivals, the Hungarians Kocsis and Czibor. In Kocsis, 'the Golden Head', Herrera discovered a player not only talented with his head, but with a sure touch and strength of foot also; in Czibor, pure speed on and off the ball, and a similar goal-scoring capacity. Only on one point did he disagree with Czibor: while the latter proudly proclaimed himself 'an engineer among workers', Herrera insisted that in his philosophy of football there were no hierarchies, only one for all, all for one. It was competitive spirit, strength and speed, together with technique, that constituted the main ingredients of the ideal team. 'You in England,' he pontificated to gob-smacked English journalists at Birmingham Airport in 1960, 'are playing now in the style we Continentals used so many years ago, with much physical strength, but no method, no technique.' Barça had just beaten Wolverhampton Wanderers 5–2 in the European Cup.

When thirty years later, shortly before he died, he was visited at his Venice *palazzo* by the writer Simon Kuper and was asked to talk about his time at Barça, Herrera commented that he had played his 'tricky foreigners in attack' – Kocsis, Villaverde, Czibor and so on – while basing his defence on a local brew, 'my big Catalans' – Ramallets, Olivella, Rodri, Gràcia, Segarra, Gensana. 'To the Catalans,' Herrera told Kuper, 'I talked "Colours of Catalonia, play for your nation," and to the foreigners I talked money . . . I talked about their wives and kids. You have twenty-five players, you don't say the same thing to everyone.' What were the differences between the nationalities? Kuper persisted. ' "Hungarians are more reserved," he [Herrera] hunched his shoulders and screwed up his face in imitation, "so I mixed them, not Czibor and Kocsis alone in one room. I wanted all to be the same, I wanted friendship. That is why we trained together, why we ate together . . ." '

Nothing perhaps demonstrates Herrera's single-mindedness more than his decision to exclude from his grand design a player who had become one of Barça's great idols, Ladislao Kubala. According to Herrera's own version of events, he had every intention of keeping Kubala as a key component of the team when he first took on the job as

Barcelona, 1901. Arthur Witty stands on the left in the back row;
an Gamper, the club founder, sits cross-legged holding the ball.

Barcelona, 1927: Catalan champions.

Pepe Samitier: the 'Lobster Man' and 1920s star.

Carlos Gardel:
tango singer and Barça fan.

sep Sunyol *(centre)*: member of Catalan parliament and President of FC
rcelona until his execution in 1936 by Francoist forces.

trick O'Connell *(centre, with hat)*: Barça manager, 1935–37.

Revolution: anarchists in Barcelona during the Spanish Civil War.

Air raid damage in Barcelona during the Spanish Civil War.

Francoist forces 'liberate' Barcelona.

Ladislao Kubala in action.

The politics of football: Franco and his wife, Doña Carmen, entertain Real Madrid's Di Stéfano *(far left)*, Barça's Kubala *(second from right)* and Real Madrid's Gento.

Franco presenting the Copa del Generalissimo to Joan Segarra, captain of victorious Barça in 1963, in the Camp Nou: 'Don't forget, this cup is named after me.'

Helenio Herrera: the Magician looks on from the bench.

Josep Lluis Nuñez: elected
President of FC Barcelona
in 1978.

Johan Cruyff: Barça player.

Johan Cruyff: Barça manager

Diego Maradona: sex, drugs and football.

Terry Venables: Barça manager, 1984–87.

Gary Lineker: the Matador.

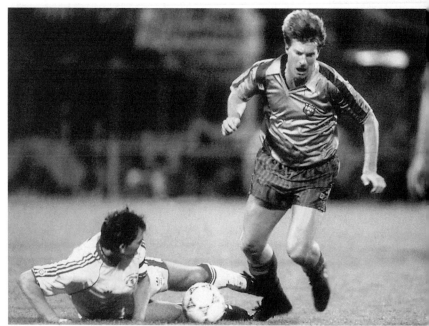

Michael Laudrup, playing for Barça, evades Manchester United's Bryan Robson, 1991.

Barça wins the European Cup, 1992: Koeman celebrates the dream goal.

The European Cup final at Wembley: Zubizarreta, Laudrup and friends celebrate.

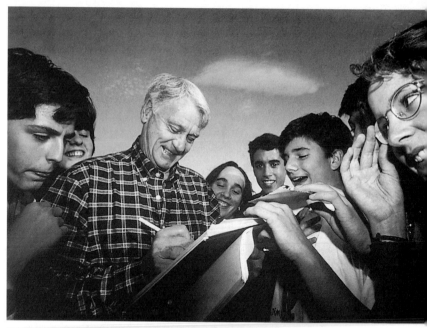

Bobby Robson, Barça manager, enjoying the fans.

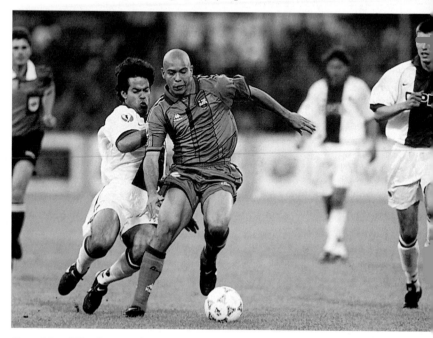

Ronaldo: 'The fastest thing I've ever seen running with the ball.'

Robson, Ronaldo and Jordi Pujol celebrate Barça's European Cup win against Paris St Germain.

Champions' League, Old Trafford: Luis Enrique vs. Ryan Giggs.

Champions' League: fan power.

A football nation.

Champions' League, 1994: 'Pep' Guardiola vs. Nicky Butt.

Rivaldo strikes.

The Camp Nou: a cathedral of the football world.

manager, but then discovered that the Hungarian's drinking bouts affected both his self-discipline and his form.

'Kubala is the greatest player I have ever known,' Herrera declared long after he had left Barcelona, to pursue a glittering career. 'When I trained other teams I always admired and feared him. To have him completely under one's orders was a great advantage, his presence in the team a sure guarantee that its path to winning a title would prove less arduous. That is what I thought in principle. Unfortunately I found myself unable to convince myself that his technique could offset his lack of speed and the loss of continuity in his efforts . . . The crowd who mill around football stadiums are conservative and above all sentimental. I realised that excluding Kubala from the first team was going against the current.'

Even Herrera could not quite stand up to the roar of disapproval from the Camp Nou, and he did occasionally play Kubala when Barça played at home, but some *cules* have never forgiven him for the tactical alliance he formed for a while with the club's authoritarian president, Francesc Miró-Sans – which at the time led to the resignation of seven directors in solidarity with the player. The resignations followed a public statement issued by Miró-Sans in consultation with Herrera in which Kubala was accused of missing training sessions 'without justification', refusing to play because of illness and injury, and of showing a 'lack of spirit of commitment which contrasts with the magnificent unity and comradeship of the rest of the team'. Those angered by the statement considered it a travesty of the truth, given Kubala's long-standing reputation as a man willing and able to make extraordinary sacrifices in order to go on playing. In the darkening climate of intrigue, they saw it simply as a cynical ploy to protect Herrera, and the president who had signed him, Miró-Sans.

Herrera's critics insist that while his arrival as manager of Barça did coincide with a temporary loss of form by the Hungarian, there was nothing failing that could not have been put right had the new manager genuinely wanted him as the star of his team. They point not to Herrera's single-mindedness but to his arrogance based on the belief that there really could be only one star at Barcelona, loved or hated by the *cules*: Helenio Herrera. As one of Kubala's biographers, Juan José Castillo, comments, 'Helenio Herrera – or HH as he was famously known – was a man who knew about football and who knew a lot of its secrets. A good psychologist and star of all the teams he managed. When he came to Barcelona he was not very keen on "Kubalismo" – the veneration of Kubala. It was not that he didn't appreciate Kubala or that he didn't recognise his qualities, but that he saw him as a rival and Herrera always wanted to be the boss. Herrera was a prima donna with all that that entailed – it was something that brought him success, as well as failure.'

It was certainly Herrera's single-mindedness based on a demand for absolute loyalty within the team that was behind the departure from Barça of another idol, Pepe Samitier. The former 'star' player was told that he could no longer stay at the club as technical secretary – a job that over the years had given him considerable power and influence over the management of the team. Samitier went to Real Madrid, convinced that he had become the victim of Herrera's jealousy, and leaving behind a club riddled with internal divisions and intrigue fuelled by one of the most controversial managers in its history. For by the late 1950s Barça was a club struggling to retain a sense of its own identity amidst its management's ambiguous attitude to the regime, and the success of Real Madrid. When Herrera arrived, the club had for several years been submerged in a political and sporting limbo, and had in some ways turned in on itself, looking for others to blame for its own shortcomings.

A symptom of Barça's schizophrenia at the time was the way the popular support for the construction of the Camp Nou had been overtaken by a divisive debate over the amount of money the board was spending and its lack of accountability – a row that was going on when Herrera arrived on the scene, demanding more money not just for the manager but also for the players.

Herrera had flown into Barcelona having narrowly escaped an air crash on an earlier flight to Lisbon where he had been managing the Portuguese team Belenenses – an escape he interpreted as a good omen for his time in the Catalan capital, and which helped him psychologically put up with the extraordinary atmosphere he encountered on arrival.

'It was an unpleasant scene that I found: conflicts and antagonisms between rival groups that seemed to hate each other. There was instability, a lack of solidarity, scepticism . . . The supporters of the team felt alienated by the political ambitions of men who inside and outside the club were fighting each other and making their lives impossible . . . Certain sectors of the media had taken to distracting the public, poisoning it with propaganda which favoured one director against another . . . Envy was the order of the day. I was up against a hard wall of vested interests, intrigue, plots, rumours . . . The public wanted titles and the healthy happiness of success, even if some groups among them were already contaminated by the tendency towards intrigue which is the serious defect of Barcelona . . . I realised immediately that it was necessary to fill one's ears with cotton wool and put on an eye-visor to avoid losing oneself in the labyrinth, and go on along the path I had set myself – the road to victory.'

In his first season at Barcelona, Herrera was confronted by a Real Madrid – still with an impressive cast of players such as Di Stefano, Gento, Puskas, Kopa and Marquitos – that was doggedly resistant to surrendering its status as Spain's best club. The whites won two matches against their old rival at the Bernabéu. The results in isolation could have brought about Herrera's premature downfall, led by those with their knives out from the day of his arrival, had Barça not played so brilliantly elsewhere. It had convincingly beaten Real Madrid 4–0 in the Camp Nou earlier in the season – 'a wonderful day played at a devilish speed which Real Madrid hates because it obliges them to defend themselves, something that champions never like to do', Herrera later commented. He also brought about some spectacular victories against other Spanish teams, including two 3–0 wins over Espanyol and Athletic Bilbao. Barça went on not only to win the League championship, breaking a new record on points achieved, with 96 goals scored and only 26 conceded, but to clinch the double, overpowering Granada in the Bernabéu stadium by 4–1 in the Generalissimo's Cup. The League championship meant that Barça was back in Europe.

In a celebratory supper in Barcelona before over 1,000 carefully selected guests, club president Miró-Sans promised that Barça would behave as champions and dedicated the League Cup to Franco.

Under Herrera, Barça went on to win its second consecutive League title, this time with the traditional 'duel' between it and Real Madrid going to the line. Both teams ended equal on points and goal average, but with Barça showing a higher total of home and away goals. Within two days of the final match of the League championship, the rivals again faced each other, this time in the semi-finals of the European Cup. To reach it, Herrera's team had convincingly beaten CDNA of Bulgaria, Inter Milan and Wolverhampton Wanderers, proving to most foreign commentators that it was once again among the best in Europe.

On the eve of the first leg, to be played at the Bernabéu, Herrera announced that he was backing a bonus-payment claim by his players, arguing that there was a risk that the much better terms being offered by Real Madrid would demoralise his team. But the claim was strongly criticised by Herrera's opponents within the club as a symptom of the financial mismanagement that had overtaken Barça under the Miró-Sans presidency. When Barça lost 3–1 at the Bernabéu, and then 3–1 at the Camp Nou, Miró-Sans hesitated not an instant in sacking Herrera, claiming that by so doing his management was showing itself to be financially sound. Before he left for Italy to manage Inter Milan to national and European glory, Herrera was paraded up the Rambla on the shoulders of his adoring *cules*. Days later, Barça won the European Fairs Cup. Within a year of his departure, Barça had lost the League and the Spanish Cup – and its president Miró-Sans.

Herrera seemed to have cast his magician's spell on his postscript, a vengeful curse, such was Barça's bad fortune. Fate turned against the club in the one competition that was still left open to it, the European Cup. Barça once again faced Real Madrid in an early round, this time beating them 4–3 on aggregate, clinching victory at the Camp Nou with a spectacular diving header by the Brazilian Evaristo. It went on to beat Spartak HK of Prague and Hamburg. The final, however, played against Portugal's Benfica in the Swiss capital Berne on 23rd May 1961, was to be remembered as one of the biggest disappointments in the club's history. Kubala, who had been brought back from the bench following Herrera's departure, remembers it as the saddest day of his life.

In the minutes prior to the game, only Kocsis and Czibor had a premonition of disaster. The last time the two had played at Berne's

Wankdorf stadium was when Hungary was beaten by West Germany
in the 1954 World Cup final. Rain had drenched the players throughout that game. Hungary had taken a two-goal lead in the first eight
minutes, only to end up losing 3–2 after the German keeper Turek had
punched clear a last desperate strike at goal by Czibor.

The Berne match proved unluckier in so many more ways for a
Barça team generally convinced they could finally clinch the holy grail
of European football. Kubala saw what seemed like two certain goals
beat the goalkeeper only to be deflected by the post. Then Czibor let fly
a strong, precise strike only to see it hit the right post, then deflect off
the crossbar, before curving past the goal mouth and round the other
post. The worst nightmare was yet to come when Barça's hugely
experienced keeper, Ramallets, missed an easy save, reminiscent of
a similar blunder committed by the Spanish international ten years
earlier during the World Cup in Brazil. Benfica, without Eusebio, won
3–2, leaving Barça psychologically in tatters.

At the start of the following season, on 30th August 1961, Kubala
played his last game for Barça in an emotionally charged testimonial
against Stade of Reims. Around the Camp Nou there were tears mixed
with applause, as Puskas and Di Stefano put on the local colours in
honour of an opponent they had always respected. The sight of the
three playing together and contributing to a 4–2 win was the fantasy of
every *cule* which circumstances had conspired against for more than a
decade.

Kubala's departure from the club proved a protracted affair. He
stayed on as the director of the youth training school before being
asked by the club president, Enrique Llaudet, to try his hand at
managing the team. The contract was cut short after a season in
which the team failed to recreate the form it had discovered during the
Herrera regime. The presidency claimed to feel the pressure of the fans,
who had once again been denied both the League and the European
titles they so obsessively craved. Kubala felt badly treated, claiming he
had not been given either the time or the resources to develop the team,
and in a fit of pique agreed a controversial contract as a player with
Espanyol, joining Di Stefano. The two veterans played there off and on
for a season, lacking the pace and the commitment to produce more
than occasional moments of brilliance.

Llaudet in his retirement recalls the Kubala years much as an ageing father does his wayward son – with a sense of frustration, mixed with affection: 'Kubala was quite a character. Once I told him to go to Germany to look at a player I was interested in. He had an airline ticket to go at ten o'clock on a Saturday morning. I was in the club getting on with my business when the secretary turned up and said that someone was trying to get me urgently by phone. I picked it up and listened to Kubala's voice. "For fuck's sake," I told him, "do you realise it's midday? Where are you?" "In a village," came back the reply. He was in fact about eighty kilometres from Barcelona and he was ringing to say that he had overslept and missed the plane. "Well, damn you," I said. "Come here and when you arrive come immediately to my office." I remember that when they told me that he'd turned up, I stormed out of my office to look for him. I found him at the end of the corridor on his knees. "Don't get cross with me, I'm sorry, I'm sorry, sorry, sorry," he said, over and over again, promising he would never do it again. "OK, go away," I said. "God knows what I'm going to do with you." You see, I knew that deep down he was a good lad. He was someone who cried only when he felt it.'

Elsewhere, inside and outside the club, it is difficult to find anyone who has a bad word to say about Laszi. They forgive his exploits – with drink, with women – as something that . . . well, that is written about when players become famous. Age has conferred iconic status on him. With the passage of years, what might at the time have seemed scandalous has become less so – the antics of one of the great personalities of the game.

It is only fitting that Di Stefano should have been the person to give him a lasting tribute that takes in his sporting qualities as well as some of his humanity: 'Kubala was, as a player, one of the best there have ever been . . . His game was pure, crystalline, a real joy for the fans. He wasn't just a star on the pitch, but in order to be one he put a lot of work into his training, which he sometimes did on his own, trying to reach a point of perfection. I learned from him in that respect. What I remember is his spirit of comradeship, the loyalty he showed as a friend. The only things I don't forgive him are that he had more success with women than any of us and that when he made films he was a better actor than I was. I guess this is the least important aspect of it. What is important is that he was a footballer who made history.'

Other players who left Barça in the aftermath of Berne included Czibor, Ramallets and Suárez. Suárez was transferred for a record 25 million pesetas to Herrera's Inter Milan. When he returned with the Italians to play a pre-season tournament match against his old team at the Camp Nou, local fans booed every move he made. It was the end of an era at Barça.

The 1960s represented another period of 'crisis', with the fading dream of Herrera's presence giving way to lacklustre performances at home and a receding presence in Europe. Having lost some of its idols, the club seemed unable to secure suitable 'star' replacements in the form of either exceptionally talented players or inspirational managers. The exception was the emergence – a natural consequence of the absence of 'foreigners' – of some good former Barça schoolboys as first-team players. Boys from the *cantera* like Josep Fuste and Charly Rexach as individuals came to be adored by local fans as personifications of the typical 'Catalan player' – unassuming, tough, and utterly dedicated to the colours they wore. But it was no less true that historically the typical 'Catalan player' had been part of a great team when he played alongside a real genius of the game. The essential star, the always hoped-for mythical figure descending on Barcelona to lift it from its melancholy, was absent in the '60s.

Under a new president, Enrique Llaudet, priority was given to balancing the club's books – mainly by securing a good sale on the old Las Corts stadium to help pay for the Camp Nou – and to ensuring more transparent administration of funds after the alleged misappropriation that had taken place in the Miró-Sans regime. Llaudet was not only an unrepentant Francoiste, he was also a hard-nosed businessman who believed that the club should be administered with the presidential single-mindedness his father had displayed when reviving his textile factories after the Civil War. His father it was, after all, who had ordered the young Enrique to spend his honeymoon working in his office, and to think about the family business before his wife's pregnancy. Although he was regarded with affection by some of the players during his time, Llaudet himself later admitted, when I interviewed him, that he grew increasingly weary of the world of football, once he had, as he claimed, taken steps to put the house in financial order.

Llaudet may have 'put the house in order', but at what price? During his presidency, once again Real Madrid laid claim to being the best club in Spain, consistently beating Barça at the top of the League championship. More often than not Barça played like a team without a sense of itself, rudderless and adrift in a sea not of its making. Less than two years after Herrera's departure, one of his successors watched his players virtually hand the Spanish Cup over to one of the country's historically less inspired teams, Elche, in a 4–0 defeat. The Catalan manager, Josep Gonzalvo, quit soon afterwards, declaring before he went, 'Thank God that I've got a few days left as trainer of Barcelona. It's about time they threw us out of the championship and stopped us looking so ridiculous in the stadiums of Spain.'

Under Llaudet, Barça moved from extravagance to austerity not just in purely financial terms but in the one area that most mattered to the fans: the spectacle of good football. For the *cules* had shown before, as they would do again, that they could honour their team even if they lost. But the team had to lose fighting, and with nobility. To lose badly was tantamount to Catalans losing a sense of themselves. Midway through the decade, the mood of the fans was summed up by an end-of-season commentary by the magazine *Destino*: 'The fans are not used to the club's not winning any titles in a season. Barça has gone far in the League and the Cup, but to go far is not the same thing as to triumph. We failed in the European Cup Winners Cup, putting in doubt our status as an international club.'

By the mid-1960s, the disillusionment had given way to long rows of empty seats in the Camp Nou. Hard to measure, but undoubtedly a factor in the alienation felt by some Barça supporters, was the politics of the club – a president who encouraged the use of Spanish at his board meetings and was on the best of terms with Franco, while claiming to have the members' interests most at heart by making sure that the club they theoretically owned could pay for itself without excessive borrowing. If not alienated, there must have been *cules* who were at the very least confused about where the club was coming from and where it was going.

Hopes were temporarily raised when Barça won the European Fairs Cup of 1965–6, beating Zaragoza 5–2 on aggregate in September 1966, only to be immediately dashed when it conceded the title in the same year. It lost in an early tie against the Scottish champions, Dundee United, before Dynamo Zagreb took the crown, beating Leeds in the final.

Two years later, and months after Llaudet had been replaced by a 'transitional' president, Narcis de Carreras, who had more inspiring credentials as a democrat and a Catalanist, Barça beat Real Madrid 1–0 in the final of the Spanish Cup in the Bernabéu. The Catalans played well, dominating the game from the outset even though the goal was scored by one of Real's own players!

When the final whistle was blown, the wife of Franco's Minister of State General Camilo Alonso Vega (nicknamed Don Camulo by some Barça supporters) turned to Real Madrid's president, Santiago Bernabéu, and sighed loudly, 'Santiago, we've lost, what a pity.' General Vega – a great admirer, like Franco, of the legendary Pepe Samitier – insisted, for the sake of diplomacy, that his wife also direct some words to the enemy. Turning to Carreras, the Barça president, she said, 'I congratulate you. After all, Barcelona is also Spanish.' The patronising assumption that the Catalan capital was Spanish without a right to its own autonomous existence left Carreras barely containing his anger. 'You must be joking,' he whispered just out of her earshot. The diplomatic smiles were as stiff as knives. Beyond, above and below, the Real Madrid fans delivered their response to the 'fucking separatists' who had robbed them of the title. They threw hundreds of half-drunk and empty bottles on to the pitch. This demonstration of local air power left the Barça team fuelled by a rediscovered defiance of the enemy and, miraculously, unscathed.

The Cup, however, was the Generalissimo's Cup, and was presented to the Barça team by the Generalissimo himself. Franco managed to hide whatever his true feelings were with the dexterity of a wily old fox. Photographs of the occasion show a smile, only marginally forced. It couldn't have been easy for the dictator, handing his cup to that team, amidst the bottles and the whistles of his most loyal supporters. Yet by then the regime's obsession with Real Madrid was not quite what it had been a decade earlier. During the 1960s, the impact of Real Madrid in Europe had faded almost as much as Barça's. The year after Real Madrid were beaten by Barça in the semi-finals of the European Cup, they in turn lost to Benfica in the final, effectively ending an unprecedented run of success in the tournament. In the mid-1960s, it was Inter Milan – coached by the same Herrera who had been sacked by Barça – that took triumphal centre stage, winning the crown in two consecutive years. Real returned to reclaim their crown in 1966, beating Partisan Belgrade in Brussels 2–1, without Di Stefano or Puskas. The club's sixth triumph still stands as a record, which Barça to this day has equalled only in its wildest dreams. However, that win marked the end of an era in the tournament, undoubtedly the most prestigious international club competition. From then on, the power base of European club football shifted from Latin countries – Spain, Portugal, Italy – to northern Europe – Germany, Britain and Holland.

During this period of changing fortunes, the Franco regime's focus had to a certain extent also shifted, away from national clubs to the national team, particularly when, in 1964, Spain hosted the final stages of the European Nations Cup and won it. The regime then found itself proclaiming victory by a Spanish team which effectively neutralised the separate identities of Barça and Real Madrid. The fact that Spain, without any star foreigners, had beaten Hungary and then the Soviet Union to claim the trophy helped boost Franco's delusion of his domestic popularity and his acceptance on the international stage.

'No longer will Barça come second. We're going to be number one from now onwards. We are going to win every title!' declared Domingo Balmanya in the aftermath of the 'final of the bottles'. Not for the first time, or for the last, would a senior figure of the club let his passion mask his judgement, in believing that beating Real Madrid was the only test of strength. Balmanya, a former player and manager of the national team who had returned to his club as its 'technical secretary', was proved terribly wrong – in the short term, at least. In the 1968–9 season which followed that final, Real Madrid once again won the League, leaving Barcelona trailing in third place behind Las Palmas. In the Spanish Cup, Barça was defeated in the opening round by Real

Sociedad. Reaching the final of the European Cup Winners Cup proved some consolation, only for raised hopes to be dashed again with the team losing 3–2 to Slovan of Bratislava. The club sank once again into self-doubt and division.

An attempt to bring back Helenio Herrera provoked a split within the management and among the fans, the debate focusing – as it had on the eve of his departure – on whether the manager was worth the price. With a track record that now included successful stints as manager of the national team and of Inter Milan, Herrera had no intention of selling himself cheaply, demanding huge bonuses for every title secured. His supporters argued that if Barça really wanted to be considered among the world's great clubs, it had to be prepared to pay whatever money was necessary to achieve success. The detractors clung on to an emotional sense of what Barça stood for: a club that was above the crude mercantilism of Real Madrid and drew its strength from its commitment to a cause.

Neither argument made total sense in the circumstances, and the unresolved nature of the debate served only to provoke resignations including those of the club president, Narcis de Carreras, and the manager, Salvador Artigas. Carreras was succeeded by Agustin Montal, while Artigas made way for an 'interim coach' – another former Barça player, Josep Seguer. As for Herrera, he returned, as far as Barça was concerned, to his former status of fading dream, his lingering presence no more than a figment of the imagination. And all the while the team played on, unable – amidst the administrative chaos, and the continuing absence of anyone who could really inspire it from within – to keep its hold on the League championship.

It was in such chaotic circumstances that a rather down-to-earth Englishman called Vic Buckingham stepped in, and began Barça's revival as a club that believed in itself. Buckingham took over on 11th January 1970, at a time when Barça's 'crisis' seemed never-ending. Three months into the season, the club was trailing badly in the League in tenth place. By the end of that spring, the team had recovered its form and was back up to fourth place. Those who played for Barça at the time describe the coming of Buckingham much as might ship-wrecked sailors glimpsing their rescue on a distant horizon: as the promise that things could only get better.

One of the players who warmed to Buckingham most was Charly Rexach: 'There are certain managers in the history of football who have stolen an excessive limelight, but Buckingham was not one of those who pretended that the team didn't exist without him and that it was only thanks to him that it won or lost. But he was the first coach I worked under who taught us the importance of (1) having good players, (2) having discipline in the changing room, and (3) having a game plan.'

Another ex-Barça player, Fuste, recalls that when Buckingham came to Barcelona the players and the fans regarded him as an unknown. 'But he made a name for himself by showing people that he understood how the game worked. With one of his predecessors, the Catalan Salvador Artigas, we'd play against a third-rate team, and it was as if we were playing against a world eleven. Such was his lack of confidence. But when Buckingham came, it was quite the opposite. For instance, whenever we played against Real Madrid, he'd say, "Don't worry, they are just a bunch of show-offs." '

Buckingham was tall and lean. He liked to dress in tweed jackets and silk ties and, in the winter months, a beige button-down jersey. He liked his cocktails, played golf, and talked about his other favourite hobby – English horse-racing. The few middle-class Catalans who couldn't understand any English or dealt with him only on social occasions were impressed by his bearing, thinking him a cross between Henry Higgins (the professor in *Pygmalion* and *My Fair Lady*) and a retired army officer, a throwback to the days of Witty and Witty – 'a true English gentleman', records Antoni Closa in his *Croniques del Barça*.

In fact, Buckingham could be *simpático* one moment, and abrasive the next. He had a sharp tongue – bad Spanish, good English swear-words. Fuste held only one thing against him: that he swore too much at the players in his team he didn't rate much. 'There was only one thing I didn't like about Buckingham. He only thought of fourteen or fifteen players. The rest he just wasn't bothered with. He wanted to forget about them, didn't even want to see them around. He didn't have time for those he didn't rate highly. There were six or seven players who if he found anywhere near the changing room he'd simply tell them to fuck off.'

But then Buckingham just as often swore at the enemy without as at the hangers-on within, which helped lift the team spirit, sometimes amidst loud laughter. On one occasion he stood during a training session with the word 'BETIS', the name of the team Barça was to encounter the next day, chalked at the top of a blank blackboard. 'Betis?' Buckingham growled. 'Who are they? Fuck Betis,' and with that kicked the blackboard to the ground.

Only sometimes did Buckingham's sense of humour fall flat among the Catalans, as when before a match against Espanyol he had himself photographed genuflecting before the rival club's manager as if pleading for a victory.

Perhaps the local man who got to known Buckingham best was his interpreter, José-Maria Minguella, who recalls, 'He had some very clear professional concepts. He had a lot of experience and he said things that would become commonplace in modern football. He used to say that once a match got under way it was like a film that constantly changed scenes. Each player had to think of himself as an actor in that film, constantly adapting to the change of scene, moving his position to deal with each move that was played. He also thought the manager had to play a part. For instance, if the game was going well in the first half, he might have to pretend that things were not so good when it came to half-time; at other times if things weren't actually going too well, he had to try and lift morale some other way.'

Barça's resurgent self-confidence and rekindled sense of mission were such as to ensure a virulent reaction at all levels of the club to the highly controversial encounter with Real Madrid at the Camp Nou – the so-called 'Guruceta case', named after the referee who gave the game away to the visitors. This was, as explained in the previous chapter, a detonating point in the politics of the club, which now entered a crucial stage in the lead-up to Franco's death.

In Buckingham's first full season at the club, Barça narrowly – by one point – lost the League championship to Valencia, although it finished ahead of Real Madrid, which it more than matched in skill and determination. The club secured a double revenge of sorts by beating Valencia 4–3 in a cliff-hanger of a final of the Spanish Cup in the Bernabéu stadium. Valencia scored the first two goals, but Barça fought back, equalising with goals by Fuste and Zabalza. In extra

time Zabalza scored his second, only to have Valencia come level
again. The match was decided in the seventh minute of the second half
of extra time, with a goal by Alfonseda.

'The victory over Valencia,' reported the magazine *Barça*, 'will go
down in the history of the club as one of the most dramatic and
impassioned games we have seen. To equalise after being two goals
down and then go on and win in extra time after 120 anxiety-filled
minutes is no ordinary final, rather an adventure worthy of being
remembered.'

Less enthusiastic were the feelings of Franco, once again faced with
the awkward task of handing his trophy to the Catalans in the stadium
constructed in his honour. By now the dictator was growing physically
more frail and his hands shook as he raised the Cup. As well as
suffering from fungal infections of the mouth, the Caudillo had a
stiffness in his legs and a vacant expression – the other unmistakable
symptoms of Parkinson's disease. He seemed touched by a nervous tic
of a death foretold – he had just over four years to live. Spain was no
longer what it had once been on the international football scene, still
less politically. The use of football for political ends was past its sell-by
date amidst the growing political isolation of the regime.

The desperation of the regime when faced with any kind of reversal
was reflected in an unconvincing printing error in a post-match edition
of the *Hoja del Lunes*: 'At last – Barcelona is champion' over an
archive photograph of a smiling Franco handing a cup . . . to the
captain of the Real Madrid youth team.

Buckingham was forced to cut his contract short soon after the
Spanish Cup final, because of a recurring severe back problem. Despite
the shortness of his stay in the Catalan capital, and the unemotional
nature of his departure – no one paraded him up and down the Rambla
as they had Herrera, nor subsequently cried 'Vic, Vic, Vic' in the Camp
Nou as they have done with icons from Kubala to Rivaldo – he remains
one of the great unsung heroes of Barça.

Buckingham's mixture of English irony and direct approach to a
game he knew well was just the tonic that Barça needed at the time to
shake it from its doldrums. He confided at times that even his
experience had not quite prepared him for the emotional helter-skelter
that was Barça. One wonders how he would have managed amidst the

mounting political passion that was to follow his departure. But he seemed to have been reasonably unfazed by the Guruceta affair. He had Herrera's single-mindedness without any of his pretences, and brought to the club an experience of northern European football which, while it had been absent for years, none the less took Barça back to its roots.

That other ex-Fulham and Barça manager, Bobby Robson, reminisced in his autobiography, published a few years later, 'The manager when I was at the "Hawthorns" [West Bromwich Albion] was that astute tactician Vic Buckingham, a manager who learned the art under push-and-run expert Arthur Rowe of Tottenham Hotspur repute [Buckingham played at fullback at Spurs]. Buckingham was vastly experienced – he also had a spell at Ajax – and was not afraid to take on board the hard lessons learned from the Hungarians and to experiment with our style of play.'

Robson was to see Buckingham very much as his role model when he himself went to Barça twenty-six years after Vic did. Probably more important still, was the role that Buckingham played in serving as the bridge for the man Barça fans to this day consider the biggest saviour of them all: Johan Cruyff. It was while Buckingham was manager at Ajax in the early 1960s that he gave the young Cruyff his first chance to play in the first team. And it was during Buckingham's time as manager at Barça that the Catalan club began its first tentative negotiations with Cruyff, paving the way for his transfer in 1973.

10

The Flying Dutchman

Part refuge, part citadel, the monastery of Montserrat has for centuries cast its influence on Catalonia's religious, cultural and political life. It stands some forty kilometres north of Barcelona, encrusted amidst craggy rocks which rise like giant stalagmites, seemingly impenetrable by man or machine. Within it is a tiny black Virgin, La Moreneta, carved, her followers believe, by St Luke and brought there fifty years after the death of Christ by St Peter. Another legend marks this as the spot where the knight Parsifal discovered the Holy Grail. Simple faith has made the diminutive Virgin the recipient of millions of prayers, the eternal oracle of hopes and thanksgiving around the world, the sacred icon that has survived the worst of persecutions, and presided over the happiest of celebrations.

On 17th November 1974, some 6,000 Barça supporters gathered at Montserrat to pray for themselves, for Catalonia, and for their club. The occasion was as much a political statement as a pilgrimage, part of a series of events celebrating the seventy-five years since Barça's foundation. The club, in the dying days of the Franco regime, was being used to press the Catalan nationalist agenda. Among those present was Jordi Pujol, a forty-four-year-old banker and former political prisoner of the Franco regime, who was taken to his first Barça game, at the age of six, in Les Corts stadium in the spring of 1936 – just days before the outbreak of the Spanish Civil War. Drawing on his experiences of repression and resistance, Pujol has written, 'Barça is like other folkloric manifestations of our people – Montserrat is another example – a reserve we can draw on when other sources dry up, when the doors of normality are closed to us.' In other words, in the absence of democracy, the club can be a vehicle for achieving it.

The match that spring in 1936 was the second leg of the Spanish Cup semi-final tie between Barça and Pamplona's Osasuna. Barça had earlier won the Catalan Cup, with an extraordinary unbeaten run of ten consecutive games, only to trail fifth in the League, behind – in victory order – Athletic Bilbao, Real Madrid, Oviedo and Santander. That day in Las Corts, the child Pujol watched his team beat Osasuna 7–1, his players courageous and defiant in the midst of cruel tackling by the Navarrines. A sweet memory, if one that has necessarily faded with the passage through turbulent times.

None the less, later football matches would come to be recalled by an older Pujol because of their coincidence with key political events, as was the case with the match between Barça and Oviedo in 1959. In the days leading up to the match, Barça supporters planned to join a protest march to the offices of the newspaper *La Vanguardia*. The previous Sunday, its editor, Luis de Galinsoga, had berated a local priest after he had delivered his homily in Catalan. 'All Catalans are a bunch of shit,' Galinsoga had screamed before storming out of the church. Galinsoga was subsequently sacked, but the Barça fans took to the streets anyway – after the match – to celebrate victory, inside and outside the stadium. Pujol had the memory with him, that day in 1974 when the fans gathered in Montserrat, crowding the pavements from wall to wall, in a fusion of religion, politics and sport that far from relegating Catalanism to the gutter, as Galinsoga had tried to do, had elevated it to the unofficial status of nationhood.

Less than four years had passed since the Abbot of Montserrat, Cassia Just, had allowed three hundred Catalan artists, writers and intellectuals to take sanctuary in the abbey, backing their manifesto in support of an amnesty for political prisoners, democratic freedoms, and the right to regional self-determination. Police laid siege for three days before the Abbot reached a deal with the civil governor under which the protesters were allowed to leave with guarantees of freedom from prosecution (an agreement that was subsequently breached by the police).

This time the abbey was witness to a mobilisation of mass loyalty that the police were powerless to do anything about. It was an opportunity that no politician as ambitious as Pujol could easily let pass. And so, 17th November 1974 was marked not just by a celebration of Barça's seventy-five years but by the founding by Pujol of a new Catalan nationalist party, Convergència Democrática de

Catalunya. The way the Barça gathering was willingly used as 'cover' for this significant development in Spanish politics was explained to me by Agustin Montal, himself a friend of Pujol's, who was there as president of FC Barcelona:

'During my presidency, the institution of FC Barcelona came to support the idea of an autonomous Catalan state, even though there were people inside the club who were against it. I saw my role as that of ensuring stability, but politics was inseparable from the club. I remember that there was a member of the PSUC – the Catalan Communist Party – who was very vocal in the members' meetings . . . I myself had personal ties with Pujol and I was politically in favour of him. His party, Convergència, really came together that day in Montserrat where groups of Barça fans led by myself and the Abbot provided a cover for a political meeting between Pujol and his people.'

Spare a thought for the poor monks, a mixed community, joined in their humanity and dedication to the Virgin, but with differing political sensitivities. Among those in the monastery that day was Fr Alejandro Olivar. By then nearly sixty years old, he had first entered the community back in 1932. I interviewed him when he was over eighty – his memory as clear as the mountain range was that brilliant spring day I took the cable-car up from the station in the valley.

Fr Olivar and all the other monks had been forced to vacate the monastery when the Civil War broke out and the anarchists started looting churches in Barcelona. He returned following Franco's victory in 1939, and after a short exile in Germany under Hitler, to discover that twenty-three of his fellow monks had been executed by anarchists. Fr Olivar has not forgotten: 'Churches were looted and burned by people who hated religion. The Gospels talk about this kind of thing . . . This was the kind of suffering Jesus Christ went through . . . Franco executed a lot of people too, but the crimes committed on the Republican side were more numerous.'

After the Civil War, Franco came to Montserrat on a number of occasions. It was his sway of telling the Catalans that their Virgin was Spanish first and foremost, and that the monks owed him a favour or two. Only rarely did the monks raise objections, as when the Abbot discreetly expressed his concern about Franco's habit of having loyal pilgrims clap him enthusiastically whenever he arrived, like a football crowd. When the Abbot left the monastery after backing the solidarity protest, he did so not because he was forced to by the regime but because during an internal conclave several of his own monks had objected to their community's becoming so politicised.

I asked Fr Olivar why, despite all this, the monastery had still allowed itself to be used by those resisting the Franco regime. He replied, 'We all thought Franco was our liberator when the Civil War began, but once it was all over what upset us was the way he oppressed the Catalan people. That's why Montserrat became something of a symbol of freedom.'

I knew that Barça's propensity to mix sport with religion extended beyond these mountains. Players prayed in the Camp Nou chapel before each game. The team dedicated every cup won to the Virgin of the Merce, the 'Mother' of Barcelona. Bishops are rarely absent from the club's major social functions. One of Catalonia's most famous monsignors is Antoni Deig, a *cule* in a cassock who likes to base his belief in the spirituality and fraternity of Barça on papal encyclicals and selected extracts from the Bible. Yet even Mgr Deig draws the line at superstition, insisting that one should pray to the team only if it leads to God, not as a substitute for him. Mgr Deig also disagrees with Bill Shankly, the one-time Liverpool coach, who once said that football is not a matter of life or death but more important than both. 'I think Mr Shankly risks committing a grave sin saying that,' Deig told the Catalan journalist Pere Ferreres. 'Football is a sport, and human life is more important than football whoever it's played by.'

Fr Olivar had his doubts, too, when I visited him in the monks' residential quarters, a building filled with tranquil conversations and smelling vaguely of incense and polish. I had told him I was writing a book about Barça, not about the Virgin, although I was interested in the relationship between the two. Call it a theology of football, or something like that. 'Not all of us here in Montserrat like the abbey being used for "pilgrimages" by Barça fans,' said Fr Olivar, 'because sometimes the religious intention is far from clear. Feelings about Barça have to do with patriotism more than with religion . . . As a monk and as a priest, I have the impression that one of the obsessions of our youth is football . . . There is a danger in that, it can be disturbing to the mind. I think there are spiritual values that are above a game of football.'

I now knew why the rumour among some of the more fanatical Barça fans was that the latest Abbot was a closet Espanyol fan, and why there was a wider concern in the club that this great bastion of freedom and nationhood was in the throes of 'redefining' its Catalanism. However, while Fr Olivar openly admitted that football did not form part of his life, he did point me in the direction of another ageing monk whom he described as the one passionate *cule* in the building. His name was Fr Boix, a very old monk indeed, who, with his scraggly grey beard and hair and whispering voice, resembled the Count of Monte Cristo at the end of a long jail term. 'After the Civil War, as a matter of Christian conscience, we helped political fugitives,' whispered Fr Boix during a conversation marked by long pauses and contemplation. He recalled the phones being tapped by the regime and the liturgical pomposity with which Franco surrounded himself. But he confessed to not being in much of a mood to discuss Barça these days. It was the first season of van Gaal, in an era of competition victories without beauty, and of so much of football's apparent domination by money. Fr Boix wanted to forget that side of Barça, to focus instead on the club as a symbol of nobility, freedom and Christian brotherhood, but he thought this aspect of it was being lost somehow. He did not, however, agree with those seeking to sever the club's links with the monastery. 'Barça will always find the gates of Montserrat open to it as long as its fans come in the spirit of democracy,' he said before disappearing, ghost-like, down the corridor.

The coupling of politics and sport, historically never far absent from FC Barcelona, had entered a new lease in December 1969, when Agustin Montal became president of the club – although one would not have thought it at first sight. Montal, a former vice-president of the club, whose father had also been president, had his candidacy endorsed by all his living predecessors, all of whom came from the same business sector, the textile industry. No matter that they had straddled years of Francoism with varying degrees of complicity and collaboration. Montal thanked them all for their endorsement, describing them as '*grandes barcelonistas*', while at the same time pledging loyalty to the wishes of a mass following who were anxious for change: '*Con el socio todo, sin el socio nada*' – 'With the fan, everything; without the fan, nothing'.

Despite being criticised by his opponents as the candidate of continuity rather than innovation, Montal was showing himself to be very much a man of the times. For 1969 was also an important turning-point in the history of the Franco regime. It was the year Franco appointed Prince Juan Carlos as his successor, when his government was hit by a major financial scandal, and when radical opposition in the form of terrorism, strikes and student demonstrations began to accelerate. Faced with a scenario of crumbling confidence, new tactical alliances began to be formed within the political and business communities with an eye to the future. Inside Catalonia, Barça became an indispensable component of most political calculations. While the club's mass support had been self-evident for decades, that of individual politicians had yet to be tried and tested.

During his eight-year presidency, Montal claimed to govern in the interest of stability, drawing on a fairly broad local political spectrum, from centre-left to centre-right – definitions not always easy to pin down in a society like Catalonia, much of which is characterised by interlocking political and financial interests. Montal occasionally reshuffled his team in an apparent attempt to appease one group or the other and to maintain a sense of dynamic in tune with the world beyond the stadium. A small group known as 'Españolistas' within the junta tried their best to hold back the tide. They objected now and again to what they saw as the deliberate 'politicisation' of the club, and maintained close links with the regime's hand-picked sporting and football authorities.

However, the pace of change was dictated by a nucleus of junta members and administrators closely identified with Jordi Pujol's brand of Catalan nationalism. Significant for the inner workings of the club during this period was not just Pujol's track record of political opposition to the regime, but his success in building up during the 1960s a seemingly strong bank with a clear Catalan identity: Banca Catalana. Pujol's banking group in its marketing consciously echoed Barça's own claim to be 'more than a club'. Catalana was 'more than a bank' in terms of how it identified with the region – all its internal memorandums were in Catalan, and the bank went out of its way to sponsor Catalan culture and industry.

As Armando Caraben, the secretary of the club at the time, recalls,

'There were two very marked political tendencies in the governing junta of the club: one was the so-called Catalan group – Catalan nationalists like Raimón Carrasco, Josep Lluís Vilaseca and Antonio Amat; the other I called the group of "delegates", people more linked to the Franco regime and a rival bank, the Banco Condal – Ignasi Brenguer, Manuel Grau and Antoni Portabella, who was linked to the Danone dairy company and very pro-Franco. This group also included Joan Gic, who had fought with the Blue Division which Franco sent to Russia to help Hitler in his war against Stalin . . .

'The first group, with its links to Banca Catalana, helped the club financially. Through the bank they organised bridging loans to cover us during dips in revenue from membership dues. But the club was also under pressure from the delegates. Portabella was among those who kept saying, "We must be careful, the club is becoming too Catalan nationalist." These "Spaniards" were always trying to block things when they got too political.'

One of the tests of strength between Barcelona and Madrid during the Montal presidency was over Spain's restrictions on the contracting of foreign players. Montal believed that the law was not only being selectively breached with the tacit blessing of the authorities, but also being deliberately manipulated to discriminate against Barça. While Barcelona was prevented from signing one South American player, Irala, and obstructed in the negotiation for another, Heredia, other Spanish clubs led by Real Madrid faced no such problems.

Matters came to a head when the Spanish football authorities, in tacit alliance with Real Madrid, decided to ratify the legislation without making any effort to deal with its glaring inconsistencies. Montal dug in, ordering the Catalan lawyer and member of the Pujol camp Miguel Roca Junyent to carry out a detailed investigation into the transfer of players from South America. While such a confrontational approach irked the 'delegates' in the junta, it proved popular with the Barça membership, who had not forgotten the humiliating climb-down over Di Stefano, and his loss to Madrid.

Roca discovered that of the sixty South American players allowed to play in the Spanish League on grounds of their alleged Spanish nationality, forty-six had their status approved on the basis of false documentation. One of the most popular tricks, with the help of a compliant Spanish consul in Paraguay, had been to pick on an unknown Spanish village as the birthplace of the player's father, claiming that it could not be traced because it had disappeared from the map of Spain during the Civil War. On occasions the fraud was so crude as to be laughable, as in the case of one player who claimed that his family had originated in Celta, Galicia, when in fact Celta is the name of the football team of the Galician port of Vigo.

Roca's report left Real Madrid officials unimpressed. They claimed that Catalan nationalism was mischievously creating a mountain out of a molehill. The Spanish Football Federation, however, was rattled by the Roca investigation, fearing that it might develop into a major exposé of the hidden workings of the Spanish League. As for Montal, he had no qualms about pursuing the politics of blackmail in the best interests of FC Barcelona. He told me, 'The Roca report helped us secure an agreement. The deal was that I promised not to bring out further information about under-hand stuff which half the Spanish football world was involved in, while the Spanish Football Federation would lift its restrictions on some of the foreigners whom we wanted.'

The strategy worked. On 26th May 1973, the Spanish Football Federation officially opened its borders to foreign players, allowing two per team. Barça signed the Peruvian international and Municipal de Lima player Hugo Sotil, and went all out for the one player it wanted more than any other, Johan Cruyff.

The Dutchman was by then already a living legend in the football world. Born into a working-class family on 25th April 1947, Cruyff had spent his childhood years kicking ball-shaped objects in the street, when not helping his father with his small fruit and vegetable stall. The Cruyff home was in the neighbourhood of Betondorp, a poor suburb on the outskirts of Amsterdam, next to the Ajax stadium where his mother worked as a cleaner. It is said that it was she who persuaded the club coaching staff to take the young Johan into its youth section when he was twelve, soon after his father's death from a heart attack. Cruyff owed part of his advancement to his parents – to his mother for persevering, and to his father for the promise he made him that he would be successful like a good dutiful son. But it was the Ajax youth trainer, Jany van der Veen, who turned him into a two-footed player, developing a hard shot in his left as much as his natural right, thanks to weight training and, again, sheer perseverance.

Cruyff was seventeen when he made his team début at Ajax, in the final days of Vic Buckingham's management. He became a regular in the starting line-up in the 1965–6 season after Buckingham had been replaced by Rinus Michels. He represented Holland in his first international a year later, scoring one of his team's two goals in a European championship match against Hungary which ended in a draw.

During Cruyff's teenage years, Holland was at the level of an amateur footballing nation, well behind the top footballing countries like England, France, Argentina, Uruguay, Germany, Spain, Hungary and Brazil. The Dutch team failed to qualify for the 1966 World Cup finals. Thereafter, a much more imaginative and innovative way of thinking entered the Dutch game. Cruyff has said that his 'first and only football master' was Michels: 'He was a perfectionist. He kept on working on a tactic until it came out the way he wanted. He was a strong disciplinarian and every night he'd ring my home to make sure I was in. Under his management, we became a machine for producing football.'

It was under Michels, towards the end of 1966, that Cruyff played a leading role in Ajax's first real achievement in the European Cup, helping the team trounce Liverpool 5–1 in Amsterdam, and scoring two memorable goals in the return tie, in front of the Kop. The following year Cruyff signed a four-year contract designed to keep him at Ajax at least until July 1971. He was emerging as the star performer of what the Dutch called 'total football'. It was the concept under which every player was supposed to have comparable technical and physical abilities and be able to interchange roles and positions at will. At its best, the system was supposed to have players in a seemingly effortless collective flow for most of the game; an exciting mixture of dribbling, first-touch passing and goals, rather than long balls or kicks into touch.

The number 14 Cruyff wore on his shirt was as surprising as his play. While he might play centre-forward, he was as often seen playing through the midfield or out on either wing, his ever-changing figure on the pitch playing havoc with any conventional concept of defence. A profile by a local Dutch journalist published at the end of 1970 noted,

'Wherever he plays, with his radius of action, his ability to run past defenders at speed, his inimitable movement, his hard shot with both feet, his running for every ball, his stamina and his sense of positioning, he should be able to make defences despair . . . His greatest pleasure is playing beautiful football.'

In that year, Cruyff announced in a Dutch TV interview that Ajax would let him go at the end of the season. Later this was expanded in local newspaper reports, which claimed that Cruyff could indeed leave at the end of the season, but only if a Spanish buyer emerged who could pay a certain amount (in the region of one million guilders).

In fact Barcelona had secretly already made its first approach. Buckingham, who had taken over as manager, had been instructed by club president Montal to make discreet contact, paying two separate visits to Amsterdam. Cruyff himself was persuaded to come over to the Catalan capital for some friendly conversations with Montal, and to pose in the Barça colours for *Revista Barcelonista* magazine in pictures that were syndicated worldwide. 'Now I want to come to Barcelona more than ever before,' Cruyff declared. In April 1971, while officially out of a Dutch team fixture because of flu, Cruyff was reported once again to have dropped in on the Catalan capital. Leaks about Cruyff's comings and goings were thought by the Dutch press to be not unconnected with the attempts by the player's father-in-law and agent, Cor Coster, to raise his market value. As far as the Barça management was concerned, there was never any realistic prospect of clinching a deal while the controversy over the transfer of foreign players remained unresolved. However, it did not allow the contacts with Cruyff to go cold, conscious that there were other European teams, including Real Madrid, ready to pounce if the Ajax management and the player were persuaded that there was an alternative more in their interests than the renewal of his contract.

The Barça man who was entrusted with the Cruyff file was Armando Caraben, the club secretary. An economist and lawyer, with a good grounding in international affairs, Caraben was one of the reformers in the Montal junta who felt the time was ripe to shake up the club both politically and in football terms. The 'Españolistas' linked to the Franco regime considered Caraben a liability and wanted him sacked. But Montal regarded him as an indispensable asset in one key respect:

married to a Dutchwoman, Caraben understood Holland well, and found little difficulty in getting near to Cruyff and establishing a good friendship.

By 1971, the Dutch were well on their way to producing a genius of the game, with Ajax – under Michels's Romanian successor, Stefan Kovacs – winning the European Cup for the first time, against the Greek Panathinaikos. In that year, Cruyff was voted European Footballer of the Year in an international poll conducted by the prestigious Paris-based football magazine *France Football*, evidence that a growing number of people had started to take notice of him beyond his native country. Caraben was certainly one of them:

'I'd watched this phenomenal player on the TV. That short fabulous sprint, that extraordinary speed of thinking, of playing the ball, of finding space. It struck me that as well as being a great executor on his own terms, a good goal-scorer, he could also organise a team around his talent, like a director of an orchestra. I don't think I was making a huge discovery. Everyone knew he was a star. Once we had Cruyff dressed in the colours of Barça, the Federation tried it on one more time by claiming he wasn't properly registered. Everyone got really rattled. We thought, here comes a repeat of the Di Stefano saga when Real Madrid and the government robbed us of a great player . . . But Cruyff really wanted to be in Barcelona, because he thought this would give him a much bigger projection than the football he'd been playing in Holland. I saw it as my one and only task: making sure that once we got him, he stayed with us.'

Cruyff's star with Ajax seemed on a never-ending ascendant. In the European Cup final of 1972, he single-handedly pulled Inter Milan apart, scoring both goals in Ajax's 2–0 victory. The following year, in Belgrade, he inspired what Keir Radnedge, the editor of *World Soccer*, has described as 'one of the greatest twenty-minute spells of football ever seen', part of the game in which Ajax beat Juventus 1–0 thanks to a goal by Johnny Rep. Yet despite the success, Cruyff's relations with other players in the team proved far from harmonious. Players who considered themselves essential cogs in the 'beautiful machine' which allowed Cruyff to shine resented his higher earnings, and grew weary of his arrogance – his habit of always wanting to be seen to be right.

Soon after the 1973 European Cup they voted against his captaincy of the club.

Cruyff later described his colleagues' taking away his captaincy as 'the last straw', and what had convinced him he had to leave Ajax. 'The other players said they didn't like it that I was changing my lifestyle, and was isolating myself. They started to live differently; they started going into town and asked me to go with them. But I never went into town myself before,' he told two trusted Dutch journalist friends, Frits Barend and Henk van Dorp.

While relations at Ajax got frostier, Cruyff became increasingly seduced by the idea of going to Barcelona. It had a climate, people and geology not unlike those of nearby Mallorca, his favourite holiday location. The club now had as its manager Michels, the man he regarded as his only football teacher, and a senior official – Caraben – to whom he could relate both personally and professionally. Nevertheless, the negotiations with Barcelona produced a financial tug-of-war once they began in earnest following the lifting of the ban on foreign transfers. According to Caraben, among those shocked at the price that was initially being asked was Cruyff's 'football teacher'. 'Michels was not very in favour of Cruyff coming for the price they were asking – three million dollars. He thought that with that we could buy three or four good players. Among the players he wanted was Bayern Munich's Gerd Müller.'

Caraben travelled to Munich with the club lawyer and member of the board, Josep Lluís Vilaseca, and to his own personal relief got nowhere with the Germans. He took an instant dislike to Müller's agent, while the German football authorities made it clear that they wanted their star footballer to remain in the country at least until the World Cup in 1974.

The record $1-million three-year contract between Barcelona and Cruyff – then the highest price ever paid by the Catalan club for any player – was finally signed on 18th August 1973. In the end, two factors appeared to have focused the negotiators' minds. Ajax agreed to the deal after Cruyff had made it clear that he was prepared to quit football altogether rather than stay on in Holland. Barcelona for its part picked up a rumour that Real Madrid, having publicly declared that the initial price Ajax was asking was beyond their means, was in fact closing in. This strengthened the resolve of president Montal and his chief negotiator, who felt that $1 million was a price worth paying for what they considered guaranteed success and the avenging of the Di Stefano saga. 'The only important thing for me was that the team win,' recalled Caraben. It was certainly a view shared widely within the club. When the 60,000-strong membership was told that annual fees would go up over the next two years by twenty-five per cent in order to help cover the cost of the transfer, there were few objections.

As for Montal, he managed to extend his term of office for another five years – but only after first dealing with the Spanish sporting authorities, who had become increasingly nervous at the growing self-confidence of the Catalan nationalist group within the club junta. On 15th October 1971, Montal and his junta were summoned to El Pardo, Franco's palace outside Madrid, and told by the Caudillo himself that they should defuse the growing militancy that was being displayed by certain elements within the club. Present at the meeting, as a member of the regime, was the newly appointed Secretary of State for Sport, Juan Gich, who had been secretary of Barça prior to Armando Caraben.

To Gich's chagrin, his successor at Barça had made a point of distancing himself from the regime as much as he could, rather than keeping Gich abreast of his administrative affairs, as the Spanish Federation of Football was only too happy to do. Caraben, a social democrat at heart from a Catalan nationalist family background, regarded Gich – a veteran of Hitler's Blue Division – as a Francoiste pawn. It was Caraben's key role in the Cruyff negotiations that saved him from the *putsch* that Gich and other officials of the regime attempted when Montal prepared to extend his term at the end of 1973. At a meeting held with Gich in the home of Manuel Grau in Palamos, Montal agreed to purge his junta of one of its more radical Catalanists, Fernan Ariño, but held his ground in insisting on retaining three others – Ramón Carrasco, Josep Lluís Vilaseca and Goncal Lloveras. The days when the regime could dictate to FC Barcelona who it should have to run it were over.

Montal's presidency had in fact got off to a stumbling start, the ray of hope kindled by Vic Buckingham soon giving way to a familiar pattern of mediocrity, with his successor Michels unable initially to reproduce the spirit of the beautiful game he had helped develop at Ajax. The Barça players lacked the individual talent and spirit to inspire any real transformation in the team, while Michels's stern, somewhat humourless style made some of the players wish they had never lost *el inglés*. Michels was nicknamed 'El Señor Marmol' – 'Man of Marble' – on account of his stiffness of expression and bearing.

It was probably thanks more to Buckingham's legacy than to Michels's arrival that Barça won the last European Fairs Cup tournament (subsequently reorganised and renamed the UEFA Cup) on 22nd September 1971, beating Don Revie's Leeds United 2–1. If nothing else, Buckingham had reminded his Catalan players of the tough, direct football that Anglo-Saxons could play. In the 1971–2 season which followed, Barça seemed a victim of creeping dysfunctionalism, with relations between Michels and the team becoming increasingly tense. Ten games into the season, Barça was third from the bottom of the table, looking over its shoulder at the prospect of relegation. It recovered, but belatedly, once again surrendering the League to Real Madrid. In the European Cup Winners Cup, it had a technically easy if politically sensitive first round against Distillery of Belfast, beating them 7–1 on aggregate, but fell at the quarter-finals stage against Steaua of Bucharest, losing 3–1 on aggregate. Barça was similarly beaten in the quarter-finals in the Spanish Cup, by Atlético Madrid, leaving the club bereft of titles and honour.

Pepe Samitier's funeral that May was a day of mourning in the Catalan capital, with thousands of Barça fans conferring iconic status on 'the Lobster Man' – the acrobatic player immortalised in the sketches of the Catalan cartoonist and *cule* Valenti Castanys. It was an emotional, though dignified, event, the coffin carried on the shoulders of Barça players past and present. (With hindsight, it presented a striking contrast with the violent clashes between drunken Scottish fans and riot police at the Camp Nou three weeks later, following Glasgow Rangers' 3–2 win over Moscow Dynamo.) The Barça mourners recalled the glory days of the 1920s. In nearly half a century, dozens of players and managers had come and gone, several dying – some, like the Irish manager of the Civil War, Patrick O'Connell, virtually forgotten. But this was one son of the city who would not so easily be dispensed with. No matter that Samitier in his later years had been a somewhat combative member of the club, and had flirted with the Franco regime; that his widow believed him betrayed by some of those who paid him public honour, and that some officials at Real Madrid probably had a closer friendship with him than they would ever admit.

El Sami had helped turn Barça into a genuine mass movement during a time when players stuck to their clubs and did not allow themselves to be marketed like commodities. He was a player at the club from 1919 to 1933. In those fourteen years, Barça won five Spanish championships, twelve Catalan championships and one League title. He scored a total of 326 goals. He loved to walk along the Rambla, and to socialise with the players and fans he really trusted. He liked to say that his university was the street. He also personified the need that the Catalan people have historically felt to break out, beyond their political frontiers, to Europe and beyond. His friendships extended from his beloved Gardel's Buenos Aires to Paris, where he befriended Maurice Chevalier. At the moment of Samitier's death, FC Barcelona needed him as a symbol of the club's greatness, a celebration of its past, and a reminder of its potential, which the club seemed temporarily to have lost sight of.

The following season, Barça again hit bottom, failing not only to win any titles, but also to play any football of distinction, scoring only forty-one goals in thirty-four League matches. The most humiliating experience in more respects than one occurred on the occasion of Barça's first-leg quarter-final Spanish Cup clash played away against Second Division Sevilla. Barça having lost the game 3–1, seven of the club's players, including the goalkeeper, Miguel Reina, and Charly Rexach, decided to relax in one of their hotel rooms playing cards. At one point, they ordered two bottles of *cava* and seven glasses from room service. A few minutes later there was a knock on the door. Opening it, the players came face to face with a stern-looking Michels holding the two bottles. In a rare display of emotion, the Dutch coach screamed at the startled gathering, 'The trouble with Spanish footballers is that they are not professional!' and with that threw the bottles at the floor, splintering them into pieces, one of which lodged in the naked foot of a player.

None of the players had been remotely drunk by British standards, and the media generally took the whole incident as a huge overreaction by a manager who simply had an obsession with discipline. Michels admitted as much in the cold light of the next morning. 'These kinds of things happen sometimes,' Michels said afterwards. 'It's the way I like to deal with things if I see things done in a way which I haven't asked for.' Barça beat Sevilla 1–0 in the Camp Nou, sufficient only to ensure its own elimination from the Cup. The Barça management could think of nothing better to do than impose heavy fines on the card-players, while confirming Michels in his post as manager. By 1973, a dismal statistic had dimmed the club's illusion of greatness: it had failed to win the League in fourteen consecutive years.

Anyone doubting that Cruyff was the player whose time had come would have had to look no further than Barcelona's international airport the day the flying Dutchman arrived that summer to an ecstatic reception formed by thousands of Barça fans. Di Stefano may have been snatched cynically away before their very eyes, but Cruyff's presence among them was living proof that FC Barcelona was a club that was taken seriously in world football. His delivery came just as Catalonia, like the rest of Spain, seemed poised to turn a political corner with unforeseen consequences. The Franco regime had dug in, with the ailing Caudillo appointing the hard-line admiral Luis Carrero Blanco as his President. At the same time, strikes became more bitterly contested and solidarity action in response to police brutality was stepped up.

In Barcelona, opposition to the regime became grouped around an increasingly active Asamblea de Catalunya, whose support ranged from the Communist PSUC to sectors of the Church. It included immigrant trade-unionists as well as several prominent members of the Catalan banking and industrial bourgeoisie, many of them passionate Barça supporters. That December, in Madrid, Carrero Blanco was blown to bits on his way to Mass by an ETA bomb, fuelling a general climate of uncertainty and agitation.

In the midst of it all the expectation generated by Cruyff was tremendous. Media coverage was typified by a breathless article in *Dicen* magazine which described his coming as a key moment in the club's history, comparing it to the arrival of Kubala, and predicting a new period of glory. 'Cruyff is a leader,' it said, 'a man who inspires people to follow him through personal example and the combination of discipline and sacrifice.'

Last-minute bureaucratic wranglings involving officials in Amsterdam and Madrid meant that Cruyff was unable to start playing for his new club at the start of the League championship. But the Barça management craftily arranged a series of international friendlies in the Camp Nou so that the fans could get an early look at the new acquisition. In the first game, a packed stadium gave Cruyff and the team a standing ovation after they had beaten Bruges 6–0. The Dutchman scored two goals, showing off his talent and speed both on and off the ball, and lifting the rest of the team to a level of play that had not been seen for a long time.

As the Catalan journalist Santi Nolla wrote in his profile of Cruyff, 'Barça fans really enjoyed the change of pace, the variety of the game, the talent of this Dutchman who alone was capable of filling the Camp Nou. The fans realised they had the best footballer in the world in their midst, and the club had guaranteed a different style of playing football, given another meaning to the word entertainment. It was at that point that there began to develop what came to be known as "Cruyffmania".'

In the friendlies, Barça went on to beat Kickers Offenbach 2–0, and Arsenal 1–0. In each match, Cruyff was the undisputed star, transforming Barça's game into something exciting and dynamic. And yet as soon as the team was forced to play without him, in the first games of the League, it seemed to lose its speed, flexibility and sense of itself, like an engine having to run without a key part and driver. The short interlude only served to underline Cruyff's importance, making his appearance in the League all the more dramatic. Barça, without him, was in the lower half of the table, having won two, drawn two and lost three. Then *el salvador* was in their midst again, as if sent from heaven to banish all that was bad and mediocre in football and replace it only with what was a dream to behold.

No one was more enthusiastic than the man who had doggedly negotiated his transfer from Holland on Barcelona's behalf. 'I remember very well,' recalled Caraben, 'the day they finally rang me from the Spanish Federation to confirm that FIFA had finally authorised the transfer. It was my saint's day. He played his first game two days later. It was a majestic League début and from that moment on he became an

idol in Barcelona. How does one explain such a miracle? I think the
team felt that with Cruyff with them they could never lose – and the
fans felt that way too. It was as if he'd come from another planet, a
man who had fallen to earth, for our sake.'

From Cruyff's first League match – in which Barça convincingly beat
Granada 4–0 – the team never looked back, within weeks positioning
themselves at the top of the League, where they resisted all rival
attempts to replace them for the rest of the season.

That Granada game prompted a simple banner headline in the
magazine *Barça*, heralding the words, 'Cruyff not only plays for the
rest of the team, he makes the team play. His quality brings out the best
in those other Barça players whose quality was never in doubt but who
sometimes stumbled rather than show the true measure of their worth.
The team has turned into a homogeneous unit, full of ideas and at ease
with itself. And what all this means is that football has become fun
again, it's recovered that special grace which makes it the favourite
sport of the masses.'

Amidst the outpouring of idolatry, only the coach Michels struck a
note of caution. Remembering how Cruyff's diva status had ended up
undermining the solidarity within Ajax, Michels told the local media
that Cruyff was nothing without his Barça colleagues – men like Sotil,
Marcial and Rexach who helped consolidate the club's offensive
capability. In fact Michels had picked up on some disquiet in the
changing room, with Marcial among those who resented suddenly
being projected as mere appendices in the shadow of Cruyff.

For every team colleague in whom Cruyff provoked envy, however,
there were several others who felt only admiration, among them
Rexach, whom he came to consider his best friend among the Catalan
players. Rexach has no doubt that Cruyff's arrival stimulated local
talent, making it more competitive in its desire to prove itself alongside
the foreigners. 'We all had our sense of pride that made us feel that we
were as good as the next one, and that meant that for a while Barça had
a team that wanted to prove it could play football.'

Barça played football that season not only with enormous self-
confidence but also with a particular vengeance against the one
opponent that had always mattered, Real Madrid – beaten in its
own Bernabéu stadium by a spectacular 5–0, with two goals by Asensi

and one each by Cruyff, Juan Carlos and Sotil. Of all the goals, it was Cruyff's that seemed guided by a dose of particular magic. In fact it was pure Cruyff. Picking up the ball from just inside Real's half, on the turn, the Dutchman dribbles first with the uncluttered, floating speed of a gazelle, then weaves in and out of the Real defence, his nimble frame turning at sharp angles, now like a cheetah chasing his prey. Skipping effortlessly over a final desperate sliding tackle, Cruyff takes the ball on his left foot and from the penalty spot strikes it home past the goalkeeper.

As usual, the Real fans packed the 80,000-capacity stadium, but unusually they were reduced to silence by the sheer mastery of it all. The thousands of Barça fans who saw the match on TV poured out of their homes and their neighbourhood bars and joined in a spontaneous celebration as if to say, we have got our Di Stefano at last, and nothing can stop us. In the aftermath of the match, the *New York Times* correspondent – in a commentary on football rare for an American journalist – wrote that Cruyff had done more for the spirit of the Catalan nation in ninety minutes than many politicians had achieved in years of stifled struggle.

There was more to come. Barça's winning of the League champion-ship, together with Cruyff's performance in the 1974 World Cup, had the Dutchman reaching his zenith as one of the best players of all time. Of the Cruyff who helped deliver the League Cup to the Virgin of Montserrat, before being knocked out in the finals of the World Cup by Germany, the English journalist Brian Glanville, who witnessed it, has left us with this description: 'So far, Cruyff had plainly surpassed Beckenbauer on the field. Though he himself denied that he was particularly fast, insisting that it was a matter of when he accelerated, what fascinated me was not only his originality, but his amazing speed of thought and execution. Müller was thought to be the goal-scoring machine *par excellence*, still deadly, despite those who felt he had passed his peak, but Cruyff was immensely more versatile, capable of roaming the field like his idol, Di Stefano, now goal-maker, now scorer, slim, long-legged, almost gawky, yet superbly elegant in motion.' The writer went on to conclude that although West Germany won the Cup, it was Cruyff's Holland that had been 'the most attractive and talented of all losers'.

*   *   *

Following the 1974 League championship, Barça won only one other title with Cruyff as player – the Spanish Cup, during his final season, on 19th April 1978 with a 3–1 victory over Las Palmas. The furthest it got in Europe was the semi-finals of the European Cup, in which Leeds United took its revenge and won. And yet Cruyff's farewell testimonial in May of that year, a match between Barça and Ajax in the Camp Nou, had the stadium full and on its feet in a warm expression of tribute and gratitude. To an outside observer it was possible to conclude that Cruyff, despite the magic of his early period, had delivered rather less than Di Stefano did at Real Madrid, where the Argentinian secured consecutive League and European titles within the same five-year span.

Indeed, following the 1973–4 season Barça not only did not win titles but also clearly did not rekindle the spirit the team had shown in that 'dream' season, giving the fans only flashes of brilliance rather than constant entertainment. Some thought that the arrival of Neeskens might re-create some of the old Ajax magic. Barça fans warmed to the aggressive sharp-tackling midfielder, who seemed to play more with his heart than with his head. But the magic tandem never quite materialised, with Cruyff blaming biased refereeing and Michels's one-year replacement by the German Hennes Weisweiler for the dysfunctionalism that once again began to pervade the team, particularly when it played away from home.

The agent José-Maria Minguella was an assistant trainer at Barça when Cruyff and Neeskens coincided and when Sotil was pulled out as second-choice foreigner from the team. He explained why it didn't work: 'Neeskens (a midfielder) replaces Sotil (a forward), and in some way, although he is an exceptional player, it alters the balance of the team . . . It's inevitable if you replace an attacking footballer like Sotil with someone like Neeskens, who despite being a very strong player is not a forward. As things turned out, Neeskens didn't agree one hundred per cent with Cruyff's way of doing things and ended up leaving.'

It was a reminder that 'total football' was a theory, an aim, with no cast-iron guarantee of success. It was a system that not only needed to be played a certain way but relied on certain players and particular teams. If you need two to tango, you need eleven to play the beautiful game. At Barça, Cruyff, Neeskens and Michels approached the game much as they had at Ajax, with the aim of playing versatile, effective football. But the chances of delivering it proved limited.

Yet for all the apparent shortcomings of the first Cruyff era at Barça, the Dutchman remained hugely popular throughout the period. Cruyff's popularity stemmed not only from his iconic status as the player who had avenged the Di Stefano case and produced some spectacular football in his first year, but from the way his presence fitted so well with the thrust of Catalan politics at that time.

A few days before Barça's historic 5–0 victory over Real Madrid in February 1974, Cruyff's first and only son was born. In a rare interview which Cruyff agreed to give me for this book, the player claimed that when he first arrived in Barcelona, 'It took me some time to understand what was happening politically in Spain although I realised soon enough how important the club was in Catalan terms.' Unwittingly, the birth of his son transformed itself into Cruyff's first political act in Spain.

Cruyff went to the Francoiste authorities in Barcelona and insisted on having his son's name registered as Jordi, the Catalan for George and the local patron saint, despite an official ruling that only Spanish names could be used for official documentation. 'We just liked the name Jordi because in Holland it didn't exist. A week after we brought the baby to Barcelona we tried to register him with that name. The officials in the register office said they just couldn't do it, because it wasn't a Spanish name. What was my reaction? I said, "Look, here are the Dutch papers and his Dutch passport with the name Jordi, just go ahead and photocopy them." The officials kept insisting they couldn't do it, that the only name they could register was Jorge, the Spanish version. In the end I just said, "Well, it's just too bad, here are the official papers and he's called Jordi whether you like it or not." It's when people tell me that something can't be done that I really want to do it.'

And he did. The duty registrar agreed on the name Jordi, seemingly after being advised by his superiors that it wasn't worth risking a major political row with the most popular guy in Catalonia. Cruyff for his part dedicated his next victory to his son, who was destined to grow up like him to play football.

It is a story that Jordi was only too happy to expand upon when I interviewed him twenty-five years later as a player at Manchester United. 'I think my father wanted to somehow thank the Catalans for the way he had been received by Barça and thought this was a nice way of doing it. The fact that I was actually born in Holland simply had to do with the fact that my mother wanted to have me in the same hospital and with the same doctors who had delivered my elder sisters. But I was brought over to Barcelona almost immediately and I've always felt as if I was born there. Catalan and Spanish were the two languages I learned first. Catalonia gave me my roots and it's something I've always felt.'

The Cruyff gesture went straight to the heart of a majority of Barça fans, confirming him from the outset as 'one of us'. Later Cruyff was asked by his Dutch friends Barend and van Dorp whether he felt intimidated by the institutional nature of FC Barcelona, the fact that people considered it to be more than a football club. 'It is a challenge,' he replied, 'but you know when people cheer you on a Sunday when you do well and you win, it means more to them than simply the pleasure of winning. It's not just a game, football; it's not just about the people on the terraces . . .' He continued, 'You know what struck me most when we won the championship? They didn't say, "Congratulations"; they said, "Thank you." That was really something. That will always stay with me. It's all they said: "Thank you," everywhere. One time we were shopping on the Costa Brava and an old woman came up to me and said over and over again, "Thank you, thank you." That made a very deep impression.'

The Power and the Glory

At 5.25 a.m. on 20th November 1975, Generalissimo Francisco Franco, Caudillo of Spain, was pronounced officially dead, the complex life-support machinery that had sustained him through the final hours of his agonisingly slow death finally switched off by order of his daughter Carmen. The most tenacious of Europe's great twentieth-century dictators had ended his thirty-six years in power suffering from Parkinson's disease, cardiac failure, blood-poisoning and massive intestinal haemorrhaging. He had had two-thirds of his stomach removed, and had had at least two heart attacks in as many weeks.

To those he had most violently oppressed, the manner of his going symbolised the disease-ridden nature of his regime. But in the transition to the democracy that was subsequently agreed to by a majority of Spain's politicians, there was to be no revenge, no bringing to account. A broad spectrum of Spaniards co-operated in what came to be known as the *pacto del olvido* (the agreement to forget). In his final political testament to the Spanish people, read out by his tearful President Carlos Arias Navarro within hours of his death, Franco wrote, 'I believe that I had no enemies other than the enemies of Spain.'

Around the country, there was mourning and rejoicing, nowhere more so than in Catalonia, which Franco had both 'liberated' and repressed, and where collaboration and defiance had formed part of the same political reality for so many years, whatever the propagandists of one side or the other might have wanted us to believe. Manuel Vazquez Montalban portrayed the duality in Barcelona on the first day without Franco thus: 'The city filled with silent passers-by, walls reflected in their eyes, their throats dried by prudent silence. Up the Rambla and down. As ever. Security guards, police and paramilitaries observed the muted demonstration while with their sixth sense they heard the "Hymn of Joy" sung by the hidden soul of the "Rose of Fire"

[Barcelona], by the cautious soul of the widowed city, by the wise soul of the occupied city. Above the skyline of the Collserola mountains, champagne corks soared into the autumn twilight. But nobody heard a sound. Barcelona was, after all, a city which had been taught good manners. Silent in both its joy and its sadness.'

At FC Barcelona, club president Agustin Montal sent three telegrams to Madrid. One to Franco's private office said that the club 'is filled with sadness at the irreplaceable loss of the Head of State'; the second, to Franco's widow, Doña Carmen Polo de Franco, and her family, expressed 'our most heartfelt condolence'; the third, to Franco's appointed successor King Juan Carlos, declared 'the personal loyalty of our club, and the hope of a future of peaceful and democratic coexistence as represented by your Royal Highness'.

News of Franco's death had been brought to the higher echelons of the club by a concierge. 'Gentlemen, the Caudillo is dead,' the concierge had announced solemnly, after interrupting a meeting Montal was having with other senior club officials. You could have cut the ensuing atmosphere with a knife. Among those present was Jaume Rosell, who had recently replaced Armando Caraben as club secretary, and who later recalled, 'There were two reactions: those who said, "Let's open a bottle of *cava*," and the others who stayed silent and scared shitless. Among the latter was a director who said he didn't feel well and who went home. Poor guy, it seems the news gave him a stomach upset. Among the happier reactions was that of his brother – he was a Communist.'

Later, when the meeting broke up, Rosell and the chief secretary of the club, Joan Granados – also recently appointed – stayed behind, looking at a bust of Franco perched on a shelf in the room usually occupied by Montal. As soon as Montal had gone, Granados got up on a chair, picked up the bust, and threw it at Rosell. 'I stepped aside so that it wouldn't hit me on the head, and the bust fell to the ground and broke up into little bits,' recalled Rosell. 'I had thought that it was made of bronze, but it was made of plaster. So I said, "Fuck me, we thought this was so solid that it could never break, and now it turns out it's nothing but shitty plaster!" ... A few minutes later some fans turned up. They were in a state of high excitement. We handed them some photographs of Franco that were hanging up in another room.

Then we gave instructions for the removal of a sign that was in the stadium remembering the Francoiste members of Barça who had fallen during the Civil War – "For Spain and for God", it read. We put the sign in a box and took it down to the basement where we put it well out of the way, for it seemed to me that such a sentiment did not belong to the history of Barça, although I didn't think we should destroy it as other things were destroyed.'

By the time of Franco's death, the administration of FC Barcelona had come under the increasing influence of the Catalan nationalist movement, headed by Jordi Pujol. It was Pujol's bank Banca Catalana (BC) that the club had turned to for help in funding the signing of Johan Cruyff. The transfer was booked by the bank in its accounts as an agricultural import, an item that was legally entitled to low-interest credit. The monetary links between BC and Barça were mirrored by the role of key officials who straddled both institutions during the Montal presidency. Montal's vice-president at the club, Raimón Carrasco, whose father had been executed by Franco during the war, was the director-general of BC. Josep Lluís Vilaseca was the legal adviser to both entities. Joan Marti Mercadel was president of the club's *peñas* while serving as an executive member of the BC board. Rosell himself, like Granados, was an active member of Pujol's Convergència Democrática de Catalunya, the party whose roots were sown at the clandestine meeting held in the abbey in Montserrat during the celebration of Barça's seventy-fifth anniversary, the year before Franco died.

Pujol had served a three-year prison sentence between May 1960 and August 1963, after being charged by Francoiste police with political subversion. Although he was not himself present, Pujol was accused of organising the singing of the Catalan national anthem during a concert in Barcelona's Palace of Music attended by government officials. After his release from jail, Pujol developed BC as the financial backbone for his movement, which drew its strength initially from sectors of the Church, academia, neighbourhood organisations and business. His political ideal was to resurrect Catalonia's sense of national identity by influencing key institutions of Catalan society and making them part of his movement. As he wrote in his book *To Build Catalonia*, 'A people is a fact of mentality, of language, of feelings. It is a historical fact, and it is a fact of spiritual ethnicity. Finally it is a fact of will. In our case, however, it is in an important sense an achievement of language. The first characteristic of a people has to be the will to exist. It is this will, more than anything else, that assures the survival and, above all, the promotion, the blossoming of a people . . .'

When it came to Barça, Pujol clearly regarded the club as a key ally and vehicle for maintaining the concept of Catalan nationalism as a living force, particularly since its president, Montal, was an easily manipulated ally. For there is no doubt that Barça during the transition to democracy was at key moments sacrificed to the political whims of the two officials entrusted with the day-to-day running of the club: Rosell and Granados, both of whom had a keen sense of their own power. As Rosell told me, 'Montal was a great president of Barça during a very difficult period. We, as members of the executive, took decisions without consulting too widely. Montal used to say, do what you want to do, and I'll try not to take too close notice.'

Among the controversial acts organised by the Rosell–Granados partnership in the dying days of the Franco regime was a friendly match in the Camp Nou between the Soviet Union and an all-Catalan team, made up principally of Barcelona players, during an international trade fair held in the city. Posters for the match, commissioned from the artist Tisner, showed a Catalan peasant embracing a Russian peasant and exchanging a Catalan flag for a hammer and sickle.

Before the kick-off, the Barcelona municipal band was placed in front of the main stand of the Camp Nou with instructions to play the Catalan national anthem. As Granados recalls, 'The band leader said he couldn't play it because it was banned and the authorities would accuse them of a subversive act. I told him that I took full responsibility. So when the Soviets came out they played the Soviet anthem and both teams stood to attention and the stadium got to its feet. In the stadium that day were several government officials, among them Samaranch. [Juan Antonio Samaranch had been named president of the Barcelona county council in 1973 before being made head of the International Olympic Committee.] As soon as they'd finished the Soviet anthem, the band struck up with the first notes of the Catalan anthem. At that point I saw a single figure leave the presidential box and run down towards the band, screaming, "Stop that, stop that!" It was Samaranch.

'The band stopped playing and then started up again, this time with the Spanish national anthem. At that point the stadium broke out into chants of 'We don't want that, we don't want that!' I thought that we were going to see a repeat of 1924 [when the Les Corts stadium was closed by government order after Barça fans had whistled during the playing of the national anthem]. What happened instead was that I was arrested and taken to the police station. I was held there all night, after which they fined me 200,000 pesetas. The Minister of State tried to get me sacked without success. The fact is that things turned out better than I could have ever imagined. From that moment on, the dying regime had me on their "danger list".'

On 21st July 1975, the minutes of a meeting of FC Barcelona's junta of directors were recorded in Catalan for the first time since before the Civil War. This, together with the gradual introduction of Catalan in announcements through the Camp Nou loudspeaker, formed part of a Rosell–Granados-inspired strategy to help restore the Catalan language and culture on a mass scale – in turn, a key element in Pujol's political project.

The synergism between Barça and the Pujol camp was stepped up within weeks of Franco's death. In December 1975, Granados, in his dual role as chief secretary of Barça and the secretary of the neighbourhood organisation the Junta of the Friends of Barcelona, held a meeting and asked that Catalan flags be prepared for an upcoming special occasion at the Camp Nou. Some present at the meeting suggested that twenty-five flags would do, others suggested twice as many. Granados overruled the lot, insisting that strength lay in more numbers rather than fewer and that it was symbolically important to cover as much of the stadium as possible. He arranged for seven hundred Catalan flags to be sewn discreetly by dozens of volunteers in their private homes. It was a time of growing political mobilisation to press for the release of prisoners and for Catalan autonomy. Pujol's party joined several other local political groupings on a common platform, as the Council of Catalan Political Forces.

On 28th December, Barça played Real Madrid in the Camp Nou. It was the first time the teams had met since Franco's death. In the run-up to the match, the seven hundred Catalan flags ordered by Granados were smuggled into the Camp Nou. The few discovered by the police were allowed to go through – a sign that the war of attrition against the continuation of Francoiste rule was finally going the way of Catalan nationalists. Minutes before the kick-off, as the players came on to the pitch, the Camp Nou was awash with the yellow-and-red striped emblems of Catalonia – a sight regarded as a sin by Franco throughout his reign, but now hugely symbolic of political change. They were waved again when Barça scored the first goal. When Real Madrid scored the equaliser, the flags were rested, and a strange silence fell on the stadium, as if the ghost of Franco had decided to haunt the game. With minutes to go before the final whistle, one senior Real Madrid club official was so confident of a draw – effectively a moral victory for the visitors – that he got up and walked out of the stadium, claiming he had other urgent business to attend to.

Just as he was getting into his car, in the last minute of the game, the official heard a collective roar erupt from within the stadium. He knew instinctively that it was Barça's goal. It had been scored by the one Barça player who had done very little for most of the game, Charly Rexach. His lack of concentration and occasional laziness made Rexach one of Barça's most exasperating players. Yet his capacity to pull one out of the bag just when all seemed hopeless was what had always endeared him to the fans. In a way he seemed just the right person to lay Franco's ghost to rest. As soon as his goal was in the net, the flags came out again, this time with a sustained display of colour that perfectly synchronised with the passion of the people.

The interlocking relationship between politics and FC Barcelona during this period extended to one of the most sensitive issues affecting the consolidation of the new democratic Spain: the return from exile of Josep Tarradellas as President of an autonomous Catalonia. Tarradellas, a leader of the left-wing nationalist party Esquerra Republicana de Catalunya, had served as Prime Minister of the Catalan government during the Civil War. Having fled Spain before the conquering Franco forces could arrest him, Tarradellas became President-in-exile, succeeding Lluís Companys, who was returned to Barcelona by the Gestapo and executed in Montjuïc. Following Franco's death, Tarradellas was visited in his exile home of St Martin-de-Beau in France by the hyperactive Granados – as always wearing two seemingly indistinguishable hats, one that of chief secretary of FC Barcelona, the other that of a close ally of the other Catalan politician who had begun to pace the corridors of power, Jordi Pujol.

Tarradellas had never been properly elected as the successor to Companys and now, in his late seventies, seemed a lonely if somewhat anachronistic figure. Yet during all his years in exile he had kept the conscience of Catalonia alive, proudly bearing the standard of the Generalitat (the Catalan regional government). Many of his fellow countrymen considered him the legitimate embodiment of Catalanism, while he himself saw his role as spiritual leader, above parties.

At the meeting, Granados presented Tarradellas with the gold insignia of Barça, and handed him the club membership card he had left behind at the end of the Civil War. During their lunch together, Tarradellas spoke about the possibility of reaching an agreement with the Spanish Prime Minister, Adolfo Suárez, a former leading Francoiste whom King Juan Carlos had appointed to negotiate the transition to democracy. Granados felt unable to share in his optimism and feared that Tarradellas was being drawn into a pact with the devil: 'Everything I heard there left me with the impression that they were planning the impossible. As Catalan nationalists we still looked upon Suárez as an enemy whom we had to fight.'

Within Barça, the Pujolistas continued to back the broad political movement aimed at securing major concessions from Madrid. In April 1977, a meeting of members' representatives issued a statement in favour of a restoration of the autonomous powers that had existed before the outbreak of the Civil War. Montal, the president, delivered an impassioned speech referring to the club's historic role in 'our collective resistance' against dictatorship and oppression. He added, 'Today, as in the 1930s, the word autonomy is being heard throughout our land and the cry "We want our statutes!" is one that belongs to a reborn Catalonia that is looking towards the future. Catalonia is ready to live for ever in freedom and brotherhood with the other peoples of the Spanish state on terms of equality and as part of a democracy.'

Within days, Montal was reminded of his club's own power, and of the latent divisions between some of Catalonia's leading politicians. In the closing stages of the campaign, in the region's first democratic elections since Franco's death, Montal was approached by the leader of the Catalan Socialist Party, Narcís Serra, and asked for his permission to stage a rally in the Camp Nou. Montal agreed. Hours later, however, he received a furious phone call from Jordi Pujol, the leader of the nationalist Convergència, insisting that his party should be lent – as of right – the Camp Nou to stage a similar rally, unless the Socialists abandoned their plans to stage theirs in the stadium. Montal could not make up his mind to cede to Pujol's pressure. While he was still considering matters, the Socialists switched their venue to the bullring and the nearby streets, drawing over 200,000 supporters in the biggest rally of the campaign. Pujol told Montal he would no longer be needing the Camp Nou.

As Pasqual Maragall, the former Socialist mayor of Barcelona and Catalan presidential candidate, recalled when I interviewed him in 1999, 'Narcís [Narcís Serra, the leader of the Catalan Socialist Party] went to see Montal . . . Montal, after thinking about it for a while, said that he could have his rally. Pujol found out and went into a rage . . . We ended up filling up the bullring and everything around it . . . Pujol ended up without his rally in the Camp Nou, having neutralised our earlier plans. That was very much his style. Then we had a spectacular victory in the elections of 15th June. People in Europe at the time described Catalonia as "the red spot of Europe" because there were so many Socialist and Communist votes. There were others, like some of Pujol's supporters, who cried bitter tears . . .'

That June, Suárez's UCD Party was swamped in elections held in Catalonia, with the highest number of votes going to the Catalan branches of nationwide parties, the Socialists and the Communists, and Pujol's party trailing behind them. At the beginning of autumn that year the cry of '*Estatut*' (the Catalan statute of autonomy) was taken up by a demonstration of nearly one million people in Barcelona, the biggest mass rally any Catalan could remember. In fact, unknown to many demonstrators, a secret deal had been negotiated between Tarradellas and Suárez. In return for the re-establishment of the Generalitat, with similar powers to those it had enjoyed during the Spanish Republic, Tarradellas pledged Catalan loyalty to King Juan Carlos, acceptance of the overall unity of Spain, and respect for the armed forces. Tarradellas had shifted considerable political ground since he was last in power. When, at the outbreak of the Civil War, Catalonia had successfully defended itself against Franco's military uprising, Tarradellas had argued that the region should turn itself into a state within a state and 'wash her hands of Spain'.

Tarradellas returned as President of the Generalitat on 23rd October 1977. '*Ja soc aquí!*' ('I am here!') he declared triumphantly to the huge crowds awaiting him. Within three days of his presidential installation he was visited once again by Barça's chief secretary, Granados, this time not in the austere French home of his exile but in the palace of his office, the first stone of which had been laid in the fifteenth century. Granados invited Tarradellas to the Camp Nou to the match that was to be played the following Sunday – an invitation Tarradellas accepted without hesitation. Granados then asked the President whether he wanted members of his party, the Esquerra Republicana de Catalunya, to act as stewards and his personal guards. Just a year earlier, Tarradellas had insisted, in his contacts with Suárez, that on his return to Barcelona he be received by the traditional guard of honour of the Generalitat, the Mozos d'Escuadra. Granados, however, was thinking not of the pomp and circumstance of government, but of Barça as the citadel of Catalan nationalism. To his surprise, Tarradellas replied that he wanted the security at the stadium to be taken care of by the Civil Guard. To many Catalans, the national police force was still a body of agents of repression, a relic of the dictatorship. But Tarradellas's answer convinced Granados that he was in the presence no longer of an exiled eccentric but of a statesman who believed that compromise was a necessary ingredient of peace and stability.

That Sunday, the Camp Nou strained and heaved to bursting point, every conceivable space around the stadium occupied by somebody. With his penchant for striking symbolism, Granados had arranged not just for the seven hundred-odd hand-held flags to spread out once again around the stadium, but for the biggest Catalan flag ever made, and commissioned especially for the event, to be unfurled as Tarradellas entered the stadium. The flag, more than twenty metres wide, was dragged diagonally across the pitch, covering its full width. With the President in their midst, over 90,000 people rose in unison to their feet and broke into ecstatic applause and cheers.

Tarradellas stood on one side of the Barça president, Agustin Montal; his wife, clutching a bouquet of flowers, on the other. Beneath him, a large sign proclaimed, '*BENVINGUT A CASA, PRESI-*

DENTE!' ('Welcome home, President!') Around him, the powers of FC Barcelona and their allies in the commanding levels of Spanish football – past and present – competed with one another to demonstrate the biggest reverence. As Granados recalled the scene, 'What was striking was watching those officials of the world of sport who had done least to help Tarradellas end his exile all running to shake his hand and embrace him – these presidents of Spanish federations, the old regime councillors, and the old Barça directors. They all wanted to embrace him because they realised he was the new power in the country. It was evidence that this was a political transition in which yesterday's enemies were today's friends. It told you something about how Catalonia works. In Catalonia, those on the left may not necessarily be that left-wing, while those on the right may not be as right-wing as they seem. People like to compromise.'

The speeches that day, of course, were played out to a different tune, a tune more in keeping with Barça's mythology. 'Today is a great day,' Montal told the assembled crowd, 'for thousands of Barça supporters who have done the impossible to keep alive the spirit of Catalonia, who have fought and sacrificed themselves to remain loyal to the institutions you [Tarradellas] represent . . .'

Tarradellas followed with a more intimate recollection of Barça's 'coming of age' playing in the 6,000-capacity stadium in the Calle Indústria, popularly known as 'the Spitting Bowl'. As a young *cule* he had followed the team during that period of 1911–22 with its hard-fought victories in the Spanish and Catalan championships – the days of Gamper, of Samitier and Alcantara, of simple loyalties and collective nobility, on and off the pitch. 'In those days we were few in number,' Tarradellas said, 'but we had the same faith as you have today. That was the Barça you have inherited, the Barça rooted in its Catalanism.'

He continued, the stadium a simmering mass of red and yellow stripes, of genuine emotion eclipsing the cynical pretence of some of the VIPs and their supporters, 'The whole of Catalonia has fought for the freedom we have now finally achieved. I am sure you will maintain yourselves loyal to this Catalanism, making this Catalonia ever rich, ever strong, ever free . . . Long live Barça! Long live Catalonia!'

As his final cry echoed around the stadium, the majority of those gathered broke spontaneously into a rendering of the Catalan hymn to the flag, the anthem banned for so many years, the cause in the past of countless fines and imprisonments, of executions even, now delivered without interruption, like a river finding its natural deliverance into the sea. In the match that followed, Barça beat Las Palmas 5–0, the home team seemingly inspired by the atmosphere of the stadium after a lacklustre start to the season.

Two months after Tarradellas's emotional return from exile, Agustin Montal resigned from the presidency of FC Barcelona, having previously announced that he was not seeking re-election. By then, the various constituent parties of the broad Catalan nationalist coalition that had been formed in opposition to Francoism had begun to separate, with individual parties reasserting their differences of ideology and strategy. With Franco dead and buried, other ingredients were thrown into an increasingly complex political brew. They included the unresolved differences of personality and politics between Tarradellas and Pujol, and divisions between the left and right of the local political spectrum.

Montal had announced his intention to resign in September 1977, in effect paving the way for an interregnum that lasted until the election the following May. The manner of his going represented a conscious break with the past, more in keeping with the democratic structures that were beginning to be restored throughout Spain. For the first time in the club's history, the new president was to be elected by a mass membership – since the end of the Civil War this had increased from 3,486 to over 77,000 – and not as part of a tacit pact between the outgoing junta and government officials. Montal himself distanced himself from the election to avoid any suggestion that he might want to influence it. 'My successor will be elected democratically by all the membership,' he insisted. The price of democracy was that the politics of Barça now became a battleground between rival candidates in an increasingly dirty campaign, the outcome of which radically changed the nature of power within the club.

A total of eight individuals, with differing professional and political backgrounds, initially announced their intention to stand for election. The list was quickly reduced to five, with three 'possibles' – Josep Pla, Francesc Perez Mateu and Jaume Pascual Cumillera – unable to muster any significant support. Of the short list, one – Victor Sagi – was regarded at the outset as the strongest contender because of his background.

Sagi, a member of Barça since 1948, ran one of the biggest advertising agencies in Spain. The grandson of Emilio Sagi-Barba, the legendary left-winger of the 'glorious' 1920s, Victor had married into one of the Catalonia's more powerful family-owned business groups. He developed close personal and business links with successive juntas at the club, as indeed with key sectors of the political and financial establishments. He was very much part of Catalonia's network of clubs and associations which grouped the more traditional sectors of the local bourgeoisie around a broadly centrist nationalist agenda. His contracts included lucrative deals on billboard advertising around the Camp Nou. His local friends ranged from Enrique Llaudet and Agustin Montal, former and outgoing presidents of Barça respectively, to close advisers of arguably the two most powerful men in Catalonia at the time, Tarradellas and Pujol (he was a member of the board of Banca Catalana). Part of his attractiveness as a candidate also seemed to be his exterior image as a youthful, fit and outward-going fifty-six-year-old – he was a Catalan sailing and motor rally champion – although other less openly declared aspects of his personal life and professional life were to prove a liability rather than an asset deeper into the campaign.

From the outset, Sagi was clearly the favoured candidate of a significant sector of Barça's long-ruling establishment – Catalans who, for all their nationalist rhetoric, on occasions had reached an accommodation with the Franco regime, and now looked towards an orderly evolution of the democratic process that would not undermine their economic interests. Despite his public claim of non-interference, Montal admitted to me, in an interview for this book, that he personally considered Sagi the best choice, describing him as 'a new man who won't lose sight of the past'. Sagi, meanwhile, told me that he had put his name forward in response to pressure from 'within the club'. He recalled, 'I was a good friend of Montal. All his directors came and said they were backing me.'

While Sagi owed his candidacy to the pressure of others, another member of the short list, Josep Lluís Nuñez, had thrown his hat into the ring motivated mainly by a burning personal ambition. Nuñez's offensive on the presidency of Barça had begun in a subtle way months before Montal had even stepped down. Unlike Sagi, and the two other main candidates – Fernando Ariño and Nicolau Casaus – Nuñez had no official ties with the club. Indeed he had a limited record of a long-term allegiance to it of any kind. It was only during the 1976–7 season, when the Montal presidency was reaching the end of its term, that he had begun to be noticed in the affairs of Barça by those who had followed the club closely for years. It was during that season that Nuñez adopted a very visible role of dedicated *cule*, following the team both nationally and internationally and developing contacts with journalists on assignment to cover Barça. For a while Nuñez himself was mute on the subject of the Montal succession. However, the idea of him as a serious candidate was increasingly filtered through the comments of his supporters, most noticeably Antonio Sala Mas, a popular figure in the world of cycling, and Luis Fernandez Abajo, a well-known radio journalist.

It was Fernandez Abajo who, during one of Barça's League expeditions to Alicante, told a group of his Catalan colleagues that *el señor* Nuñez would very much like them to join him for supper. The journalists were subsequently wined and dined on an assortment of luxurious local seafood, with the cost of transport and the meal fully covered by Nuñez. During the meal, the most inquisitive journalist in the group, Josep Morera Falco of *El Correo Catalan*, asked Nuñez what the purpose of the evening was, and whether it had anything to do with the Barça election. Nuñez stonewalled, before letting slip a tactical hint. As Morera Falco later recalled, 'He replied that his only aim was to get to know us better, and in that way he was paying a kind of tribute to a profession that he respected and in some way envied . . . Whenever I asked him whether he was standing for the presidency he gave an evasive answer, like "I don't know . . .", "Perhaps", or "I recognise I am under pressure to do so, but we'll see . . ." '

Such contacts could not easily be ignored by the journalists involved. For while Nuñez had never previously been identified with the club, he was not by any means an unknown. He was, after all, the president of the family-owned Nuñez y Navarro, the biggest construction company in Catalonia, especially known in Barcelona for its involvement over more than two decades in the redevelopment of important parts of the city. Aged forty-six, he was his sector's unrivalled business success. In most other parts of Spain, indeed Europe, such credentials would have made him an obvious candidate not only to be president of but also to own the biggest football club in his area of business. That Nuñez had to struggle to attain the presidency can only be understood in the particular context of who he was, where he was, and what others thought of him.

Although he adopted the Catalan name after Franco died, he was christened, brought up, and made his first fortune registered with the name José Luis Nuñez Clemente. With his ancestry from other parts of Spain, much further south, Nuñez was born on 7th January 1931 in the small town of Baracaldo, near the Basque city of Bilbao. The fact that he was born the day after Epiphany may have left his mother thinking of his birth as a good omen for the future – full of unexpected gifts, perhaps. But the reality surrounding the Nuñez household at the time was somewhat more mundane. His father was a customs officer, working for the Spanish state and with no particular loyalty to the concept of Euskadi – the Basque nation free and independent from the control of Madrid. When José Luis was seven months old, the family moved, with the father's new posting, to Port Bou, on the French border. 'The Civil War had broken out and they were hard times, with the town bombed every now and then,' Nuñez recalled when I interviewed him in 1999. 'We used to take shelter in the railway wagons.' In 1938 the Nuñez family moved again, this time to Barcelona, just as the Civil War was drawing to an end and as Franco's troops converged on the Catalan capital. With his family seemingly untouched by the repression of the Franco regime, Nuñez went to a state school. 'My life really began when I was fourteen. It was then that I began to look after my own future,' he told me.

At the age of fourteen José Luis took a course in accountancy, then did odd jobs here and there before his first full-time job working in a state pensions department. In his early twenties he increased his salary and his knowledge of how companies operate by working as an insurance agent. However, it was his marriage to Maria-Luisa, the strong-charactered daughter of Francisco Navarro, a financially liquid property developer, that proved the real turning-point. While it was his father-in-law who initially had the assets, it was José Luis who set about keeping the company accounts and looking at ways of boosting profits, when not visiting individual sites on his Vespa. José Luis, encouraged by his wife, gradually took over the running of the family firm, which, during the late 1950s and early 1960s, went through various changes in title – Navarro y Nuñez, Navanu SA, Construcciones Navarro and Construcciones Navarro y Nuñez. In 1966, the family firm was wound up, and its assets realised and distributed around the family. The following year, the Franco government brought out a decree liberalising the property market, a measure that guaranteed growth in the construction sector. Fifteen days later, a seemingly prescient Nuñez registered eleven new companies with his name and that of his wife as president and company secretary respectively. Over the next ten years the new holding, called Nuñez y Navarro, came to register more than 100 different companies, some of which were set up simply to administer a specific project.

Nuñez made a fortune out of the unconstrained and unplanned urban growth that took place in Catalonia in response to an influx of immigrants from other parts of Spain. The most notorious developments were those of 1957–73, when the City Hall was run by a Franco appointee, Josep Maria de Porcioles Colomer. As Robert Hughes has written, 'Sins of omission, as much as those of commission, were what depressed the urban fabric of Barcelona in the Franco years.' His writing paints a vivid portrait of how Porcioles massacred parts of the landscape of what was once considered Spain's most elegant city: 'So the visitor [is] locked in the roaring mass of traffic between the indifferent high-rise walls of the *autovia* that cuts north towards France and is called the Meridiana (1971), or gazing at the brutal gashes of the Via Augusta and the Avinguda General Mitre . . . incisions that tore out so much of interest in the upper parts of nineteenth-century Barcelona . . .'

Among the more notorious developments or rather destructions involved buildings in the Eixample district, ironically conceived in the nineteenth century by the Catalan designer Cerdà as the 'Ideal City' which would save urban man from the dehumanisation of the industrial age. In order to increase floor and parking space within a highly valued area, Nuñez's bulldozers flattened old walls and built new ones, reducing the ratio between open and built space that Cerdà wanted the residents to enjoy. The crude monotony that was imposed throughout – and the company's habit of boasting its presence with large billboards – earned Nuñez the title of 'the Man of the Four Corners' or, worse, 'the Beveller'. Among the later buildings of historic and artistic interest that Nuñez destroyed was the Palau Trinxet, the work of Josep Puig Cadafalch, one of Catalonia's architects of the early half of the twentieth century. In 1975, the year of Franco's death, Nuñez y Navarro constructed a housing block next to Gaudí's Sagrada Família, in the exact place where the original plans conceived an extension of the church.

Hughes argues that what Porcioles allowed – and what men like Nuñez built in Barcelona during the Franco years – was no worse than the urbanisation that took place during the same period in the United States and democratic Western Europe. The difference, however, was that what was done in Barcelona occurred under a regime that flouted its own laws and repressed any opposition in a city justifiably proud of its architectural heritage. And men like Nuñez were only too happy to take advantage of the situation to enrich themselves. As a former employee of his company recalled, 'During the Porcioles period, Nuñez had important contacts with architects and councillors . . . Nuñez was a man without real feelings, without any politics, although in the way he operated he was a man of the right.'

By acting the way he did, Nuñez fuelled a growing political opposition of left-wing architects, sociologists, academics and writers, some of whom were also *cules* and would remain critical of the constructionist's attempts to extend his power base within Barça.

By 1977, however, Nuñez had proved himself capable of overcoming adversity. He had moved well beyond the modest family environment into which he had been born, no doubt making best use of his new family's money, but investing it wisely through his own talent for business and finance. His ability to reconvert large swathes of Barcelona, despite the opposition of conservationists and tradeunionists, boosted his sense of achievement, of being a 'winner'. And yet if there was one obstacle that Nuñez had to overcome it was the trauma of alienation. As an immigrant, and a largely self-made millionaire, he struggled for social acceptance in a society that maintained closely knit forms of hierarchy. Money had not so far bought him the social status that in Catalonia was interlocked with political power. He did not belong to the so-called 'civil society' – that network of clubs and associations – where senior Catalan executives discussed more traditional businesses like textiles, while maintaining an influence on local culture and politics as a concession to the nationalist ideal.

'I am a man who has never got involved in party politics,' Nuñez told me. 'I presented myself as a candidate who wanted Barça to be completely independent politically. I always believed that the club had to appeal to all the immigrants who come and work in Catalonia.' And yet during the Franco years, when it seemed that the dictator would never die, Nuñez's ambition had been to be *alcalde* (mayor), in a sense appropriating for himself the power that had fuelled his own growth in the construction industry. The City Hall Nuñez identified with – authoritarian in its refusal to respond to criticism, liberal in its attitude towards planning permissions – became an anachronism almost from the day of Franco's death. With the coming of democracy, and in a city as conscious of its architectural history as Barcelona, it was only a matter of time before the ideology of preservation reasserted itself. If there was one institution, one focus of power, that had shown itself through the years to be both resistant to change and adaptable to it, it was FC Barcelona. It was a club that had absorbed thousands of immigrants as fans, while keeping its own power structure intact. To get to the top of Barça, for Nuñez, represented the most important goal of his life. The election called by Montal was the perfect opportunity to make his boldest move.

Far from directly challenging the Barça establishment from the outset, Nuñez had at first tried to negotiate with it, hoping that he could turn tradition on its head and be accepted by it. During the 1976–7 season Nuñez had got himself introduced to Raimón Carrasco, the then vice-president of Barça who became president of the club during the interregnum preceding the election. The two men met at the seaside resort where Nuñez took his summer holidays alongside the Catalan bourgeoisie. Nuñez told Carrasco that he was interested in joining the junta of directors of Barça, a move he clearly saw as a stepping-stone to becoming president.

Carrasco didn't commit himself one way or the other. But the meeting left him harbouring a deeper social bias towards Nuñez. 'Nuñez had a way of expressing himself that I found difficult to understand,' Carrasco said, in an interview for this book. 'Because of his social background he couldn't really speak either Spanish or Catalan properly. He was pretty uncultured. What I did understand was that he wanted to be a director of the club. I felt that he was a person who wanted the post simply to further his own ambition and not to serve the club, which is why I thought he'd make a bad director, and a bad president. Nuñez had been successful financially and wanted a social status he didn't have – because money can't buy you everything. It can give you assets but it doesn't give you social standing. It was when he realised that he wasn't going to be made a director that he decided to present himself as a candidate for the presidency.'

Once the candidates had been declared, Nuñez tried one more time to negotiate with that sector of the Catalan bourgeoisie that had sought to exclude him from its social circle. He approached Victor Sagi. According to Sagi, Nuñez proposed what he considered a straightforward deal: 'Nuñez came to see me to make me a proposal. "The only ones who really matter in this election," he said, "are you and I. I'm sure we can reach an agreement." What he proposed was that we would sign an agreement in which I would be president for four years, at the end of which I would hand over to him. I refused. One of the reasons I was fighting the election was that a lot of people didn't want Nuñez. So I couldn't play such a dirty game.'

And yet Nuñez was already demonstrating that he was a man for whom the ends justified the means, however questionable the means. At the beginning of 1978, soon after declaring his candidacy, Nuñez was approached by an anonymous fixer and offered a list of all the members of Barça with their addresses. According to Nuñez, the fixer initially asked to be paid two million pesetas, but after much haggling handed over his file for less. He told the Catalan journalist Josep Morera Falco, 'I've bought the electoral register for 70,000 pesetas. They wanted more money, but I managed to get it for that price and I know that as a result the other candidates are getting really flustered. What I can tell them is that I am quite prepared to sell them copies of the register for the same price.'

On 13th April 1978, three weeks before the election, Victor Sagi announced that he was pulling out of the race. At a press conference attended by incredulous journalists, Sagi argued that the existence of five candidates who could not agree between themselves threatened to confuse and divide the membership, and would make it difficult for anyone to emerge with a convincing majority. He was therefore retiring for the sake of the unity of the club, which he said was dangerously close to experiencing an election that 'because of either democratic experience or personal vanity could turn into an economic and social battle for the presidency'.

It may have sounded noble but it barely made sense. Of all the candidates, Sagi appeared to be the one who until then was publicly feeling the least pressure. Nothing in the campaign so far had altered the widely held perception of him as the firm favourite to win. Indeed, some of his strongest supporters were so unconvinced by the announcement that they asked privately for a better explanation. Among those unconvinced by Sagi's public explanation was Carrasco, the interim president whose job was to supervise the election, and the first person to whom Sagi had to communicate his decision officially. Carrasco was among several senior Barça figures at the time who later told me he believed that Sagi had decided to pull out after hearing that Nuñez had accumulated a compromising dossier about his private life and his business affairs. To this day there is no evidence that such a dossier existed, although highly placed sources within Barça at the time maintain that the devastating blow to Sagi's self-confidence was delivered not by an actual dossier but by his fears as to the alleged contents. According to their version, Sagi was terrified at the prospect of his public life becoming the subject of electoral controversy.

I raised the subject with Sagi at a meeting we had at his luxurious home in Pedralbes in 1998. The house was filled with family portraits, between which Sagi walked – bronzed skin, taut muscles, easy available smile – seemingly utterly relaxed, a king in his castle, still the publicist after all these years. Whatever may have belonged to his past, he seemed to have put the darker sides of it well behind him, like someone who had survived a nightmare to see the dawning of a sunny day. Without a hint of nervousness, he told me, 'Although I had made up my mind to pull out of the race, Nuñez tried his best to stop people thinking that the reason I had done it was as an act of loyalty to the club. That is why he spun the rumour that there were secrets that might put me in a compromising situation. There were even rumours that he had hired some private detectives to follow me. Nuñez thought that money could buy everything, but that dossier never existed.'

When I asked Nuñez about the campaign, he showed no inclination to apologise for Sagi's downfall. On the contrary, he seemed still intent to sow doubts about the whole affair. 'When a candidate stands for president, the first thing he has to have is complete transparency in his personal and professional life. Unfortunately, there was one candidate who had things he wanted to hide . . .'

Following Sagi's withdrawal from the race, Nuñez pulled off another strategic *coup* – persuading another candidate, Joan Casals, to declare his open support for him. Casals never really had any chance of winning on his own. But Nuñez held out the prospect of giving him an important post in the future junta were he to be elected, arguing that in that respect the six million pesetas Casals had spent on his campaign would not be wasted.

In fact, an opinion poll of the Barça membership showed that Nuñez was trailing in third place, behind the two remaining candidates – Nicolau Casaus, second, and Fernando Ariño, now emerging as a strong front-runner. Casaus was a relatively modest businessman (his firm manufactured kitchen cloths) whose main credentials were a long and loyal association with the club and his semi-legendary status as the man who had survived imprisonment and an execution order soon after Franco took power. He was the club 'insider' who claimed to know its strengths and its weaknesses and how to put them right, better than any of his rivals. His manifesto appealed to the club's roots – his preference was for a team made up largely if not wholly of Catalan players – while showing itself open to innovation in terms that would in time prove prophetic: he wanted the creation of a European champions' league to boost the club's international profile.

Ariño had also developed stronger if more recent ties with the club structure, having served for a while on the junta during Montal's presidency. He, like Casaus, appealed to the club's roots, speaking a language that mirrored the politics of Jordi Pujol with its vision of the club as an integral part of a Catalan civil society. And yet members of

Convergència, including Pujol himself, drew back from supporting Ariño outright. With an eye on the future Catalan parliamentary elections, they calculated that the party would be better served by being seen to be above Barça's divisive battles than in backing a candidate who might end up losing. They were reluctant to be drawn into a campaign that was increasingly being portrayed as involving the left against the right. They were also not so sure that Ariño would win, after he and Sagi had failed to agree on a joint candidacy. Although Sagi had the support of some of Pujol's camp, Ariño considered the publicist to be tainted with Francoism because one of his main clients, apart from Barça, had been the state radio station under Franco.

With only half-hearted support coming from his natural ally, Ariño found his campaign at grass-roots level increasingly dominated by the local Communist Party, the PSUC. Throughout the Franco years, the party had encouraged its cadres – many of them immigrant members of the working class with strong trade-unionist ties – to support Barça as part of the resistance. The party's analysis, as explained to me by one of its leaders, Gregorio Lopez Raimundo, was that although the club had been managed and controlled by members of the Franco regime together with a resurgent bourgeoisie, it was in essence a mass movement that had played a historical role, at given moments, in challenging the forces of reaction, and therein lay its political potential. As Raimundo observed, 'During Franco's time, Barça became for a majority of Catalans, including those who didn't go to matches but simply tuned in to the radio, an emblem of nationalist feeling and of the struggle for self-government and freedom. This attitude was endorsed by the fans independently of what the directors wanted.'

The PSUC believed that Ariño's manifesto pledge to increase the role of a greatly increased membership in the future running of Barça held the key to transforming the club's power structure. Its optimism was fuelled by the strong Communist vote in the city of Barcelona in March 1977 in the Spanish elections. The PSUC had emerged as the party with the second-most votes, behind the Catalan Socialist Party.

The involvement of the PSUC in the Barça election and the way that the 'Communist Ariño' allegation was used by Nuñez's supporters to scare off middle-class members of the club were recalled by Ricardo Huguet, a businessman who was one of Ariño's campaign strategists.

He told me: 'The PSUC, from its general secretary to the ordinary militant, got very involved in the Ariño campaign. I remember being with Ariño when he told me, "The PSUC have jumped on my bandwagon." We felt we couldn't reject them just because they were Communists. It was, after all, a time when we were aspiring to a more democratic Spain, so it wasn't right to have such an attitude. The Nuñez faction, however, had no problems with exploiting the suggestion that Ariño was the "Communist candidate". He appealed to the middle-class members of the club. The fact was that Ariño was a practising Roman Catholic and sociologically right-wing. As you can see, the campaign was pretty dirty.'

Nuñez knew that the anti-Communist card also had its drawbacks. To play it too hard or exclusively would make him an easier target for left-wing Barça supporters who had long viewed Nuñez y Navarro as the construction arm of Francoism, its bulldozing of all that was special and precious in the urban landscape symbolic of a chilling disregard for life. So Nuñez added another barrel to his strategic gun: the idea that he was the only candidate who represented a real break with the past. Now the target became the closely knit group of businessmen from the textile sector that had produced the majority of Barça presidents since the Civil War. One of the favourite campaign mottoes of the Nuñez camp became '*Romper con el porron*' ('Break with the wine jar'). Previously the running of the club had been passed from one textile boss to another just as peasants pass their wine from one to the other. Nuñez represented a break with that tradition, or so he told his electorate, as if power that was moved from one sector of the bourgeoisie (textiles) to another (construction) was essentially any different, and as if the fact that he had made his fortune thanks to Franco before trying to gain acceptance by those who had the *porron* didn't matter either.

Nuñez's campaign started somewhat clumsily. His tendency to launch personal attacks on the Barça trainer, Michels, and individual members of his team exposed not only a vindictive nature in the man but also a judgement of football that was far from faultless. It left many Barça supporters feeling uneasy. Some also found distasteful a poster of a large key superimposed on the club colours which suggested that only Nuñez had the key to its soul.

But with the opinion polls not looking too good, Nuñez took corrective action. He brought more actively into his campaign a group of journalists and other individuals with an inside knowledge of the club. What became known as the 'Team of Ten' advised Nuñez on what to say and how to say it in a way designed to attract the greatest number of votes from a politically diversified membership. The 'spin doctors' included three of Catalonia's most prestigious sports journalists – Domingo García (then sports editor of *La Vanguardia*), José-Maria Casanovas and Antonio Hernaez – and a one-time nobody who had gradually worked himself into the administrative structure of the club, first as interpreter and then as assistant trainer, José-Maria Minguella. Between them they elaborated a new language of collective seduction for Nuñez. It was based on a rewriting of years of Barça history to make it look like failure, and contrasting it with the pledge of a brave new world in which Barça would reclaim its peaks of glory – and stay up there.

Nuñez promised he would find the money not just to finance some of the best players in the world, but also for an expansion of the Camp Nou, making it beyond doubt one of the great stadiums in the world. Two slogans were added to the Nuñez lexicon: 'For a triumphant Barça' and 'Barça will once again make history'. And in another strategic variant, Nuñez claimed that he was 'apolitical' – not in the sense of being disloyal to Barça's Catalan roots, but in being beyond and above the party/political interests of his rival candidates. In a way, Nuñez was playing the typical card of a demagogue, appealing to the broadest common denominator for support: a promise of power and conquest. Looked at from another perspective, he was also cleverly turning the political uncertainties and fears about the transition to democracy to his own advantage, as well as appealing directly to those members to whom all that really mattered was that Barça win and win well.

Years later, Domingo García, a member of the 'Team of Ten' who went on to become Nuñez's head of press, when I interviewed him he summarised what he believed were the main strengths of the Nuñez campaign he was so instrumental in backing: 'Nuñez is a product of a rebellion by a small sector of Barça against the establishment, against those families who had between them maintained control over the presidency for decades. The club had been a political instrument from

Helenio Herrera's day until the coming of democracy, but had been a disaster in football terms for most of that time. It was true that a lot of people felt sentimentally attached to the club as an expression of their nationalism, but there were also people who were fed up to the back teeth of seeing Real Madrid win the League too often and calling itself the best team in Spain.'

As election day approached, Johan Cruyff, who had already announced his departure from the team, made a brief reappearance in the politics of Barça, declaring that in his view the one candidate who did not deserve the vote of the membership was Fernando Ariño. The candidate himself had no love lost for the Dutchman, even though he had deliberately avoided attacking him in his campaign, knowing the popularity he enjoyed among the fans. But it was an open secret that of all the former directors of the club, Ariño was the one who got on worst with Cruyff. One of the points of tension was Cruyff's habit – he was a chain-smoker at the time – of lighting up cigarettes in the changing room, something that no previous player at the club had ever done. Ariño was also critical of the way Cruyff was always pressing for more money, not just for himself but for the rest of the team too, claiming that this demonstrated a lack of loyalty to the club and a measure of financial irresponsibility.

In the eyes of the Ariño camp, however, the tension that existed between the two men did not seem a convincing reason for Cruyff's bolt from the blue. They suspected that Nuñez had reached a deal with him – a suspicion they believed was confirmed once the election was over when Cruyff moved into a new office in Barcelona, built by Nuñez, to start up a new business venture. However, there is no evidence specifically pointing to a reward for services rendered. Cruyff told me that he backed Nuñez quite simply because he had been advised by some former directors of the club that he was now the best man for the job.

As controversial as Cruyff's involvement in the election was that of Charly Rexach, one of the Catalan members of the Barça team who was also hugely popular among the fans. The day before the vote, the man regarded by many members at the time as the essence of the club declared his unequivocal backing for Nuñez, claiming that he was clearly the candidate for the future. Again Nuñez's opponents suspected dirty tricks: at best a deal whereby Nuñez had promised Rexach – then reaching the end of his career as a player – a job on the club's technical staff. Again there was no evidence. Although Rexach did eventually join the technical staff, José-Maria Minguella, the man who claims the credit for pushing the player into the Nuñez camp, offers another explanation. He told me, 'I enlisted Rexach's support for Nuñez because I knew it would have a huge impact on the vote. I knew how popular Rexach was among the fans at a time when Catalanism, after Franco's death, was still a strong force. I told Rexach, "Look, this is a critical moment in the history of the club and it's important that we elect the person who has the ability to take it into the future. The business of football is entering a period of change. It's going to stop being something that can be handled by a group of friends. It's going to involve some tough company management to keep afloat." Rexach understood it completely. He wasn't paid for his vote. I can swear that on the Bible.'

On 6th May 1978, Barça finally staged its election. The results: Nuñez 10,352 votes (39.38%); Ariño 9,537 votes (36%); and Casaus 6,202 (23.41%). The total number of votes represented only forty-one per cent of the 53,688 members in the election registry, suggesting that the campaign, for all its tortuous and dubious strategies, had left many members cold. Within the Ariño camp, however, there was a deep sense of foreboding about the future under Nuñez, and a commitment by some of those who had backed him – and Sagi before him – not to give up the fight in support of the club's democratic values.

Nuñez himself quickly moved to bolster his position by drawing Casaus into his team as vice-president, and making four of his leading campaign managers directors of his junta. Having achieved the ambition of his life, he was not going to surrender it easily.

aftermath of Spain's first democratic elections, Madrid had agreed to hand over self-governing powers to the regions, and Catalonia was preparing to elect its government on the basis of a broad agreement among local political leaders. So the European Cup Winners Cup final was widely seen as an opportunity to show Europe that the Catalan nation was once again coming into being, as well as to demonstrate to Madrid that the final push for self-government had the backing of the people.

Some 30,000 *cules* – of all ages and social backgrounds – travelled to Basle, waving as many Catalan flags as they did Barça flags, and chanting, '*Visca el Barça! Visca Catalunya!*' It was the biggest foreign expeditionary force ever assembled by the club; one that would never be repeated on such a scale. Before departing, the fans had been urged by politicians and club officials to act like diplomats not predators. The sleepy Swiss town had never seen such an invasion of fans. There was no doubting the passion of the Catalans, the flag-waving and the chants intensifying as the game approached, but there was no outbreak of violence of any kind – in striking contrast to the reputation for hooliganism that other European fans, led by the English, were gaining. The *cules* seemed genuinely bent on celebration rather than conquest, and there was not a paralytic drunk among them.

The match against Fortuna of Düsseldorf handsomely rewarded the fans – a cliff-hanger of a game, touched with nobility, which turned into the highest-scoring final in the history of the competition. Barça was the first to score, a perfect pass in the fourth minute of the game from Rexach finding an unmarked Sanchez, who then struck at goal. Three minutes later Fortuna equalised, the German international Klaus Allofs taking advantage of a fumbled catch by the Barça goalkeeper Artola. The stadium was at fever pitch and the game had scarcely begun. In the 12th minute, Barça's talented new recruit from the youth team, Carrasco, broke through the Fortuna defence only to be brought down by Zewe. A penalty was awarded. It looked like being a certain goal. Barça's main penalty-taker, Charly Rexach, never seemed to fail with the dead ball. He did on this occasion, his nerves cracking under the strain of the collective emotion. The game kept moving from one end to the other in a tough duel of equal strength and skills. In the 31st minute, the Barça captain, Asensi, scored off a rebound from a

Carrasco strike, and just before half-time the Germans came level again with a goal by Seel.

There were no goals in the second half, with both teams nervous of committing too many players forward, but the excitement returned in extra time. In the 13th minute Neeskens showed his true worth – a player with good vision as well as touch – by delivering a perfectly angled centre for Rexach to pick up and score with. In the 24th the Dutchman did it again, this time picking out Carrasco from inside his own half and setting the young player off on a bold bruising run, ducking and diving as he drew what seemed the entire Fortuna defence to him. Carrasco had just beaten his last man to the right of the German goal when he spotted Barça's Austrian striker, Krankl, in the centre. Krankl volleyed powerfully into the net: 4–2 to Barça. With Krankl's goal, many of the *cules* thought it was all over, but it wasn't. Seel scored his second for Fortuna with three minutes left, and Barça was forced to end the game pulling back into its own half and putting up an extraordinary last-ditch defence. It was a nail-biting finish which left the older *cules* – veterans of the Civil War now enjoying the liberation they had fought for and lost so many years ago – gasping for breath.

When the final whistle blew, the Barça fans erupted, the younger among them – with no hindrance from the police – running on to the pitch and lifting the players on their shoulders. Among the 'souvenirs' taken from the stadium that night was one of the corner-flag posts. Dislodged by a *cule*, and signed by the players, it was later smuggled out of Switzerland and placed in the Barça museum, like a tribal totem – a symbol of the enthusiasm that was generated by the match.

The chemistry between supporters and players was nowhere better identified than in the comments subsequently made by Migueli, one of the toughest defenders in Spanish football, who had sacrificed the most to play in that final. Many years later, Migueli revealed how he had gone out to play with an injured collar bone, the pain dulled by a local anaesthetic, ignoring medical advice that he risked long-term damage. Migueli had managed to persuade the coach, Rifé, to let him play after telling him that he had not come all the way to Basle to have a rest. With passion, Miguelli had insisted that this was the most important game of his life and he was prepared to commit his all to it.

In order to prolong the effect of the anaesthetic, Miguelli left his appearance on the pitch to the last moment, avoiding the warm-up before the game. During the match he proved as good as his word, an anchor in defence, and a perfect complement to Neeskens. He played on throughout the game, even though the anaesthetic had worn off by the time it had gone to extra time. In an interview with TV3, he explained, 'When I came out on to the pitch and saw all those fans with their Barça and Catalan flags, I felt really moved. It really boosted my spirits seeing all those people who had come all this way to support me. I thought about how much these fans were giving the team, and realised that we had a duty to give them something back. I think it's at that point that I understood the importance of this link between club member and player.'

The team's home-coming was unprecedented in its scale and emotion. Over a million people took to the streets of Barcelona in a massive extension of the scenes that had been witnessed in Basle. Again there was an underlying sense of political affirmation in this, the biggest popular demonstration since Franco's death, with the cries of *'Visca el Barcelona! Visca Catalunya!'* reverberating along the Rambla. Flanked by members of the team and Narcís Serra, Barcelona's newly elected Socialist mayor, the man who had returned from years of exile to become provisional President of Catalonia, Josep Tarradellas, delivered a heartfelt speech of gratitude from the balcony of the Generalitat. Tarradellas, a lifelong member of Barça, declared unhesitatingly that the win in Basle had been a victory not just for the club but for the whole of the Catalan nation at a critical moment in its history.

The event was to prove memorable in one other important respect. As the team took their places on the balcony, the words 'Neeskens, Neeskens' began to emerge from the crowd, a tentative murmur turning into a full-fledged chant that gathered increasing support among the thousands packed in the Plaça Sant Jaume. The Dutchman was not visible among the first line of players who had appeared on the narrow balcony, holding the Cup. He was in fact just inside, behind the window, waiting to take his turn. The chanting became louder and at one point reached such a crescendo that Tarradellas, seemingly fearing an outbreak of public disorder, turned to Neeskens and gestured to him to take his place alongside him. Seeing the Dutchman, a sector of the crowd burst into spontaneous applause. Neeskens, in tears, undid his Barça tie and threw it into the masses, a gesture that was greeted with an even greater ovation. Later that evening the chant was taken up afresh, with Neeskens once again bursting into tears, as the team ended its tour of honour in the Camp Nou.

It did not take a great stretch of the imagination for anyone witnessing the affair to realise that its significance went far beyond the expression of support for a popular player who had played his last game for the club. It was also a gesture of defiance by those who had voted against and remained opposed to Josep Lluís Nuñez. The president in the short time he had been in office had already adopted a higher profile than any of his predecessors, and had made a special point of taking centre stage in the celebrations surrounding Basle. Prior to the match he had had the TV cameras film him testing the pitch as though he were one of the players or the team's manager. Among those who subsequently invaded the pitch were loyal supporters who put Nuñez on their shoulders too. Nuñez's self-importance made itself most felt, however, when the team returned to Barcelona. When they were picked up at the airport, Nuñez made a point of sitting next to the driver, and close to the cup. Many fans couldn't believe their eyes when they saw the team bus making its triumphal progress fronted by the diminutive Nuñez, waving to the crowds like a triumphant Napoleon. And later it was Nuñez who led the team out of the tunnel at the Camp Nou.

But Nuñez's efforts to turn the team's victory into an unqualified endorsement of his presidency were wrecked by the slogan that developed during those dramatic hours: 'Neeskens si, Nuñez no'. He returned home from the ultimate humiliation at the Camp Nou publicly prepared for the first and only time in his life to admit defeat. In a statement, Nuñez declared, 'I thought this was going to be the happiest day of my life, but it has turned out quite the opposite. I'm feeling sunk.' Yet by insisting that his opponents were only in a minority, and offering to resign rather than resigning outright, he showed that his ambition together with his political instinct for survival had not diminished one jot. In the hours that followed, the Nuñez camp, using its allies in the media, launched a counter-offensive boosted by a personal telegram of support from Tarradellas. The provisional President of the Generalitat had been almost as shocked as Nuñez to see the celebrations in the Plaça Sant Jaume disrupted. He feared that a resignation by Nuñez and a fresh election in the club would destabilise his careful politics of consensus in the rest of Catalonia.

The campaign not only to save Nuñez but to turn the whole controversy to his advantage involved tactics that ranged from gentle persuasion to outright intimidation. The members of the Barça board unanimously backed Nuñez, feeling that they owed their positions to him. Among them was the club's vice-president, the veteran Nicolau Casaus, who used his influence in the *peñas* – Barça's fan clubs – to rally the grass-roots behind Nuñez. Meanwhile, opponents of Nuñez denounced his supporters' alleged use of groups of *morenos* – the nickname given to mainly working-class unemployed Catalans who both acted as bodyguards and gave vociferous support, threatening violence against anyone who disagreed. Within days of Basle, Nuñez was back in the Camp Nou to watch a League match against Real Sociedad. This time he made his entrance into the stadium surrounded by supporters who chanted and waved placards in his favour. If there was anyone around still prepared to shout 'Neeskens' they were not heard. Nuñez stepped into the directors' box to be greeted with huge signs of affection by each member of the board in turn, while thousands of members gave him a standing ovation lasting over half a minute. Nuñez smiled and waved his acknowledgement. It was as if the emperor, having regained control of the senate, had returned to the circus to popular acclaim from the plebs – with a little help from the gods. In Nuñez's case, Tarradellas's endorsement had assured his survival just as the backing of Cruyff and Rexach, during the campaign, had swung the election behind him.

Nevertheless, only time would show that those who opposed Nuñez's authoritarianism had not surrendered but simply beaten a tactical retreat.

If Nuñez had pledged a triumphant Barça, he had done so anticipating what was to become the guiding principle of most wealthy clubs in Europe: success is only possible with star players, and star players cannot be bought without money. Or, to borrow the catchphrase coined by the former advertising executive and football writer Alex Fynn, the name of the game is the price of success.

Nuñez had come to the presidency of Barça knowing a lot about making money and being successful. He would have had to be pretty stupid not to know about either, coming from the construction business during a development boom unrestricted by government regulation or the wishes of the citizen. More limited, however, was his knowledge of football – not in the sense simply of knowing how to run a club as big as Barça, but of knowing how to identify what motivates people when they passionately follow it.

When Nuñez took over Barça he took charge not of a company but of a club owned by its membership. He asked for a major audit to be done on the accounts inherited from his predecessor, and discovered that the club had hugely overborrowed to cover its costs. Nuñez instructed his treasurer, a bright young banker called Carlos Tusquets, to draw up a plan that would allow him both to reduce the debt and to generate additional revenue to cover investment in star players and an expansion of the Camp Nou. Tusquets drew up a scheme whereby members would advance the annual payment for their season tickets by a year, and this sum would be repaid by the club over the following five years. In effect the scheme represented an interest-free loan for the club, and a saving for the members. The scheme was extended to include parking season tickets, and a plan to convert and enlarge the VIP area, pricing the seats as the most expensive in the stadium.

What made the scheme financially viable was that the demand for season tickets far outstripped availability, and that having a season ticket was often the only way many people had of getting into the Camp Nou. Tusquets was therefore able to offer the scheme not only to the club's existing members who had season tickets but to aspiring members too, on the basis of a further expansion of the Camp Nou – an increase in its seating capacity from 90,000 to 120,000. Underpinning the whole scheme was the search for a player the club felt it could afford and with the ability to fill the stadium and win titles on a scale never seen before.

The player called upon to play such a role, Diego Armando Maradona, was first brought to the attention of senior officials of Barça early in 1977 – a year before Nuñez's election to the presidency. Nicolau Casaus, who had special responsibility for the *peñas*, received a transatlantic phone call from one Beltrán, an old Catalan friend who ran a cake shop in the Argentinian coastal resort of Mar de Plata. Beltrán, a self-exiled *cule* who made up for not being able to go to the Camp Nou by following Argentinian football, had just watched Maradona aged sixteen help his club, Argentinos Juniors, to a spectacular win against the local team. 'This Maradona is an absolute genius. You've got to come and see him for yourself,' Beltrán told Casaus. Another equally enthusiastic report reached the club from José-Maria Minguella, Vic Buckingham's former interpreter, who had set himself up as an agent in South America. He tentatively suggested that the player might be bought for one million dollars. Minguella got a message back from Barça's then secretary, Jaume Rosell, saying that the club felt that this was too much to pay 'for a teenager'. With the evidence of hindsight it was a missed opportunity to get Maradona cheaply.

Only when Nuñez came to power and after the 1978 World Cup – which Argentina without Maradona won – did serious negotiations get under way. They were to last, off and on, for four years, with the Argentinian military authorities reluctant to surrender their most popular asset, and Nuñez holding out for what he believed was the price he could afford. Carlos Tusquets, the club treasurer, remembers being told by Nuñez in the final stages of the talks, 'Save us as much money as you can but make sure you get him as soon as possible.' Tusquets, with the same imagination he had applied to raising money from the *socios*, took advantage of Argentina's weak financial situation by purchasing bonds quoted in dollars on the New York Stock Exchange and trading them in for Argentinian pesos. Large bundles of the local currency were then put in a security van hired by Tusquets and delivered to the Argentinians.

According to Barça's official records, the club formally agreed to pay a total of $7.3 million. Maradona himself was guaranteed $50,000 per season, excluding perks and bonuses. In an appendix to the contract signed between FC Barcelona and Maradona's own company, Maradona Productions, the latter was described as having the only 'legitimate and exclusive rights to all advertising rights and merchandising of the name Maradona'. Discounting the advantage he secured on the exchange rate, Tusquets believed the real cost of the transaction to Barça was in fact just over $5 million.

By the time Maradona finally arrived in Barcelona to sign his record-breaking contract at the beginning of June 1982, Nuñez had got through four managers – one for each year of his presidency. He had dispensed with some popular players and taken on others who had yet to prove themselves fully. The onus of financing the stadium's expansion had been transferred to the membership, some of whom had yet to take their seats in the Camp Nou. Following Basle, Rifé was replaced by Kubala, under whom Barça was knocked out of the UEFA cup and failed to win anything at home. Nuñez then recalled Helenio Herrera for a brief period, hoping against all the odds that history could repeat itself. On his first day back, 'the Magician' used his characteristic psychology, chalking up on the training board one phrase, 'We shall be champions!', and then getting each of his players to repeat it. Herrera took the club to victory in the Spanish Cup, although it failed to win the League championship. In 1982, Barça under German coach Udo Lattek fared badly in the League again and also in the Spanish Cup, but managed to regain some honour beating Standard Liège 2–1 in the final of the European Cup Winners Cup.

It was a mixed record that Nuñez had achieved so far – the peaks and troughs in his presidency seemingly no different from those in the years of his predecessors. Now he had signed a huge transfer deal with Maradona, a player still untested professionally in any club outside his own country, and who had failed to live up to his promise in the 1982 World Cup. Yet Nuñez was determined to prove wrong the sceptics – most of them in Madrid – who accused the Barça president of mindless extravagance. 'I am running a business,' he declared the day before he signed Maradona. 'If the politicians don't understand it, well, then they can go home. Maradona is going to revitalise football and thanks to him we're going to avoid a financial crisis. We deserve a monument to be built in our honour over this.'

On 28th July 1982, three weeks after Argentina had been knocked out of the World Cup in Spain, Maradona took to the field at the Camp Nou with the rest of the Barça team for the traditional start-of-the-season presentation ceremony. There were 50,000 fans there that day – a record for such an occasion – although Maradona's popularity was temporarily eclipsed by that of Bernd Schuster, the star of West Germany's triumph in the 1980 European Nations Cup, who had transferred from Cologne to Barça. It was cries not of 'Maradoooona' but of 'Schuuuuster' that reverberated around the Nou Camp.

Maradona had yet to earn his colours, having not exactly ingratiated himself with the Catalans with his petulance and inconsistent form during the World Cup. Schuster by contrast had shown himself a tough and skilful midfielder during his first season under the inspirational Herrera, despite having a highly temperamental character. The third recent foreign purchase was the Danish international Allan Simonsen. Because of pre-Bosman rules restricting the number of foreigners playing in a Spanish club side to two, it was widely expected that the Dane would give way to the German and the Argentinian. Maradona seemed only too aware of the challenge he was facing, declaring in one of his early press conferences, 'The moment of truth has arrived for me. I haven't come here to convert myself into the star of the team, but to be a member of it, because Maradona cannot win matches alone. That is why I hope that I and my team-mates can help each other and ensure that Barça becomes champion.'

From the outset, Maradona won the confidence of his team-mates on account not just of his uniquely talented play on the field but of what several of them perceived as his essential humanity. 'El Lobo' Carrasco, who shared a room with Maradona during a pre-season training session and developed a friendship with him, told me, 'I was very impressed by his humility, and his humanity. In Argentina he was a demigod, but when I was with him he seemed all too conscious of his roots. I realised how much he'd struggled to get where he was and how much he felt he still had to achieve to secure his family's future. He came across like a boy full of dreams. He seemed still to be very innocent and hungry. His eyes were like two big plates. He wanted to eat the world, and that frightened me. The more I got to know him, the more friendly we became, the more I worried about him too, the more I feared it would all end in tears.'

But whatever insecurity showed itself in the privacy of their shared room instantly dissipated when a football came into the equation. As

Carrasco put it, 'He was like a chameleon. On the football pitch, he was transformed. He suddenly became really sure of himself. He had complete mastery of the ball. When Maradona ran with the ball or dribbled through the defence, he seemed to have the ball tied to his boots. I remember our early training sessions with him: the rest of the team were so amazed that they just stood and watched him. Only he could create such a feeling of expectation around him. We all thought ourselves privileged to be witnesses of his genius.'

The respect of his team-mates in turn helped boost Maradona's self-confidence in the early games he played for Barcelona, during which he demonstrated some of his magic. In one memorable game against Real Madrid, Maradona pick up a pass from Carrasco just outside his own half, and dribbled through the Real defence until he was just a couple of metres away from the goalkeeper. Instead of tapping the ball past him, he kept it close to him, dribbled past the goalkeeper and then tapped it in.

Maradona had played just over a quarter of a season when he appeared before the cameras, ashen and unshaven, to announce that he had hepatitis. In his extended absence from the game (he missed fifteen matches) Maradona's rising star stopped in mid-flight. Both the *cules* and club officials felt let down by the player amid rumours that the illness was the result of Maradona's undisciplined and chaotic private life, much of it played out within the palatial home the club had rented on his behalf in the rich neighbourhood of Pedralbes. Maradona for his part became depressed, as he usually did whenever he was unable to play. 'It was the unhappiest period of my career,' he later recalled of that first Christmas in Barcelona.

One way Maradona dealt with his feelings of alienation was to create around himself a world of personal alliances based on unwritten codes of loyalty and self-protection, not unlike those that had helped him survive growing up in a shanty town on the outskirts of Buenos Aires. As well as having close friends among the players, such as Carrasco, Luis Alberto and Marcos, Maradona imported his own personal doctor, Ruben Oliva, and trainer, Fernando Signorini, and numerous friends and relations who soon turned the house in Pedralbes into a virtual colony. They came to be known locally as the Maradona 'clan'.

For any outsider wishing to deal with Maradona, the point of contact was not the player himself but his childhood friend and agent Jorge Cyterszpiler. The corpulent, Afro-haired, bad-mouthed Cyterszpiler cut an awkward figure among the sophisticates of Barcelona. Nor did his ruthless handling of every aspect of Maradona's copyright – from T-shirts to film-shots – through Maradona Productions endear him to sectors of the local media used to having a more direct relationship with the players. For their part, both Maradona and Cyterszpiler came to view the majority of local journalists as lackeys of Barça's senior management, acting either as informants or as purveyors of false information. Cyterszpiler told me he considered his media enemies analogous to 'members of the Gestapo or CIA agents'.

However sympathetically Maradona wished to be judged, the world he created for himself was viewed with increasing disdain by senior officials at FC Barcelona. They were rarely invited to Maradona's home, and when they were they were alarmed by what they saw. Carlos Tusquets, the club treasurer, remembers turning up at the Maradona home in the middle of the day to discuss some contractual matters. He was ushered into a large room by a member of the 'clan' to find Maradona in bed with his wife and a dog. Even Casaus, the Argentinian vice-president of the club who considered himself something of a father figure in Maradona's life, grew increasingly weary not so much of the player as of the world he had allowed to envelop him: 'Maradona arrived in Barcelona saying that he was prepared to give it his best in football terms. I believed him. It struck me that the promise was very typical of him – all heart and little head. But then after a while I realised that he didn't really control his own life. It was Cyterszpiler who did. I realised that the first time I visited Maradona in his Barcelona home. He was surrounded by seven or eight people, including the woman he was to marry, Claudia. It was a human wall that I was unable to penetrate.'

And yet it was Maradona's willingness to break out of this insulated state in defence of his colleagues that made him a focus of alternative power with the club. As the Barça Basque goalkeeper, Urruti, recalled, 'The importance of Maradona was that despite leading the life he led, and earning more than anybody and being the number one in the world, he still treated his team-mates like mates. That is to say that he was prepared to stick up for them and defend their rights and wishes. Maradona became our representative, the person we channelled our demands through to Nuñez. When it came to dealing with officials, we could always count on Diego's helping hand.'

With Maradona adding workers' rights to his extended injury periods and defiant social life, it was hardly surprising that no one grew to despise him as much as Nuñez. In a sense, Maradona represented a challenge to the kind of club Nuñez was trying to create – his own state-within-a-state where everything and everyone was subordinate to his rule. The tension between the two was epitomised by an incident that developed around a friendly match that Barça played away against Paris St Germain. Prior to the match Maradona insisted that he would play only if all the other members of the team received the same bonuses as he did. When they got what he asked for, the team went on to win 4–1.

That evening, Maradona persuaded half the Barça team to celebrate the victory by spending all night and most of the next morning in Parisian night-clubs. When word got back to Nuñez, the president was furious and in a statement publicly rebuked Maradona. The player replied – also publicly – that the way he conducted his life was his concern only, and that he intended to go on doing what he liked as long as it didn't damage his abilities as an athlete and a player. After reading Nuñez's statement, Cyterszpiler, with Maradona's blessing, went one step further. He rang Nuñez and over the phone called him an 'hijo de puta' – a 'son of a bitch'.

And yet Nuñez knew that to cut short Maradona's contract would have cost the club millions and signified a huge loss of face which the sceptics would have relished. Instead he tried to improve the situation in March 1983 by sacking Lattek – blamed by the media for losing control of both Maradona and Schuster – and replacing him with César Menotti, the Argentinian coach who had won the 1978 World Cup.

Maradona's recovery from illness and injury followed within days of Menotti's landing in Catalonia. There is a telling image in the TV coverage of Menotti and the team's presentation in the Camp Nou. While Nuñez and Casaus stand stiffly in their white jackets and dark ties, Maradona can be seen larking around in the back row with one or two of the other players, at one point losing his balance and giggling like a naughty little boy who has succeeded in wrecking the annual school photograph. Maradona seemed to be acting not just out of defiance towards the stiff-necked officials, but with a sense of relief and joy at having the relaxed, libertarian Menotti with him at last.

Whereas the German Lattek had insisted on morning training sessions, Menotti opted for a 3.00 p.m. start, an hour he argued was more compatible with a football player's natural biorhythms. It certainly suited Maradona and Menotti's lifestyle off the pitch – both enjoyed Barcelona's night life. In Maradona's case, it was not just women, it was booze and drugs, as the player confessed years later. And yet in Barcelona Maradona's drug-taking did not reach the addiction levels of later years. In an interview in January 1996, he said, 'The first time I tried cocaine was in Barcelona in 1982 when I was only twenty-two years old. I did it because I wanted to feel alive. In football, as in other walks of life, drug-taking has always existed. I was not the only one who began taking drugs. Lots of others were at it as well.'

When he was in Barcelona, Maradona's coke-taking remained a secret known only to a close circle of friends. Menotti has always insisted that he knew nothing about it, while conceding that the player 'like any young guy could have occasionally committed an act of foolishness'. Some club officials I have talked to had their suspicions but kept them under wraps, judging the matter not serious enough to make a public fuss over.

What is certainly true is that with the coming of Menotti, Maradona for a while recovered an instinctive enthusiasm for the game, which in turn contributed to reviving Barça's form. While the League and European titles remained elusive, the Argentinian partnership did the next best thing by making sure that Barça beat Real Madrid in the final of the King's Cup in June 1983. The match played in La Romareda stadium in Zaragoza had all the ingredients of a classic encounter between the two rivals. Each side wanted to redeem itself after a mediocre season. Nuñez used the occasion to rally the players and fans in a language he knew they would respond to: 'I hope that the team will be conscious during the match that it is representing a country and therefore it must be guided by a spirit of unity and strength.' Some 25,000 *cules* had converged on the Aragón capital, outnumbering the Madrid fans by nearly two to one.

It was a beautifully timed and visionary pass by Maradona in the 32nd minute of the first half that helped create the first goal of the match, scored by Victor. Real Madrid equalised soon after half-time when Santillana took advantage of a terrible mix-up in defence between Gerardo and the goalkeeper Urruti. Barça dominated what was left of the game, with both Maradona and Schuster showing their quality as players and inspiring the goal of the match: nine minutes into injury time, and with the referee about to whistle extra time, Julio Alberto dribbled down the left wing, centred, and the unmarked Marcos delivered a volley of such precision that Real's goalkeeper, Miguel Angel, stood wondering how it had ever happened. Schuster had no doubts and in the full view of the King of Spain delivered two Spanish equivalents of the 'fuck off' sign at the opposing side. Barcelona had won the Cup.

Nuñez looked a man who had grown in his shoes as his captain, Sanchez, led Maradona and the rest of the team to pick up the trophy from King Juan Carlos. All seemed forgiven and for the next night and day Barça celebrated in characteristic style, Maradona, Menotti and Schuster among the heroes of the hour. Only *La Vanguardia* dared utter a word of caution, wondering when, if ever, Barça would once again win the League and the European Cup.

Menotti failed to win either. Instead he opened up a potential new minefield for Maradona, by drawing him into a bitterly fought public controversy with Xavier Clemente, then manager of Athletic Bilbao, over how football should be played. Menotti claimed to be an admirer of a free, creative style of football which he contrasted with the 'tyranny' of the defensive, destructive play favoured by authoritarian managers. In Menotti's view, tyranny in football had its most brutal exponent in Clemente's team, which had a reputation for brutal tackling and little else. Clemente made it clear that he was not prepared to take any lessons from an ageing Argentinian hippie who seemed to spend more time pursuing women than teaching football skills.

The row intensified after a League match in the Camp Nou on 24th September 1983 in which the Bilbao defender Goikoetxea tackled Maradona from behind, breaking a run that could easily have ended in a goal. The tackle, one of the most brutal ever seen in Spanish football, so shocked Edward Owen, a Spain-based freelance tabloid English journalist, that he dreamed up the memorable description of Goikoetxea as 'the Butcher of Bilbao'. This was no consolation to Maradona, who spent three months recovering from a severe injury to his left ankle.

Barça's own surgeons initially operated on Maradona while he was under a haze of anaesthetic, implanting three pins they thought would aid recovery. Instead the operation had Maradona in agony and threw him into a new bout of depression. He recovered from it thanks to the unorthodox treatment of his own doctor, Oliva, who distrusted surgery and believed in the power of psychology. Within two months of the match Oliva had persuaded Maradona to throw away his crutches and show his strength of will by walking on his injured foot.

Maradona was declared fit to play again in the New Year of 1984. In his first match, against Sevilla, he played like a man reborn, scoring two goals and leading his team to an impressive 3–1 victory which had the Camp Nou celebrating once again. Three matches later, for the first time since his injury, he faced the Basques again, in Bilbao's San Mames stadium. Maradona now played like a man possessed, fearless in the face of the opponents who had nearly wrecked his career. He managed to score two goals, securing a 2–1 victory for Barça. But the game showed the tension between the two fanatically nationalist teams to be greater than ever. They committed a record of more than fifty fouls between them.

Perhaps had Maradona been playing for any other team, these two performances alone would have been sufficient to earn him praise and honour. Not for the first nor the last time in his footballing career, he had hit the lowest point only to pick himself up again and prove he could still be among the best. But Barça was Barça, and no amount of personal heroism on Maradona's part could make up for the club's failure to win the League or, in Maradona's final season, any European title.

Barça was eliminated from the European Cup Winners Cup by Manchester United in March 1984. United won the first leg at Old Trafford 3–0. In the second leg at the Camp Nou, Maradona insisted on playing despite developing one of his recurrent back pains. He played part of the game heavily anaesthetised; both his concentration and his reflexes were plainly affected. Just before half-time Menotti decided to substitute him, and as Maradona walked off the pitch and into the dressing room he was booed and loudly jeered by the Barça fans. A few minutes later, in the presence of Cyterszpiler, he threw a tantrum, raging against a world he felt had betrayed him. At one point, Maradona screamed, 'Why do I sacrifice myself if when I struggle to play I'm treated like this?' That evening all the bitterness and frustration that had been simmering below the surface from his early days at Barcelona boiled over. He decided there and then that he wanted to quit. But there was worse to come.

On 5th May of that year, Barça faced Athletic Bilbao in the final of the King's Cup in Madrid's Bernabéu stadium, with King Juan Carlos himself the guest of honour. The war between the two clubs that had been declared by Menotti and Clemente had by now drawn in an increasingly paranoid Maradona. On the eve of the match the Argentinian engaged in a much-publicised exchange of insults with Clemente. 'Clemente hasn't the balls to look me in the eye and call me stupid,' Maradona declared. 'Maradona is both stupid and castrated. It's a shame that a player like him who earns so much money has no human qualities whatsoever,' came Clemente's retort. The scene was set not so much for a football match as for the battle to end all battles – and this came at the end, once Bilbao had won 1–0. Maradona exploded when one of the Bilbao players, Sola, provocatively gave him a 'fuck off' sign as the Barça players were making their way off the pitch. As Maradona retaliated, he was promptly set upon by some of Sola's team-mates, led by 'the Butcher' himself – Goikoetxea – who lashed out with his foot as if intent on crippling Diego all over again. It was the signal that some of the Barça players had been waiting for. The toughest among them, Migueli and Clos, waded in with a series of kung-fu kicks. The brawl, which drew in more players on both sides and some of the fans, was eventually brought to a stop by officials and the police, having been watched with expressions of total horror by the King and his VIP entourage.

The episode left the directors of FC Barcelona seething, convinced that the reputation of one of the world's best-loved clubs had been tarnished by the irresponsible thuggery of an uneducated Argentinian –

13

Meester Venables and Archigoles

At the end of the summer break of 1984, two Barça players – a small, taciturn Scotsman and a tall, stubborn German – sat in the first team's dressing room, arguing about a shirt. With the minutes ticking away before the match – a pre-season tournament game against the Argentinian champions Boca Juniors – the two players had put on identical shirts with the number 8, each arguing that it was his lucky shirt, each trying to persuade the other to wear the number 10 instead.

The smaller of the two was Steve Archibald, the Scottish international whom Barça under its new manager Terry Venables had just signed from Tottenham Hotspur. The other player was the German international Bernd Schuster, who had been at the club for nearly four years. The number 10 had last been worn by Diego Maradona, before his transfer from Barcelona to Napoli. Archibald recalled the scene:

'It didn't matter to me but people wanted it to matter to me. Ever since I had arrived in Barcelona, every question was about how I felt about substituting Maradona. I kept saying, "I'm not substituting anybody. I'm Steve Archibald." Then when I arrived at the club Terry said I could wear the number 8 shirt, but then come the first game and what do I find but Bernd with the number 8 in his hands.

' "He's got my shirt," I tell Terry. He says, "Do you want me to get it for you?" I tell him, "No, it's OK, I'll do it myself." So I go over to Bernd and I say to him, "Bernd, I've got to have that number 8. It means a lot to me. I've worn it for ever, I've always scored goals with it, at Aberdeen, at Spurs . . ." But Bernd starts off saying it means a lot to him, too, that he played with it for Germany, for his old German club, for Barça . . . and I can see Terry waiting for us to sort things out, knowing that we've got to go soon. And I know that any minute I can say to him, "Terry, I want my shirt," and he'll do it for me, but that will cause a big problem in the dressing room, a big problem because all the other players are sitting watching . . .

'So I say to Bernd – and at this point I'm not just saying, I'm really trying to force the issue, using the limited English he might understand – "Bernd, I really *need* it," hoping that bringing in the "need" factor will convince him. But Bernd says it's the same for him, he needs it too. And then he leans over and says, as if he really means it, "I'm not going to wear Maradona's shirt."

'It was then that I understood the Maradona factor. It had finally entered my head not only what Schuster was thinking, but what the whole team was thinking – the influence Maradona had had on them, this world-class player with the magic at his feet. And I realised that for Schuster to change into that shirt was going to mean a much bigger thing for him than for me. Because in the end I thought, I don't care if Maradona and his granny have worn that shirt. I can respond to the challenge.'

In that summer's Gamper tournament Barça beat Boca Juniors, Maradona's old Argentinian club, 9–1, with Archibald scoring two of the goals. Barça went on to win the tournament, beating Bayern Munich 3–1 in the final. But it would take a while yet for Maradona's ghost to be laid to rest.

Maradona had flown in to a hero's welcome at Napoli's San Pablo stadium just four weeks before, on 5th July 1984. No sooner had he left the Catalan capital than the Barça president, Nuñez, jumped to defend the move, pointing to the difference between what Napoli had paid for him and what he had originally cost, a difference of 450 million pesetas. Speaking later to an assembly of the membership, he accused Maradona of lacking respect for the club and of trying to run it himself. 'For him,' Nunñez told the members, 'playing for Barcelona was a secondary consideration. That is why when he wanted more money he wanted to leave. It was all for the best.'

Judged simply in terms of a short-term return on investment, Maradona had clearly proved himself not only socially controversial but also a disappointment in footballing terms, only occasionally showing the promise he had demonstrated in his native Argentina. The success of his comeback from injury in the second half of the 1983–4 season had not prevented Barça's elimination by Manchester

United from the European Cup Winners Cup, nor Clemente's Athletic Bilbao from getting the last laugh in its gruelling battle of football ideology with César Menotti's Barça. The Basques won the League, pushing Barça to a humiliating third place behind Real Madrid.

While researching my biography of Maradona in the mid-1990s, I was struck by how little the player was recalled by Catalan fans, as if his time at Barcelona had been a painful interlude best forgotten. And yet I couldn't help feeling that Nuñez's responsibility in mishandling the best player in the world, and the fans' own inability to prevent Maradona's breakdown, had produced a collective amnesia to deal with a collective sense of guilt.

That other Argentinian 'star' and bane of Barça history, Alfredo Di Stefano, commented once that in his opinion the younger Maradona had only played at twenty per cent of his potential while at Barcelona. If so, and I believe Di Stefano was right, one is tantalisingly left with the what-if question. What if, for instance, Maradona had not been so felled with illness and injury? Perhaps the personality clash between him and Nuñez might still have led to trouble. And yet it is equally arguable that, had he stayed, Maradona not only might have been saved from the drug addiction of later years, but also would have contributed to the kind of genius mixed with guts at the Camp Nou that the discerning *cule* is hungry for.

Terry Venables and Josep Lluís Nuñez were the right men meeting in the right place at the right time in that summer of 1984. Each man's ambition complemented the other's. So far, while Nuñez's successes had yet to earn him respect, Venables's reputation had always exceeded his achievements. Within the UK Venables had won no trophies either as a player (Chelsea and Spurs) or as a manager (Crystal Palace and Queen's Park Rangers), and his record hardly compared with that of other British managers such as Alex Ferguson, George Graham, Howard Kendall or Bobby Robson.

Among the British managers, it was in fact Robson who had always been Nuñez's first choice. Nuñez's English-speaking vice-president, Joan Gaspart, had first offered Robson the job over the telephone during the 1980–1 season. Both Nuñez and Gaspart were impressed by the way Robson's Ipswich Town had played against Barça in two

successive European competitions: the 1977–8 UEFA Cup, in which
the English had lost to the Catalans only in a penalty shoot-out; and
the Cup Winners Cup, which Ipswich had again lost on aggregate by a
narrow margin – winning 2–1 at home and losing 1–0 away. The
negotiations had foundered because Barça felt they were too big a club
to have to pay the £200,000 the chairman of Ipswich, John Cobbold,
was asking, partly as a compensation for breaking into Robson's ten-
year contract. However, Robson was retained as an unofficial scout for
Barça, and was approached again in 1984 when Menotti told the club
he was not prepared to renew his contract.

This time, Robson's conversation with Gaspart did not even reach
the money stage. Robson was then managing England, and felt that to
walk out at that point would be seen as as much an act of betrayal as
Don Revie's walking out to manage the United Arab Emirates in 1977,
a year before the World Cup in Argentina. When asked to suggest an
alternative English coach, Robson recommended Venables, as he later
recalled: 'I told Gaspart that I thought Terry Venables could be the
answer, that he was a bright, young, thinking coach who was destined
to go a long way in the game. He was maybe a bit inexperienced but
made up for this by being intelligent and progressive. Gaspart listened
but told me he had never heard of Terry, and he even asked me to spell
out his name . . .'

Another key recommendation came from Menotti, who in turn had
previously consulted a Spanish-speaking British journalist he had
befriended during the World Cup in Spain, Jeff Powell of the *Daily
Mail*. 'I talked to Powell and asked him which English manager is
competent. Barça is a team of important players. He mustn't be a
dictator. They've already had a German [Udo Lattek]. He must be able
to win the players over.'

Finally, a politically important word was put in on Venables's behalf
by Jaume Olive, the Catalan coach of Barça's youth team and a keen
follower of English football, who had watched a video of Crystal
Palace and been impressed. Olive felt that although Menotti had
structured his team around the inimitable talent of Maradona, the
majority of the players who remained would adapt to Venables's style
and strategy without major trauma. According to Olive, the last thing
Nuñez wanted to be seen doing, after the Maradona saga, was making

another decision that risked subsequently proving a huge mistake. 'Nuñez was very nervous at that time,' recalled Olive. 'He was very stressed. The Maradona thing had gone badly and the fans were not happy.'

Thus did Venables – a man few Catalans had ever heard of – come to be short-listed for the top job at Barça, alongside two heavyweights of international football: Helmut Benthaus, who had just won the German championship with Stuttgart, and Michel Hidalgo, who was about to win the European championship with France. The cockney candidate – referred to by the Catalans as Meester Ben-ah-Bless – told me how he came finally to be picked as the belated successor in an interrupted line of connection between England and Barça via Vic Buckingham and dating back to the early players: 'So there I was with some pretty high-flyers and I was just manager of QPR and I actually didn't know what I was doing in such company. And then I discovered they wanted an English guy. They thought the team wasn't fit and needed hammering and the English had a reputation for being quite tough. With Menotti they had had the experience of someone who had won the World Cup in 1978 and was not so motivated. They wanted someone who had yet to become successful.'

The job was offered to Venables with a salary in excess of £150,000. It was a sum that Barcelona could afford, a considerable saving on Menotti, and less than the value put on either Benthaus or Hidalgo – a shrewd financial decision as far as Nuñez was concerned. It was nevertheless also twice anything that was on offer in the English First Division. For Venables, who from his earliest days had seemed to be stimulated by a burning ambition both to succeed and to deal with large sums of money, the offer could not have been better in the circumstances. As he told British journalists on accepting the job, 'I am looking forward to the challenge, the excitement and the experience. I am going to be running a great club in a foreign country where the game is a religion. You know, too, you are working with players of a different nature and temperament from the English player, with potential superstars. If I want ultimately to manage England, which I do, and hope then to win the World Cup, which I would, then I need to discover all I can about international football.'

From the outset Venables was made aware of the scale of the

challenge that faced him. Since Nuñez had become president in 1978, seven managers had come and gone. It was a reminder of where the buck had traditionally stopped whenever the team seemed on a losing streak. Those sacrificed had included men of the stature of Helenio Herrera, Rinus Michels and Ladislao Kubala. One failure above all others loomed over the club like an albatross of dark fate: Barça had not won the League in eleven years.

Venables had picked up on the mood as he prepared to take on the job. He later recalled, 'Things were going so badly when I arrived that it was as if a conspiracy was in the air. Everyone in Barça thought that the rest of Spain was against them, and that everything was being controlled from Madrid. Everyone, from directors to players, thought there was no chance of winning . . . and yet football seemed a complete way of life, the vehicle for their lives. There was a cause that was strong in the head and in the heart – so that while everyone was against them, there was also a will to fight back.'

As was common elsewhere in Spanish football, the job Venables had taken on was that purely of coach, not of manager. In other words, he was expected to concentrate exclusively on selecting and coaching the players, leaving it up to the directors and chief executive to negotiate the contracts. The arrangement was waived slightly in the case of Steve Archibald, whose transfer to Barcelona proved the first test of strength for Venables, along with the decision over Maradona's future.

Venables had decided not to argue the case for Maradona's staying, after sounding out the player, his team-mates and the senior club directors. The picture he had gathered was of an immensely talented player who could no longer be trusted to show loyalty and deliver at this particular club, both because of his hatred of Nuñez and as a result of the financial crisis he had got himself into while living in Barcelona. The fact that Maradona was facing a three-month suspension at the start of the season because of a match punch-up was also put into the equation. Venables was under pressure to show himself successful, quickly. Venables told me that what proved decisive was an unre-ported meeting he had with Maradona in which the player conveyed all the frustration and anger his experience of playing for Barça had brought him. 'From what Maradona said to me, I felt that the situation in Barcelona if he stayed would become very difficult. The damage was perhaps irreparable.' According to Nuñez, it was Venables's unwillingness to use his own influence to persuade Maradona to stay that finally made up his mind to sell him.

Venables's decision to push for Archibald as Maradona's replacement was initially viewed by local opinion – from fans to directors – as a dangerous eccentricity which risked plunging the club further down the League and away from its cherished dream of winning the European Cup. It was not Archibald (also unknown to most Catalans, despite the fact that he had played at the Camp Nou with Spurs) whom people in Barcelona wanted, but another Latin American, Hugo Sanchez, the agile and visionary Mexican forward.

Those pushing for Sanchez included José-Maria Minguella, the Catalan agent who had come to wield increasing power under the Nuñez regime. It was Minguella who had been negotiating for the Mexican's transfer to Barcelona from Atlético Madrid, drawing up an agreement with Atlético's president, Vicente Calderón, while he was recovering from an operation in Houston, Texas. Further negotiations aimed at concluding the deal continued in Barcelona at the same time as Archibald arrived to sign his. So tense and distrustful was the atmosphere that at one point it provoked an extraordinary scene involving Archibald and Dennis Roach, the English agent whose range of interests – through his close association with Minguella – extended to Barcelona. Roach had made a career out of turning other people's problems into business opportunities, building up an impressive portfolio in cross-border transfers. In addition to picking out dissatisfied players and matching them with predatory clubs, he represented the commercial interests of international stars with a marketable name. For example, during Johan Cruyff's time playing for Barça, Roach acted as the Dutchman's agent in the UK.

But Roach's attempts to sort out the Archibald deal proved stillborn. As Archibald was on his way to sign his agreement, together with Barça's vice-president, Gaspart, he was joined by Roach, uninvited and unexpected. Roach got into the car that Archibald was in, seemingly so intent on getting in on the negotiations that he suggested that the Scotsman's wife might make room for him by taking an alternative car. Incensed, Archibald turned to Gaspart and asked who Roach was. Gaspart replied that he worked for Barcelona. 'Well then, you pay him, I won't,' said Archibald and delivered Roach a two-word expletive.

Archibald was not only a self-confident Scot not prepared to suffer fools easily, he was also, in Venables's eyes, 'a top player, a fine goal-scorer, intelligent, quick, good with his head, and nearly always on target'. He was costing the club only marginally less than Sanchez, but Venables felt this did not matter 'because we had a lot of money to spend'. In the end, Nuñez agreed to take him, but only on the condition that Venables sign an addendum to the contract assuming full responsibility for it – undertaking to carry the can if things went wrong, in other words. 'It wasn't easy for Terry to do,' recalled Archibald. 'All Catalonia seemed to want was Hugo Sanchez, and so did the board of directors, but he held firm. I think he got away with it because he had just been appointed as manager and it was his strongest time. When you start at the club, it's your strongest time.'

Certainly Venables wasted little time in asserting his presence, focusing on the two things Barça fans appreciated: good football and learning to speak their language. Soon after getting the job of coach, Venables had been told by Menotti that there were only three players worth mentioning in the whole squad: Maradona, Migueli and Schuster. After watching the team fall apart in front of Real Sociedad in San Sebastián a few days later – in one of the last games of Menotti's last season – Venables felt less than reassured. 'There was this young Catalan sitting in front of me who turned to me and said, "How do you think you're going to win the League with this lot? If Menotti can't do it, you won't." Watching them play, I thought to myself, you might be right.'

But after that initial shock, Venables began to study the team more closely, watching videos and compiling his own files on individual players. It was then that a team that had initially seemed to him 'made up of bit-part actors and a couple of stars' began to open itself out to him with all its potential. He cut the first-team squad of twenty-seven players down to twenty-three, and then re-examined the goods. The player he felt closest to and trusted most was Archibald, in a sense making him a bridge with the team which he could ill afford to see collapse.

The Scotsman's own deadpan recollection of the lack of excitement he had felt the first time he played at the Camp Nou belies the ease with which he later adapted to his new life in the Catalan capital. 'The first time I played against Barcelona was while playing with Spurs in the UEFA Cup two years earlier. I had no feelings towards Catalonia whatsoever, and no interest in it. All I did as a Spurs player was do my business. I can't remember most of the Barça team I played against. It was a big stadium and there were lots of people watching but when we came out I was struck how numb the local fans seemed to be; it just didn't seem to compare with White Hart Lane. I was used to always giving recognition to my home support, but in this away game I just switched off . . .'

Even in his first days as a player with Barça, Archibald kept his emotions in check, his aloofness helping him survive the scepticism with which the local community greeted his arrival. 'When I came here I didn't feel I had to prove myself in anything, because I was a person who for the past five years had scored goals on a consistent basis for two different clubs and had helped one of them win the League. I was confident in my ability, and all that mattered was that Venables had confidence in me too.'

And yet Barcelona had a transforming effect on Archibald. Like Venables, he warmed to the climate, the geography and the people, and forged warm friendships in the club dressing room. Archibald's early training days were spent sharing a room with the Basque goalkeeper, Javier Urrutikoetxea, known as Urruti. Very popular with the fans and the rest of the team, Urruti had achieved almost legendary status in a club that had historically prided itself on having some of the best and most loved goalkeepers in the world. Like so many of his fellow countrymen, Urruti owed his quick reflexes and solid handling of the ball to having played the fast, tough Basque ball game *pelota* from an early age. Quite apart from his skill at second-guessing the intentions of even the best strikers, and his eccentric habit of venturing well beyond his area and occasionally scoring goals, Urruti was widely respected on a personal level. He was one of those, the fans liked to tell you, who really knew how to sweat for his team-mates, who made you laugh and think, and who was simply a genuinely nice guy.

There certainly could have been few people in the Barça team better qualified to bring an instinctively suspicious character like Archibald out of his shell. Having played at Real Sociedad and Espanyol before coming to the Catalan capital, Urruti had a healthy objectivity about Barça's place in Spanish football together with an understanding of the club's peculiar social character. Urruti liked to recall, with that sense of the picaresque that many goalkeepers tend to share, how in his early days at Real Sociedad they used to flood the ground prior to a match against Barça so that the muddy surface would break up the Catalan team's play. Urruti also believed that Barça was the most potentially individualistic of any club he had ever been in 'because each player thought he was a star'.

None the less, Urruti always accepted that playing for Barça was not like playing for any other club, and that he had a responsibility that extended way beyond the goalposts. 'I felt that we had a duty to give our best for those colours every time we played because of what the club represented. Whenever the team travelled beyond Catalonia, I felt somehow that we were ambassadors not just of the club but of Catalonia. We had to dress smartly, be courteous, and be sportsman-like. If a player didn't understand that this was his role, that he had to give his all, then there was little point in his staying with Barça.'

Urruti also had a realistic sense of the limitations of football, making a point of getting involved in business from his early twenties as an insurance against the future. And when it came to teaching a taciturn Scotsman about Barça he knew what wavelength to tune in to. Language was all-important, but making it interesting required in-stinct. Archibald knew no Spanish when they first met. After the obvious introductions – '*Yo Javier*,' '*Yo Steve*' – Urruti took a piece of paper and drew a man and a woman. Sex seemed to the Basque as good a place as any to start. Later, the phrases Archibald was taught had the advantage, from Urruti's point of view, of being orders that had to be complied with. For instance, when Urruti pronounced, '*Steve, apaga tele*,' or '*Steve, enciende luz*,' Archibald would dutifully switch off the TV, or switch on the light. Equal status was achieved between the two the day Archibald suddenly blurted out in almost perfect Spanish, '*Javier, apaga tele.*'

A few words of Catalan is what Venables made an effort to speak when he walked out into the Camp Nou to be presented to the local fans on 1st July, the first training day of the season. It was, as Venables later recalled it, somewhat modestly, 'little more than "If we all work together, we can do it. Let's go." ' But it was enough for the fans – a symbolic token of recognition, an indication that the latest *Meester* in their midst had a sense of just how important language was in a nation where for so many years it had been repressed.

Elsewhere on the pitch that day, a no less important gesture of reconciliation was taking place between Archibald and Schuster, two players with totally different backgrounds whom destiny had brought to the same club. While Archibald had to prove himself to an unfamiliar audience, Schuster had been in Barcelona long enough to have become too exposed. Controversy had dogged Schuster ever since the semi-nude body of his model wife had been splashed across the pages of a local magazine. Schuster's subsequent relationship with Barça's Udo Lattek had proved so brittle that he found it hard to dissociate himself from one celebrated interview in which he was quoted as calling the German coach a drunkard. Now, after surviving Maradona, Schuster was faced with a personal appointment of the new English manager, a tough dynamo of a Scotsman with a tremendous sense of self-belief. And yet on the day of Venables's presentation, Archibald did something that with the evidence of hindsight can be judged to have secured the immediate future for Barça as much as the coach's pep talk. Sitting down next to Schuster in a break from training, Archibald went out of his way to reassure the German. 'Bernd,' Archibald said, 'you and I are both foreigners here and we are both under a lot of pressure. So what we have to agree on is that we are going to stick together. We've got to help each other.'

Archibald and Schuster were to complement each other well in Venables's Barça, the paranoia of who should wear what shirt when soon dispelled. The Scotsman co-ordinated the attacks, while Schuster organised things from behind. About Archibald what stood out were his selflessness and his positioning. As Venables put it, 'He was not concerned with trying to look that good himself by going past opponents. If he could pass, get into the box and then take the return pass when he was in a scoring position, that suited him fine.' As for Schuster, for a while captain of the team, Venables judged him as good as any midfield player he had ever worked with: 'He operated on the basis there were two ways to get possession – from your own team-

mates or by winning it from the opposition . . . He would attract the
ball and when he got it he could deliver the killing pass.'

What both Archibald and Schuster helped Venables do was mould a
team that he could recognise as his. As part of that strategy, Venables
promoted some players and made different use of others, bringing
about the subtle transition from the Menotti period that the youth-
team coach Jaume Olive had predicted. He drew from the *cantera* (the
youth team), unable to understand the tendency the club had shown all
too often in the past to let young players reach their early twenties
before giving them their chance in the first team. Of the two players he
introduced from the youth team, Caldere and Rojo, it was the latter
whom Venables particularly admired as the most consistent member of
the team. Others brought in from the second team by Venables
included the Moroccan 'Nayim' (who was later to follow the coach
to Spurs). Among the players inherited from Menotti, three were later
singled out for praise by Venables: the left back Julio Alberto – 'very
quick, reminded me of Kenny Sansom' – and the two centre-halves
Miguelli – 'with the possible exception of Tony Adams, the strongest
and bravest I have ever worked with' – and Alexanco, 'a good goal-
scorer, with a gift for instigating successful set pieces'.

When Venables first arrived on the scene, Barça fans and players
resigned themselves to what local commentators had predicted would
be a typical English game: long-ball 'route one' football with a coach
disciplining anyone not willing to play kick-and-rush. Instead they
found a coach prepared to devise a strategy that brought out the best in
the team as a unit and produced results. If Venables brought an
'English look' to the side, it was in disposing of the sweeper system,
replacing it with a 'pressing' game, not unlike the 'total football'
favoured by the Dutch: Venables attacked with three while aiming
to get five or six going forward. As far as Venables was concerned, the
main obstacle he faced with many of the players he inherited was one
of attitude: 'They had the tendency to want to show off their indivi-
dualism in an area of the pitch where it was going to do us the most
harm . . . I had to drum into them that there are times and places on the
football field when passing is more productive than trying to beat
people. I told them to keep their ball skills up their sleeves so they could
suddenly hit the opposition with the unexpected in areas where it

would do the most damage. I worked hard for them to press the ball, hustling the man in possession with three to four players at one time and trying to rob him in parts of the field where we could counter-attack quickly, efficiently and effectively instead of falling back and only winning it when the their whole team was in front of us. If you can win the ball half-way through their team, you may only have five guys to get past to reach their goal. It sounds very simple, but when you get players to do that, life becomes an awful lot easier.'

While Venables thought that the team had some new tactics to learn on the pitch, he was generally impressed by what he found at Barça, a strong sense of professionalism and loyalty to the colours which extended from the management to the schoolboys. The latter were, and still are, educated and trained next to the Camp Nou, in a residence built in the style of the old Catalan farmhouses that have traditionally provided a home for visitors and strangers. The boys, who have been scouted for all over Spain, are put in the care of Catalan families to help them get to know the city and its culture. In the gardens of the Masia is a statue of a bearded old gent, a Santa Claus figure dressed in football shorts. Called the 'Abuelo' ('Grandfather') and bearing a vague resemblance to the club's founder, Joan Gamper, the statue stands as a symbol of the traditional Catalan belief that a close family life holds the key to a more stable community.

On his arrival in the Catalan capital, Venables had quickly picked up on the rumour mill surrounding the crazy goings-on at the Maradona residence, which undoubtedly involved other players too on party night. 'Towards the end, players, women and bottles of champagne all ended up floating in Maradona's swimming pool,' one Barça player recalled. But after the Argentinian's departure, Venables was left with a squad who both before and after matches showed extraordinary self-discipline. To Venables, coming from England, the encounter with the players, as much as with the fans – no drunks, few hooligans – proved a revelation. As he later commented, in an incisive comparison between two football worlds, 'When I was at Barcelona we would travel to San Sebastián by coach, a journey of seven or eight hours, and the players would just drink water, all the way there and back. In England, the players would drink water and Coca-Cola on the way to a match, but on the way back they would be swilling beer. In Spain, I did not see a single player smoke or drink until we won the League, and then they all got absolutely smashed. They were professionals and the job was done. In England we do it every Saturday, after the match . . .'

Venables went on, 'The Spanish footballers care about their condition, their fitness and their behaviour. They enjoy showing off their skills. The British are more functional, they get the job done, and are professionals from that point of view, and if they lack the technical ability of the Spanish players, they do have resilience. If the Latin teams are 1–0 or 2–0 down, then, as a rule, you can forget it, but the British will fight till the death. We both have our strengths and weaknesses, but the sight of a squad of highly skilled, motivated and disciplined footballers waiting for me at my first training session with Barcelona was a very welcome one.'

Under Menotti, the team's training sessions had taken place in the afternoon. When Menotti had first met his successor, he had said to Venables, greeting him through a cloud of cigarette smoke, 'If you like women, Terry, welcome to paradise.' Venables was no stranger to the good life. None the less, he thought Menotti's philosophy on training complete nonsense, a convenient smokescreen for his – and Maradona's – weakness for pleasurable late nights that required rest the morning after. And given the professionalism of many of the Barça players, Venables found little difficulty in restoring training to the morning.

The first big test of Venables's regime came sooner than the English coach would have liked: a game at the start of the new season against Real Madrid. In any other country, a new coach would be granted several matches over which to settle in and be judged. But this was Barcelona, where any game against the eternal rival represented the resumption of hostilities, with huge potential consequences for all involved. The fact that the game was away meant less pressure than that imposed by the collective fanaticism of the Camp Nou, which would countenance nothing less than victory. Even so, for Venables's Barça, travelling from Barcelona's Camp Nou to Real Madrid's Bernabéu stadium was like going from the Roman circus to the lion's den. It was ninety degrees in the shade that 2nd September, with over 90,000 Real Madrid fans baying for

Barça's blood, and the sprinkling of *cules* present as yet unwilling to risk their necks for the new coach.

Few players had their future more on the line that day than Steve Archibald, the unknown Scotsman who had displaced both Diego Maradona and Hugo Sanchez! There to give him moral support was a group of family and friends who had come over from Scotland, and who miraculously managed to watch the match safely. Archibald recalled, 'I felt apprehensive. I felt it was too big a test too early for Terry. But I didn't feel scared and I think that was thanks to my upbringing in Aberdeen – playing against Rangers and Celtic had got me used to the aggression of partisan crowds. Our coach at Aberdeen was Alex Ferguson. He bred such an arrogance and self-belief among us that we just went out and did the business.'

Archibald certainly did the business at the Bernabéu, scoring the second goal and helping out with the other two in a convincing 3–0 victory. The second, a classic Venables set move, reflected some early hard work in training: an interplay on the edge of the box involving Schuster and Caldere, the ball played through to Rojo, and then cut back to Archibald, who, having run and lost the defender, was perfectly placed to hit home. It was a nice easy goal against a difficult opposition, which confirmed Archibald's nickname as 'Archigoles'. Unsurprisingly, the Real fans didn't like it.

Venables and his team left the stadium under heavy police protection, as the fans vented their frustration by throwing coins and bottles, and later stones at the Barça bus as it headed off into the night. When the team returned to Barcelona, it was to a heroes' welcome: dancing in the streets and fireworks and thousands of *cules* delighted that *el Meester* had kicked ass in Madrid.

The opening game set the pattern for the rest of the season, with Barça subsequently enjoying an unbeaten twelve-match run. Six months later Barça had successfully fought off challenges to its position at the top of the table and was eyeing the championship that had eluded it for eleven years. And yet even in the midst of mounting expectations, a familiar paranoia returned to haunt Barça. The team's progress in the Spanish League was hindered by the award of an unusually large number of penalties in favour of opposing sides, the majority of which seemed unjustified from Barça's perspective. The penalty awards fuelled the long-standing belief held by anyone remotely associated with Barça that Spanish referees were biased against the Catalans. The fact that the penalties were usually awarded during away games, when the referee did not have to face the collective power of the *cules*, simply strengthened the conspiracy theory.

In such a context, the role played by Barça's Basque goalkeeper, Urruti, became all-important: he was the last bastion of defence against the sinister forces emanating from Madrid. Early in March, with six games in hand, Barça played away against Hercules, knowing that if they emerged from the match unbeaten, the championship would almost certainly be theirs. The two teams were holding each other to a goalless draw when, three minutes from the final whistle, the referee awarded a disputed penalty for a foul by Schuster. Hercules scored, leaving Barça convinced once again that it had been robbed.

The next away game Barça played was on 24th March 1985 against Valladolid. With four games in hand, the team played knowing that a win would clinch the League trophy. In the hours leading up to the match, the whole of Catalonia seemed paralysed by a huge groundswell of hope mixed with scepticism. The match was reaching the 88th minute; the score was 2–1 in Barça's favour, with goals by Clos and Alexanco. Around the country, Catalans were watching in bars and in their homes convinced that, yes, they had finally been allowed to do it this time, when the referee blew his whistle and ordered a penalty. Again it seemed to have been awarded for a non-existent foul; again the Barça players and the whole of Catalonia protested.

Only this time, Urruti felt that he would not bow to what seemed to be the inevitable. Instead he felt that this was one of those moments in football when you live or die, and he conjured up a hidden reserve of instinct, experience and training to confront it. Like all good goalkeepers Urruti had, on a good day, an incredible memory which allowed him to register in the course of the game the moves of particular players and their shots at goal. The Valladolid player who prepared to take the goal, 'Mágico' González, had scored his team's earlier goal from the same distance. Urruti believed it most likely that the player would aim in the same direction with the penalty, given the success of his previous shot. He guessed right, leaving it up to the last possible moment of the kick before diving in anticipation of its direction.

Urruti's save was immortalised in the commentary of Catalunya Radio's Joaquim-Maria Pujal, whose voice transmitted the feelings of a nation: 'The 41st minute-and-a-bit of the second half. From deep within its own half, Valladolid plays the ball . . . Barça is now three minutes away from the League championship. Valladolid has possession, it is attacking down the left flank . . . Mágico passes to Aracil, Aracil to Yanez . . . Julio Alberto tackles . . . and the referee has indicated a penalty . . . the referee has invented a penalty! The referee has invented a penalty against Barça! I can't believe it! A penalty against Barça! I honestly believe this is a penalty that the referee has invented. I have not seen a foul committed . . . Julio Alberto touched the ball with his foot and the Valladolid player threw himself . . . We are in the 42nd minute of the second half of the match. Penalty against Barça. I honestly don't believe it was . . . This is a bad decision . . . Barça was winning by two goals to one, and has now been punished by the referee with a penalty which, quite frankly, my friends, is designed to wreck Barça's chances. This is a bad decision by the referee Mr Sanchez Arminio, which forces Urruti to have the fate of the championship in his hands. Just think if Urruti stops it, just think if Urruti manages to hold it . . . Here it comes . . . and – yes – Urruti has saved it! Urruti has saved it! Urruti, I love you! Urruti, I love you! Urruti, I love you! . . .'

Among the thousands of *cules* listening to Pujal that day was fourteen-year-old José-Maria González Blasco, a member of a generation who, consciously at least, had never experienced Barça winning the League. It had always seemed as if Real Madrid were the only ones who did it fairly consistently. And yet with a mounting sense of expectation, José-Maria had cut short a day in the country and gone to a friend's house in Barcelona to listen to the match on the radio. The passion in that commentary touched a deep chord in him, so much so that in 1997 José-Maria, by then a young architect student, wrote a short but moving biographical portrait of Urruti – undoubtedly one of the most loved players in Barça's history. In it, Blasco describes the spontaneous celebrations in the streets of Barcelona that began as soon as the match was over:

'During the car ride home, after the game had finished, I witnessed for the first time how the balconies of the city suddenly filled with the colours of Barça and the colours of Catalonia; how the streets filled with the sound of car horns hooting and the cries of people coming out of their homes, who seemed to be expressing a happiness that hadn't been felt for eleven years. I asked my father, a man who never liked making too much noise, to blow the horn too. He did. I wound the window down further, waved to the people, cried along with them, feeling part of a shared joy. What I learned that day was that the people of Barcelona can show themselves more than willing to assert their sense of community, which is almost tribal, but which is more like one giant *fiesta*, a ritual of engagement that is set instinctively in the collective subconscious . . .'

Elsewhere in the city, thousands more *cules* took to the streets in a party that continued well into the following night. The next day a massive crowd converged on the airport where the team were due to fly in on their return from Valladolid. Before they arrived, Steve Archibald had told Barça's vice-president, Joan Gaspart, that much as he'd like to join in the celebrations, he wouldn't be able to stay in Barcelona that day because he was wanted by Jock Stein for Scottish international duty.

'You can't miss this, Steve, it's going to be a really important celebration,' Gaspart told him. Gaspart ran a chain of hotels. He had learned the trade and the English language working in his youth as a waiter in London's Connaught Hotel, an experience he claimed had taught him how to deal with every class of British man or woman, from Terry Venables to the Queen. He had taken Archibald under his wing since his arrival. The Scotsman referred to him as his 'Catalan brother'. Now the question of the celebration was not so much a heated argument as a bit of personal plea-bargaining by Gaspart, who knew the symbolic value of having the once-disputed Archibald in the victory parade. Gaspart also considered himself a *cule*, among the few members of the ruling junta who claimed to be genuinely in touch with grass-roots feelings. He needed Archigoles to be there, as much as the other *cules* did.

And yet Steve Archibald was, well, Steve Archibald. He had too much Scots blood in him to surrender one nation for another just like that. 'Believe me, Joan, I can't,' he told Gaspart. 'Jock Stein is not the kind of man I can ring up and say, sorry, Jock, I can't come, I've got a party to attend in Barcelona.' It was then that Gaspart pulled his magic bunny out of the bag. He told Archibald not to worry about scheduled flight connections. The club would lay on a private jet for him. That way he could celebrate *and* get to his training session with Stein. The offer was accepted by Stein in a subsequent phone call to Scotland. Archibald then sat back and enjoyed himself, just like all the others.

Venables told me about the scene that followed, which he said would be engraved in his memory for ever: 'When we arrived at the airport and got into the bus, there were so many people that a journey that should have taken twenty-five minutes ended up taking over seven hours. People were raising their children up to our windows, old ladies were on their knees. It was incredible, as if we were the triumphant army that had returned after achieving the impossible . . . It brought home to me that the suffering of the past was something that had stuck these people together, through generations. I felt it had nothing to do with sport at all.'

The bus made its way first to the Church of the Merce, where traditional thanks were offered to the Virgin of the city. From there it continued to the administrative centre, the Plaça Sant Jaume, where finally the victors alighted from the bus. Players and their training staff then ran a gauntlet of wildly enthusiastic fans who had packed the square. It was hard to believe that this had been the setting, before the advent of democracy, of violent protest and brutal repression. The players were touched and fondled like rock stars as they ran laughing along the route, swimming in a sea of joy, lines of policemen clumsily protecting them on either side, uniformed fish out of water. Local government in Catalonia was now shared between a Catalan Socialist mayor and a Catalan nationalist President. Each wanted his share of Barça, neither wanted to surrender his claim to the masses. So the route took the players first to the balcony of the City Hall and then across the square to the balcony of the regional President. A tale of two halves politically negotiated beforehand. Claiming to owe his allegiance to neither seat of power, Barça's president Josep Lluís Nuñez was none the less happy to be honoured by both as he stepped on to one balcony, then the other, clearly basking in the glory of the occasion.

Across the pages of *El Mundo Deportivo*, Nuñez declared his
admiration for the perseverance and loyalty of the club's mass social
support, while at the same time emphasising his own role in the club's
development. He recognised that in the seven years of his presidency
there had been disappointments, but insisted that the best way to
overcome adversity was with *seny* – the word meaning common sense,
almost natural wisdom, which certain Catalans think belongs only to
them. Nuñez, it seemed, wanted everyone to see a method in his firings
and hirings, to see them as part of an ordered scheme.

And yet much as Nuñez would have liked that day to be his day, it
did not turn out that way. It was *Meester* Venables and the players to
whom the masses paid tribute, Archigoles and Schuster among them,
although it was Urruti the fans cheered more than any other – the crazy
Basque who had let in one penalty one week and blocked another the
next, glorying in nothing except the sweat of his shirt.

The next day, once the players had finished celebrating and the
crowds had dispersed, Steve Archibald boarded a Lear jet bound for
Glasgow. He was greeted personally by the pilot: 'Welcome aboard,
Mr Archibald, just sit back, relax and enjoy the flight.' With the
passenger compartment all to himself, save for the flight staff, Archibald was told he would be served a luxury three-course meal, and all
the champagne he wanted. He sat back in a big brown leather arm-
chair, as the jet rose sharply and turned towards the Pyrenees.
Archibald thought on the post-match celebrations and now the flight,
and a big smile came over his face as he said to himself, 'Fuck, this is
incredible, and it's probably as good as it gets, so why not sit back and
enjoy it.'

Little did he know the rumpus his saga had provoked back at HQ.
Nuñez was so furious about the special arrangements laid on for the
canny Scot that he insisted that Gaspart pay the estimated $8,000 cost
of the flight out of his own pocket rather than out of club funds.

14

The Matador and the Bull

Adrenalin is pumping through Gary Lineker's veins. One of English football's smoothest operators, Lineker has never been one to give the appearance of living in the fast lane. Yet the match he is about to play is no ordinary match. There are more than 90,000 Barça fans out there in the Camp Nou waiting for the game that can break or make not just a player but a whole team: the League derby match between FC Barcelona and Real Madrid. Although the clubs belong to different cities, the word 'derby' has been appropriated by the Spanish language to denote a game traditionally identified with intense rivalry. No other encounter in the football calendar compares in scope and scale with this expression of local fanaticism.

This is not Lineker's first game as a Barça player, but it is his greatest challenge since he joined the team. A few weeks earlier, after walking out into the stadium for the first game of the season against Real Santander, he had scored a goal in the first two minutes and a second thirteen minutes later, in a 2–0 win. Lineker had felt elated by the goals, but unimpressed by the atmosphere. The excitement of the crowd in the match had seemed a little too *tranquilo* compared with his experience as an Everton player, playing at Goodison Park on a Saturday afternoon. 'There was no crescendo, no huge roar of the kind I got used to at Goodison,' recalled Lineker. 'I took in the audience – it seemed to have pretty wealthy people in it, more comparable to the kind of people who go to the theatre or opera.'

But now the sense of anticipation that had gripped him before that game is with him again, as he watches his new team-mates begin to step out from the dressing room and make their way towards the pitch. The players walk as if in a dream, through a part of the stadium that is insulated from the sound of the outside world, the eerie silence contributing to the sense of ritual as the team passes the chapel, signs of the cross completing the opening act of the drama. The chapel is at the top of a staircase that plunges downwards as if towards hell. Deliverance comes in the form of six steps that rise upwards at the end of a curving tunnel. As Lineker climbs them the silence gives way to a sound that shakes the ground beneath his feet, and draws his eyes upwards to the awesome sight of a packed multi-tiered stadium honouring the home team. 'This is no derby,' thinks Lineker, 'this is Catalonia against the rest of Spain, and I'm one more soldier in the Catalan army.'

Lineker goes on to become the undisputed hero of a battle which Barça wins 3–2. He scores a hat trick, putting two goals in the net in the first five minutes. 'When I scored that second goal was one of three times in my life when it's felt as if the hairs on the back of my head were standing up,' Lineker told me after he retired from playing football. While his agent John Holmes had a few years earlier diplomatically chosen not to get his client involved in my unauthorised biography of Maradona, Gary seemed only too happy to reminisce about his own time at Barça, despite a hectic TV schedule.

Over the previous months of researching this book, I had at times felt myself sinking into the self-absorbed obsession that renders so many *cules* seemingly unable to see their team in the wider context of world football. Now Gary Lineker's hairs-on-end analogy struck me as as good a statement as any with which to measure the passion of a people. So what were the other times, Gary? I asked him. He told me that the first time had been a few weeks before that Barça–Real Madrid encounter: the second goal of his hat trick in England's 3–0 win over Poland in the Mexico World Cup. The third time had come later: the equaliser against Germany in the semi-final in Italia '90. He continued, 'In the Camp Nou, I felt something extra when I scored that second goal. If there had been a roof in the stadium it would have blown off. The sound was unbelievable. I remember the challenge, the massiveness of the game, the incredible atmosphere, the explosion of noise . . . I'd done reasonably well until then by scoring a few goals. But that second goal in that particular game is what launched me in people's hearts. The name "*LEEEENEKER*" echoed round the stadium seemingly for ever.'

Lineker transferred from Everton to Barcelona at the start of the 1986–7 season for a fee of £2.2 million, in a deal agreed before the player's success in the World Cup in Mexico. During the championship, Lineker, twenty-five years old, had confirmed himself the undisputed star of English football. Although England was beaten by the 'Hand of God' in the quarter-finals against Argentina, Lineker returned home with the Golden Boot, having scored more goals than Maradona. Unsurprisingly, Lineker had gone down well with the team coach and long-term 'friend of Barcelona' Bobby Robson, not just because of his warm and adaptable personality, but thanks to his playing skills. 'Not a sophisticated technique,' Robson would note later, 'but very instinctive, knowing when the ball was going to come in and where to be so that he was on the end of it.' Sometimes it was the near post and other times the far post. 'He could always read it well and he never minded how he scored or which part of his anatomy he used to put the ball in the net.'

For Lineker, success had come in a whirlwind rush. He had played eight years for his home club, Leicester City, then one year at Everton, and he was now, a few days after getting married to Michelle, on his way to the biggest club in the world. When the final offer had come from Barça's top honchos, Gary and Michelle had sat up half the night turning over in their heads and between them the pros and cons: the money against the stability; the excitement of going abroad against the vertigo of displacement; the challenge of breaking into European club football with one of the best teams in the world; and the anticipation of playing against a very different kind of opposition from that encountered in Britain. Quite apart from their mutual respect, neither of them felt sufficient certainty to impose a unilateral decision, so both scribbled a choice on separate pieces of paper. Both opted for going to Barcelona.

No one was more pleased by the decision than Terry Venables. He was in desperate need not just of a goal-scorer but of a player who could settle down to a change of lifestyle and game without controversy. 'I knew about Lineker, because we had met a few times and I was impressed with his intelligence, which for a player moving abroad can be quite important,' Venables would later comment. 'If you wanted him to do something he would respond, and his running and positioning became better. There were things he couldn't do and his heading ability was only adequate. What I liked about him was that he had everything worked out. He preferred it when he knew what he was supposed to do as a player.'

At the time, Venables's star was in desperate need of rekindling. It had been dimmed dramatically by Barça's defeat in the final of the European Cup by Steaua Bucharest – 'the most disappointing day of my life', recalled Barça president Nuñez in an interview with me. The defeat, combined with Barça's losing the Spanish Cup and ending up once again behind Real Madrid in the League, had meant some disillusioned *cules* redubbing 'the Historic Dream' – 'the Historic Nightmare'.

The 1986 European Cup final was held on 7th May in the Sanchez Pijuan stadium in Seville. The Andalusian capital is a popular venue for Barça football fans, partly because of its inhabitants' sense of humour and partly because many Catalans are descended from immigrants from the region. The city and the stadium were virtually taken over by some 50,000 *cules*, the biggest expedition of Barça fans since the European Cup Winners Cup final in Basle. The fans behaved impeccably, with good humour mixed with genuine passion that at no point turned violent. Around the stadium sat detachments of police in the new casual uniforms brought in since Franco's death, unruffled by the copious Catalan and FC Barcelona flag-waving and rhythmic jumping in the stands. Coming as the match did just a year after the tragedy at Heysel, where thirty-nine people had died after a group of Liverpool fans had charged at Juventus fans, the atmosphere in Seville that day was a welcome reminder that loyalty to a cause does not necessarily have to be accompanied by thuggery.

Not even in defeat. For the fans who saw Barça lose that day reacted not violently but rather with resigned sorrow, a stoicism informed by the collective endurance that had developed in the face of all too frequently broken dreams. The match which FC Barcelona had been the clear favourites to win had turned into a tragedy in three parts. The tragedy had begun a few weeks earlier when Archibald had been temporarily dropped from the team. He had developed hamstring problems after helping his team beat Juventus in the quarter-final with a winning goal. The Barça doctor Carlos Besit recommended surgery. Archibald, with Venables's support, refused, fearing that the Catalans would end up crippling him for life. Instead he decided to put his trust in a Dutch physiotherapist who had been recommended by Bryan Robson, the English international who had managed to achieve extraordinary footballing success despite repetitive injury.

Archibald's suspicion of local doctors, encouraged by other members of the team whom he consulted, was a legacy of Maradona's time. The Argentinian player's distrust of orthodox medicine had been fuelled by the operation performed on his foot by Catalan surgeons after he was severely injured by Bilbao's Goikoetxea. Maradona subsequently allowed himself to be treated by Ruben Oliva, a fellow Argentinian who had acted as physio to his country's national team during the 1978 World Cup.

The recovery programme applied to Archibald by the Dutch physio Richard Smith when the Scottish player flew into Amsterdam proved a challenging one. As Archibald told me, 'Bryan had recommended this guy but warned me not to go if I couldn't suffer pain. "I'm not talking about ordinary pain, I'm talking about real pain. But he'll sort you out," he'd said. So I went over there because I really wanted to play in the final, and I did suffer real pain. What Richard Smith does is break fibres to make them bleed and cause a new healing. You're talking about eight hours of massage – knuckle massage, bone massage, deep massage – but also of someone standing on you until he is relieved by his partner, an expert kick boxer. I've never had to suffer so much in my life – but I was sprinting within four days.'

Archibald had arrived in Amsterdam with five injuries to his right leg, and feeling, in his own words, 'like a dead body'. He returned to Barcelona telling the English media that, thanks to Messrs Robson and Smith, he was much more at one with his body, and mentally more content than ever. Had he been returning to a British club side or a British national squad, then perhaps Archibald's ability to deal with pain would have won him an accolade. It certainly convinced Venables that he should put him back in the team. But this was Barça, with a different concept of what constituted a fighting spirit. Fighting had to do with survival and resistance, sure, but also with loyalty, good entertaining football, and winning the League and the European Cup.

Archibald, just like Maradona, had broken club rules by turning his back on its doctors. And his reinstatement by Venables was at the expense of a popular Spanish player, 'Pichi' Alonso, who had brought the Camp Nou to its feet by scoring Barça's three goals in the second-leg victory in the semi-finals against the Swedish club Göteborg. It was a controversial decision that was not justified by Archibald's performance in the final. Venables, who had declared him fit enough to play, later reluctantly concluded that the Scot had been 'some way short of his best'. Archibald claimed that Venables had made a mistake by taking him off before the end of the game, 'when I was just getting into it, warming up'. Neither argument convinced the Barça supporters, who looked upon the whole Archibald affair as a management blunder from start to finish.

The second part of the Seville tragedy involved Bernd Schuster. The volatile German's honeymoon period with Terry Venables had lasted less than a year. Having survived Lattek and Menotti, and won the affections of a significant section of the *cules*, Schuster not only considered himself a star but expected to be treated as such. Venables for his part considered him the most talented player in his team, and in his early days at Barça certainly had no doubts about his commitment. The coach was impressed by Schuster's habit of staying on at the end of training sessions and practising on his own, particularly the curling shot into the net from the corner flag that was his trademark. 'It is sometimes difficult to convince players at the highest level that they can improve still further, because they are already stars in their own right. They might say, "Why should I need more?" . . . You *can* keep improving – Gary Lineker did it, because he was smart, and Bernd Schuster did it too,' Venables later reflected.

And yet by the end of the first season something had changed, with Schuster striking an increasingly discordant note within the club. One cause of Schuster's problems was the extrovert and dominating German model to whom he was married, a source of periodic disruption in the dressing room. She had a habit of marching through it when the players were stark-naked, on her way to Venables's office – usually to protest about something. Schuster seemed increasingly tense, while conveying a sense that he had lost faith in his team and his manager. Despite Barça's League championship win, Schuster clashed with Venables in the aftermath of the team's defeat by Metz in the European Cup Winners Cup. In a dressing-room showdown, Schuster blamed the defeat on the lack of support he had got from Archibald. Venables, angry at the breach of team spirit, hit back and told Schuster not to underestimate his own contribution to the defeat. The row turned out to be a mere prologue to what was yet to come. During the European

Cup final in Seville, Venables subbed Schuster before the end of the game, having concluded that he was playing at half his normal ability. Schuster, furious, walked off the pitch and straight out of the stadium.

By then the third and final act of the Seville tragedy was unfolding. The game had reached the end of normal time with no evidence of the stylish and attractive football Venables had promised in a pre-match press conference. Steaua Bucharest's solid defence broke the rhythm and flow of Barça's game, ensuring a sterile 0–0 draw. The scoreline remained the same after extra time; the match was to be decided by a penalty shoot-out. For the second consecutive season, the outcome of a critical game rested on the shoulders of Urruti, Barça's goalkeeper.

Urruti's hero status had been reaffirmed by popular acclaim in the second leg of the semi-finals against Göteborg. An early goal by the Swedes had been disallowed thanks to his protestations. Urruti had followed the referee to the half-way line where he argued that the goal had been scored by a player after the ball had gone out of play. The referee consulted the linesman nearest the incident, confirmed that it was indeed as Urruti had spotted it, and disallowed it. During the final stages of the penalty shoot-out, Barça went one down, when Carrasco failed to score. Urruti next not only saved what could have been the winning shot by the Swedes, but went on to score himself. He then challenged the Swedish goalkeeper to do the same. Disconcerted by Urruti's psychological game, the Swede misfired the next shot, leaving it up to Victor to score the winning goal. The whole of the Camp Nou roared, 'Urruti, Urruti, Urruti!' The goalkeeper would later recall, 'There is not a bullfighter in the world who has come out of a bullring the way I came out of the Camp Nou that day. It is something I shall never forget.'

(Venables never quite understood the bullfighting analogy: 'Spanish players have a little bit of the matador in them, an inclination to show off, which was one of the traits we were trying to get them to play down,' he told me. And yet with its history and its politics, few clubs had a better understanding of matters of life and death than FC Barcelona.)

In Seville, a town where bullfighters had been badly gored and sometimes killed, Urruti faced his ultimate challenge. One week before, in a decision that thousands of *cules* could not understand, the club had signed up Zubizarreta, the Spanish international goalkeeper.

Urruti had no doubt that if Barça won this match, and so the European Cup, it would be difficult for even Zubizarreta to replace him. If they lost, it would be his last game. In the penalty shoot-out, Urruti saved two goals. But the Romanian goalkeeper saved four. The European dream had evaporated.

Venables always insisted that he had bought British players not to turn Barça into an Anglo-Saxon fiefdom, but simply to ensure that he had players he knew would score goals. His objective was to blend British and local styles of play, rather than impose one on the other. He felt that this was the ideal formula to produce a game that had both flair and toughness. Following the 1986 European Cup débâcle, however, Venables emerged with the popular support he had enjoyed in his first season considerably reduced, and with his decisions subjected to increasing scrutiny and criticism. Part of the opposition he faced had less to do with him than with club president Nuñez, whose enemies resurfaced whenever the club hit a losing streak; but there was also a growing sense that Venables was losing the plot, even though he was spending a not inconsiderable amount of Barça's money.

During the European Cup, and with Barça still on a seemingly unstoppable run, Venables had let it be known that he might not stay on beyond the end of the season. His position was being carefully monitored by Arsenal's chairman, Peter Hill-Wood, and by Spurs' Irving Scholar. Within the club, Nuñez panicked and began sniffing around for a replacement. He travelled to London, accompanied by his vice-president, Joan Gaspart; the club secretary, Anton Pareda; and the youth-team trainer, Jaume Olive. According to Olive, the Barça high command held informal talks in the Connaught Hotel with Bobby Robson, Howard Kendall and Alex Ferguson.

No one had as many stories about the Connaught as Gaspart, who had worked there as a waiter in his youth. His favourite was one about a dinner given at the hotel by the Mayor of London for Grace Kelly, Princess of Monaco. Gaspart was serving the Princess some poached salmon in boiling water, when he lost his balance. Fearing that he would spill water on the Princess, he steered the dish over himself, subsequently fainting with the pain of the scalding. Gaspart was hospitalised for three days, during which he was sent a note of gratitude by the Princess. For his suffering, Gaspart was named Employee of the Month by the hotel management.

Much as he liked to dine out on such stories, it was the business of football rather than fairy-tale princesses that was on the menu the day Gaspart returned to the Connaught. Both Ferguson and Kendall came across as knowledgeable no-nonsense guys, according to Olive, but nothing was offered them, nor indeed did they advertise their availability. The real significance of the meeting was in strengthening the existing bond between Robson and the club which would in time materialise in contractual terms. As Olive told me, 'Robson was the last of three we talked to and the one who stayed behind for supper. When we had finished eating, he began to lay out the glasses across the table, explaining some tactics. Nuñez was very impressed. He thought Robson was great.'

Before the summer was out, Venables had agreed to stay, after getting Nuñez to pay him more than the £200,000 plus bonuses he had been paid for winning the League championship. After failing to deliver the European Cup, Venables told British journalists, 'If I had won the trophy, what would I have had left to prove at the club? Now I have to get off the floor and prove myself.' But locally some fans and members of the Barça staff thought that Venables was putting too high a price on success.

Olive had by now turned into one of Venables's most vocal critics. He described Venables as 'an absolute mercenary' for the way he had bargained for a higher salary, and was also outspoken in his criticism of the decision to sign up Lineker and Mark Hughes. Olive thought that Lineker was a good player, but one who would have to adapt a lot to the Spanish game if he were to prove at all successful at Barça. But it was the Hughes signing from Manchester United, arranged through Dennis Roach – the agent with whom Archibald had refused to involve himself – that angered him most. Olive saw Hughes as a tough player with limited ball skills and predicted that he would be nothing but a failure in the Catalan capital. When Venables went to Nuñez and put forward the names of Lineker (£2.2 million) and Hughes (£1.7 million), Olive countered with the names of van Basten and Gullit, arguing that they were more talented, more suited to the Spanish game, and cheaper, but he was overruled. He was subsequently forced out of any training responsibilities by Venables, following a public row in which Olive was pictured by many sectors of the local media as a destructive element within the club. His friends suspected a stitch-up. To this day Olive has stuck by his original judgement, claiming that he was vindicated by subsequent events.

Certainly Hughes proved a failure during his time at Barça. The Camp Nou had always demanded a good spectacle. Hughes played a tougher, rougher game than the Barça fans were used to or even wanted. They nicknamed him 'El Toro' – the 'Bull' – not so much because he was brave but because they saw only physical force, without skill. Lineker by contrast was nicknamed 'El Matador' for his goal-scoring abilities, and for the graceful figure he cut both on and off the pitch. In Barcelona, Hughes found the football of the effortless touch difficult to master. As Venables himself later recognised, when it came down to it, it was really quite simple: the football he got away with in English football was frowned upon in Spain.

It did not help that Hughes, never the greatest of communicators even back home, found learning the local language difficult. His poor communication extended to the early days of training with Barça when he also found it difficult to engage in the *rondas*, the small highly tactile groupings of players into which the team was divided to test individual dribbling and passing skills at close quarters. Once a match was under way, Hughes would inevitably find his game interrupted by a referee's whistle – a situation that had him being sent off in one of the early games of the season. Barça had a long tradition of players – both local and imported – who contested referees' decisions, but they were 'star' material and their antics were perceived as part of the spectacle. Hughes was simply seen as a bad-tempered plodder undeserving of a club with an ego as big as Barca's.

The *cules*, who were never convinced that his transfer was justified anyway, showed little patience with Hughes. From an early stage in the League championship they shouted insults at him. It didn't matter that he couldn't understand what they said. Like any player with even a minimum experience of deeply partisan fans, Hughes could instinctively feel that he wasn't loved. Gary and Michelle Lineker tried to look after him as best they could, but, as Gary told me, it proved a hopeless endeavour: 'He used to go home after training and sleep in the afternoon and think about things too much. We tried to get him out as much as we possibly could, but in the end I think he got embarrassed about relying on us. Because he couldn't communicate with the other players, he got very solitary, and that weighed on his shoulders. The problems began on the field. Because he was struggling on the pitch, the crowd got on his back. When he was sent off and missed the following game, people were saying out loud, "Don't you think things are better without Hughes?" '

In striking contrast, Lineker – like Archibald before him – took to Barcelona readily, playing off the pitch and on it. The newly-wed Linekers found little difficulty in discovering the romance and excitement that was on offer in the Catalan capital. They mastered the language quickly, and forged close friendships within the team and beyond it. In a city that appreciates beauty, the handsome Lineker couple were accepted easily into the local social scene. If, as Bobby Robson later remarked, Lineker 'was one of those footballers who could get by on a minimum amount of training', Barcelona certainly proved the city for him in other respects – at least while Venables was there. For Venables was a manager who could understand occasional indulgence, as long as this did not affect a player's underlying commitment to the game.

It was Venables who introduced the Linekers to his and what became their favourite Barcelona drinking and eating places: a beer bar at the top end of the Rambla, and a beach club along the coast in the retirement resort of Castelldefels which served excellent seafood, both owned by a man named Manolo. When I interviewed Lineker in the final stages of researching this book, he had taken a break from a hectic and tense schedule as a BBC TV sports commentator. But his eyes lit up when he recalled his life in Barcelona, as if those had been some of the happiest moments of his life:

'I love the place. It's got everything – charm . . . a fabulous location – mountains on one side, beach on the other. We had such a wonderful life when we lived there. I'd train in the morning, then go to the beach or into town and have a big lunch, followed by a siesta from five till eight. Then about ten, most nights, we'd go out for dinner. It was such a lovely relaxing lifestyle, and it proved very difficult to get out of it. It was a rude awakening when children came along.'

Lineker's contentment off the pitch during his first season with Barça held the key to his success in footballing terms. Healthy and relaxed, he learned to make his game more subtle and varied to beat the European-style man-to-man marking. He learned pretty quickly that he couldn't just wait for the ball to come to him: he had to go looking for it and lose his marker. For nearly a year he maintained a goal ratio of one every two games, scoring twenty-one goals in forty-one games in his opening season, not a bad record in Spanish football. Between them, Hughes 'El Toro' and Lineker 'El Matador' were two sides of a mirror that reflected a thing or two about the nature of Barça – a massive club in a city of contrasts, which can as easily destroy as seduce, such are the expectations generated by history.

Much as Venables had hoped to pick himself up from the rubble of Seville, it didn't quite turn out that way. During the 1986–7 season, Lineker's goals were the only bright spot fans perceived in a period that was marked more by loss than by achievement. The 'renewal' of the team with Zubizarreta, the Valencian forward Roberto Fernandez and the Lineker–Hughes tandem had meant the sidelining of two popular players, Urruti and Archibald, and the transfer of two others who commanded respect widely among the fans, 'Pichi' Alonso and the former captain Sanchez. Because of the Spanish Federation's restrictions on the number of foreign players who could play in a team, Archibald reluctantly agreed to 'sign off' the first team in order to make way for Hughes – although he never hid his anger at having to do so. 'I was really disappointed with Terry for doing that; I was really pissed off,' Archibald told me, 'although later I analysed the situation and thought that if I'd been the manager and I'd had to decide whether Archibald, lying in hospital with an ankle injury at the time, was really fit to play for the biggest club in the world, I'd probably have done the same.'

The most controversial absentee that season was Bernd Schuster. The German had launched a legal action against the club on the grounds of unfair dismissal. While he remained living in Barcelona, Venables was under orders from Nuñez not to bring him back into the team as a punishment for his walk-out at the end of the European Cup final.

For all the changes, the team failed to deliver. They were knocked out of the Spanish Cup early on, and despite a good start in the League championship ended up behind Real Madrid. In the UEFA Cup, they were beaten by Dundee United in the quarter-finals. Barça lost the first leg away 1–0, while the Scots followed up in the second leg with a 2–1 victory at the Camp Nou. Without Schuster, Barça seemed to lose a lot of its creativity, at a time when Real Madrid were gearing up to one of their better periods; and Hughes's ultimate humiliation came with a sending-off during the UEFA Cup tournament, from which he never recovered his place in the team.

The following season began with a sense of collective hangover. Nothing makes a manager at Barça more vulnerable than a season without titles, and in 1986–7 this was coupled with a resurgent opposition to the president led by Ricardo Huguet, the businessman profiled in an earlier chapter. Huguet was the most vocal figure of an alliance of former Barça directors and businessmen with links to Jordi Pujol's Catalan nationalist party, an alliance that claimed that Nuñez had overspent on the wrong players and lost touch with the membership and its Catalan roots. Barça kicked off the season with a 2–1 win away against Las Palmas, but followed this up with two defeats at the Camp Nou, and a third defeat away. The growing opposition demanded that heads roll. Nuñez offered to resign, but it was an empty gesture which he knew would be turned down by his hand-picked junta. It was. Instead he turned to Venables for the role of sacrificial lamb. When I interviewed Nuñez eleven years later, he had no regrets about the speed with which he ended up sacking the coach who had won the club its first League championship in fourteen years. 'I am the kind of person who . . . when I need to make a decision I don't hesitate,' Nuñez said. 'A case in point was Venables's departure. I had come to the conclusion that Venables wasn't capable of winning any more titles.' So much for gratitude. *El Meester* bowed out officially on 23rd September 1987, after securing what is thought to have been a not ungenerous pay-off during a series of meetings with Nuñez and his vice-president Gaspart.

Venables had seen the storm clouds approaching, and turned the other way towards the sunset. His time at Barça had secured the experience and reputation he had sought when he first took on the job. Beyond Catalonia his managership was generally judged a success,

bringing with it not just one of the most coveted League championships, but a final in the European Cup. Spurs and England now
awaited him. But in the intense, demanding and obsessive world of
Barça, Venables's departure was not widely mourned. Moreover, the
atmosphere of internal strife at the club, far from abating, now sank to
new unprecedented depths of crisis with a bitter row between Nuñez
and the team over payments.

The row had developed as a result of a Spanish government clamp-
down on tax evasion. Evidence had been gathered by tax inspectors
during Schuster's legal wrangling with the club over his own financial
arrangements. It had emerged that the German had signed two contracts with the club, although only one had been fully declared to the
tax authorities. Further investigation by the tax inspectors revealed
that the majority of the players at Barça had reached similar deals
behind the scenes with the club, in order to minimise the amount of tax
they had to pay on their earnings. When Barça was ordered to pay
back what had been evaded, Nuñez insisted that it should be paid by
the players and not the club. The players were furious, claiming that
they had signed the double contracts with the club's full approval and
encouragement, and that it was therefore the club's responsibility to
make provision for the loss.

On 28th April 1988, the bulk of the team held a press conference in
the Hotel Heredia, calling on Nuñez to resign. It came to be known as
the mutiny of Heredia. 'Nuñez has deceived us as people and has
humiliated us as professionals,' the players said in a joint statement
that had half the Barça management thinking a revolution was in their
midst. Among those absent was Lineker. Call-up for England squad
duty had provided a convenient excuse for a player who claims never
to have signed a dubious contract and who certainly felt he had
nothing to gain from getting involved in that particular row. 'You
just couldn't imagine such a mutiny taking place in England, the fans
just wouldn't buy it,' Lineker told me when we discussed the incident in
1999. Nor could Luis Aragones, Venables's successor as caretaker
manager, deal with the row. According to Lineker, Aragones broke
down during a pre-match strategy meeting with the players, the stress
of managing one of the biggest clubs in the world exacerbated by the
unprecedented mutiny within its ranks.

Hughes and Archibald had left the club by the time of Heredia, although the Scotsman later declared himself quite sympathetic towards the mutiny. When I asked Archibald about Heredia, he said, 'It's always the club's responsibility to resolve a contract. We were guided by the club in signing our contracts. They knew what was going on. I signed a contract, they told me how the contract worked, end of story. The players felt let down. The club should have absorbed the loss. Instead they transferred it to the players' wages.'

Two days after the mutiny of Heredia, the Barça players, Lineker among them, played Real Madrid in a League match at the Camp Nou. Of all the extraordinary encounters between the two teams, it was probably one of the most surrealistic. The home team was loudly whistled as it came out into the stadium, the membership showing its disgruntlement even when Carrasco scored the first goal. In the stands, Nuñez supporters held up placards accusing the players of being *peseteros* – money-grubbers. The Real Madrid team was applauded. Only in the second half did the mood change as the Barça team began to play better than their rivals for the first time in months. By the time Lineker scored the second goal, familiar loyalties had been re-established. The Matador got a big ovation and from then on the Camp Nou directed the usual insults at the men in white, particularly Real Madrid's Hugo Sanchez.

The signals emanating from that game were too mixed to provide any comfort for Nuñez. The players had clearly not endeared themselves to part of the mass membership by their rebellion, a challenge to the *seny* – the level-headedness and pragmatism that Nuñez claimed to have brought to the club and which middle-class Catalans appreciated. Yet they had won back hearts and minds by appealing to a more profound sentiment of Catalan pride and playing some good football; and all the while an organised opposition was still knocking at Nuñez's door, calling for his head.

In was in these circumstances that Josep Lluís Nuñez delivered a master-stroke, by bringing back to Barça the one person who seemed to be able to guarantee the success and spectacle that so many *cules* pined for: Johan Cruyff.

15

Dream Team

It was a second coming that was to prove more successful and far-reaching in its influence than the first.

When he signed as Barcelona coach on 4th May 1988, Johan Cruyff ushered in a period of football glory that few clubs in the world had enjoyed before, or have experienced since. For Barça supporters the Cruyff reign seemed truly sent from heaven, bringing together and sustaining, during an extended period of hugely entertaining football, skills and talent of a kind that had been experienced off and on for most of the club's history. It was as if the shooting stars of times past had been reincarnated, and fixed in a more lasting firmament. In seven football seasons under Cruyff, Barça won four consecutive League championships, the European Cup, the European Cup Winners Cup, the European Super Cup, the Spanish King's Cup and three Spanish Super Cups. The football club's success was the icing on the cake of the social and cultural renaissance that Barcelona as a city experienced in the late 1980s and early 1990s as a result of its hosting, in 1992, what was to become one of the most successful Olympics of all time – an event that stimulated an extraordinary architectural transformation of the Catalan capital under Pasqual Maragall, its visionary democratically elected mayor.

Cruyff returned to Barcelona with his reputation preceding him. As a player at the club in the 1970s, Cruyff had joined the pantheon of 'stars' who command huge support among the fans. Nothing that had happened since had deterred the fans from the view that now, as then, *el salvador* would raise the game from the dire depths into which it had fallen at the Camp Nou. After his first departure from Barça, Cruyff had embarked on a disastrous agribusiness venture with an Eastern European of dubious reputation called Michel Basilevich. Cruyff lost most of the money he invested in circumstances that have never been fully explained. He vowed never again to invest in things he did not understand, and thenceforth to stick to making money on what he regarded as certainties: his knowledge of football and himself. In fact as a footballer Cruyff had never allowed himself to be underpaid, discovering early on in his career the important part that sponsorship and advertising can play in boosting a star sportsman's wage, at a time when football was still relatively green in this area. He always rejected accusations that he was mercenary, insisting that all he was standing up for was a fair wage based on a player's market value.

Cruyff became an even tougher negotiator in matters financial after a short spell playing in the United States, first with the Los Angeles Aztecs and then with the Washington Diplomats. He then returned to Europe, defying those football commentators at home and abroad who had suggested that at thirty-three he could no longer handle the pace of the European game. He won the Dutch championship twice with his old team Ajax, and once with its old rival Feyenoord. Cruyff's move into management had him back at Ajax once again, making up for his brief betrayal by leading the team to victory in the European Cup Winners Cup. Marco van Basten, the player Terry Venables had chosen to overlook in favour of Mark Hughes, scored the winning goal, before moving to Milan.

Although it was his own choice finally to leave Ajax, Cruyff's departure had been embroiled in controversy. The Ajax management, led by chairman Tom Harmsen, had claimed, not for the first time, that Cruyff's arrogance had got the better of him, leading him to interfere excessively in every aspect of the club, from the food that players ate to the terms of their contracts. Against the background of Cruyff's disastrous business venture in pig farming, management had resented all the more Cruyff's habit of arguing over what the club paid players, and in particular his criticism that van Basten had been undervalued before transferring to Milan. Cruyff hit back by drawing on his US experience and, while never claiming to be a businessman, insisted that he now only involved himself in things he understood.

Nor had his relations with the Dutch media been universally positive. He caused resentment as a result of his habit of trusting a select group of journalists, and using them to increase his influence within the club. Among other things it appeared to be more than a coincidence that *De Telegraaf*, the paper he was under contract to write a regular column for, also happened to get most of the scoops.

Some Catalan journalists had been reminded of Cruyff's brashness in April 1987 when a group of them had gone to Zaragoza to cover Ajax's semi-final encounter with the local club in the European Cup Winners Cup. According to a story told by the Dutch journalists Frits Barend and Henk van Dorp, on the day before the match a team from Catalan TV had caught up with Cruyff and van Basten during the final training session – as had, separately, a party of local schoolchildren, given the day off in honour of the Dutchmen. Catalan TV wanted to interview Cruyff and then use him as interpreter for a further conversation with van Basten. Cruyff refused. The Catalans pleaded. He agreed to answer just one question. The Catalans asked Cruyff to ask van Basten what kind of player he thought he was. Cruyff turned away instantly, followed by van Basten, and left the Catalans without a word. It was the children who confronted Cruyff next as he tried to get on to a bus, bombarding him with questions such as whether Jordi, his son, spoke Spanish and whether he'd stay and live in Zaragoza if the local club made him an offer. Cruyff chatted to them casually for about ten minutes. Later, when his Dutch journalist friends asked him why he had been prepared to talk to the children for ten minutes, after walking away from the Catalan TV crew in less than ten seconds, Cruyff gave them what they described as a 'typically enigmatic answer': 'It's very simple,' Cruyff said; 'television is press, children are not press, so for them the fact we weren't giving any more interviews wasn't relevant.'

Defiance of management, wrangling over money, tricky relations with the media, all or any of these would in different circumstances have signified from the outset a passport to disaster in a club like Barça. But Cruyff's potential for controversy was a subject that a majority of Barça fans, the local media and the club management found little difficulty in temporarily downplaying when the Dutchman signed his contract to become manager in May 1988. Cruyff's reputation was one of a gifted player and manager, enjoying the kind of internationally recognised star status that Barça took pride in bringing back into the fold. If anything, his extraordinary self-belief was just the tonic the club was seeking in the midst of one of the worst internal crises of its history. Poor results combined with the players' unprecedented act of insubordination – the so-called mutiny of Heredia – had alienated the team from a sizeable part of the club membership. Attendance at the Camp Nou had dropped to an all-time low, with the stadium less than half full for most home matches.

Sectors of the membership were once again giving a public airing to their opposition to club president Nuñez. Backed by the ruling Catalan nationalist party, Convergència, and sectors of the media it controlled, such as Catalan TV and the newspaper *Avui*, one of Nuñez's most eloquent opponents, Ricardo Huguet, threw down the gauntlet, claiming – as the opposition had always claimed – that Nuñez was the man primarily responsible for the club's ills and for abandoning the Catalan cause. The opposition forcefully demanded Cruyff's presence, but much to their chagrin it was Nuñez who signed him, a year before the presidential elections, taking a significant wind out of their sails. With a typical eye on opportunity, the besieged Nuñez had calculated correctly that, in the shorter term, ignoring the loose cannon of Cruyff's personality was a price worth paying for the club's resurrection and his own survival as president. Cruyff for his part signed up with Barcelona conscious that from the strong position in which he found himself he would be able to pursue his own agenda, relatively unrestricted, as long as he delivered success. Although the arrangement in time became unhinged, the Nuñez–Cruyff partnership initially came into being as a marriage of convenience.

On 22nd July, Cruyff told some 20,000 Barça supporters gathered in the Camp Nou for the pre-season presentation of the team, 'I like the fact that you have applauded the president because we are beginning a new season, but what I like less is the way you have whistled at the person I have chosen to be captain of the team . . . We need the support of the fans, not their protests . . . Because there is no point in looking back, we must only look forward.' The speech was extraordinary in its presumption of pre-eminence, Cruyff so self-confident as to present himself to the fans and the membership as the man with the power to reconcile the divisions of the club, to seek clemency on behalf of the president, and to stifle any criticism of his choice of captain. Not since the early days of Helenio Herrera had Barça taken on a coach who laid claim to such total control of the club.

The captain, Alexanco, had been the spokesman of the mutiny of

Hesperia, when the players had asked for Nuñez's resignation. There is no doubt that if Cruyff had not intervened, Nuñez would have got rid of him. For the majority of the other players involved – ten in total, including Schuster – had been culled from the team by Nuñez before Cruyff took up his new job. Archibald had been transferred to Hibernian, Hughes to Bayern Munich. Caldere and Nayim would leave soon afterwards, the latter following Venables to Spurs. In addition to Alexanco, the only well-known players left from the previous regime were Lineker, Carrasco, Julio Alberto, Zubizarreta and Migueli.

According to Cruyff, the decision to purge over half the team was taken the day before he signed his contract. He certainly did not intercede on behalf of any other player, insisting that he did not want to deal with anything from the past. On the day he started, there were still some players left who wanted to carry on the fight. Cruyff refused to indulge them. Instead he seems to have been only too pleased to have Nuñez act the way he did, without involving him. The purge effectively gave him an almost clean slate from which to start constructing a team more suited to his style of football.

From the outset Cruyff made it clear that a central plank of his philosophy was the concept of fair value for money and equality of treatment. One of his first moves was to make Carrasco and Julio Alberto's survival in the team dependent on their renouncing a special bonus payment they had arranged with the previous management: the bonus was paid regardless of whether the team won or lost, which struck Cruyff as lacking any justification. Cruyff also made it clear from day one that he considered himself to be the only authority in the dressing room, insisting that neither the players nor Nuñez had the right to tell him how he should coach the team. As he told Barend and van Dorp in an interview conducted in January 1989, six months after he had taken charge, 'On the day I started, there were a number of players who wanted to have fights about the past. I had to tell them that the trainer is the boss in the dressing room, not the players, and, however strange it may sound, that was news to them. But at the same time you couldn't blame them, because they weren't used to anything else. The conflicts might have been solved but the wounds had not healed. The tension between the players and the board was obvious.

On both sides there was a lack of discipline so bad that the board had a sort of meeting room in the dressing room. And I said, "The words 'dressing room' mean it's a dressing room. If you want to talk, do it in the office." And I said to the board, "If you want to talk to me, I'll come to your office, you don't come to my dressing room." To an outsider it seems explosive, but it's something normal. Maybe in one way Nuñez didn't like it. But in another way, maybe he was happy someone else did the hard work.'

In the dressing room, Cruyff did allow himself two allies to help him navigate the stormy waters of FC Barcelona. He brought with him from Ajax his assistant Tonnie Bruins Slot, a sharp scout with a photographic memory, to help him select players and discard others. He also took on his old friend and Barça team colleague Charly Rexach, still hugely admired by the membership. As well as helping out with the training, Rexach became Cruyff's eyes and ears within the club, keeping him in touch with what management, membership and players were saying about him behind his back.

The conspiratorial atmosphere that would in time again take hold at Barça was partly fuelled by Cruyff's selective use of the media. Cruyff's preferred strategy was to have a few Dutch and local journalists to whom he could give a story confident that they would either put a spin on it in his favour or at least report it uncritically. But like all his predecessors he found that nothing he had experienced before had prepared him for the obsessive media coverage, with several local newspapers, magazines and TV programmes devoting the bulk of their coverage to the club's affairs. After his first year he abandoned his daily press conferences, considering them both too time-consuming and potentially destructive – 'one little slip and a minute later it's around the world'. He held the work of several local journalists in quite low esteem, and felt demeaned by having to answer a stupid question with a stupid answer. In time he would make as many enemies as allies, this crazy Dutchman who would never admit that he was wrong.

It was those who felt left out of his entourage who would sharpen their knives whenever Cruyff's fortunes dipped. Cruyff himself always considered that the Madrid-based national paper *El País* was conducting a vendetta against him, although in fact it tended to report relatively objectively on developing tensions and, in particular, the struggle for power between Cruyff and Nuñez that would simmer and occasionally bubble to the surface. Indeed the extraordinary paradox of the Cruyff era was that despite his conflictive style, he nevertheless managed to secure titles, the manner in which they were won restoring the confidence and passion of thousands of Barça supporters.

Cruyff was able to succeed probably because he had played and lived in Barcelona before, and had also played and managed one of the most difficult European clubs, Ajax. From the moment of his return to Barça he showed an instinctive feel for the club's roots, and its transformation under Nuñez, and was absolutely clear where he wanted to stand in relation to the fans and the president. He realised, as Herrera had realised, that Barça's biggest enemy, in times of internal crisis, was the club itself: that when, for instance, an election was round the corner, there was a tendency on the part of some of the membership and the media to exaggerate the seriousness of a bad result; and equally that Nuñez was an authoritarian by nature, and a potential paranoid when challenged. Cruyff felt there was no point in taking part in the human drama that is FC Barcelona unless he delivered the best on his own terms, and that in order to win in style it was necessary to maintain a creative tension, changing things all the time, but for the best. Cruyff was a fulfiller, with a sense of mission. Historically, Barça had had plenty of promises, but too many of them had been broken.

As Barend and van Dorp wrote on encountering the first signs of tension of the Cruyff era within a year of his taking over, 'Cruyff knows where he's going and doesn't want to be followed. He is controversial by definition because he sets trends, unlike ninety per cent of coaches, who follow them. He doesn't know how to kowtow, and compromise does not exist in his way of thinking.'

As a player, Cruyff had helped introduce the concept of 'total football', halting the trend towards defensive football; as a coach he once again added a new dimension to the game, challenging those who instructed their players in a more cautious method of football. As Cruyff put it to me when I interviewed him for this book, 'I like positioning of the ball, I like attack, I like to see the team dominating the situation . . . The "other" game was basically: play the long ball, close it down, and take it from there. It's a different approach but I think my way brings out individual skill.' Cruyff divides the world of football between white and black. There is no room for greys.

The Cruyff system depended on the role played by key players. Its heart was the so-called central axis, the contact between the centre-forward and a free central midfielder – connected, as van Basten used to say, by an invisible cord. Other parts of the central axis were the goalkeeper and the two central defenders. The remaining six players were supposed to cover the two flanks: two wingers playing wide and close to the touch-line, and two defenders and two wing halves watching the flanks. Overall the system was designed to produce a seamless rhythm of attacking play, each player responsible for keeping the ball moving forward.

During his time as coach at Barcelona, Cruyff crafted a team that could best play his system in stages, all along both consolidating and developing. He brought in new players, got rid of others, as if each player represented a piece of an elaborate jigsaw known only to him. Some pieces fitted better than others, several not at all. It took him three seasons before he created a group of players that worked like magic, a moulding of individual talents into a wholeness of commitment and skill, truly a 'dream team'.

The purge of the Hesperia mutineers gave him an unprecedented opportunity to recruit new players. In his opening season he presented the membership with no fever than eleven, all Spaniards from Spanish First Division clubs, among them Bakero from Real Sociedad and Julio Salinas from Atlético Madrid. He also promoted five players from the *cantera* – the youth team – including Milla, Amor and Sergi. The only foreigner in the starting line-up was Aloisio, a Brazilian who was transferred from Internacional do Port Alegre.

Experience and political instinct appear to have inspired Cruyff's initial choice of players. Barça had had three managers in five years: Lattek (German), Menotti (Argentinian) and Venables (British). The fact that the fate of the club had also fallen on the shoulders of German (Schuster), Argentinian (Maradona) and British (Archibald, Lineker and Hughes) players had disorientated many fans' sense of identity, as if the club had simply become a vehicle for imported talent or failure. Cruyff came from a country, Holland, where players like him had been the product of a conveyor belt for producing young talent. Once back in Barcelona, Cruyff had little difficulty in turning a perceived loss into an opportunity, as he later told me: 'Before I came as coach, Barcelona had been experiencing all kinds of players and strategies – English, German, Argentinian . . . It just happened that when I arrived there was a new crop of local players who had come up through the *cantera* and were ready to join the first team. There was the kind of availability that comes at the end of a cycle, every five or six years. But there was another situation that I understood. Fans the world over like to see good players who share their mentality, and preferably come from their country, and if a coach has to choose between a foreign and a local with equal qualities, he should go for the local. That way the fans are less likely to whistle him if things go wrong. In Barça, people like seeing players from the *cantera* in the first team; it makes them feel that the coach somehow is more a part of Barcelona that way. So I tried to do it the way they liked, to produce a game that they could claim as Catalan. Because I'd been here as a player I think I knew what they liked.'

Well, not completely, Johan. Some of Cruyff's critics thought that he had a tendency to suffer from a Michels complex. As a player both at Ajax and at Barça, Cruyff had been impressed by the toughness with which Rinus Michels stuck to his system – a system in which Cruyff had flourished and which he had made his own. Michels had been the psychological master of his Ajax team, knowing what made them tick as players, knowing what positions they could play best in. To what extent Cruyff either respected all his players or treated them like cogs to fit into a machine is open to dispute, although he never lost an underlying sense of humanity.

Gary Lineker's personal experience of the Cruyff era was certainly a far from happy one, and you need something pretty terrible to make Gary Lineker admit openly to even a hint of non-fulfilment. Lineker was unable to play at the beginning of Cruyff's first season because he was ill with hepatitis for three months. Once he was fit enough to play, Cruyff insisted on making him play wide on the right wing. 'At the beginning you never know what a player's real possibilities are. Perhaps I was distracted a little by the European championship [which Holland won under the coach Michels],' Cruyff told me. 'I knew that Lineker was a goal-scorer and that is good for any team. But I also knew that with a more attacking system, and more players moving forward, the field was smaller up front. That is why I moved him from the centre to the right side, to give him more space in which to use his sprint.'

That was not how Lineker felt about it. 'It became pretty apparent to me relatively quickly,' he told me, 'that Cruyff basically wanted his own people in, and me out. But instead of coming along and saying to me, "You're not my type of player," he tried to mess me about by making me play on the wing. What really made me feel disappointed was that his system was actually perfect for me in the centre-forward position. It was made for me. With one player behind him, the centre-forward had to play as far up as he could, if possible not go out of the width of the box and make near-post runs. That way there was the potential to score a bundle of goals. But Cruyff gave the job to Salinas. Instead I was one of two wide players. I wasn't an individual, I was just a number, just like number 4 – the centre-back – was part of the system too. You wouldn't have thought in a million years that Gary Lineker could play on the wing, but I know why he did it – he did it so I would kick up a fuss, then the crowd would turn against me and he'd get rid of me that way.'

Another forward forced to play wide and who felt himself dislocated by what he perceived was Cruyff's game of numbers was Carrasco, a player who had been at the club since the age of sixteen, and would therefore have been expected to qualify for Cruyff's notion of a 'Catalan team'. Yet as Carrasco admitted in an interview with Spanish TV recorded after he had left the club, 'I couldn't stay stuck on the flank, not because I didn't want to co-operate with the team but because two minutes would pass without me touching the ball and I felt like running up the terraces to find it. I need to be near the ball all the time. I have it in my blood.' Carrasco transferred to the French club Sochaux after just one season with Cruyff at the helm, a season in which relations between the two men were further strained by a disagreement over bonus payments.

With the evidence of hindsight, the departure of Lineker and Carrasco proved far less disastrous for Barça that some thought at the time. As they went out of one door, two players entered through another who seemed from the outset much better fits in the Cruyff jigsaw: Ronald Koeman and Michael Laudrup. The first to be signed was Koeman, for 1,000 million pesetas. The Dutchman was transferred to Barcelona after a double triumph: a European Cup final victory over Benfica with his club PSV Eindhoven, and the 1988 European championship – Holland's first international success – with a national side trained by Michels and composed of the likes of Ruud Gullit, Frank Rijkaard and Marco van Basten.

Koeman was brought in as veteran sweeper with that number 4 so crucial in Cruyff's overall strategy. To this day he remains in that privileged league of Barça players whom Cruyff can be persuaded to relate to and talk about as individuals. 'Koeman's quality was his personality, his behaviour in the field,' Cruyff recalled. 'He would always make the other players in the team feel comfortable. If they ever had a problem they could rely on him. Second, he had a fantastic touch: with one of his passes he could get all the forward players to work playing one to one with that one pass, and then there was real rhythm of play, and all sorts of possibilities opened up . . .'

Beyond the stadium, Koeman integrated himself quickly with the local scene, just as Lineker had done – something that Catalans respected. He made a point of learning the local language, and despite his friendship with Cruyff – the two would play golf regularly, together with van Basten who would fly over from Italy to relax – he made a point of also forging his main social circle from among the local and Spanish players.

Koeman was followed by Danish international Michael Laudrup, transferred from Juventus for a mere 220 million pesetas. His arrival had not been anticipated with universal approval within the club – one of its vice-presidents had openly questioned it in front of local journalists. 'How can we buy a player who has not triumphed in Italy?' he had bleated. But Cruyff had taken a broader view of Laudrup's potential, going back to the future, remembering the untapped Danish talent that had been released in Mexico 1986, and confident that Laudrup's lightning counter-attacks would prove more devastating under his system. Michael, the son of a widely respected and popular former player in Denmark, Finn Laudrup, was, in the words of World Cup commentator Brian Glanville, 'an attacker of tremendous, fluent gifts but slightly suspect temperament'.

Like Koeman, Laudrup settled down well in Barcelona. The fanaticism and intrigue of Italy's Serie A football made Barça seem curiously civilised, with the exception of the encounters between the club and Real Madrid – which the Dane was to experience from both sides. Laudrup's memories of his time at Barça are tarnished by what he remembers as one of the worst experiences of his career in football: the night he played at the Camp Nou against Barça after he had transferred to Real Madrid. The moment he appeared, the whole stadium erupted in a chorus of boos and whistles, with fans holding up placards accusing him of betrayal or shouting further abuse at him. The protest reached such a volume that Laudrup totally lost his nerve once the match got under way. He was unable to control the ball or initiate any action and soon found himself substituted in an act of mercy.

As Laudrup recalled in an interview for Catalonia's TV3's series celebrating the centenary of Barça's foundation, 'When I returned to the Camp Nou with Real Madrid I expected the fans to be divided in their feelings towards me; after all when people love you, they hate you also. I thought some of the fans would take the view "All right, he's changed teams – that's just too bad." Instead it turned into one of the worst days of my life. The fact that part of me still felt loyal to Barça was what made the reaction of the crowd hurt me even more.' It is something of a tradition that Barça fans give ex-players in white shirts a rough ride at the Camp Nou. Similarly Real Madrid fans do not take too kindly to defections. But Laudrup was considered by *cules* to have committed an exceptionally incomprehensible sin by choosing Real Madrid over the dream team of Johan Cruyff.

It was said that although Cruyff was unique, Laudrup was the player who came closest to his image. Cruyff in his prime as a player was not just a brilliant individual, he inspired a whole team; like the director of an orchestra he gave shape and structure to the music of the game. In Barcelona, Laudrup for a while came to personify the character and aspirations of the team: it came to be said in Spain that if Laudrup played well, Barcelona excelled. 'I am enjoying my football here more than ever before,' Laudrup told Guy Hodgson of the *Independent* once he had settled into his second season at Barça. 'That is not a reflection on the players or the supporters from my time in Italy, rather an appreciation of the tactics here. I have a freedom I've never had before and the emphasis is

always on attack.' With the number 9 shirt, Laudrup was given a free role
by Cruyff, proving as pivotal in launching a counter-attack from deep
within his own half as in linking up front in a series of one-twos with
Koeman that could similarly play havoc with the opposition.

*   *   *

In the weeks leading up to the start of Cruyff's third season as coach at
Barça, Luis Milla was transferred to Real Madrid, and negotiations to
bring Jan Molby, Liverpool's Danish international midfielder, to
Barcelona came to nothing. Both eventualities involved a flexing of
muscles in the power struggle between Cruyff and the club management. Nuñez always liked to recall the Molby controversy as an
example of how he knew more about the business of football than
Cruyff did. When I interviewed Nuñez early in 1999, he went into
great detail over Molby – a player whom most *cules* have probably
never heard of, and Cruyff himself has almost forgotten.

'When Koeman got injured,' said Nuñez, 'I asked Cruyff to suggest
various alternatives. Cruyff said he wanted Molby. I told him I had my
doubts, firstly because I thought we were being used by Liverpool. I
knew that the English club was trying to sell some of its players in order
to get some new ones because it had qualified for the European Cup. I
didn't see why we should help Liverpool resolve its problems by taking
on a player who wasn't suitable. The fact was that Molby had never
played as a *libero*, which was Koeman's position. I said to Cruyff,
"Look, it's your decision, but I'm also warning you that if we take on
Molby and he doesn't resolve our problems then I will expect you to
end your contract at the end of the season. In other words, if I'm
proved right and you're proved wrong, you're sacked." '

Following that exchange Cruyff decided against buying Molby, and
said that he wanted to give 'Pep' Guardiola, a player from the youth
team, an opportunity to play in the first team instead. To this day
Nuñez claims that Guardiola's promotion – a move that came to be
widely popular with the fans – was all down to him. Cruyff naturally
disputes this. In the case of Milla, Cruyff prevailed with his policy that
no player who did not want to play for Barça should be forced to do so.
Part of the management, led by vice-president Joan Gaspart, were

strongly opposed to allowing a player they considered a star in the making to go to their old rival. The whole Di Stefano saga, in which the Argentinian player had been lost to Real Madrid, even after more than thirty years still weighed heavily on the psyche of many Barça officials and fans.

Guardiola's appearance at the Camp Nou for a while reconciled Cruyff's desire to forge a team capable of playing his system and pleasing the fans with Nuñez's reluctance to surrender control of the club purse-strings. Guardiola was a tall, gangly youth who had joined the club's youth section at the age of thirteen, and who had made something of a mark during his apprenticeship playing in the second team. Born into a relatively poor background, and effectively adopted by the club, Guardiola was luckier than many other young boys who were separated from their families but never succeeded in making it to the first team. Guardiola owed his talent to the street, and his stardom to Johan Cruyff.

The former Argentinian international Jorge Valdano was a huge admirer of the young Guardiola, whom he had got to know while coaching Tenerife and then Real Madrid. Valdano, a middle-class graduate, always had as a point of reference for his judgement of players Diego Maradona, another poor neighbourhood kid who had kicked his first ball over the dust and stones of Villa Fiorito, a shanty suburb of Buenos Aires, gradually turning his anarchic first toy into a source of skill and inspiration. In an interview with Guardiola after he had joined the first team, Catalan journalist Pere Ferreres quoted Valdano: 'In Guardiola's game one notices the pride of the poor neighbourhood kid.'

Guardiola agreed he had been lucky to be born in a village and not a huge city. 'It's true that the fact of being born in a village and being able to play in the streets among the stones has a certain advantage. Using the wall of a house to practise one's game against is easier than in the centre of a city where it's almost impossible to play football in the street. I can't remember when I started playing. I feel I've had a football with me all my conscious life. Everyone remembers me as a kid always with a football.'

He also maintained that the other key to his life as a player was Cruyff himself. 'Cruyff didn't invent me. He took a bet on me and believed in

me and pointed a finger, saying, "It's you I want." I accept that I was
helped by circumstances. There was a hole in the team that needed filling
– Koeman was injured, and Guillermo Amor was suspended because
he'd collected too many cards, and Milla had left the club. But Cruyff
also believed that I could do it, and gave me the opportunity. I think
there are a lot of people with talent who sometimes miss out simply
because they are not given that chance. I owe it to Cruyff.'

Cruyff himself had few doubts that Guardiola had the technique that
would fit into the system he was developing. As he told me, 'Guardiola
could control the ball quickly and pass it quickly. He could deliver the
ball in good condition so that another player could do something with
it.' Guardiola's début with the first team was in a game against Cadiz,
nine days before Christmas in 1990. By then he was already a popular
figure with the local media, the fans and his own colleagues. He was
considered a necessary antidote to the foreign stars once again dominating the Barça firmament. When Cruyff had reacted to Ronald
Koeman's injury by immediately thinking of replacing him with another
foreigner, the Spanish centre-forward Julio Salinas had protested, 'We
don't need anybody. We are twenty-two players, many of us internationals. You would think we were no one without Ronald.' In such an
environment, Guardiola was respected as a player who had lived and
breathed Barça for most of his life. He had been brought up among
Barça veterans, led by the popular Juan Ramón Fuste, and nourished on
the stories of earlier stars such as Samitier, Kubala and Ramallets.
Among Guardiola's more recent heroes was the Asturian forward
Enrique Castro 'Quini', who emerged as the Spanish League's top
scorer in the 1980–1 season despite having been kidnapped by a group
of common criminals and not having reappeared for nearly four weeks.

Guardiola had lived in his teenage years near the Camp Nou, never
quite catching up with his curriculum studies. He liked Catalan poetry
and the protest songs of Lluís Llach, whose defiant concerts marked the
end of the Franco regime. Most of all he liked learning about football,
using the spare time he was left with after training to spy on the first-team
players. His earliest and clearest image was of Terry Venables gently
encouraging his Catalan players in Spanish. He would in time look up to
Andoni Zubizarreta and Laudrup as his examples of what is good and
noble in football – in the dressing room and out in the field.

The earliest and clearest image a lot of *cules* have of Guardiola is of a skinny, unshaven waterboy running out from the touch-line and embracing Pichi Alonso the night Venables's team qualified for the European Cup final. Guardiola had broken the rules but claimed afterwards that he had acted just like any fan who happens to be there at a sublime moment of victory. When Barça lost the final, he would also go silent like all the other fans. As he later remarked, 'With Barça it always seems that there is no alternative to winning. Therein lies some of the club's greatness and its misery. Because it's so important to win, when you lose everyone cries about it more because they think they are not used to it.'

For most of the Cruyff era, Barça fans lived with the expectation of victory. From the moment of his arrival as coach, there was a collective will that he succeed. You don't invest in legends only to shoot them down. And Cruyff for a long time managed to project an image that seemed larger than life.

Catalans learned a lot about Johan Cruyff, and through him something about themselves, early in 1991. The world, it seemed, had become a less secure place. Spain had joined the Western alliance to confront the threat of a nuclear and chemical annihilation threatened by Saddam Hussein. In Barcelona, police intelligence had warned that an equally ruthless enemy commando, the Basque terrorist organisation ETA, had plans to bomb its way to the negotiating table in the run-up to the Olympics. Inside Barça, some club officials and supporters were experiencing a sense of *déjà vu*, while others took comfort from Cruyff's apparent ability to rekindle faith just when all seemed lost. During his first season, 1988–9, Barça had ended five points behind Real Madrid in the League championship, and had been eliminated from the King's Cup by Atlético Madrid. And yet 25,000 *cules* had once again turned a dour Swiss city into a carnival when Barça had gone on to beat Sampdoria 2–0 in Berne in the European Cup Winners Cup final. The following season, Barça failed to win the coveted League title which again went to Real Madrid, with Valencia in second place. In the European Cup Winners Cup it lost to Anderlecht, having reached the last sixteen. This time consolation came in the form of a convincing 2–0 victory over Real Madrid in the final of the King's Cup, after a typically bruising encounter in which Zubizarreta was stoned by a Madrid fan, and Aloisio similarly put out of action by a crude tackle from the Mexican Hugo Sanchez.

The victory over the eternal rival restored a measure of confidence within the club, but dark murmurings resurfaced with the start of the 1990–1 season. The rumour mill of some sectors of the local press focused on the apparent chaos in the dressing room, with players unhappy and wanting to leave. Dutch journalists visiting Barcelona became the object of derision in some quarters. When they mentioned Cruyff and Koeman, they were given the thumbs-down and told to take coach and player back to Holland. Even Cruyff's defenders were finding it difficult to make sense of his turnover of players. His critics suggested that he had simply lost the plot. All *cules* were furious at the malicious pleasure that Real Madrid's Barça-hating chairman Ramón Mendoza took in parading his new acquisition, Milla, who Cruyff had claimed had asked for too much money.

Cruyff let it all brush past him. The same Dutch journalists who had earlier been ridiculed on his account found him calm and well rested. 'If things are going badly, you've got to protect the players and give them the impression everything's going to be fine soon . . . When things are good I don't need publicity. Internally I need to be calm.' The media were convinced that this was the season that would make or break him. Cruyff remained ethereal.

'Every day he surprises you,' commented his assistant Bruins Slot. 'You think he's settled on a team and then suddenly he will say, "I want this player in, that player out," when you're least expecting it.' In addition to Milla, Cruyff had got rid of Alonso, Valverde and Roberto, another international who had gone to Valencia after publicly claiming that no one at Barcelona understood a word the coach said any more. In their place, Cruyff brought back Goikoetxea and Ferrer, who had been on loan, to join Guardiola and Busquets, who had both been promoted from the second team. Ferrer took it upon himself to introduce Guardiola to the team, and to act as his guardian angel during the first months.

But the key new input came not from Spain but from Eastern Europe: the rising Bulgarian star Hristo Stoichkov. In a deal brokered on his behalf by the Catalan agent José-Maria Minguella, he was transferred from CSKA Sofia for $3 million. Minguella recalls 'dealing with colonels while soldiers guarded the room outside' – CSKA was run by the military on behalf of the Communist Party. Stoichkov's monthly earnings as a footballer rocketed from £600 to £20,000. Everyone on the Bulgarian side made more money than they had ever dreamed of, and Minguella, for a good commission, delivered the missing piece for the Cruyff jigsaw. Stoichkov had a history of throwing tantrums and abusing officials. But with the temperamental character came a reputation as Europe's leading striker. In 1990 he had been voted Bulgaria's Footballer of the Year, and had won the coveted European Golden Boot (jointly with Real Madrid's Hugo Sanchez) for his thirty-eight League goals in thirty matches. While some experts claimed he was a liability, Minguella had no doubt that he was a player who was more than ready for the biggest club in the world. He had speed off the mark, dribbling skills, goal instinct, and a cracking shot. Cruyff needed no convincing.

Cruyff's reasons for wanting Stoichkov had as much to do with the Bulgarian's personality as with his all-round technique, as he later told me: 'Before Stoichkov came we had a team of very nice people, but you can't just have a team of very nice people. You need someone like Stoichkov who is aggressive in a positive way, and who can pass this aggressiveness on to other players . . . He goes for the ball, and when he gets the ball he shoots at the goal. There are other players who might wait and see if there is a more beautiful way of doing it, or maybe pass it, but he just went ahead and hit it in.'

In January 1991, Barcelona – without the injured Koeman and without Stoichkov, suspended for stamping on a referee's foot – beat Real Madrid 2–1 in the Camp Nou. The first goal, scored in the first twenty minutes by Laudrup, drew such an explosion of sound and orange and blue flares from the *boixos nois* stand behind the north goal that Zubizarreta asked for play to be temporarily halted. The stadium was bathed in luminous fog. David Miller of the *Times* doubted whether Barcelona had scored more spectacularly since Kocsis was in full cry thirty years previously. 'Goikoetxea, who was persistently tormenting Chendo, Real's right back and captain, danced through on the flank before crossing low into the goal mouth. Laudrup, though heavily challenged by Spasic, met the ball at top speed two feet off the ground. As his shot bulged in the back of the net, a momentarily delayed roar rose from the stadium like a train emerging from the tunnel.'

It was not just in the encounters with Real Madrid that the *cules* were breaking the sound barrier. In an earlier League match against Logrono, one of Spain's less exciting teams, they had begun to do something that was virtually unprecedented: cheer Barça when it was losing. As for attendances, the Camp Nou was once again packed on a regular basis, in striking contrast to the post-Venables *crise* which had seen under 45,000 people turning up at the 120,000-capacity Camp Nou. With Cruyff, fans were beginning to get used to the idea of success, and the achievement of it.

A month after the Real Madrid game, Cruyff's son, Jordi, then a teenager, was training near the stadium with Barça's youth team when he was approached by his brother-in-law and told that his father had been taken to hospital with a suspected heart attack. 'I suddenly felt very scared,' recalled Jordi. 'I felt I was going to lose him. I wouldn't find out until later what was really happening, but I knew that somehow that was a critical moment: I realised just how important the family was to me.'

In the hospital of Sant Jordi, the patron saint of Catalonia who had given Cruyff's son his name, Johan had been diagnosed with coronary fatigue brought on by the narrowing of an artery. The illness had almost certainly been provoked by Cruyff's heavy smoking habit. He agreed to submit himself to a four-hour double-bypass operation by one of Catalonia's leading surgeons, Oriol Bonin, after joking with the nurse who shaved the hairs on his chest, 'They'll take ten years to grow again.'

Cruyff emerged from the operation with his optimism unshaken. Although his father had died of a heart attack when he was only twelve, Cruyff had grown up with a Calvinist belief in predestination, convinced that God was on his side; a belief shared by his family and close friends. As Jordi told me years later during his final days at Manchester United, 'I have always felt that my father had a guardian angel on his shoulder keeping him on the right side.' Unlike the England manager Glenn Hoddle, however, Cruyff never brought his religion into the dressing room, still less attempted to convert his players. His belief was instinctive rather than doctrinal, something that he kept quite separate from the game. When, in his first press conference after his operation, he talked about his scrape with death, he did so with humour: 'If it had been a fatal attack, I wouldn't be here. It's one's good fortune to have a God watching over one and making sure when something like this happens that there happens to be a hospital nearby.'

Cruyff's heart condition and his manner of dealing with it touched an emotional chord among the fans, and strengthened their faith in him. Unlike Maradona and Archibald, he had trusted in local doctors. There was something seductively sentimental in the sight of his family rallying round him. But most of all there was a strength of will and enlightenment in his recovery that seemed to personify the resurrection of the club itself. The anti-smoking poster drawn up by the regional government was a brilliant piece of marketing: a tanned, relaxed Cruyff alongside the words 'In my life I've had two vices: smoking and playing football. Football has given me everything in life. Smoking nearly took it away from me.' From that time on, Cruyff replaced his chain-smoking during matches with some chain-sucking, the Catalan lollipop – the Chupa Chup – becoming a disarming trademark of *el salvador*. Cruyff's anti-smoking campaign certainly proved more honest than the Generalitat's previous attempt to engage a Barça megastar on a matter of public health: Maradona's anti-drugs campaign!

While Cruyff recuperated, training was temporarily put in the hands of Charly Rexach. Without Cruyff but inspired by him, Barça beat Valdano's Tenerife 1–0 in the Camp Nou, and Clemente's tough Athletic Bilbao 6–0 away, with four goals scored by Stoichkov. Thashing the all-Basque team coached by the man Nuñez had once considered as an alternative to Cruyff proved particularly gratifying. Barça also progressed in the European Cup Winners Cup, beating Dynamo Kiev and Juventus on the way to the final. Cruyff watched the games on TV while recovering at home. He later commented, 'I myself asked myself if I was going to get overstressed. I sat down in front of the TV to watch the match between Barça and Dynamo. When it was over I took my own pulse, and found that it was the same as when the match had started. Yet again it made me feel that luck was on my side.'

Barça went on to win the League, situating itself at the top of the table with 57 points, ahead of Atlético Madrid (47) and Real Madrid (46). Such was the collective euphoria that not even defeat at the hands of a seemingly more committed and better-organised Manchester United in the final of the European Cup Winners Cup in Rotterdam three days later dampened the widely held perception among fans and officials that Barça was embarking on glory days. The match against Manchester United, which Barça lost 2–1, had Mark Hughes showing the *cules* what they had lost by scoring two goals. On a wet blustery evening of a kind regularly experienced at Old Trafford, Hughes together with Sharpe demoralised a vulnerable Barça defence with their willingness to run for every ball directed forward. Gary Pallister added to his team's domination of the game by also frequently involving himself in attacking movements. In the 68th minute Bryan Robson set up the first goal from a free kick. Steve Bruce ran forward to beat the goalkeeper Busquets with a header, and Hughes delivered the final touch. Hughes struck again six minutes later, dribbling round Busquets from a Robson pass and striking at a sharp angle into the left-hand corner of the net. It was Manchester United's 100th goal of the season. The *cules* fell silent, leaving the few thousand Manchester United fans – well oiled on local *cerveza* – to scream, shout and bounce with customary defiance.

Barça's only goal came in the then typical Continental style which Manchester United players like David Beckham would later master: Koeman bent a free kick over United's defensive wall. The rest of the game was generally marked by the contrast between Ferguson's intelligent game and Cruyff's questionable tactics, such as only belatedly putting Ferrer on to mark Sharpe, and making Laudrup play on the left wing. But local analysis focused less on the team than on the mood of the club. Typical was Cruyff's post-match comment to English journalists: 'The biggest problem against Manchester United was that everybody was already satisfied because we had won the Spanish championship and had the opportunity to play in the European Cup. With Barça, when something happens everything is exaggerated. It's never normal, it's either big ups or big downs. So when we won the League everyone was so happy that the Cup Winners Cup became unimportant.'

The following season, 1991–2, saw the consolidation of the so-called 'dream team', a phrase invented by the local media and adopted by the fans to express a wish-fulfilment. Barça won both the League and the European Cup, and a majority of fans came to look back nostalgically on this period as one in which they experienced a rare combination of entertaining football and success.

Even by the standards of the club's own star-studded history, the players whom Cruyff could call upon that season represented an impressive array of talent and skills: youthful local promise, symbolised by Guardiola; strength and conviction in the traditional tough Basques, Bakero, Goikoetxea and Begiristain; and three proven super-stars, Koeman, Laudrup and Stoichkov. With the additional mix of experience and skill represented by Zubizarreta, Eusebio, Salinas, Alexanco and Ferrer, one would have thought that Cruyff would have been spoilt for choice. And yet stability was not a concept that fitted in neatly with Cruyff's world. So this was a season when he brought in Richard Witschge – the Dutch winger formerly under his tutelage at Ajax – and two impressive Spaniards, Miguel Angel Nadal (Mallorca) and Juan Carlos Rodriguez (Atlético Madrid), to keep his options as fluid as possible.

Barça reached the final of the European Cup to face Sampdoria, after beating Sparta of Prague, Benfica and Dynamo Kiev. It was a warm and clear evening that 20th May 1992, as if Wembley had suddenly been transported to the Mediterranean for the occasion. The stadium, filled mainly with rival supporters of all ages, created a carnival atmosphere: while not short of voice, the fans also showed themselves typically creative, the *cules* producing a large mosaic in their club colours thanks to a synchronised display of red and blue cards. The popularity of the two teams ensured a Eurovision audience of some 500 million.

As the players prepared to walk through the tunnel, Cruyff was on hand to calm nerves with a typical gesture of poetry in motion. In an impromptu last-minute pep talk he told the team, 'We are in Wembley. The pitch is perfect, the stadium is full. We are going to play in the final of the European Cup. So go out and enjoy it.'

The match was billed beforehand by some commentators as a straight fight between two less than level-headed strikers, matched as much in their goal-scoring abilities as in the passions they aroused in their respective fans: Hristo Stoichkov and Gianluca Vialli. The Bulgarian had certainly shown the nasty streak that Cruyff had declared the team needed. The Spanish referee who had been deliberately stamped on by Stoichkov's studs could vouch for that. But Stoickhov, in the midst of an ongoing row between his agent and Cruyff over money, had yet to prove himself as prolific a goal-scorer as he had been at CSKA, despite an outstanding display in the Republican stadium in Kiev. The Bulgarian's contribution, according to the *Daily Telegraph*'s Graham Turner, was not restricted to shooting. He had 'worked, harried, distributed, and created havoc with his pace and mobility'. For his part, Vialli was quite simply out for revenge: his unhappiest memory was of the 2–0 defeat by Barcelona in the 1989 Cup Winners Cup final when he had been dropped from the team because of a recurrent muscle injury.

As things turned out, Vialli was among the least impressive performers in a contest that turned out to be far broader in its excitement than had been predicted. Vialli thought he had scored in the 69th minute when, after gathering a pass from Mancini, he chipped a ball past Zubizarreta. But the ball bounced on the wrong side of the far post. Stoichkov produced some of the most thrilling moves in the match, at one point running down the left wing and delivering a perfectly struck angled pass which just failed to find Laudrup; at another, testing the Italian keeper Pagliuca with a firm header from Eusebio's centre. Two minutes past the hour, Stoichkov's shot, delivered from a Laudrup pass, beat Pagliuca – only to rebound off the inside of the far post, Kubala-style. The missed opportunities came from an exciting series of attacks and counter-attacks. Neither side stooped, as Eastern European clubs had tended to do in previous finals, to strangling defensive play followed by a penalty shoot-out.

Barça in particular showed no inclination to repeat the humiliating experience of its last European Cup final in 1986 when the team coached by Venables had lost on penalties to Steaua Bucharest. Instead they produced the kind of final Cruyff had promised, 'celebrating all that is best in football', pushing without let-up for a goal. The performance included superbly weighted long passes out of defence by Koeman, brilliant combinations by Stoichkov and Laudrup, persistent attacks by Salinas, and a wonder save by Zubizarreta from a strike by Attilio Lombardo, Sampdoria's best player of the match.

The breakthrough came with a set-piece goal of genius with seven minutes left of extra time. Stoichkov touched the ball to Bakero, who teed it up for Koeman to drive the ball over the wall with such force and so deep that it looked as if he'd broken the right side of the net, once it had sped past Pagliuca. More than 30,000 Catalans in the stadium and thousands more watching it on TV around the world erupted. Koeman was mobbed by his colleagues. Cruyff and Rexach leapt to their feet with similar jubilation, although the Dutch coach was soon back to shouting orders from the touch-line. 'When we scored that goal, all I remember thinking was, please, *please*, Barça, don't lose your mind. I knew that if my players hung on to theirs we would win.' And they did.

That night, *cules* went dancing all the way from Wembley to the Rambla via Trafalgar Square with minimum trouble. The club threw a party for its officials, the players and a host of Catalan VIPs – including the President of Catalonia, Jordi Pujol, and Barcelona's elected mayor, Pasqual Maragall – in a country club near St Albans in Hertfordshire. The club's incorrigible vice-president Joan Gaspart had promised that if Barça won he would celebrate by throwing himself into the Thames. He duly did so just before dawn and miraculously survived.

Later that day, the team returned to be greeted by over a million supporters in the streets of Barcelona. In the Church of the Merce, they gave customary thanks to the local Virgin in a prayer led by Augusto Santamans, the club's oldest surviving member. Later, as had become the custom since the coming of democracy, they took their latest trophy to the Plaça Sant Jaume, showing it separately from the balconies of both the Generalitat and the City Hall. Three years earlier there had been a failed attempt by Sixto Cambra, a businessman with close links to President Pujol, to topple Nuñez and put the management of the club in the hands of officials clearly identified with Pujol's nationalist party. But no one on this day was prepared to surrender their political identification with one of Barça's greatest victories. From his balcony Pujol shouted, '*Visca el Barça, visca Catalunya!*' Maragall, the Socialist mayor, opted for a more neutral 'Barça is no longer simply "more than a club" – it has become the best club in Europe.' It was left to Guardiola, however, to touch the real emotional nerve of the gathering. He paraphrased the historic words of the Catalan President Josep Tarradellas on his return from exile after Franco's death – 'Citizens of Catalonia, I am here!' – declaring, '*Ciutadans de Catalunya, ya la tenim aquí!*' – 'Citizens of Catalonia, you have it here!'

The following month, Barça won the League championship again, in a nail-bitingly tense competition involving Real Madrid, who had led the League table for the bulk of the season. The title was decided on the last playing day of the season, with Real Madrid losing 3–2 away to Tenerife, and Barcelona winning 2–0 against Athletic Bilbao at the Camp Nou.

For the club's supporters, its players, its officials and its coaching staff, Barça's victory at Wembley was the one that assumed legendary status. To this day, Koeman and Cruyff are among those who remember it as an achievement, the nature of which can only properly be understood within the specific political and social contexts of the club. Thanks to that one goal, which thousands of *cules* continue to replay in their minds like a ritual, Catalans felt they had dealt with the bogyman. Barça had become the first ever Catalan champions of Europe, and the first Spanish champions since Real Madrid had won the title more than a quarter of a century before. Barça had finally achieved the holy grail it had been pursuing without success since the competition had started. In so doing the club had laid to rest the bitter memories of its defeats in the finals of 1961 and 1986, while matching Juventus's feat of capturing all three European trophies.

Cruyff himself had achieved his personal ambition of leading Barça to the title he had won as a player with Ajax twenty-one years earlier. But he had also given the Catalans his own lesson on the meaning of success.

16

The Passion of Being Boss

On 2nd November 1994, All Souls' Day, Barça swamped Manchester United with a 4–0 Champions' League victory before a 112,000 capacity crowd at the Camp Nou. 'We were well and truly slaughtered,' commented Alex Ferguson on the heaviest defeat suffered by the English champions since the Scot had taken over its management eight years previously.

Barça's memorable performance involved the latest version of Johan Cruyff's 'dream team', this time spearheaded by international football's version of Butch Cassidy and the Sundance Kid: the unlikely combination of Stoichkov and the brilliant Brazilian forward Romario, the latter recently bought from the Dutch team PSV. Both men ran riot with the United defence, the Bulgarian scoring two goals, the Brazilian one, with fullback Albert Ferrer completing the humiliation. Few watching that match that evening would easily forget Romario's goal. It was dispatched effortlessly into Walsh's net, after the Brazilian had chested down a forty-yard pass from Stoichkov and left Pallister and Steve Bruce floundering. Among the surprise selections of the night was Cruyff's son Jordi playing instead of Koeman after his recent promotion to the first team. Jordi's presence in the Barça dressing room was destined to become problematical, but there was nothing to suggest such a scenario on that night. Cruyff confused the crowded United defence by playing the right-footed Jordi on the left flank, with Stoichkov on the right, the two men funnelling their forces towards the centre. It was the young Cruyff, moreover, who set up the first goal of the match, with Stoichkov moving on to his pass and then cannoning in a left-wing shot which entered the goal courtesy of Gary Pallister's heel.

Since winning the European Cup, Cruyff had not rested on his laurels, winning the League for a third consecutive season, with

Romario the top scorer of the competition with thirty goals. Four days later his team had been beaten 4–0 by AC Milan in the European Cup final in Athens. Now, the victory over United had once again demonstrated Cruyff's ability to produce entertaining attacking football. However, the euphoria proved short-lived. In the team reshuffle that followed the humiliating defeat in Athens, many Barça fans mourned the departure to Valencia of the goalkeeper Zubizarreta, one of a handful of Barcelona players who played regularly in the Spanish national squad. Cruyff claimed that Busquets was more suited to his system by virtue of being a better ball-player and more thrusting beyond the box. But the promotion to the first team of Cruyff's son-in-law as reserve keeper following Zubizarreta's exit fuelled an uneasy feeling of nepotism in the dressing room.

The other important player to go was Laudrup. Any doubts that there was no sin in the world greater than sharing part of your dream with your rival was dispelled in Laudrup's first appearance in the Camp Nou dressed in Real Madrid white. I don't think I have ever personally witnessed such intensity of hate directed at a single player in the Camp Nou as that experienced by Laudrup in that game. To Cruyff, watching from the sideline, Laudrup's verbal lynching should have served as a reminder of the huge passion he had stirred up with his dream team, and the difficulties he faced once Barça had been brought down to earth. But he was not one to regret any decision he'd ever taken, still less publicly to admit doing so. Laudrup had failed to play the numbers game as developed by Cruyff at Barça. He had taken Laudrup on to play forward but the Dane had shown an increasing tendency to play deep. That is why Cruyff let him go. It was as simple as that.

When, in Barça's first season without Laudrup, the club got knocked out of the Spanish Cup and once again started dropping below Real Madrid in the League, Cruyff had this to say: 'I will not denigrate Laudrup. He was and remains a very good player. I myself bought him from Italy when everyone had written him off. Everyone called me crazy because at Milan – or was it Juventus? – he was always on the bench. When he came to us, he played very well, but at a certain moment, we noticed he was playing less well than in his early years. I can't prove it, but I don't think we'd have had better results if Laudrup had been with us this season, which doesn't take away from the fact that I think Laudrup is still a very good player. I always want to win, and I'm not going to get rid of someone if I think he's still the best!'

In the second half of his final season at Barça, Laudrup had effectively become the 'fourth' foreigner, which, given the pre-Bosman restrictions of three to a team, meant more time on the bench than off it. Cruyff gave a more prominent role to Romario. 'They wanted me to score goals when I came here; that is what I did,' Romario would later remark on his fleeting presence in the Catalan capital. It was Romario's goals that helped Cruyff to his fourth League championship in the 1993–4 season. At the age of twenty-seven, the Rio-born Romario was probably at the height of his physical powers. Only five feet six inches tall and solidly built, he had a low centre of gravity which made his runs effective rather than elegant. 'Romario was a footballer who could do everything, a real quality player. His passing and scoring were very good, he was skilled in one-to-ones,' recalled Cruyff when I interviewed him in the spring of 1999. And yet, in a rare admission of failure, Cruyff also commented on what had gone wrong: 'He lacked discipline and that was one of the problems we had to deal with. If you have a lot of stars in a team, there has to be a limit as to what each does as an individual. Each has to respect the others, which means that you don't do what the others don't because otherwise everything ends in chaos.'

Perhaps Cruyff would have saved himself a lot of trouble if he'd had a word with Bobby Robson, Romario's coach at PSV. 'The Brazilian was an exciting player, who was capable of turning a game in an instant with his skill around the penalty area, but he could also be frustrating, disappearing for long periods of the game, rarely shouldering any responsibility and sometimes socialising and dancing late into the night before important games,' Robson later recalled. Romario's problem – if you can call it a problem – was that he was a typical Carioca, who owed his way of life as much as his football to the fact that he had been born and bred in Rio de Janeiro. 'I'm the face of Rio,' Romario said in his second season at Barça. 'I'm the type who likes samba and carnival. I love life, I want to enjoy it. I love the sun and the beach. That's what the Carioca is like.'

Barcelona was certainly an improvement on Eindhoven. In his first game with PSV, Romario had been substituted after thirty minutes after being numbed by the cold. Despite wearing a leotard and gloves, he was shivering so much he could hardly focus on the ball. But he chose to make the Catalan capital simply a staging post for his international career, turning down a longer-term contract than the minimum two years he had signed up for. Instead of taking up the club's offer of a private residence, he moved himself and his entourage into two rooms and a suite on the seventeenth floor of the Hotel Princesa Sofia, near the stadium. In all his time in Barcelona, he rarely moved accommodation – only briefly staying at the Hilton, and then in the seaside resort of Sitges, when the Spanish press began to run stories that he was using the Princesa Sofia not for himself and his family but for one of his numerous girlfriends.

Just before Christmas 1994, Romario played in a match against Blackburn Rovers in Almería, the last of six friendlies which he was contracted to play for Barça as part of his transfer deal from PSV. It was a Tuesday evening. Because they were playing an international match midweek, the Barça players had been excused from playing a League match the following weekend. Cruyff had given the whole team a week off, from the Wednesday. Romario played brilliantly in the first half, but when it came to half-time made out that he was exhausted. He convinced Rexach, who was acting coach for the night, that he should substitute him. Romario showered, changed and, as his colleagues walked out on to the pitch, dashed from the stadium. He took a taxi to the nearest airport where a private jet he had hired for 1.5 million pesetas was waiting to whisk him off to Rio. Romario's great escape, witnessed by Dutch journalist Leo Verheul, is illustrative of just how drawn the player felt to his birthplace. But it wasn't just nostalgia that ended up undermining Romario's performance at Barça. In his second season with the team, he saw it as his priority to play for Brazil in the World Cup in the US. He had had a bad experience of Italia '90, only belatedly and unconvincingly playing for his national team after months recovering from a broken leg. He was determined not to do anything that might put his presence in the US at risk, which meant that while he was with Barça he played well only when he felt like it, not when Cruyff wanted him to.

Romario's commitment to the club got no stronger once the World Cup was over. With Maradona busted yet again for drugs, Romario's inventive brilliance was one of the high points of the tournament, in which he scored five crucial goals. But he had lost whatever incentive he had ever felt for staying on at Barcelona. At PSV, Robson recalled, he had not been able to stay cross with Romario for long because 'he had such an angelic face and such a nice temperament', and anyway his off-the-pitch problems were not of his concern, as 'he was on a six-year contract earning a lot more money than I was with my two-year contract' and winning games and titles. Such an attitude was anathema to Cruyff, who from his early days at Ajax had insisted on ruling his roost, and who had taken up the coach's role at Barça more determined than ever to control the dressing room. For Cruyff, the beautiful game he aspired to meant money and it meant achievement – without making concessions about either. His sense of betrayal at the hands of Romario was not helped by the eventual manner of his going: the Brazilian's longed-for return to his beloved Rio, oiled by a lucrative sponsorship deal signed between the city's Flamengo club and Nike.

Cruyff's single-mindedness in fact had been nowhere more brutally expressed than in his treatment of his close friend Koeman, soon after Romario's arrival at Barça. Koeman, as calm and skilful a character on the field as he was gentle and kind off it, had been gutted by Cruyff's decision to put him on the subs' bench, playing Romario straight away. The two Dutchmen's friendship survived this and subsequent substitute humiliations, with Koeman finally putting it down to Cruyff's management style. However, by the autumn of 1994 Koeman had made up his mind to leave Cruyff's team, despite his enormous popularity among the fans. Since scoring that goal at Wembley, Koeman had retained the status of a football demigod among the fans – which has continued to the present day. 'Every year, on the anniversary of Wembley, I get dozens of phone calls and cards from fans around the world who have not forgotten,' Koeman told me in 1999! And yet the same fanaticism that that goal had aroused had also represented a constant source of collective pressure. There was also a sense of wanting to keep a memory sweet, a dream special, before it risked being spoilt by events.

Among the emerging sources of tension within the club was the appearance of Cruyff's son Jordi in the first team. Memories of Cruyff defiantly taking on the Francoiste state by insisting on registering his first-born with a Catalan name seemed to belong to a distant past. The young Jordi was now a grown-up footballer, sporting the colours of the biggest club in the world with all the intrigue, conspiracy and jealousies that came with them.

Jordi had been fated to carry the weight of his father's fame on his shoulders from birth. His delivery by Caesarean on 9th February 1974 – a few months after his father had moved as a player to Barcelona – was timed in such a way as not to disrupt Cruyff and Rinus Michels's plans for winning the League. Barça did not have any games that weekend. From cradle to school, and beyond, football remained an inescapable part of Jordi's existence. His father shared his enthusiasm and knowledge of the game with Jordi from early childhood days, taking him to watch his first League games at Ajax's De Meer stadium and encouraging him to join Ajax's famous youth training scheme at the age of seven when the family returned to Holland in 1981. It was as a young adolescent, at a time when Cruyff began to fall out with the Ajax club management, that Jordi first experienced the negative pressures that went with his surname. Although he was already proving himself as a player of potential, he was treated coldly by some officials and others on the youth team.

When Jordi was fourteen, Cruyff returned to Barcelona as manager, and his son went straight into the club's youth system. Two miserable years followed, during which the soft-natured and slender Jordi struggled to keep afloat amidst the macho culture of Spanish football and the public obsession with his father. He suffered periodic pangs of homesickness for Amsterdam. His father kept him going. As Jordi told David Winner of the *Independent* in October 1994, 'My family wouldn't let me give up. When you think or talk about it, you really think you can't do without football. There are people around you who have expectations of you. You can't let it pass.'

Jordi had every reason to feel grateful to a father he has always idolised. Under Cruyff's guidance, and with an inherited will-power, Jordi had finally begun to blossom. Three months earlier, during Barça's pre-season tour of Holland, Jordi had made his début for the first team, scoring hat tricks against Groningen and De Graafschap. When the Spanish League opened he headed an important goal against Santander and secured a decisive penalty. By then Jordi was embarked on a two-year training and dietary programme designed by specialists to add pounds to a frame that, despite topping six feet, tipped the scales at around ten stone eight pounds. 'What we have to avoid,' Cruyff senior had told long-term Barça friend the English journalist Graham Turner, 'is putting him in the centre of the stage before he is something like a finished product and capable of doing himself justice.'

According to Turner's observations, Jordi's 'frugal frame, wiry legs, close control of the ball and a shoulder dropped here and there' were visible chips off the old block. Yet Jordi was not then, nor would he ever become, the genius in the field his father had been, lacking either Cruyff's passionate sense of his own superiority or his range of technical and physical ability. At Barça Jordi always sensed he was playing on borrowed time, knowing that his surname, while in some ways advantageous, could just as easily turn into a millstone round his neck. As Jordi told me when I interviewed him for this book, 'Being the son of my father turned into a big disadvantage while I was at Barça. If I played well, people said I had played unbelievably well. But if I didn't play too good, people would say I had played incredibly badly. They would judge me with my father as reference without judging me on my own terms. And if people got unhappy with my father, they took it out on me.'

As Barça entered the 1995–6 season, time was running out for the Cruyffs. One by one, the players who between them had represented aspects of Barça's most glorious game had left the club – Laudrup, Zubizarreta, Salinas, Goikoetxea, Salinas, Romario, Koeman, Stoich-kov. With the silverware no longer coming in as often as it once had done, Nuñez no longer felt he had to put up with Cruyff. The tension between the two men got worse, with Nuñez increasingly interfering in Cruyff's plans for restructuring the team and claiming that his coach and trainer was losing a sense of longer-term strategy. When Cruyff presented Nuñez with a 'wanted' list of new players including British players of the calibre of Steve McManaman, Ryan Giggs and Robbie Fowler, the president accused him of wanting to waste money.

Cruyff suspected that a palace *coup* was in the making, as he later told me: 'When I came back to Barcelona, I insisted that I was in charge of the dressing room and didn't want interference from the presidency. But I was losing that freedom towards the end. Nuñez was increasingly talking and drawing up contracts behind my back without consulting me. The problem with that was that once that process began with one player, a sense began to spread across the team that the coach was no longer in control. I was surprised because I thought things were going quite well. You can't just say you've had a bad year because you haven't won a title. I didn't feel tired of Barcelona – the place was still special and nice. I had had six years with a lot of good football, and a lot of cups, and now I had been spending two years building up the team again. There were players who had played at the highest level who were getting old, but a lot of young players waiting to come on, and I felt that I was one step away from forming another great team. I was quite prepared to go on as long as I could do what I said I wanted to do. But they thought, let's get rid of him so we can start making decisions. The way they finally did it showed they didn't simply want to sack me, they wanted to harm me. All they said about me was rubbish; they tried to blame me for everything when all they wanted to do was create a bad image.'

The end, when it came, was as brutal as it was swift. On Saturday 18th May 1996, Cruyff arrived at the Camp Nou for a training session with the team. The next day Barça was due to play a game against Ceula, the penultimate match of the season. The headline news in the sports papers that morning was that Nuñez together with his vice-president Joan Gaspart had met with Bobby Robson in Madrid the previous day and signed him as Cruyff's replacement. It was not unusual for Nuñez, his vice-president or one or other of his ruling junta to spin a tale or two through trusted journalists, but Cruyff had never in his life suffered the indignity of being fired through the media. Cruyff had been with Nuñez on the Thursday, and the president had dropped not even the merest hint of what he was about to do. But he now had no doubt as to the meaning of the visit Gaspart paid him that Saturday in the stadium. Charly Rexach, who was with Cruyff in the technical staff's dressing room, takes up the story:

'Gaspart arrives, and he's about to offer Johan his hand when Johan says, "You're Judas!" Then Cruyff starts accusing him and Nuñez of being false, of being traitors, and of stabbing him in the back. How was it possible, he screamed at him, that Nuñez didn't have the guts to deal with whatever problems there were with him face to face? The scene was very heated indeed. Gaspart got angry and told him that he was throwing him out of the club and threatened to call the police. He said that he was leaving and coming back later, and that when he returned he didn't want to find him still there. Gaspart said it as straight as this to Johan: "You no longer belong here." '

It was ten o'clock. Johan Cruyff, one of the greatest footballers of all time, who had won Barça more titles than any other coach in its history, had been given his marching orders like a part-time lavatory attendant who had overslept.

To this day Nuñez claims to have no regrets. When he agreed to be interviewed for this book, Nuñez said of Cruyff's sacking, 'Cruyff's contract was coming to an end. The fact that one week before that contract expired he was told that the following season his services would no longer be needed seems to me quite normal in the world of sport . . . The club had decided that after spending two years without winning any title and instead creating a lot of problems in the team it was time for Mr Cruyff to leave.'

Seconds after Gaspart's departure, Rexach walked on to the training ground and told the players that he was assuming temporary management of the team until the end of the season. The reactions of the players ranged from anger to relief. Only a handful threatened to walk out in solidarity with Cruyff, but in the end they too buckled under to what seemed irreversible. For months the players had felt themselves mere pawns in a power struggle over which they had no real control.

On the evening before the match day, only Jordi failed to turn up for the final training session. He was both deeply hurt and furious at his father's treatment. Rexach rang Cruyff senior and begged him to persuade his son to play. 'Your problem is your problem, but Jordi is still a player with Barcelona,' he told him.

Cruyff was in no mood to do Rexach any favours. The speed with which his assistant had taken over smacked of disloyalty. Although in fact Rexach had always maintained enormous respect towards the Dutchman, together with loyalty to the club, in Barça's developing equivalent of the Battle of the Titans, Cruyff, like Nuñez, divided the world into those for him and those against him. And yet Cruyff appears to have glimpsed an opportunity in Rexach's impassioned appeal. Together with Jordi, he worked out a compromise designed to help Rexach over a potential crisis of discipline while at the same time providing the Cruyffs with a sense of restored honour. The agreed strategy was that Jordi would be in the starting line-up but would be substituted before the end of the match. 'I talked to my father,' recalled Jordi, 'I was feeling very hurt with the way they had treated him. We understood each other's feelings, but he convinced me that the game provided an opportunity: "Give it your best shot," he said, "and the fans will understand." I knew in my heart that this was going to be my last game with Barça.'

The game against Celta turned into one of the more memorable matches played at the Camp Nou, an occasion probably only Nuñez and Gaspart would prefer to forget. Barça played for most of the first half like a team in mourning: poor passing, gaps in defence and a pedestrian offensive play reflected not so much a tactical flaw as psychological paralysis. The team was 2–0 down when Jordi began to help lead a remarkable second-half comeback, bringing Barça level, and then ahead 3–2. Five minutes from the end of the match, Rexach called Jordi to the subs' bench. As he left the pitch, the stadium gave him a standing ovation, which had the Camp Nou for neither the first nor the last time reverberating with the name of Cruyff, as if the very name was an inseparable part of its soul.

*   *   *

In March 1998, I was sitting with Bobby Robson in his office at FC Barcelona when a club official barged through his half-open door and, without offering the slightest excuse for the interruption, queried his application for an airline ticket to Paris: 'The president thinks that any flight under four hours should be tourist class, not business,' the official snapped.

It would be hard to imagine a more subtly calculated put-down to a man whose illustrious career had spanned more than forty years in the playing and management of international football, embracing some of Europe's leading clubs and one of England's more competent national squads. He had won eight European and national cup titles, and still commanded an enormous following around the world. Yet Robson's standing in Barcelona was clearly not what it had been when, eighteen months previously, a beaming Nuñez had emerged from the Cruyff débâcle to confirm him as Barça's new coach. For in June 1997, half-way through a two-year contract, Robson had been replaced by the Dutchman Louis van Gaal and told – in a much-publicised act of humiliation – that he could stay on as the club's *director de fichajes* or head of recruitment.

'I've been using this as a sabbatical really, as an adventure,' Robson told me, after he had diplomatically chosen to ignore the insult over the Paris trip. 'I've done things that I've been wanting to do for years but never had the time, like spend some time in Africa and South America looking at players.' A not inconsiderable incentive was that the club had agreed to keep him on his full manager's salary. The longer we talked, however, the clearer it became that being the best-paid talent scout in the world was poor compensation for having to survive one of the most frustrating periods of an otherwise fortunate life. In the weeks leading up to our interview, Robson had become an increasingly unappreciated and isolated figure at Barcelona; indeed, I had come across him by chance in the otherwise deserted grounds of the Camp Nou, after he had been excluded by Nuñez from the delegation that accompanied the team to their European Super Cup final in Germany.

Nuñez seemed to have forgotten that it was thanks to Robson that Barcelona had qualified for the Super Cup in the first place, and that in his first and only season as coach, Barça had won the European Cup Winners Cup along with the King's Cup, while coming a close second to Real Madrid in the League championship. 'It was a phenomenal year. We played good football, we scored over 100 goals in the League and 140 in all competitions . . . but a sector of the media here kept saying I had no system!' Robson told me. A year earlier, when Barça were snapping at the heels of the League leaders Real Madrid, and progressing well in the King's Cup and in Europe, he had voiced similar frustration in an interview with Amy Raphael for *Esquire* magazine: 'We won 3–0 yesterday but that's not good enough . . . If I was second place in England and in the last eight of the FA Cup and European Cup Winners Cup with a great chance of going through, I'd be a hero and king of the city. But you have to win *every* game *and* be above Real Madrid. You know, when I took over from Johan Cruyff, he was a legend both as a player and as a manager, and no one remembers that he hadn't won anything for two years. We've scored sixty goals in half a season and they're still bitching . . .'

When we talked, Robson seemed to have no doubts that the real reason he had been pushed aside had nothing to do with football, and everything to do with the politics of the world's most politicised club. I couldn't bring myself to ask him where he thought he'd been all those years during which he had served off and on as an unofficial adviser to Nuñez on issues such as whether Terry Venables was a good manager or not. But there was no underestimating the importance he put on the Cruyff legacy. 'I came here after Johan Cruyff. He was a god, a hero here, he'd been here eight years and during it had been magnificent. I didn't realise the political battle I was coming into, to be honest – what he meant to the city, with half the club thinking he should have gone, and half thinking he should not have gone, and how those who were with him were against the president and were therefore against the new coach . . . And this is what football here is all about, it's about power, about the necessity of winning, it's about this city and about Catalonia. The army cannot be defeated . . . It's a good job I was experienced because a younger coach would have cracked under the pressure. It was relentless. Meeting the press every day, seeing the power of the press, half of it attacking me all the time, hoping that I'd fail. I used to say to myself, "Do I need this in my life? I didn't come here for this political battle; I came here to try and win football games." '

Maybe the thing about Robson was that essentially he occupied a different world from the Nuñezes or even the Cruyffs; that, as Amy Raphael commented after meeting him, he was quite simply 'an honest bloke, a football addict passionately loyal to his clubs, who has never let ambition get the better of him'. When I saw him, he was trying to be as circumspect as possible about what he had to say about the club. A few days earlier, Nuñez had exploded with rage when the local media had reproduced some unguarded comments – some of them off-the-record – made during a year of Robson's being assiduously tracked by British freelance Jeff King. Still, Robson was nothing if not human, and the hurt fuelled even more indiscretion and subsequently another threatened reprisal from Nuñez when the local press reproduced part of my interview published in the *Financial Times*. It seemed as if the power struggle had no cut-off point, and journalists, like managers, were simply further pawns in the game. Robson told me, 'If I'd known what was going to happen to me, I wouldn't have turned down the offer Newcastle made me in January 1997. At the time I wasn't looking to leave Barça. I'd only been in the job a few months. I felt that by the end of the year we'd get things right and win things, and that as long as people were patient and gave me the opportunity I would do it. I turned down megabucks to stay. Nuñez and Gaspart could have said at that point that I should take the money and go, but they didn't. They said, "You're doing very well, we want you to stay." '

The first contact from the Newcastle management had come on 7th January with a phone call from its chief executive, Freddie Fletcher, confirming that Kevin Keegan was on his way out. A few days later, and after Keegan's departure had been confirmed publicly, Fletcher – together with Freddie Shepherd, the vice-chairman; Douglas Hall, the chairman's son and a director of the club; and Mark Corbidge, the man Newcastle had appointed to look after the stock-market flotation – arrived in Barcelona and offered Robson a five-year contract with a two-year option. The next day Sir John Hall, the chairman, turned up to back up the bid. 'My salary clearly didn't frighten them, as they offered me a comparable salary,' Robson reflects in his autobiography, *An Englishman Abroad*. At a separately reported £5 million over three years, the offer would have made Robson the best-paid manager in the Premier League.

The offer played as much havoc with his heart as with his calculator. Robson had lived and breathed Newcastle from childhood. Born in 1933 – three years before the outbreak of the Spanish Civil War – in Country Durham, into a working-class Methodist family, Robson had played his early games of street football kicking pieces of coal before being taken by his miner father to see the first of many matches at St James's Park. It was seventeen miles to the stadium from the Robsons' two-roomed terraced house in Langley Park which Bobby shared with his parents and four brothers, but father and sons always made a point of arriving early enough to be at the front of the queue. That way Robson was assured of seeing his childhood heroes, players they've never heard of in Barcelona such as Jackie Milburn, Albert Stubbins and Alf McMichael.

When that phone call came through in January 1997, Robson had reacted like any other true Geordie fan – with a sense of loss at the departure of Keegan, the man earlier considered 'the second Messiah' on Tyneside. Robson thought about his roots. Not only did he still bleed black and white; his wife, also a Geordie, did too, and she wanted to go back home.

For all Robson's dilemma, people in Barcelona who knew a thing or two about footballing passions saw things differently. As *Sport*, one of the two biggest local sports newspapers, put it, 'The football world must have gone crazy if Newcastle seriously think they can lure a coach away from FC Barcelona. Newcastle may be a big club in English terms, but you can't possibly compare their international prestige or potential to Barcelona's.'

By this time Barça had joined in the post-Bosman transfer frenzy and spent a record-breaking £27 million on five new foreign players – Ronaldo (£12.8 million from PSV Eindhoven), Giovanni (£5 million from Santos), Baia (£5 million from Porto), Stoichkov and Couto (£2 million each from Parma) – in addition to making substantial investments in Pizzi, Blanc and Luis Enrique. Robson had had some thoughts of his own, Emmanuel Amunike and Alan Shearer among them. Shearer he'd been unable to get, having been told by Blackburn Rovers that he was not for sale. Amunike would join Barça later. But Robson wasn't complaining. Nuñez could have his power as long as Robson could play his football. As he told me, 'They want success badly in Barça, and at first I felt they were going to give me what I asked for to give me the chance of giving them the success that they wanted. I never had full control because the control was always above me, among the directors. They liked to wheel and deal and they bought the players. I could recommend and suggest but they did the negotiations, they did the finances; I never got to touch or see a player's cheque. It's not like in England, where a manager is at the apex, at the helm.'

Among the inevitable sacrificial lambs of the new era was Jordi Cruyff. He had rung Robson as soon as he had taken over as manager. Jordi said he wanted to go on playing for Barça, and hoped that Robson would not be swayed by politics but base his decision on technical criteria alone. Although Robson later claimed he had acted with equanimity in transferring Jordi out of Barça's first team and on to Manchester United's subs' bench, the decision was taken essentially on political grounds. In his autobiography, Robson says that keeping Jordi at the club would have risked turning him into a spy: 'He would have gone back home and his dad would have asked him what had happened at the club . . . if a story had leaked from the dressing room he would have been seen, unfairly or not, as the prime suspect.' Even the one technical argument he puts forward – that Jordi may have effectively become surplus to requirements with players around of the calibre of Ronaldo, Giovanni, Stoichkov and Figo – is underpinned with a political consideration. 'It was a no-win situation, for if I hadn't picked him [to play] it would have been seen as getting back at his father and I couldn't let people think that way. Even though it wouldn't have been true, it would have been manna from heaven for the anti-Robson, anti-Barcelona brigade.' The use of the phrase 'anti-Barcelona' is either a slip of the pen or a deliberate evasion of the fact that many genuine Barça fans were anti-Robson not because they felt themselves anti-Barcelona but because they were anti-Nuñez.

As an editorial in *Sport* suggested, the club's pre-season press release stating that it was Robson's decision alone to get rid of Jordi was a convenient smokescreen for Nuñez and Gaspart. According to Jordi, the player had been told personally by Gaspart that even if there were twenty-five players injured, there were still fourteen he would want to play at the Camp Nou rather than him. 'I had been caught up in a personal war, and I was being made to pay the price. It was clear that they wanted to wipe out all trace of Cruyff from the club,' Jordi told me.

As the 1996–7 season got under way, Ronaldo seemed the one player endowed with the potential to bury the ghost of Johan Cruyff. (While Jordi left for Manchester, Cruyff senior in fact remained very much alive and well and living in Barcelona, ever watching over developments at Barça like an avenging eagle, when not in Amsterdam commentating on Dutch football and looking after his non-Spanish business interests.) No one felt more enthusiastic about Ronaldo than Robson. It was while he was managing Porto, prior to his arrival at Barça, that Robson had begun to take note of reports that a child prodigy was playing at his former club PSV Eindhoven. Ronaldo had been transferred to the Dutch team from Cruzeiro for US$6 million. He was then eighteen years old. One year later, after trying to buy Shearer three times from Blackburn and being told he was not for sale, Robson went for the boy wonder.

As Robson later wrote in *FourFourTwo* magazine, while he was still managing Barça, 'He was still only nineteen but I told Barcelona we must have him, that we would be buying not only a wonderful player, but a player for the future. And he was much more than an alternative to our other front men: he was rare, different and exhilarating. He has different skills from other centre-forwards. He's an incredible dribbler; he dribbles like George Best, Tom Finney and Chris Waddle. He has an amazing ability to just plough his way through. Part of that is his natural talent and part is his amazing physique. He's incredibly strong, tall and beautifully balanced. And, of course, he has astonishing pace. I have never seen a player as fast as him when he runs away from people on the turn, or turns into the ball. He just explodes.'

Ever since Ipswich days, Nuñez had looked on Robson as one of the wise men of football who would cause him minimum hassle. With the Cruyff menace hovering around him, and TV revenues pouring into Barça coffers, the president was psychologically primed to be convinced. If the name of the game was the price of success, then Robson and Nuñez were prepared to play it with Ronaldo, as Robson made clear in a separate comment he made for Amy Raphael's *Esquire* profile of him published in June 1997: 'I made Nuñez buy him. Started at $12 million, went to $13 million. The president asked, "Are you sure about him?" I said I was. It went to $17 million. The president went crazy. PSV kept upping the price, until we said, "What do you want?" They came back with $20 million. I told the president that he was more than worth it. I told him, "He's barely twenty; it's not as though he's thirty and losing it, pet. He's on the incline, not the decline." I promised he'd be laughing at the money in two years. In fact he's laughing now.'

On 7th September 1996, the Camp Nou's most fanatical section, the *gol nord*, was awash with Brazilian and Catalan flags as Ronaldo made his début in the Spanish League. The presentation of Barça's star-studded team and of one superstar in particular had raised the excitement stakes around this opening encounter against the long-discredited local rival Espanyol. In fact the game was handicapped by the appalling state of the ground, its uneven surface the result of a mixture of adverse weather and poor seeding. The sight of Robson spending his pre-match walkabout gingerly treading the pitch, and of the multimillionaire players subsequently having a hard time passing the ball in a way designed to do minimum damage, would have been farcical had it not seemed to many of the fans a potent symbol of mismanagement and waste. Things livened up towards the end. Espanyol was looking at a surprise victory of 1–0, when six minutes before the final whistle Giovanni stole the equaliser. Then, two minutes into injury time, the man everybody was there to see picked up the ball thirty yards from the opposition goal. Ronaldo slalomed in and out of the Espanyol defence and delivered a powerful strike. The keeper parried it but to no avail. The ball spun from his hands into the waiting feet of Pizzi for a mere formality of a finish.

The former Liverpool player Michael Robinson, now a Spanish media pundit, later commented that the match had reminded him of the games he had played in his school days, when the 'good' team had deliberately let the 'bad' team score the goals until the teacher's announcement that it was five minutes before the end. Only then had the 'good' team played for real, making up for lost time with a mad scramble for goals. 'It's the same with Barcelona, they gave me that unbelievable sense of "This is a powerful football team when they put their minds to it." '

The problem Robson faced was that even with the longest-ever start-of-season period at the top of the League table, he still didn't manage to win the unqualified support of either the fans or the media. As Jeff King noted in his diary, a month later, 'There are still question marks against overall performances . . . great players, not so great team is the general feeling.' The jury remained out on the boy wonder. Ronaldo had scored his first goal in the League in Barça's second match of the championship, away against Santander: an enlightened piece of play, killing a long ball from Guardiola on his chest, before sweeping past his marker and wrong-footing the keeper. Robson described it as 'a marvellous example of how you make goals out of nothing'. However, his Portuguese assistant, José Mourinho, put it less tactfully: 'We've told Ronaldo it's no good scoring a wonder goal and spending the other eighty-nine minutes sleeping.'

By way of contrast, perhaps at this point one should quote from Robson's own appreciation of the Cruyff years: 'Cruyff had created a very special style of football, adapting the Ajax way with his own ideas and weaving them around three of the world's best players in Ronald Koeman, Michael Laudrup and Hristo Stoichkov – and, later on, Romario,' he writes in *An Englishman Abroad*. 'He had a group of Spanish and Catalan players who fitted in perfectly with fast, one-touch, total football, with the emphasis very much on attack. For six glorious years the people of Barcelona were thrilled and delighted.'

As soon as he faced criticism at Barça, the only concession that Robson was prepared to make was that any problems were down to the players' form and not to his system. Yet there was perhaps a telling irony in the fact that the match in which Barça under Robson achieved its most flowing game of the season involved a team depleted of megastars, including Ronaldo, Stoichkov and Figo, through a combination of injury and international duties, and instead featured a starring performance by Luis Enrique, a recent 'free' transfer from Real Madrid, and Ivan 'Little Buddha' de la Peña, from the Barça youth team, who had between them cost the club a fraction of what had been spent on the foreigners. The match, played against the reigning champions, Atlético Madrid, at the Camp Nou on 9th November 1996, had 90,000 fans enthralled as Barça held the visitors to a 3–3 draw. (Among Robson's forced choices that day was Arnau, his fourth keeper!)

Robson was still bubbling with enthusiasm for Luis Enrique when I interviewed him nearly a year and a half later: 'I felt he was unbeliev-able as a player, also a rare guy with a great spirit. He was multi-functional . . . if there was ever a problem with the team, he was like a missing piece of a jigsaw that I could put in and know it would fit. He could fill holes all the time and perform exquisitely . . .' On Ivan de la Peña he was more cautious, at a time when the Little Buddha's days in the Barça of van Gaal were already numbered: 'With guidance he could be an outstanding player . . . but he needs more maturity, more knowledge of the game. His particular talent is his passing of the ball and he has good vision, but he needs to have more self-confidence.'

Three weeks after Luis Enrique and de la Peña's enlightened performance in the Atlético match, Ronaldo, with some fatherly advice no doubt from at least one of his three representatives, let it be known that he was not in Barcelona to be taken for granted. He stirred the pot by confirming as fact rumours that he was being headhunted by Italian and English clubs. 'The offers are real and we're talking about incredible amounts of money,' he told the enthusiastically receptive local media. 'We've got to sort out this situation as soon as possible so I can settle down and concentrate on my game.'

Ronaldomania was by then very much on a roll, the hype of it distracting from a sober analysis of his performance as a player. It was perhaps best summarised by the comment a Catalan bishop made after celebrating Mass on the thirty-ninth anniversary of the Camp Nou: 'Where there used to be paintings of the Last Supper, now there are posters of Ronaldo,' he complained. Ronaldo was certainly proving a more accessible superstar than Maradona had been. Notwithstanding his assortment of bodyguards, assistants and agents, his easygoing personality made him perfect sponsorship material. He was in constant and great media demand and tried his best to meet much of it, even when this involved soapy TV quiz shows. In October 1996, Ronaldo crossed to the United States, or at least his image did – no small achievement given that following the 1994 World Cup the majority of Americans had failed to maintain their enthusiasm for 'soccer'. *USA Today* gave him shared front-page billing with José Girardi, the New York Yankees catcher, as the Bronx team celebrated their first World Series triumph in eighteen years.

Then, just before Christmas 1996, Ronaldo's superstardom ensured that Barça arrived in Madrid for the first and only time in its history to an enthusiastic reception: over 2,000 screaming fans, mainly females, packed the international airport to greet Ronaldo's arrival with the team. It was widely reported that Barajas Airport had not played host to such hysteria since the Beatles' reception in 1966. Few were as amazed as Nicolau Casaus, Barça's oldest director, who had seen a thing or two in more than sixty years' service at the club. 'Two thousand people at Barajas cheering Barcelona: it's more like Passeig de Gràcia [in Barcelona] than Madrid.'

The traditional encounter between the old rivals was watched by millions from Madrid to Rio, and helped boost the ailing coffers of both clubs, which, like the rest of the Spanish League, were beginning to wake up to the costs of a more liberal transfer market as a result of the landmark Bosman ruling. Capello's Real Madrid won 2–0. Ronaldo had three chances at goal and missed the lot, leaving the Barcelona Spanish-language daily *La Vanguardia* to headline the next day, 'Barça are going backwards'. The growing consensus among the critics was that Robson's lack of a clear system was evident from his continual tactical shifts. It was also claimed that several players were not being used in their best positions. And, perhaps worst of all, Robson's personality was judged to be at fault. Robson may have come across to some of his British pals as a genuine down-to-earth straight Geordie, but he'd failed to learn Spanish or Catalan in any convincing way, and seemed much too eager to do Nuñez's bidding at a time when the stirrings of discontent within the club had far from abated.

In February 1997, Barcelona newspapers were filled with photographs of Ronaldo and his girlfriend Suzanna at play in the Brazilian carnival. According to Ronaldo's latest unofficial biographer, Wensley Clarkson, the shots of the player clad in a gold lamé jump suit, glittering green shoulder pads, a star-spangled headband and enough blue feathers to fill a duvet and, when not dancing, crashed out in the back seat of a limo with Suzanna, went down like a lead balloon back at the club.

Catalonia would not have produced artists like Gaudí, Dali and Miró if it didn't appreciate the creative force of the extrovert, and the Catalan word for irrational or sometimes just plain dumb activity, *rauxa*, is part of the culture. But Barça that season was looking for different standards from its players, not least the one who had cost a then record sum, and a better sense of control from its coach. 'The photos are an insult to everyone connected to FC Barcelona. The club is in the middle of a raging crisis and its biggest star is given special leave of absence to parade around at a carnival,' commented Miguel Rico, journalist with *Sport*. 'It's beyond belief that Robson gave him permission to go.'

Arguably Robson's most poignant tragedy was that in the end he was unable to keep control over a player he had shown so much faith in, and this during a period when the fans needed to be convinced that the player was worth the money the club had paid for him. Ronaldo produced some magical moments of football during his season with Barça, scoring a total of forty-five goals for the team. His finest and most sustained performance came early on in his time there, in a match played away against Compostela, which Barça won 5–1. Ronaldo helped fellow Brazilian William – playing for Compostela – score an own goal within the first minute of the game after strolling through the right flank of the team's defence. Fifteen minutes later, Ronaldo had moved down the left wing before delivering Giovanni such a well-timed and visionary pass that the goal that followed might have just as easily been scored blindfold. But it was Ronaldo's first direct goal after half an hour of play that had a truly historic quality about it. Picking the ball up in his own half and keeping it so close to his boots as to make it seem glued to them, Ronaldo carved his way through half the Compostela team before delivering a goal of effortless precision. In its beauty of balance and execution, the goal was reminiscent of Maradona's second goal against England in the World Cup in Mexico in 1986. It seemed only appropriate that Robson, who had been in Mexico as England manager, should now be on the winning side.

Robson was not lost for words once the match was over. 'You can go anywhere you want in the world, and you won't find a player who can score goals like that,' he said. Even before the game, Ronaldo had scored five League goals; each had had him dribbling towards the net and leaving a keeper sprawling on the deck. While playing with Barça he scored more goals than Romario had in his first season under Cruyff. Nevertheless, at the end of January 1997, one week after picking up his FIFA World Player award in Lisbon, Ronaldo polled only seventeen per cent of the vote against Luis Enrique's massive sixty-eight per cent in a Barcelona newspaper's Best Player poll.

Four months later Barça faced Paris St Germain in the final of the European Cup Winners Cup in Rotterdam. The last time Barça had played there was in 1991 under Cruyff when they lost 2–1 in the final against Manchester United. Now 12,000 *cules* were treated to victory courtesy of Bobby Robson's team, and a penalty by Ronaldo. I remember being struck by the air of surrealism that hung about the Barça camp that day. The *cules* were vociferous enough, the colours and their drum beats more impressive than the French supporters'. All the troubles of the previous months seemed abandoned for some blissful minutes once the game was over and the Catalans in the team – Guardiola, Sergi and Ferrer – unfurled their national flags and stirred up the fans into a chorus of celebration, with undoubtedly the most popular chant '*Madrid cabrón, salut al campeón!*'

Yet the game itself was the kind that doesn't register for long in memory: no particular acts of brilliance, no real champions' play by either side – although I do remember Luis Enrique pressing and chasing relentlessly before being inexplicably substituted two minutes before full time. What most struck me was the lack of passion in Ronaldo. Soon after his arrival in Spain, Valdano said that the player seemed to him like someone who had landed from another planet. In Rotterdam, his whole demeanour was that of a man apart and beyond the club he was playing for and what it represented. As for Robson, he not only seemed removed from the event but looked and sounded exhausted, as if the power politics and lack of faith of his critics had irreversibly wounded him. At a post-match press conference he claimed not to know how much longer he had in the job, his enduring sense of nobility managing to break through the weariness of it all with a phrase that also belonged to another world: 'The word revenge is not part of my vocabulary,' he said. 'Tonight was just a great opportunity that we've grabbed with both hands. It's not about me, it's a success everybody deserves for their efforts over a very complicated season.'

The following month, on 28th June, Barça beat Betis 3–2 in the final of the King's Cup held at Real Madrid's Bernabéu stadium. The temporary take-over of the Bernabéu stadium by over 35,000 ecstatic *cules* waving their flags and singing their anthem – '*Tot el camp es un clam, som la gente blaugrana . . .*' ('The whole stadium is clamouring, we are the red and blue people . . .') – before breaking out into '*VISCA EL BARÇA!*' and '*VISCA CATALUNYA!*' would have been considered the equivalent of a gang rape by the absent *ultra surs*, Real Madrid's hooligan element. The *cules*, however, regarded the victory as a small but not insignificant compensation for the fact that Real Madrid had clinched the League. It might have been different had Ronaldo not been absent from the team when Barça played against Hercules. The shock defeat towards the end of the season had finally sunk its championship bid. After months of negotiations with the

Barça directors, Ronaldo had finally quit, after deciding that Inter Milan would both pay and treat him better. Robson never even got a chance to say goodbye because the player was in Brazil when the deal was completed. Instead Robson was left on his own to give his final press conference as manager of the team, his sense of humour sticking by him even at the point of maximum incomprehension. 'I've made history,' he said. 'I must be the first coach to win three out of four titles in his first season at a club and not get the chance to carry on.'

When I met him again nine months later, Robson had yet to come to terms with the loss of Ronaldo. 'I have nothing but admiration for that player, the fastest thing I've ever seen running with the ball – a great *chico*,' he told me, 'but how was it possible that having bought the finest, best goal-scorer in the world at a cost of $20 million, we let him go one year later? How did anyone let it happen? Nobody here has had the courtesy to sit down and explain this to me.'

Outside, the Camp Nou loomed huge and empty, awaiting the conclusion of the team's next championship bid under Robson's successor Louis van Gaal. At the age of sixty-five, and having survived a gruelling battle with cancer – less openly shared with the *cules* than Cruyff's heart problem – Robson claimed he had lost none of his ability to tough out the most adverse of circumstances. He was on his way back to PSV. Before we said goodbye, I asked him the same question I had asked countless people in the course of researching this book: what did he *feel* about the experience of FC Barcelona? He replied like a man still possessed with a dream that had somehow eluded him: 'It is the evening of a European tournament . . . an electric atmosphere, a hair-tingling scenario . . . and you know that if you lose you're going to get whacked and people are going to be unhappy and the press is going to be out there waiting for you . . . and the tension brings the adrenalin and the excitement . . . The army cannot be defeated.'

17

Beyond the Millennium

On the evening of 29th November 1998, FC Barcelona marked the start of its centenary year with a style and emotion worthy of the phrase 'more than a club' with an extraordinary ceremony held in the newly refurbished all-seater Camp Nou.

President Nuñez and his royal guest – the youngest daughter of King Juan Carlos – had only just seated themselves in the directors' enclosure when the stadium's massive floodlight system dimmed, giving way to a laser-driven extravaganza of sound, light and movement. It was hard to forget those colours that evening. They spread across the pitch in a reflected map of the world – with the Barça fan clubs around the globe pin-pointed like so many friendly satellites – which gradually transformed into the bulbous crest the club's founders had agonised over all those years ago. Across it and extending to the four corners, hundreds of local schoolkids dressed in blue track suits formed circles around players past and present, as some of the trophies won by the team were held aloft.

Few sequences produced a louder roar of excitement than the projection of Barça's historic goal at Wembley on a large screen followed by the European Cup once again being held aloft in the middle of the Camp Nou by the man who had scored that goal: Ronald Koeman. Local fans who had packed into Catalonia's cathedral of football effortlessly created a giant mosaic – the entire height and circumference of the stadium – thanks to over 80,000 coloured cards sponsored by a local sports newspaper. They had done the same at Wembley but on a much smaller scale. Now the cards had been produced on cue and in perfect synchronisation as the fans sang the chorus of the centenary anthem led by the Orfeó Catalá, the choral society which is another emblem of Catalan cultural pride – '*Cent vegades, més fort, cent vegades més gran, Fútbol Club Barcelona, per molts anys, endavant* . . .' ('One hundred times, and we're stronger, one hundred times and we're bigger, FC Barcelona, may you continue to be so for many years . . .')

But nothing quite matched the emotional punch of Juan Manuel Serrat. Catalonia's most famous singer was renowned for speaking out against dictatorships around the world, and had dedicated his most lyrical and melodious football song to the Barça of the 1950s. Under Franco he had refused to represent Spain in the Eurovision Song Contest because the government wouldn't let him sing in Catalan. He now walked alone to the centre of a deserted pitch and with trembling voice led the stadium into a slow and soulful rendering of the Barça anthem that generations of *cules* had sung in Catalan through the best and worst of times. Serrat had made it clear that he was singing for Barça, not for Nuñez. His natural sympathies lay with the people, not with the president. 'I feel for this club as I have done from birth . . . I don't need to rehearse this,' he had said before the ceremony.

As Serrat and 99,999 other *cules* delivered the anthem's final lines – '*Blaugrana al vent, un crit valent, tenim un num el sap tothom, Barça! Barça! Barça!*' ('Red and blue colours flying in the wind, and a cry of courage with a name that we all know, Barça! Barça! Barça!') – thousands of fireworks broke out across the sky, illuminating it in sweeping brushstrokes of red and blue. It was a fitting climax to an awe-inspiring ceremony that had focused on spectacle rather than speeches, and briefly united officials, membership and fans in an outpouring of loyalty and faith. Choosing to follow the ceremony with a scheduled League tie between Barça and Atlético Madrid was a calculated risk by the club management – which badly backfired.

In the weeks preceding the ceremony, Louis van Gaal's Barça had got off to a bad start in the League championship and was eliminated from the Champions' League, blowing apart the dream of winning it in the centenary year at the Camp Nou. However, it was hoped that the general euphoria surrounding the evening would aid the team to victory in a match that by virtue of being a League tie was bound to prove more competitive than a friendly. In some ways Atlético Madrid seemed perfectly suited for the occasion, the only real incongruity being the presence among the VIPs of Atlético chairman Jesus Gil, who was facing a prosecution for alleged financial fraud. Although

Barcelona usually won, matches between the two had a reputation for being among the more entertaining – certainly high-scoring – encounters of the Spanish championship, with none of the traditional animosity that Real Madrid provoked. As things turned out, however, Barça managed to play probably its worst game of the season, with poor passing and virtually nothing threatening the opposite goal, as if the minds of the players had somehow disappeared into the sky along with the rockets.

The Barça captain Figo's runs, mostly up the right flank, were constantly neutralised by the Atlético defence, a somewhat brutal, basic man-to-man marking encouraged by the club's Italian manager Arrigo Sacchi. With Giovanni asleep most of the time, and Zenden as erratic as Ciric was impotent, only flashes of individual skill from Kluivert suggested that there was anyone dressed in red and blue with a minimum sense of the meaning of attack, let alone entertainment. The fact that Atlético's Kiko was struggling on the pitch with a latent injury, and his team-mate Juninho was brought on belatedly from the subs' bench, suggested that both the gods and the managers had conspired to make this an unequivocal dog's dinner of a game.

The only thing that seemed to be in abundance on the pitch were fouls, another factor that contributed to both wrecking the flow of the game and provoking the one and only goal – a penalty taken by Jugovic after a crude tackle by Reiziger on José Mari. By then most people in the Camp Nou, myself included, were rubbing their eyes with incredulity that we were still in the same place, and hoping that things would return to the customary level of excitement in the second half. They didn't. Instead they went from bad to worse, and, gesticulating and claiming that we were all a bunch of ungrateful *hijos de putas*, the Barça defender Sergi only fuelled the flames further.

Minutes from the end, the same phrase was being screamed repetitively by an anonymous *cule* after he had walked a few steps towards the directors' box. Nuñez engaged himself in conversation with the Infanta as if he hadn't heard. But there was now no mistaking what had begun to spread in a rising volume around the stadium: '*Fuera van Gaal, fuera van Gaal*' ('Van Gaal out, van Gaal out'), thousands chorused, bringing out the white handkerchief. In bullfighting, the gesture can symbolise forgiveness (the pardon of a good bull) or triumph (a petition for the bull's ears to be given as trophies to a successful matador). In the Camp Nou it signifies quite the opposite: the sentence of death for whoever it is directed at, like the crowd of the Roman circus pointing downwards.

When the final whistle blew, boos and whistles resonated through the stadium. The players left the pitch quickly and with heads bowed. The fact that some of them narrowly missed being hit by flying jets which fans had manufactured from the coloured mosaic cards was symbolic of just how much the mood had changed in the course of the evening. It was not over yet, though. Security staff and police had to clear an escape route for the VIPs, and the Barça directors in particular, through a crowd who at one point looked bent on lynching them, as they chanted, *'Nuñez, Pinochet! Nuñez, dictador!'* and *'Johan, Johan, Johan!'* There was widespread resentment of the fact that Cruyff was the great uninvited absentee of the celebrations, sharpened by his enduring power as a symbol of the glory game that today's Barça clearly was not.

And yet only four days earlier a slightly different Barça line-up had brought the Camp Nou to its feet. The hearts and minds of the fans had been truly won over at the end of the season's second thrilling encounter with Manchester United. The final whistle had just gone on the European Champions' League tie between the two clubs when 70,000 Barça fans found common cause with the 3,500 Mancunians present and broke into spontaneous applause. In an instant the Catalans seemed to have forgotten the anger at seeing – once again – one of their city's most popular bars trashed by drunken English hooligans. For their part, the visitors had set aside the anger some of them had felt at being marshalled by riot police and corralled into one of the more remote areas of the huge stadium. Instead, the ovation was a tribute to ninety minutes of extraordinarily exciting football played by the world's two biggest clubs, where sheer spectacle and emotion took precedence over everything else. It was as if the two clubs had previously made a secret pact with each other and with UEFA to market the future of European football to a worldwide audience who rarely believe that the game these days gives true value for the money involved.

Unlike the first game at Old Trafford, when Barça had only really got going in the second half, this had been all-out attacking football from both sides from the outset, as reflected in the 3–3 scoreline and the dozens of near misses. 'It is not always easy to play attractive football and win titles,' van Gaal had said afterwards. By failing to beat Manchester United after a shaky start to the competition, Barça were effectively out of European football's final stages for the second consecutive season. And yet despite the defeat in terms of points, the match remarkably seemed to have restored Barça's sense of self-worth just when it most needed it. It had taken comfort in a noble defeat.

The player most responsible – and subsequently the other great absentee from the Atlético match, owing to injury – was undoubtedly Barça's brilliant Brazilian star Rivaldo. He produced two magical goals, some of the best ever seen at the Camp Nou: one a swerving free kick with the left foot, which sent the ball flying over the United wall and past Peter Schmeichel like a Patriot missile in slow motion; the other an overhead kick after he had turned and controlled a cross on his chest. This move brought the Camp Nou to its feet with cries of 'Rivaldo, Rivaldo, Rivaldo!' Given free rein by van Gaal to roam through the midfield, Rivaldo dribbled and weaved his way effortlessly through the opposition, leaving it mainly to Michael Reiziger and Gbenga Okunowu to hold as best they could the often devastating counter-attacks spearheaded by Andy Cole and Dwight Yorke. The Brazilian had been called an egotist in the past. But on that Wednesday night his individual talent perfectly complemented a team in which every player appeared to be in touch with a colleague's ability suddenly to switch position.

The fans who applauded Barça's performance on the Wednesday only to shout abuse at the team by the weekend were not guilty of flippancy or disloyalty. On one level they quite simply liked and appreciated good football, and felt cheated when it wasn't played. When the cules went home after the Manchester match, it was clear that they had accepted the notion that there can be a nobility in losing and not winning a title; that the football can be worth it on its own terms; and that UEFA's calculations and politics count for naught without the talent and courage of good players, and the sheer passion for the game of the fans who support them. But behind their protests lay much broader concerns about the changing nature of the modern game and the part that Barça under the presidency of Nuñez was being forced to play in it.

When Nuñez was elected president of FC Barcelona in 1978, he replaced a somewhat benevolent if patriarchal style of management with a sharper if more ruthless administration, with the emphasis on maximising the club's economic potential. He was blatantly an outsider, coming into a club that had made a point of surviving the Franco years on the basis of traditional values and cultural sentiment. Nuñez believed that the presidency of Barça would earn him the social recognition that had been denied him as an immigrant who had made his fortune relatively quickly in the construction industry. He thought he could achieve this by proving himself a better businessman and manager than his predecessors. 'My first ambition was to be a footballer, but I learned from an early age that this was not to be. So I became a businessman instead,' Nuñez told me in January 1999. In fact the ambition for status is what drove Nuñez from an early age. His undoubted capacity to understand money and how to make it work was the vehicle for fulfilling it. 'What I wanted to develop was a new style of management. Until I took over, to think in economic terms was not something that was very common in the club. But I wanted to show that we were professionals,' Nuñez said.

Much as Nuñez tried to rubbish the financial management of his predecessors, however, it is difficult to make a valid comparison, given the radically different political circumstances in which he came to power. Despite having been founded by foreigners, the club from its beginning was intimately linked to the development of Catalan nationalism, and therefore became much more than simply a football club. It cut across class divisions from an early stage in its development, and was a focus of social reconciliation for generations of immigrants. During the Franco years some of its directors collaborated with the regime, but the club never ceased to be regarded by its membership as a shelter for traditional Catalan values. Politics was Barça's emotional life-blood. It was what gave it a sense of mission. It also ensured that the club was never really short of funds, or excuses. Its own loyal membership – defined by Barça's own founding statutes as the effective owners of the club – was the permanent cash lifeline, together with the local business community usually more than adequately covering the cost of players, technical staff and general administration. The construction of the Camp Nou stadium in 1957, with an initial capacity of 100,000, demonstrated the club's ambition. However, it also contributed to the club's earning a reputation internationally for enjoying relatively little success for the amount of money it spent. Between 1958 – the year after the Camp Nou was completed – and Franco's death in 1975, Barça won the Spanish League championship just three times, winning no League title between 1960 and 1974, and the European Fairs Cup three times. It was not until 1992 that it won the European Cup.

As part of Barça's political and cultural tradition, the Spanish League championship always meant something more than a mere trophy. It became a matter of identity, even if some parts of history had to be mythologised and others simply overlooked. Beating its main rival, Real Madrid, meant a victory of democracy over a politically centralised and culturally repressed Spain. It also meant opening a door on the world beyond Spain's borders, by taking Barça into international competitive football of the highest order. Yet politics was not always the reason why Real Madrid was more successful on the pitch during much of the Franco period. At times Real simply had better players and better managers. The conspiracy theory moreover cannot really explain why it was that in the first two decades of Franco's dictatorship, Real Madrid didn't win the League championship once, while FC Barcelona won it three times.

What is certainly true is that from its early days, Barça has been at its most popular as a football club when it has played with style, and style there has been in abundance throughout its history, both cosmopolitan and innovative. Some of the best football in the world has been taught and played within the club, which is one of the reasons why generations of visitors have felt such a sense of awe on arriving at the Camp Nou for the first time. It is not surprising that the club's museum is one of the most popular in Spain, so filled is it with character, incident and creativity – quite apart from silverware.

Between 1978 and 1998, with Nuñez as president, the club membership rose from 77,000 to over 103,000, and the club's annual revenue from 817 million pesetas in 1978–9 to 14.9 billion pesetas in 1997–8. According to a survey of the richest football clubs in the world published by Deloitte & Touche and *FourFourTwo* magazine in early 1999, Barcelona had the edge over its historic rival Real Madrid in financial terms. Barcelona was second and Real Madrid third in a table topped by Manchester United. Barça's annual turnover of £58.9 million compared with Manchester United's £87.8 million. Despite the growth in Barça's membership, the percentage of total revenue represented by members' fees and ticket sales had fallen since 1978 from 87 per cent to 35 per cent. During the Nuñez years the big new source of revenue had been in the form of TV contracts, particularly lucrative whenever the club played in international tournaments, and without which the club would have been unable to cover the spiralling cost of transfers. In the club's 1997–8 accounts, the cost of players was put at more than 7 billion pesetas.

The economic transformation of the club began under the first democratically elected president of the club. Nuñez was elected in 1978 in the first election since before the Spanish Civil War that involved the whole Barça membership. Throughout his presidency, the administrative structure of the club has been supposed to reflect the grass-roots nature of its support. The assembly of delegates, the highest governing body of the club, is made up of 3,000 members, picked through a computerised lottery of members' numbers. The assembly appoints an economic committee which in turn is supposed to supervise the running of the club's budget. Although Barça has historically found the local banking system more than happy to lend it whatever money it needs, its borrowing is limited to below twenty per cent of its turnover. Because Barça's founding statutes define the club as a non-profit association of its members, any annual surplus is reinvested in the team and its stadiums and installations. One of the developments of recent years has been the setting up of a foundation through which Catalan companies and institutions can channel funds into the club's educational and non-football activities, which do not in themselves generate much revenue but which historically have been a drain on FC Barcelona's main budget.

Nuñez likes to point to the fact that he has periodically been re-elected, and has seen off votes of no confidence, as evidence of his democratic mandate. 'It is the club member who has wanted me to continue in office. Each time there is an election, more vote for me than vote against me,' Nuñez told me in January 1999. He was sitting in his office in the unobtrusive headquarters of Nuñez y Navarro, his family construction business. In the building's entrance lobby was a large model of a residential estate, carefully landscaped and filled with green space. As it entered a new environmentally conscious millennium, the firm wanted to be identified with quality and care. And yet to spend two hours in conversation with Nuñez was to experience at close quarters the abrasive manner that has made him such a disaster in PR terms. He sat behind a large desk, occasionally barking orders down a mobile or an office phone, depending which rang first – and they both rang constantly, day and night. Beneath his desk, within easy reach was a security button, with which he controlled who came in and who went out. He controlled movement the way he tried to control conversation. When pressed on controversial subjects, he adopted the tactics of the bar-room bully, hitting the desk and repeating himself in order to drive home his point. The office was decorated with photographs of him with important people, including the Pope – whom he made a member of the club when he visited Barcelona in the early 1980s – and the King of Spain. Nuñez remains loyal to Church and State, and distrusts the nationalist politics of some of his fellow Catalans in the post-Franco era. In his office were two small statues: one of Don Quixote, the other of a construction labourer. Power, ambition, hard work, and a desperate desire to be socially accepted – they are all part of Nuñez's world.

Towards the end of the twentieth century Nuñez had remained in office far longer than the president of any other club or organisation in the world, politicians included. I asked him whether he hadn't learned the lesson of history: that it is sometimes more advisable to walk out voluntarily through the front door, with your head held high, than to wait until you are forced out through the back, in the midst of scandal. 'I have offered my resignation on certain occasions. The problem is that every time I do so, people have come forward who want to control the club in a way that would do it no favours,' he replied.

Such an attitude furthers the perception of Nuñez as a man who cannot separate the club from himself, and who believes deep down that politics should have no place in the business of football. Those who 'would do the club no favours' include the Catalan nationalists linked to the President of the regional government, Pujol, who have periodically challenged Nuñez electorally. Over the years, Nuñez and Pujol – each acting like a viceroy running his own mini-state within a state – have reached a kind of political accommodation. Thanks to this, club and regional government have supported each other. And yet it has never been anything other than an arrangement of convenience between two men who mirror each other's obsession with power. In the words of a senior official at the Generalitat, who agreed to collaborate on this book on condition that he remain anonymous, 'There is no chemistry between Pujol and Nuñez, no friendship. Both men are small physically, with strong personalities. Each of them jealously guards the world he dominates. But although relations between the two have never been easy, they support each other in times of need. Now and again they'll pose for a photo opportunity. Occasionally one has made a speech attacking the other, but it's the image captured in the photographs that has had as great an impact politically.

'Towards the end of the twentieth century, a certain understanding was reached between the two men. For example, Nuñez incorporated individuals who were politically in Pujol's party – such as Sixto Cambra, the candidate he'd beaten in the club election – into his management board. At the same time, Barça under Nuñez has been a vehicle through which the Pujol government has developed many of its urban and educational programmes.'

Apart from former election rivals, Nuñez also brought into his ruling junta key businessmen and members of other parties, making Jaume Sobreques – a one-time spokesman of the Catalan Socialist Party (PCS) – the club's official historian. The PCS connection extended to Jordi Parpal, who joined Nuñez's junta as 'member in charge of institutional affairs' after working for Pasqual Maragall when he was mayor of Barcelona. Another PCS member brought into the Barça junta was Jordi Vallverdu, who was made vice-president in charge of one of the club's main fund-raising ventures, the foundation to which local businesses are encouraged to contribute financially. Vallverdu was also involved in one of the commercial spin-offs of the 1992 Olympics, developing land and property linked to it, a business he continued while working for Nuñez.

In an interview with the author, Maragall recognised that Nuñez had proved himself very able at developing a system of 'divide and rule', effectively neutralising the potential for opposition from individual parties by making some of the key political players part of his Barça mini-state. He described Sobreques as 'a maverick who doesn't represent our party any more', and said that he had personally tried – unsuccessfully, as it turned out – to dissuade Parpal and Vallverdu from joining Nuñez.

During the Catalan presidential campaign in 1999, both Maragall and Pujol signed a petition drawn up by Barça members supporting the idea of a Catalan national football team, for which players born locally would be able to play instead of playing for Spain. But Maragall accused his rival Pujol of going further in exploiting the politics of football to serve his own interests. As Maragall told me, 'Pujol has always wanted to take control of Barça . . . and even his support for the idea of a Catalan national team is a way of pressurising Barça to become more nationalist, more Catalan. I think that kind of political interference by the Pujol camp is something that was justified in the days before Franco fell, but is less so now that we have democracy. I think generally I have tried to keep our party and Barça independent of each other. I share the feelings of Barça supporters but I don't want anything to do with political manoeuvrings. I think the club should remain independent of party politics. Barça is a symbol that is above party politics. I think it's not good these days to use football for political reasons.'

Maragall, an academic first and foremost, who won international recognition for the way, as mayor, he presided over Barcelona's urban regeneration in the 1980s and 1990s, was in a minority among Catalonia's political establishment. The regimes of Nuñez and Pujol coincided in making the control, exploitation and promotion of Barça one of the prime objectives of Catalan politics during the 1980s and 1990s, along with the restoration and obligatory extension of the use of the Catalan language throughout all sectors of local life. Football became a vehicle for political influence and distraction as great as, if not greater than, it had been in the Franco years, its power strengthened by the expanding role of television.

In an article published in *El País* in July 1996 Arman Caraben, a former club secretary and opponent of Nuñez, asked whether Catalonia had become anything more than a football club. The question arose out of the spectacle of the mass presence in the presidential box at the Camp Nou of party politicians and/or their aides whenever there was an important match at the stadium. Caraben wrote, 'In Franco's time, one had the impression that football depended on the Secretary-General of his political movement. It was a very efficient trampoline which people used as a means of getting closer to the regime. Everyone thought that democracy would change all that. Instead, quite the reverse occurred. Just when democracy gave people greater access to political life, the trampoline remained the main focus of political activity, Barça the main objective of most politicians. Forget about constitutional reform, taxation, and even the language: senators, congressmen, ex-ministers, most honorary gentlemen were more interested in getting on TV and getting a post in Barça.'

On his record of the 1980s and 1990s alone, Nuñez showed himself extremely able to make use of politics to serve his own ends, making his junta submissive to his overall management. As Carlos Tusquets, a leading Catalan banker who served in the Nuñez junta, described it to me, 'At the beginning, when Nuñez was elected president, there were only a few of us in the junta and we were free to speak and take our own decisions. Over the years, Nuñez took more and more control of the club's affairs, and his junta became mainly decorative, made up of people who could provide him with political backing or whom he simply trusted as friends. Nuñez was always a clever and very intuitive person, with an extraordinary ability to work out sums without using a calculator. He could also act impulsively, with one major defect – he was a lousy public speaker. You just needed to have a few microphones in front of him for him to get very heated and lose the plot . . .'

His shortcomings in the realm of public speaking notwithstanding, Nuñez was in many ways typical of the new breed of businessman taking charge of football in the 1990s. In style and management he echoed the political ambition of AC Milan's Silvio Berlusconi, the abrasiveness of Tottenham Hotspur's Alan Sugar, and the pragmatism of Fergus McCann, the managing director of Celtic Football Club. McCann had tried to dilute the deeply entrenched traditions of the

Glasgow club – Irish nationalism and Catholic sectarianism – and concentrated instead on turning it into a commercial vehicle that would make money and be successful. And yet in one key respect Nuñez was handicapped: he did not have, nor was he allowed to have, the power that came with being a majority shareholder in a club. Much as he tried to control Barça as his own fiefdom, he continued to be faced with a widely felt and deeply entrenched tradition of nationalism and fan power.

In Barça's centenary year, Nuñez's dilemma was that despite being instinctively a bully, he still desperately wanted to be respected, even loved, by the fans, to have the hard work and financial good sense he claimed to have brought to the management of the club's affairs recognised and appreciated. His hope above all else was that van Gaal would deliver on another dream team that would be the best in Europe and would eclipse the ghost of Johan Cruyff once and for all. Yet Nuñez seemed unable to grasp an enduring reality of football – that it is the players, and their trainers, not the bosses of clubs, whom the fans follow when days turn glorious.

And so, despite signs in the spring of 1999 that the Barça of van Gaal was finally proving its worth, with a League championship in its sights and an assured place in Europe the following season, the opposition to Nuñez showed no signs of dissipating. Questions continued to be raised by the grass-roots members' association Elefant Blau about the true identity of the members of the assembly of delegates, and about the decision-making process of the economic committee, both of which bodies seemed to rubber-stamp most plans put forward by Nuñez. The 15,000 votes obtained by the Elefant Blau in its vote of censure against Nuñez in March 1997, against the 25,000 cast in his favour, were a warning to the president that he could not take the membership for granted, while it was hard to gauge the true feeling of the many thousands who had abstained.

As Barça entered a new millennium, the price of success remained a question that produced divisive debate within the club. When Nuñez replaced Bobby Robson with van Gaal, he did so with an eye to delivering a system that would operate over the long term, much as Ferguson had done at Manchester United. The Old Trafford model was that of a big club that had grown from a position of strength, developing young talent, winning trophies, and making packs of money at home and abroad.

That Nuñez and some of his advisers saw Manchester United as a commercial model during the late 1990s was apparent in countless consultancy papers and feasibility studies they examined behind the scenes, which drew comparisons with the English club's more developed merchandising and corporate hospitality, and its marketing overseas. It was estimated that the gap between Barça and Manchester United in terms of merchandising revenue was around thirty per cent. In order to help realise what he saw as Barça's economic potential, Nuñez signed a deal with Nike, and several TV contracts – including one for a match against Real Madrid – with the pay-TV channel Canal Plus. The importance of TV revenue to Nuñez was underlined by the way he insisted on securing as lucrative a deal as possible with UEFA over its revised plans for a European super league, which effectively promised to give big clubs like Barça an important share of the international market.

Nuñez also pushed ahead with Barça 2000, a 40-billion-peseta project to convert the area surrounding the Camp Nou into a huge theme park and leisure centre to attract seven million visitors a year – more than double the number of people who currently visit the stadium and its nearby museum. For several years, Nuñez on behalf of the club had been buying up land in the outskirts of Barcelona with the idea of using it for sports facilities and freeing up more space for development near the Camp Nou.

Where Nuñez insisted he had drawn the line, however, was in not carrying sponsorship on the Barça shirts. Tradition has it that the colours would be besmirched by a commercial name. More importantly, he publicly rejected any plan to float the footballing arm of the club on the stock exchange as a way of raising further finance. The idea is thought to have featured in at least one feasibility study drawn up for him by the merchant banking group Rothschild through their Madrid office, but was ditched on the grounds that it would prove too controversial among the fans. And the bid for Manchester United by Rupert Murdoch if anything strengthened the hand of those within the club who had argued that flotation carried the risk of a take-over by an 'outsider' who would never have the club's true interests at heart.

In the financial arena Nuñez had acted in ways that were not much different from those of the new business culture that had taken hold in the English Premier League and other European clubs over the preceding decade or so. When I interviewed him he insisted that his job was to ensure the club's financial viability: the playing of good football he entrusted to others. 'I have never spoken in the changing room about technical aspects of the game. When I go and see the players I simply want to give them moral support.' Tell that to Diego Maradona, Ronaldo, Terry Venables, Bobby Robson and Johan Cruyff – to name just a few of the players and managers who have been at the receiving end of Nuñez's power politics. Nuñez's intervention in the lives of players and managers over the years, his creation of a junta filled with directors he knew he could control, and his tendency to divide the world into those for him and those against him, have all been reflections of his own very particular brand of megalomania – his own passion to be boss.

Arguably it was Nuñez's relentless war of attrition against Johan Cruyff both before and after he sacked him as manager that showed the greatest lack of sensitivity to what the Dutchman had come to represent in terms of genuine grass-roots feeling. In March 1999, three years after Cruyff was sacked as manager, 98,000 fans packed the Camp Nou to honour him and players of the 'dream team' who had given them such joy earlier in the decade. Nuñez had belatedly agreed to the staging of the testimonial not because he wanted to, but because he had little choice. Once the event was over, he tried as best he could to make it seem like the final chapter of the Cruyff era, which the membership could now relegate to the history books. And yet Cruyff's iconic status was the product of a collective feeling that seemed to defy rational analysis and monetary calculations.

The anti-Nuñez Elefant Blau with which Cruyff was still identified approached the new millennium determined to ensure that Barça come to provide the brave new world of international football with a model of how things can and should be done: not by selling its soul but by being proud of its democratic tradition and drawing strength from it. Its manifesto called for a greater transparency of the club's accounts; the limiting of the presidential mandate to terms of four years; and more care with the money spent on the purchase of foreign players, which towards the end of the twentieth century was absorbing half of the club's annual budget, with questionable results. The lesson of the Cruyff years was that Barça could have foreigners and Spaniards in its team, produce hugely entertaining football, win titles, and make money. It was a time when fans rediscovered why the club mattered to them. Barça was, above all, a people's passion.

Bibliography

Rafael Alberti, *La Arboleda Perdida* (Seix Barral 1975)

Joan Josep Artells, *Barça, Barça, Barça* (Laia 1972)

Antony Beevor, *The Spanish Civil War* (Orbis 1982)

Frits Barend & Henk van Dorp, *Ajax, Barcelona, Cruyff* (Bloomsbury 1998)

Jimmy Burns, *Spain: A Literary Companion* (John Murray 1994)

Jimmy Burns, *Hand of God: The Life of Diego Maradona* (Bloomsbury 1996)

Jimmy Burns, *The Land That Lost Its Heroes* (Bloomsbury 1987)

Tom Burns, *The Use of Memory* (Sheed & Ward 1993)

Rossend Calvet, *Historia del FC Barcelona* (Hispano Europea 1978)

Armando Caraben, *Catalunya es mès que un club?* (Ediciones 62 1994)

Daniel Carbo, *Historia del FC Barcelona* (Barcelona 1924)

Juan José Castillo, *Ladislao Kubala* (Barcanova 1998)

Nicolau Casaus & Joan Villarroya, *Joan Gamper* (Barcanova 1998)

Wensley Clarkson, *Ronaldo* (Blake Publishing 1998)

Hunter Davies, *The Glory Game* (Mainstream 1992)

Paul Dempsey & Kevan Reilly, *Big Money, Beautiful Game* (Nicholas Brealey 1998)

Xavier Diez-Serrat, *Paulino Alcantara* (Barcanova 1998)

Frederick Draper, *Four Centuries of Merchant Taylors' School* (London 1962)

Lluis Duran & Magda Oranich, *Sunyol y el Barça de su tiempo* (Barcanova 1998)

Manuel Escofet, *Kubala* (Alcides 1962)

Morera Falco, *Un Barça Triomfant?* (Expres 1988)

Felipe Fernandez-Armesto, *Barcelona* (Sinclair-Stevenson 1991)

Pere Ferreres, *Cien Años Azulgrana* (El País/Aguilar 1998)

Alex Fynn & H. Davidson, *Dream On* (Simon & Schuster 1996)

Eduardo Galeano, *Football in Sun and Shadow* (Fourth Estate 1997)

Julian García Candau, *Madrid-Barça: Historia de un desamor* (*El País*/ Aguilar 1996)

Brian Glanville, *The Story of the World Cup* (Faber & Faber 1997)

José-Maria González, *Urruti, t'estimo* (Ninfa 1997)

Robert Graham, *Spain: Change of a Nation* (Michael Joseph 1984)

Harry Harris & Steve Curry, *Venables: The Inside Story* (Headline 1994)

Helenio Herrera, *La Mia Vita* (Mondo Sport 1964)

Robert Hughes, *Barcelona* (Harvill 1992)

Garbriel Jackson, *A Concise History of the Spanish Civil War* (Thames & Hudson 1974)

Andrew Jennings, *The New Lord of the Rings* (Pocket Books 1996)

Jeff King, *Bobby Robson's Year in Barcelona* (Virgin 1997)

Simon Kuper, *Football against the Enemy* (Orion 1994)

Jaume Llaurado, *El Barça d'un club, d'un país* (Columna 1994)

Gregorio Marañón, *El Conde Duque de Olivares* (Espasa-Calpe 1980)

Cataluña, Al Doctor Marañón – In Memoriam (Barcelona 1964)

Carmelo Martin, *Valdano: Sueños de Futbol* (*El País*/Aguilar 1995)

Tony Mason, *Passion of the People* (Verso 1995)

Blas Matamoro, *La Ciudad del Tango* (Galerna 1982)

Manuel Vazquez Montalban, *Barcelonas* (Empuries 1990)

Miguel Angel Morena, *Historia artistica de Carlos Cardel* (Corregidor 1990)

Josep Massot I Muntaner, *Els Creadors del Montserrat* (Serrador 1979)

Santi Nolla, *Johan Cruyff* (Barcanova 1998)

Josep M. Novoa, *Jaque al Virrey* (Axal 1998)

Carles A. Rabasso, Yo Acuso (Vosgos 1988)

George Orwell, *Homage to Catalonia* (Penguin 1989)

Hamlet Peluso & Eduardo Visconti, *Carlos Gardel y La Prensa Mundial* (Corregidor 1990)

Paul Preston, *The Triumph of Democracy in Spain* (Methuen 1986)

Paul Preston, *Franco* (HarperCollins 1993)

Keith Radnedge, *The Ultimate Encyclopedia of Soccer* (Hodder & Stoughton 1996)

Ignasi Riera, *Los Catalanes de Franco* (Plaza y Janes 1998)

Margarita Rivière, *Serrat y Su Epoca* (*El País*/Aguilar 1998)

Bobby Robson, *My Autobiography: An Englishman Abroad* (Macmillan 1998)

M. Sole I Sabate, Carles Llorens & Antoni Strubell, *Sunyol, l'autre President afusellat* (Pages 1996)

Duncan Shaw, *Futbol y Franquismo* (Madrid 1987)

Jaume Sobreques I Callico, *FC Barcelona: Su Historia y Su Presente* (Edilibro 1995)

Jaume Sobreques I Callico, *Historia del FC Barcelona* (Labor 1993)

Hugh Thomas, *The Spanish Civil War* (Penguin 1990)

Jason Tomas, *Soccer Czars* (Mainstream 1996)

Andre Merce Varela, *Josep Samitier* (Barcanova 1998)

Terry Venables & Neil Hanson, *Venables: The Autobiography* (Michael Joseph 1994)

Leo Verhuel, *El Clan de Johan* (Campos 1995)

Colin Ward, *Steaming: Journal of a Football Fan* (Pocket Books 1994)

Edwin Winkels, *De eenzame kampioen* (Hard Gras 1998)

Index

A Note on the Author

Jimmy Burns was born in Madrid in 1953 and educated at Stonyhurst College, Lancashire, and the London School of Economics. His early days in journalism were with Yorkshire Television and the BBC and as a correspondent for The Economist and the Observer. He has worked as a foreign correspondent for the Financial Times and on the newspaper's labour staff, winning the Industrial Reporter of the Year Award in 1990. He is currently social affairs and employment correspondent at the FT. His previous books are *The Land That Lost Its Heroes*, winner of the Somerset Maugham prize for non-fiction; *Beyond the Silver River*; *Spain: A Literary Companion*; and the internationally acclaimed *Hand of God: The Life of Diego Maradona*.

A Note on the Type

The text of this book is set in Linotype Sabon,
named after the type founder, Jacques Sabon. It
was designed by Jan Tschichold and jointly
developed by Linotype, Monotype and Stempel,
in response to a need for a typeface to be
available in identical form for mechanical hot
metal composition and hand composition using
foundry type.

Tschichold based his design for Sabon roman on
a fount engraved by Garamond, and Sabon italic
on a fount by Granjon. It was first used in 1966
and has proved an enduring modern classic.